BTEC First

REVISED EDITION
Now includes Unit 9

Health and Social Care

D0319209

Laura Asbridge • Siân Lavers

Neil Moonie • Jade Scott

www.heinemann.co.uk

✓ Free online support
✓ Useful weblinks
✓ 24 hour online ordering

01865 888058

Heinemann is an imprint of Pearson Education Limited, a company incorporated in England and Wales, having its registered office at Edinburgh Gate, Harlow, Essex, CM20 2JE. Registered company number: 872828. www.heinemann.co.uk.

Heinemann is a registered trademark of Pearson Education Limited

Text © Laura Asbridge, Siân Lavers, Neil Moonie, Jade Scott 2008

First published 2008

12 11 10 09 08

10 9 8 7 6 5 4 3

British Library Cataloguing in Publication Data

A catalogue record of this book is available from the British Library

ISBN 978 0 435 50026 9

Edited by Susan Ross
Designed by Wooden Ark Studio, Leeds
Typeset by Saxon Graphics Ltd, Derby
Original illustrations © Pearson Education Limited, 2008
Cover design by Wooden Ark Studio, Leeds
Printed in China (CTPS/03)
Cover photo: © Corbis
Picture research by Maria Joannou

Acknowledgements

The authors and publishers are grateful to those who have given permission to reproduce material. Every effort has been made to contact copyright holders of material reproduced in this book. Any errors or omissions will be rectified in subsequent printings if notice is given to the publishers. The publishers would like to thank Tony Cicco and Diane Goff for their invaluable comments.

Photos

Alamy Images/Paul Doyle 349
Alamy Images/ David Hoffman 150
Alamy Images/Hugh Jones 295
John Birdsall Social Issues 21, 149
Corbis 113
Corbis/Chen Jianli/China Features 62
Corbis/Ashley Cooper 164
Corbis/Reuters 69, 392
Corbis/ROB & SAS 247
Corbis/Tom Stewart 321
Mary Evans Picture Library 324
Getty Images/Photodisc 101, 166, 225, 248, 299, 367
Pearson Education Ltd 252
Pearson Education Ltd/Jules Selmes 253, 355
Pearson Education Ltd/Richard Smith 2, 223 (left), 298, 332

Pearson Education Ltd/Martin Sookias 340
Pearson Education Ltd/Tudor Photography 250
Imagestate 316
Jade Scott 317
Photofusion/Crispin Hughes 351
Photofusion/Caroline Mardon 132
Photofusion/Paula Solloway 47
Photofusion/Christa Stadtler 187
Photos.com 1, 163, 260
Rex Features/David Hartley 104
Rex Features/Stills Press Agency 170
Science Photo Library/Biophoto Associates 388, 394
Science Photo Library/BSIP, Chassenet 327
Science Photo Library/Neal Grundy 191
Science Photo Library/Gusto 67
Still Pictures 393

Text

Cancer Research 55
Food Standards Agency 336

Help the Aged 123
Prevention Source BC 73
The National Blood Service/Department of Health 112

Contents

About this book

This book has been written specially to support you studying on the Edexcel BTEC First Certificate and First Diploma in Health and Social Care course. For many of you this will be the first time you have studied this subject and so we have included many features to make your learning experience an interesting and stimulating one. There are nine units in the book.

The BTEC First Certificate requires you to study the two core units (units 1 and 2) plus *one* specialist unit to be chosen from units 3, 4, 5 or 6. The Diploma requires you to study the two core units plus *four* units selected from the seven specialist units (units 3–9).

● Over to you
Questions or problems designed to encourage reflection or practical activities that may increase understanding of important issues.

● Diagrams and tables
Ideas and information are presented in diagrams in order to make them more accessible and easy to use in class activities.

● Think about it
Key issues for individual reflection.

● Talking point
Questions that might form the basis of discussion activities.

How you will be assessed

Each unit is assessed through the achievement of specified outcomes designed to measure pass, merit or distinction grades. You are expected to achieve a higher quality of outcome at the merit and again at distinction level. Your tutors will develop tasks or assignments designed for each unit so you can achieve the grade which is right for you. There is plenty of help towards assessment in this book. The authors of this book hope that you enjoy the BTEC First in Health and Social Care course and that you will enjoy using this book and find it informative. We wish you every success in achieving the qualification.

Features of the book

This book is designed to be easy to access. Throughout the text there are a number of features that are intended to encourage reflection and help you to understand how what you are learning relates to the world of health and social care.

Real Life Care ●

Case studies that link theory with practice followed by differentiated questions designed to help you to identify key issues and then encourage the greater depth of learning and understanding required at the merit and distinction grades.

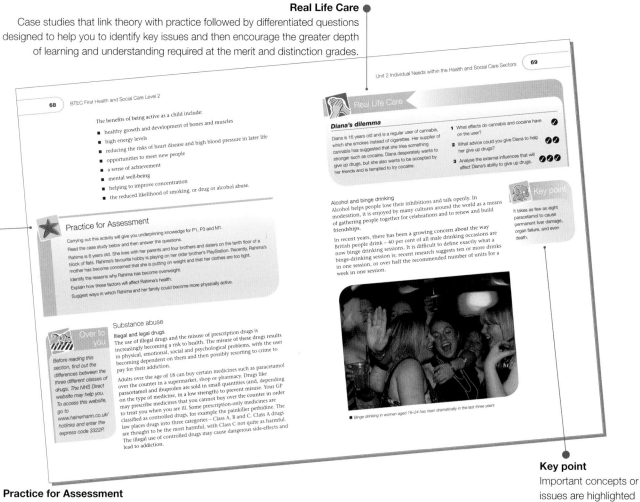

The benefits of being active as a child include:

- healthy growth and development of bones and muscles
- high energy levels
- reducing the risks of heart disease and high blood pressure in later life
- opportunities to meet new people
- a sense of achievement
- mental well-being
- helping to improve concentration
- the reduced likelihood of smoking, or drug or alcohol abuse.

★ Practice for Assessment

Carrying out this activity will give you underpinning knowledge for P1, P3 and M1.

Read the case study below and then answer the questions.

Rahima is 6 years old. She lives with her parents and four brothers and sisters on the tenth floor of a block of flats. Rahima's favourite hobby is playing on her older brother's PlayStation. Recently, Rahima's mother has become concerned that she is putting on weight and that her clothes are too tight.

Identify the reasons why Rahima has become overweight.

Explain how these factors will affect Rahima's health.

Suggest ways in which Rahima and her family could become more physically active.

Over to you

Before reading this section, find out the differences between the three different classes of drugs. The NHS Direct website may help you. To access this website, go to www.heinemann.co.uk/hotlinks and enter the express code 3322P.

Substance abuse

Illegal and legal drugs
The use of illegal drugs and the misuse of prescription drugs is increasingly becoming a risk to health. The misuse of these drugs results in physical, emotional, social and psychological problems, with the user becoming dependent on them and then possibly resorting to crime to pay for their addiction.

Adults over the age of 18 can buy certain medicines such as paracetamol over the counter in a supermarket, shop or pharmacy. Drugs like paracetamol and ibuprofen are sold in small quantities (and, depending on the type of medicine, in a low strength) to prevent misuse. Your GP may prescribe medicines that you cannot buy over the counter in order to treat you when you are ill. Some prescription-only medicines are classified as controlled drugs, for example the painkiller pethidine. The law places drugs into three categories – Class A, B and C. Class A drugs are thought to be the most harmful, with Class C not quite as harmful. The illegal use of controlled drugs may cause dangerous side-effects and lead to addiction.

Real Life Care

Diana's dilemma

Diana is 16 years old and is a regular user of cannabis, which she smokes instead of cigarettes. Her supplier of cannabis has suggested that she tries something stronger such as cocaine. Diana desperately wants to give up drugs, but she also wants to be accepted by her friends and is tempted to try cocaine.

1. What effects do cannabis and cocaine have on the user? ✔
2. What advice could you give Diana to help her give up drugs? ✔✔
3. Analyse the external influences that will affect Diana's ability to give up drugs. ✔✔✔

Alcohol and binge drinking
Alcohol helps people lose their inhibitions and talk openly. In moderation, it is enjoyed by many cultures around the world as a means of gathering people together for celebrations and to renew and build friendships.

In recent years, there has been a growing concern about the way British people drink – 40 per cent of all male drinking occasions are now binge drinking sessions. It is difficult to define exactly what a binge-drinking session is; recent research suggests ten or more drinks in one session, or over half the recommended number of units for a week in one session.

Key point

It takes as few as eight paracetamol to cause permanent liver damage, organ failure, and even death.

■ Binge drinking in women aged 16-24 has risen dramatically in the last three years

Practice for Assessment
Ideas for activities that will contribute towards the achievement of outcomes at the pass, merit and distinction levels.

Key point
Important concepts or issues are highlighted as key points.

1 Communication and Individual Rights within the Health and Social Care Sectors

Introduction

Working in health or social care is all about working with people. Care workers may encounter a variety of service users throughout their career. At a nursery, service users are young children and their parents. At an antenatal clinic, pregnant women are the primary service users. At a day care centre, care workers work with elderly service users. Care workers can have a great influence on how patients and service users feel, so it is very important that care workers have good communication skills. Communication is about helping others to feel safe, involved and cared for, as well as about passing on information. This unit explores the importance of communication and ways of overcoming barriers to communication. Good communication skills help people to feel confident when they work with others and they may help to make your own life exciting and enjoyable.

Working in health and social care involves treating people with respect and dignity and using good communication skills. These are examples of 'care values'. Care workers

▶ Continued from previous page

■ *Care workers need to be able to communicate clearly with service users*

have to value the diversity and rights of the people that they work with. This unit explores the issues of diversity and care values that are central to all caring relationships. Understanding these issues is important for a career in caring work.

How you will be assessed

This is an internally assessed unit.

In this unit you will learn about:

- ways of promoting effective communication
- barriers to effective communication
- diversity and equality in society
- the care value base.

Ways of promoting effective communication

One-to-one conversations

When you start a conversation with someone you do not know very well, you should always try to create the right kind of feelings. It may be important that the people you talk with feel relaxed and happy to talk to you. Very often people will start with a greeting such as 'Good morning'. Formal conversations have to have a beginning, middle and an end. You will need to help other people to relax by showing that you are friendly and relaxed.

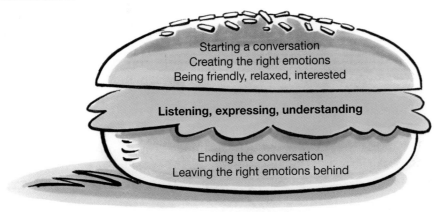

Starting a conversation
Creating the right emotions
Being friendly, relaxed, interested

Listening, expressing, understanding

Ending the conversation
Leaving the right emotions behind

■ *The conversation sandwich*

Once you have created a good feeling, you can move onto what you want to talk about. When it is time to finish the conversation, it is usually important to end with the right kinds of feeling, perhaps saying something like 'See you soon' to show that you value meeting with this person.

One-to-one conversations are influenced by non-verbal communication and the communication cycle. There is more information on these issues later in this section.

Group communication

Taking part in a group discussion involves some special issues.

Group feeling

Group discussion only works well if the group's members want to be involved. Sometimes people feel threatened if they have to speak to a formal group of people. Sometimes people stay quiet because they worry about the reaction of others. It important that the group has the right

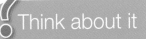

Think about it

Imagine you walked into a care home and you were greeted in the following way:

'Who are you? What do you want?'

Now, imagine, you were greeted like this:

'Good morning, my name is Saroshe. I am a care worker here. How can I help you?'

What are the advantages and disadvantages of each approach?

Over to you

Try to remember the last time you started a formal conversation with someone you did not know well. How did you start and finish the conversation?

emotional atmosphere. Formal groups often use humour or other friendly behaviours to create the right group feeling to encourage people to talk.

Group leaders

Some groups such as team meetings or classroom discussions have a leader or a chairperson. Having a leader is very useful because they can help people to take turns in talking and encourage people to express their ideas.

Thinking through what you are going to say

In formal groups, such as at work meetings, it is important to think through the points you are going to make before saying them to the whole group. Talking to a group can feel very different from talking in an informal one-to-one situation, such as to a fellow careworker, because of this extra preparation.

Turn taking

When a group does not have a leader or chairperson, it is important that group members have the skills to take turns in talking. When a speaker is finishing, they usually signal that they are finishing by lowering their voice tone and slowing the pace of talking, and looking around at other people in the group. The next person to talk knows that it is their turn by watching the eyes of other group members. People often fail to take turns in speaking and then everybody talks at once. If everybody is talking, then nobody is listening!

Use of space

If the members of a group all sit in a circle, then everyone can see everybody else's face. This is very important because group feeling and

 Over to you

Form a group of four or five people. Take four matchsticks each and agree on a topic for group discussion. The rules of the discussion are that only one person may speak at a time. Whenever that person is speaking, they must place a matchstick on the table. Once a person has run out of matchsticks, they may not say anything more. No one may speak unless they place a matchstick on the table. No one should speak for more than one minute.

You might find this task very difficult. Although using matchsticks stops everybody speaking at once, each person has to think through what they are going to say before they put their matchstick down. Preparing what you are going to say takes time and mental energy, but if you can do this, it will help you to communicate in groups.

turn taking often depend on people being able to understand the messages in other people's faces. If some people sit behind others or people sit in rows, then some group members will not be able to see others' faces. Poor seating or standing positions can make group communication harder.

Formal and informal communication

You will often use informal communication when you know people well such as friends and family. Some friends or family members may use terms that only their own group would understand. Local groups might have their own ways of speaking, for example some people in southern England might say things like 'Hi ya mate, how's it going?'. If you belong in this group, you will appreciate this as a warm friendly greeting.

Health and social care work often involves the need for formal communication. For example, at a hospital reception you might expect the receptionist to say something like: 'Good morning. How can I help you?' This formal communication might be understood by a wide range of people. Formal communication also shows respect for others.

Non-verbal communication

Non-verbal means without words, so non-verbal communication is the messages that you send without putting them into words. You send messages using your eyes, the tone of your voice, your facial expression, your hands and arms, gestures with your hands and arms, the angle of your head, the way you sit or stand – known as body posture – and the tension in your muscles.

Within a few seconds of meeting a service user, you will usually be able to tell what they are feeling. You will know whether they are tired, happy, angry, sad, frightened, even before they say anything. Another term for non-verbal communication is **body language**. You can usually guess what people feel by looking at their body language.

When a person is sad, they may signal this emotion with eyes that look down; there may be tension in their face and their mouth will be closed. The muscles in the person's shoulders are likely to be relaxed, but their face and neck may show muscle tension. A happy person will have 'wide eyes' that make contact with you – their face will smile. When people are excited, they will move their arms and hands to signal their excitement.

Most people can recognise emotions in the non-verbal behaviour of others. As a care worker, you will need an extra skill – to understand the messages you send with your own body when working with other people.

Body language
Messages we send with the body; the language of non-verbal communication.

Non-verbal messages

Your body sends messages to other people, often without you deliberately meaning to send those messages. Some of the most important body areas that send messages are shown below.

Over to you

Make a list of all the informal greetings you use, and all the formal ones. Could you use the informal ones in a formal setting?

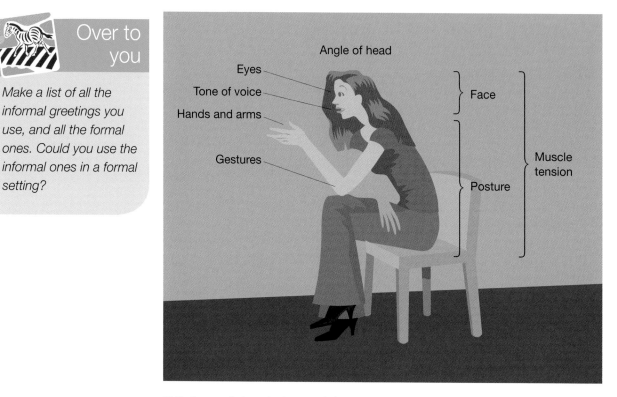

Angle of head

Eyes

Tone of voice

Hands and arms

Gestures

Face

Muscle tension

Posture

■ *Body areas that send out non-verbal messages*

The eyes

You can guess the feelings and thoughts that another person has by looking at their eyes. Your eyes get wider when you are excited, attracted to, or interested in someone else. A fixed stare may send the message that someone is angry. In European culture, looking away is often interpreted as being bored or not interested.

The face

Your face can send very complex messages.

Voice tone

It's not just what you say, but the way that you say it. If you talk quickly in a loud voice with a fixed voice tone, people may see you as angry. A calm, slow voice with varying tone may send a message of being friendly.

Body movement

The way you walk, move your head, sit, cross your legs and so on sends messages about whether you are tired, happy, sad or bored.

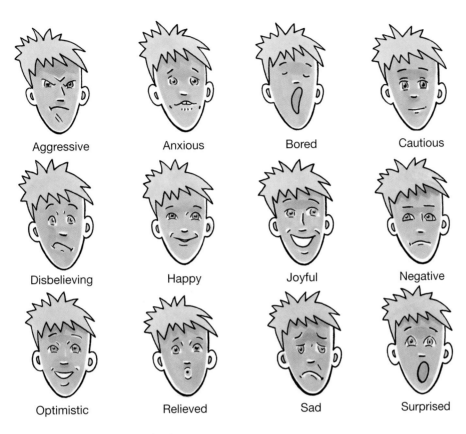

Aggressive   Anxious   Bored   Cautious

Disbelieving   Happy   Joyful   Negative

Optimistic   Relieved   Sad   Surprised

■ *Facial expressions that send out messages*

Posture

The way you sit or stand can send messages. Sitting with crossed arms can mean 'I'm not taking any notice'. Leaning back can send the message that you are relaxed or bored, while leaning forward can show interest. The body postures shown below send different messages.

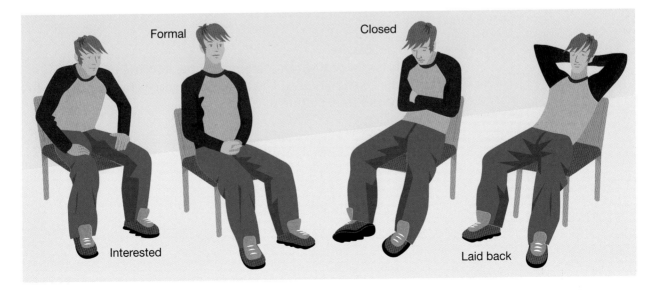

Formal   Closed

Interested   Laid back

■ *Body postures can send messages*

Muscle tension

When you are having a conversation with someone the tension in your feet, hands and fingers can tell others how relaxed or tense you are. If someone is very tense, their shoulders might stiffen, their muscles might tighten and they might sit or stand rigidly. A tense face might have a firmly closed mouth with lips and jaws clenched tight. A tense person might breathe quickly and become hot.

Gestures

Gestures are hand and arm movements that can help us to understand what a person is saying. Some gestures carry a meaning of their own. Some common gestures are shown below.

■ *Some common gestures*

Touch and contact

Touching another person during a conversation can send messages of care, affection, power over them or sexual interest. The social setting and other body language usually help people to understand what touch might mean. As a carer, you should not make assumptions about touch. Even holding someone's hand might be seen as trying to dominate them!

How close people are

The space between people can sometimes show how friendly or 'intimate' the conversation is. The amount of space between people who are talking varies from culture to culture.

Face-to-face positions

Standing or sitting eye to eye can send a message of formality or hostility. A slight angle can create a more relaxed and friendly feeling.

Verbal communication

Active listening

You can understand other people's emotions simply by watching their non-verbal communication, but you will not usually be able to understand what is on someone's mind without being good at listening.

Formal   Relaxed

■ *Face-to-face encounters*

Listening is not the same as hearing the sounds that people make when they talk. Listening skills involve hearing another person's words, then thinking about what they mean, then thinking what to say back to the other person. Some people call this process **active listening**. As well as thinking carefully and remembering what another person says, good listeners will make sure that their non-verbal behaviour shows interest.

Skilled listening involves:

1   Looking interested and ready to listen.
2   Hearing what is said.
3   Remembering what is said.
4   Checking understanding with the other person.

Active listening *Active listening involves being interested, hearing, remembering and checking what you have understood with another person.*

 Over to you

Divide a piece of paper into four and write out a heading in each area, for example 'Where I live', 'An important thing that happened in the past', 'Something I am looking forward to', 'Where I work or study'. Any four headings will do, as long as you can talk in detail about them. Think through what you can tell another person about yourself. Then get together with a colleague who has planned their speech. Explain the four areas to each other. This should take at least ten minutes. Then see what you can remember about the other person and how detailed and how accurate it is! How good are you at listening, understanding and remembering?

Variation between cultures

Skilled carers use a range of conversational techniques when working with others. These include being sensitive to variations in culture.

Culture means the traditions, values and beliefs of the family environment that you are brought up in. Different social groups will have different traditions, values and beliefs. People from different regions of Britain use different expressions. Non-verbal signs vary from culture to culture. White middle-class people often expect people to 'look them in the eye' while talking. If a person looks down or away a lot, it is a sign that they may be dishonest, or perhaps sad or depressed. In other cultures – among some black communities – looking down or away when talking is a sign of respect.

Real Life Care

Is Nisha shy?

Nisha is a resident in a hostel for people with learning difficulties. Nisha looks at the floor when she talks with people, and care workers sometimes describe her as being 'shy'.

1 Identify how culture could be influencing Nisha to look away from people. ✓

2 Try to think of other possibilities that might cause Nisha to look away from people. ✓✓

3 Explain some ways in which you might find out more about Nisha's culture. ✓✓✓

Ethnic group *People of the same race or nationality who share a distinctive culture.*

Class *A social grouping whose members share economic, social or cultural characteristics.*

Care workers have to be careful not to assume that statements and signs always have the same meaning. Culture, **ethnic group**, **class** and geographical location can alter what things mean. There are a vast range of meanings that can be given to any type of eye contact, facial expressions, posture or gesture. Every culture develops its own special system of meanings. Carers have to respect differences in culture, but it is impossible to learn all the possible meanings that phrases, words and signs may have.

It is possible to learn what service users mean when they communicate. One way to do this is to remember what people say or do and try to understand what they really mean, but this understanding will need to be checked. Usually, it is possible to ask polite questions, or to work out what people mean over time by watching and listening to other things they say or do.

The important thing to remember is that your own way of behaving and communicating is not the only way!

Other ways of communicating

Using signs and symbols

Gestures made with hands or arms, written symbols or diagrams such as traffic signs all communicate messages to people. Braille (a system of raised marks that can be felt with the fingertips) provides a system of written communication based on the sense of touch for people who may have limited vision.

Signed languages

Language does not have to be based on sounds that are heard. Signing systems such as British Sign Language provide a full language system for people who do not use spoken language.

Written communication

There is an old saying in Chinese culture that 'the faintest ink is stronger than the strongest memory'! Written records are essential for communicating formal information that needs to be reviewed at a future date. When people remember conversations they have had, they will probably miss some details out and also change some details. Written statements are much more permanent and if they are accurate when they are written, they may be useful at a later date.

Pictures and objects of reference

Paintings, photographs, sculptures, architecture, ornaments and other household objects can communicate messages and emotions to people. People often take photographs or buy souvenirs to remind them of happy experiences and emotions.

Technological aids to communication

Humans can communicate across distance and time by using written messages, email, text messages and so on. Information can be recorded electronically, enabling us to communicate more rapidly and efficiently than writing, on paper. Electronic aids to communication can turn speech into writing, such as the mini com for people with a hearing disability or voice typing for people with dyslexia.

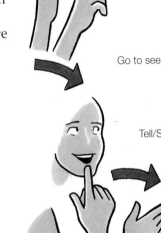

wait

Go to see

Tell/Say

■ *BSL signs*

Think about it

When you send text messages to friends, do you use symbols and shortened words that would not be acceptable in more formal academic work? If you send emails, do you use abbreviations, symbols and special terms or do you only use formal English? Why is it acceptable to use symbols and abbreviations when texting your friends but not when you do academic work?

Over to you

Check the labels of common food products. How many of them have Braille?

The communication cycle

Communication is not simply about giving information to people. While you are talking you go through a process or 'cycle' of thinking and interpreting what another person might mean, for example:

1 **Ideas occur** – you have an idea that you want to communicate.
2 **Message coded** – you think through how you are going to say what you are thinking. You put your thoughts into language or into some other code such as sign language.
3 **Message sent** – you speak; or perhaps you sign or write or in some way send your message.
4 **Message perceived** – the other person has to sense your message. They hear your words or see your symbols.
5 **Message decoded** – the other person has to interpret or 'decode' your message, i.e. what you have said. This is not always easy as the other person will make assumptions about your words and body language.
6 **Message understood** – if all goes well, your ideas will be understood, but this does not always happen first time!

The communication process might look something like this:

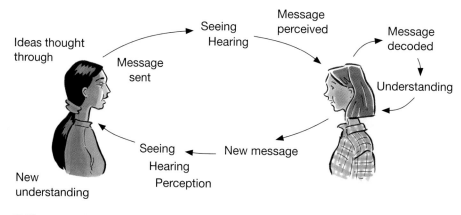

■ *The communication cycle*

Communication is a cycle because when two people communicate they need to check that their ideas have been understood. It is often easier to understand people who are similar to us. We can learn about different people by checking our understanding of what we have heard. Checking understanding involves hearing what the other person says and asking questions.

Another way is to put what a person has just said in your own words and say it back to them in order to check that you did understand. When listening to complicated details of other people's lives, you will often begin to form mental pictures based on what you are told. Listening skills involve checking these mental pictures to make sure that you understand correctly. It is important that the care worker shows that they are listening and involved with service users, not just making assumptions about people.

Real Life Care

Listening carefully

A service user is explaining her beliefs and choices about food. She says, 'I'm a Buddhist and a vegetarian.' Since most Buddhists are vegetarians, the care worker has an instant understanding of the service user's requirements. He checks his assumptions by saying, 'I will make sure you get vegetarian food then.' The service user replies, 'But I also eat fish.' The care worker now has to change his understanding – vegetarians do not normally eat fish! The care worker then says, 'So any vegetarian or fish meal will be OK, but you don't eat meat or poultry.' The service user explains, 'Yes, that's right. I believe that eating meat and poultry is wrong, but I interpret my religion to allow eating fish – perhaps I'm the first person you have met who does this?'

1 Why is it so important for care workers to repeat back what they think they have heard? ✓

2 Explain what might have happened if the care worker had just walked away after receiving the first answer? ✓✓

3 How does the communication cycle help care workers to provide high-quality interpersonal care? ✓✓✓

Good listening involves thinking about what you hear while you are listening and checking your understanding as the conversation goes along. Sometimes this idea of checking understanding is called 'reflection', because we reflect or mirror the other person's ideas.

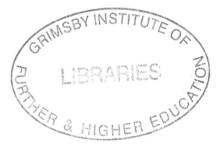

Practice for Assessment

Carrying out these activities will give you valuable knowledge and understanding of the evidence needed for Pass 1, Merit 1 and Distinction 1 criteria for Unit 1.

1 You need to plan and carry out both a one-to-one and a group conversation (also called an interaction) and identify the communication skills that you used to make the interactions successful. If you are spending any time in a health, social care or early years setting you could talk this over with your supervisor and plan to do these interactions with service users. Make sure that you treat all service users with respect and dignity and that you understand the importance of the setting's policies on confidentiality. It is important that you plan what you are going to talk about. Check this plan with your placement supervisor.

If you are not at a placement you can plan and carry out both interactions as role plays. Your tutor will help you plan these. Make sure that you take the role of a carer and that your peers take the roles of relevant service users.

One idea for doing this practical work in a classroom would be to get a voice recording or video of your interactions. If you have a recording of your work, you can hear it through again or see how you performed. It is then easier to identify your communication skills.

Identify how good you were at using the range of verbal and non-verbal skills set out in the grid below. Give yourself a mark out of five for how well you used each skill.

Skill	Mark out of 5
Using eye contact effectively	
Using facial expression effectively	
Using an appropriate tone of voice	
Using other aspects of body language	
Organising your conversation or taking turns in group conversation	
Using the conversation cycle and active listening	
Recognising cultural differences	

At merit grade

To achieve M1, you will need to go further than simply identifying the skills that you used. At this grade you will need to be able to describe the communication skills that you used in your one-to-one and group work – you will then need to be able to suggest additional ways in which you could improve your communication skills. You will need to think about your recordings and use ideas from this section of the book in order to help you to do this. You should then write an account of how you used communication skills and then write about your ideas for improving the interactions.

Practice for Assessment (continued)

At distinction grade

To achieve D1, you will need to be able to explain how communication skills can be used in a health or care setting to assist effective communication. One activity that could help you to prepare for this would be to interview a qualified nurse or social worker about the importance of communication skills in their work. You might be able to listen to a talk given to your class and ask questions; or you might take part in a group discussion or role plays of situations involving service users. You will then need to be able to explain the importance of some communication skills when working with service users.

Barriers to effective communication

What affects communication?

There are three main ways in which communication can become blocked:

- If a person is unable to see, hear or otherwise receive the message.
- If a person is unable to make sense of the message.
- If a person misunderstands the message.

Message not received

The first kind of block where people do not receive the communication includes:

- visual disabilities
- hearing disabilities
- environmental problems such as poor lighting, noisy environments, speaking from too far away.

People may not be able to sense a message – this is known as sensory deprivation. Visual and hearing disabilities may result in a person having feelings of isolation.

Message makes no sense

This may be as a result of the following:

- The use of different languages including foreign languages and signed languages.
- The use of different aspects of language such as:

Expression

Problems with seeing and hearing

■ *Environmental problems like noise and poor lighting can create communication barriers*

jargon – technical language

slang – language that only certain groups of people use

dialect – people from different areas make different sounds when they speak

acronyms – initials that stand for words, such as GSCC (General Social Care Council).

- The person receiving the message has physical and intellectual disabilities such as memory loss or learning disability.

Message misunderstood

The reasons for misunderstanding a message include:

- **Cultural differences** – different cultures interpret non-verbal and verbal messages and humour in different ways. Assumptions about ethnic group, gender, disability and other groupings can lead to stereotyping and misunderstanding.

- **Emotional issues** – very angry or very happy people may misinterpret communication from others. Aggression, distress or inappropriate behaviour may lead to misunderstanding.

- **Social setting** – statements and behaviour that are understood by friends and family may not be understood by strangers. People might use different types of language in different situations.

Because people are different from one another the communication cycle can easily be blocked if professional listening skills are not used.

The effects of communication difficulties

If a person cannot communicate effectively, there might be a danger that they will not receive appropriate physical care. Imagine you were in

Real Life Care

Talking to Frank

Frank has recently had a stroke which has left him unable to walk, use his left arm or speak clearly, although he may get back some of these abilities in time. Frank can understand everything that people say to him, but he cannot respond clearly. People often try to guess what Frank is saying and he has to shake his head if this is not right.

1 How might Frank feel having suddenly developed this communication difficulty? ✓

2 Identify some ways in which carers might help Frank to feel less stressed by his communication difficulties. ✓✓

3 Explain how carers might use non-verbal communication and the communication cycle to improve communication with Frank. ✓✓✓

pain, or that certain foods made you unwell, but you could not communicate this information to anyone. People might not respond to you – you might not get the right help to make you comfortable or receive the food that you would like.

Communication difficulties can cut people off, making it difficult for them to interact socially. A person unable to communicate might not be able to express their choices and wishes. They might end up feeling that they have not been respected; they might feel threatened and become frustrated or angry. It is very important to try to overcome barriers to communication in order to meet the physical, social and emotional needs of service users.

Ways of overcoming communication barriers

Visual disability

- Use spoken language to describe things and confirm information.
- Assist people to touch things, e.g. touch your face to recognise you.
- Explain details that sighted people might take for granted.
- Check what people can see – many registered blind people can see shapes or light and dark.
- Use materials in Braille or technological aids such as glasses, magnifiers or computer programs that enlarge information.

Hearing disability

- Don't shout; keep to normal, clear speech and make sure your face is visible for people who can lip-read.
- Show pictures, or write messages.
- Use alternative communication such as sign language (for people who use signed languages).
- Clarify communication using effective body language and eye contact.
- Employ a communicator or interpreter for signed languages.
- Use technological aids such as hearing aids and equipment.

Environmental factors
Adapt the environment by:

- improving lighting
- reducing background noise
- moving to a quieter or better lit room
- moving into smaller groups to see and hear each other more easily
- altering the layout of the room, e.g. by moving furniture.

Language differences

- Understand language needs and preferences, and use an individual's preferred spoken language.
- Communicate using pictures, diagrams and non-verbal signs, symbols and expressions.
- Use signers, translators or interpreters.

■ *Most people use signs to guide everyday life*

Jargon, slang and dialects

- Re-word your messages – find different ways of saying things.
- Try to speak in short, clear sentences.
- Make sure you understand the dialect of the service user.

Physical and intellectual disabilities

- Use pictures and signs as well as clear, simple speech.
- Be calm and patient; allow sufficient time to get the message understood.
- Repeat messages if needed. In some situations you might ask the service user to repeat the message.
- Set up group meetings where people can share interests, experiences or talk about the past.
- Check that people do not become isolated.

Misunderstandings

- Look out for different cultural interpretations.
- Avoid making assumptions or discriminating against people.
- Use active listening techniques to check that your understanding is correct.

Over to you

Use the sign language demonstration in a website about British Sign Language in order to work out how you would sign your name using British Sign Language. The BSL website will help you. To access this website, go to www.heinemann.co.uk/ hotlinks and enter the express code 3322P.

- Stay calm and try to calm people who are angry or excited.
- Be sensitive to different social settings and the form of communication that would be most appropriate.

Advocates, interpreters, translators and signers

An **advocate** is someone who tries to understand the needs and wishes of a service user, and argues on their behalf. Advocates are often needed when people have a very serious disability that means that it is not possible to communicate clearly with them. An advocate will try to get to know the service user and understand their culture and background. The advocate tries to understand the service user's needs and communicate these needs to care workers. Advocates should be independent and separate from the professional carers who are working with the service user.

Interpreters communicate meaning from one language to another, while translators change recorded material from one language to another. Translating and interpreting involve communicating meaning between different languages. Translating and interpreting is not simply a technical process of changing the words from one system to another. Interpreters and translators have to grasp the meaning of a message and find a way of expressing this meaning in a different language system. This is rarely a simple task even for professional translators.

Interpreters can be professional people but they may also be friends or family members. For example, a mother might learn sign language in order to communicate information to a deaf child. It is possible for family members to interpret for each other.

Interpretation and translation are vital in any setting where communication is blocked due to different languages or communication systems. For example, many people may not use English as their first language.

A signer is someone who can communicate using a sign language such as British Sign Language.

Advocate *An advocate argues a case for another person. In law an advocate argues a legal case for a client. In care work an advocate tries to understand and argue from a client's perspective.*

Key point

The Mental Capacity Act 2005 created a new mental advocacy service which began in England in 2007. Now there are specially trained 'independent mental capacity advocates' who can speak for vulnerable people.

Practice for Assessment

Carrying out this activity will give you the knowledge and understanding of the evidence needed for P2.

You must identify potential barriers to effective communication and suggest examples of how they can be overcome.

Start by designing a poster which identifies some of the barriers that patients and service users may experience. You could then design a second poster that identifies ways of overcoming these barriers. Provide a short presentation to explain your work.

Diversity and equality in society

Social factors that create diversity

You are special and no one is exactly the same as you. But you will be more like some people and less like others. Many of the differences between people occur because of the different cultural influences on us. Culture means the values and beliefs that different social groups have. We try to make ourselves individual, but we are also influenced by the groups that we belong to. Some ways in which people are different, or diverse, from each other are shown in the table on page 22. Sometimes diversity can lead to discrimination, where one group of people treats another group unfairly because of their differences. (Discrimination is discussed in more detail in the section on Equality on page 23.)

■ *Britain is a diverse society*

Ways in which people are diverse from each other and the risk of discrimination	
Social factor	**Diversity and the risk of discrimination**
Ethnicity	People may understand themselves as being black or white, as European, African or Asian. Many people have specific national identities such as Polish, Nigerian, English or Welsh. Assumptions about ethnic characteristics can lead to discrimination.
Gender	People are classified as male or female. In the past, men generally had more rights and were seen as more important than women. Assumptions about gender still lead to discrimination.
Sexuality	Many people see their sexual orientation as very important to understanding who they are. Gay and lesbian relationships are often discriminated against. Heterosexual people sometimes judge other relationships as 'wrong' or abnormal.
Age	People may identify others by their age group, viewing them as children, teenagers, young adults, middle aged or old. If some age groups are seen as better than others, or assumptions are made about the abilities of each age group, this may lead to discrimination.
Family structure	People choose many different lifestyles and emotional commitments, such as: marriage; having children; living in a large family; living a single lifestyle but having sexual partners; being single and not being sexually active. People live within different family and friendship groups. Discrimination can happen if people think that one lifestyle is 'right' or better than another.
Social class	People differ in their upbringing, the kind of work they do and the money they earn. People also differ in the lifestyles they lead and the views and values that go with different levels of income and spending habits. People may discriminate against others because of their class or lifestyle.
Geographical location	People develop different customs based on the area where they live. Sometimes people from another area are thought of as being outsiders, as being different and strange. People may make assumptions that they are only safe with people who belong to their own local community.
Religion	People grow up following different religious beliefs. For some people, spiritual beliefs are at the centre of their understanding of life. For others, religion influences the cultural traditions that they celebrate, e.g. many Europeans celebrate Christmas even though they might not see themselves as practising Christians. Discrimination can take place when people assume that their customs or beliefs should apply to everyone else.

Equality

Your own culture and life experience may lead you to make assumptions as to what is right or normal. When you meet people who are different from you, it can be easy to see them as 'not right' or 'not normal'. Different people see the world in different ways. Your way of thinking may seem unusual to others. Look at the illustration below. Which is the 'normal front of the cube'?

■ *Which is the 'normal' front of the cube?*

If a person was used to seeing the cube from one direction only, they might be sure their view was right. A person's culture may lead them to think that some habits are more normal than others. In order to learn about other people's culture and beliefs, you will need to listen and watch what other people say and do. A person's own culture and beliefs may feel challenged when they realise that different beliefs exist. Emotions may block their abilities to learn.

Skilled carers have to get to know the service users that they work with in order to avoid making false assumptions. In getting to know an individual, you will also need to understand the ways in which they are influenced by class, ethnicity, age, gender and other social categories. A person's culture may include all the social groups that they belong to.

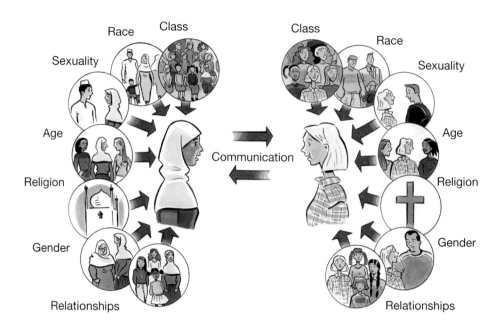

■ *The groups that a person belongs to will influence their beliefs and behaviour*

You can pick up background knowledge on different ethnic and religious customs, but it is impossible to study and learn all the differences that can exist for individual service users. The best way to learn about diversity is to listen and communicate with people who are different from you.

Real Life Care

Jayda's shoes

Jayda has recently gone to live in a hostel. She is puzzled that the other residents do not remove their shoes when they come in from the street. Jayda says that you have to have different shoes for indoors.

1 Try to identify why Jayda thinks that it is normal to change shoes when entering the home. ✓

2 Describe how care workers should respond to Jayda's need to change shoes, bearing in mind that the other residents do not think it is normal to change their shoes. ✓✓

3 What might be the consequences for Jayda if care workers simply ignored her views and told her to keep her outdoor shoes on inside? ✓✓✓

Differences between people should be seen as a good thing, but discrimination can result in a lack of equality between different people.

The word discrimination means to tell things apart – to know the differences between similar things. It is all right to discriminate between, say, a sandwich filling that you do not like and one that you do. Telling things apart is an essential part of life – if people did not do this, then they would not be able to live independently. But discrimination against people has a very different meaning – it means to treat people unfairly because of their differences. It is important to realise that people are all different, with different life experiences.

If an employer did not want to appoint a woman to a job – because she might leave to have children – the employer would be illegally discriminating against her. The discrimination would not be that the employer treated her unfairly because she was female; it would be because she was treated differently from a man who might want to start a family. A man in the same situation would be appointed while the woman receives unequal treatment because the employer thinks she might leave or take maternity leave to have a baby.

Discrimination can take place against people who belong to any group. Common forms of discrimination are based on ethnicity and culture, gender, age, disability and sexuality.

How does discrimination come about?

People usually feel that they belong to certain types of group such as friendship groups, families and so on. Some teenagers belong to gangs or clubs. People start to feel that there are 'people like me who I belong with'. Groups tend to include people who share the same views, who look similar and who think in the same way. But we all meet people who are different. There is a danger of seeing people who are not like us as being threatening, stupid or disgusting. Many people then divide their social world into Us and Them. 'Us' is the group we feel safe and OK with, i.e. 'Our Side'. 'Them' are the people who are different – people we don't like.

People who work in care have to be interested in learning about other people – including their diversity. Care workers must not divide people into 'types that I like' and 'types that I don't like'. As a care worker, you must never exclude service users from receiving a good service because they belong to a different ethnic group, culture, religion, gender or age group, or because of their sexuality or abilities.

Discrimination sometimes comes about because of assumptions that people make in their thinking. People will sometimes stereotype or label others.

Stereotyping

Life is very complicated for everyone. Sometimes people try to make life simpler by seeing people as being 'all the same'. Perhaps a younger person meets an 80-year-old who has a problem with their memory or they see someone like that on television. It is easy then to think that 'all old people are forgetful'. This would be a **stereotype**.

People may make assumptions based on stereotyped thinking. For example, a carer working with older people might say, 'I'll just go in and wash and dress this next one. I won't ask her what she would like me to do because she's old – old people don't remember – so it doesn't matter what I do.' Stereotyped thinking may cause us to discriminate against people.

Key point

Discrimination means to treat some types of people less well than others. In health and social care, discriminating against service users means to give them an unequal service or treatment because of their differences.

Over to you

You can probably think of groups of people who lead very different lives from you. Do these people seem interesting and exciting because they are different, or do these people seem frightening, wrong, disgusting and so on?

Stereotype *An assumption using a fixed set of ideas.*

■ *An example of stereotyped thinking*

When people say, 'All women are …,' or 'All black people are …,' or 'All gay people are …,' they will probably go on to describe a stereotype of these groups.

Skilled caring starts with being interested in people's individual differences. Stereotyping clumps people together as all the same. Thinking in stereotypes usually stops a person from being a good carer.

Labelling

Another way in which thinking can lead to discrimination is labelling. Labelling is similar to stereotyping but labels are simpler. Instead of having a set of thoughts about a group, a person gets summed up in just one word or term.

Over to you

Many years ago, there was a school for children with learning difficulties. When it came to meal times, the 'slows' were allowed to start first because they took longer. Staff would label children 'slows'. The 'slows' sat down when the word 'slows' was called out. Some children were not very skilled at holding plates, etc. These children were labelled 'clumsies'. Children would describe themselves as 'slows' and 'clumsies'.

What effect do you think being called a 'slow' or a 'clumsy' would have on a child?

Labels can be words like:

- aggressive
- emotional
- disgusting.

These words might be used to describe ethnic groups, women or old people. Labels can be used to say that a group of people are all the same. Labels may say that people are all only one thing, such as aggressive, emotional or disgusting. When individuals are labelled, it is almost as if they stop being people; they are simply the label – no other details matter. Labels take away people's dignity and individuality.

Prejudice

When people live in a world of 'Us' and 'Them', it becomes easy to judge people who are different. For example, people who are unemployed might be judged as lazy by people who have not experienced unemployment. People who do not lead healthy lifestyles might be seen as 'stupid' by people who can manage to do the right things. Judging other people involves thinking that we are better or superior, our views are right and that people who do not meet our standards should be criticised or punished for failing to meet our expectations.

The word prejudice comes from the term pre-judgement. Prejudice is when a person has decided that they can judge other people and that they have all the knowledge they need to judge, even though the 'knowledge' may be wrong. No new information or understanding can alter their judgement; it is a 'pre-judgement' that is not open to being changed. If people believe stereotypes about groups, they may go on to make judgements about individuals. For instance, if a health care worker believes that 'all Asians are vegetarians', they may not offer an Asian service user the full range of available menus.

Once people develop prejudices against groups of people, they are likely to discriminate if they are in a position to make decisions.

Key point

Prejudice is to pre-judge a person without examining the facts fairly. A person can be prejudiced against a group of people simply because they are different.

Forms of discrimination

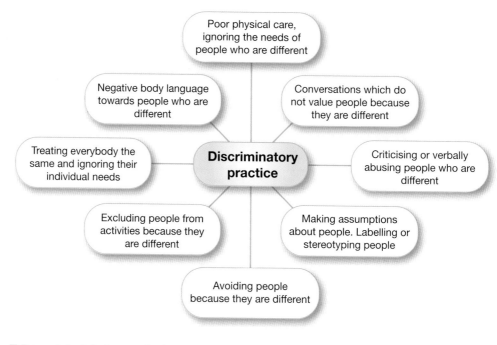

Discriminatory practice

- Poor physical care, ignoring the needs of people who are different
- Conversations which do not value people because they are different
- Criticising or verbally abusing people who are different
- Making assumptions about people. Labelling or stereotyping people
- Avoiding people because they are different
- Excluding people from activities because they are different
- Treating everybody the same and ignoring their individual needs
- Negative body language towards people who are different

■ *Types of discriminatory practice in care settings*

Real Life Care

Setting people apart

Many years ago, a care worker explained that people with learning difficulties were not allowed to leave the hospital where they were cared for because 'these people are not normal and they would become distressed if they were let out'. These service users were never given a choice about their clothing or meals 'because it would only confuse them'. Sometimes, service users were shouted at and ordered to fit in with activities that care workers wanted them to do. There was an attitude that 'these people' should be kept away from 'normal people' so that 'normal people' would not have to look at them.

1 Identify some examples of discrimination in this story. ✓

2 Identify examples of labelling/stereotyping and explain how these labels or stereotypes contribute to discrimination. ✓✓

3 Explain how the idea of 'normal people' is likely to result in discrimination. ✓✓✓

People are often discriminated against because of their class, ethnicity, gender, religion, sexuality or age. Discrimination may take a variety of forms as shown in the following diagram.

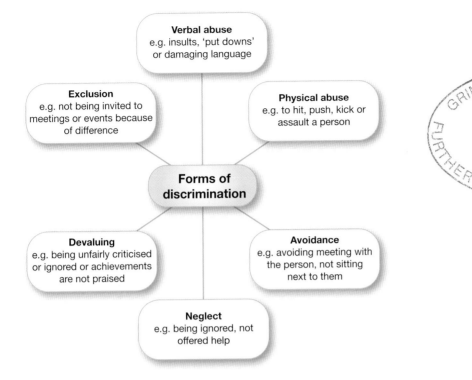

■ *Forms of discrimination*

Physical abuse

Physical abuse means to hit, push, kick or otherwise assault a person. People may commit assault because they hate certain groups or simply because they feel frustrated or annoyed by people who are different.

Verbal abuse

Verbal abuse means any insults, 'put downs' or damaging language which is spoken. Physical and verbal abuse may happen because individuals feel that they are more powerful if they can hurt other people.

Neglect

Sometimes people are discriminated against by being ignored or not offered the help that others might receive.

Exclusion

Exclusion is a more subtle form of discrimination which may be hard to prove. Exclusion means to stop people from accessing services or jobs because they belong to a certain class, ethnic group and so on. People with physical disabilities may still be excluded from certain services because access is difficult. Some buildings still do not have full disabled access facilities. Some jobs may not be advertised in all local areas, so excluding certain communities.

Avoidance

People sometimes try to avoid sitting next to people or working with people who are different from them. People who decide to discriminate

> **Abuse** *This covers a range of negative and damaging behaviour, including hitting, humiliation, exploiting, stealing from or neglecting others.*

against others may try to avoid contact, perhaps so that they do not need to learn or to re-think any of their prejudices.

Devaluing

Discrimination may involve seeing some types of people as less valuable than others. Some people are helped to build a sense of self-esteem because they receive praise and their ideas are valued. People who are 'different' may be criticised and their ideas ignored. People who are subjected to constant discrimination and prejudice may develop a low sense of self-esteem (see Unit 6 Human Lifespan Development, page 278).

The effects of discrimination

Discrimination that results in abuse can have permanent and extremely damaging effects on people. All forms of discrimination will harm service users. Some of the effects of discrimination are shown in the diagram below.

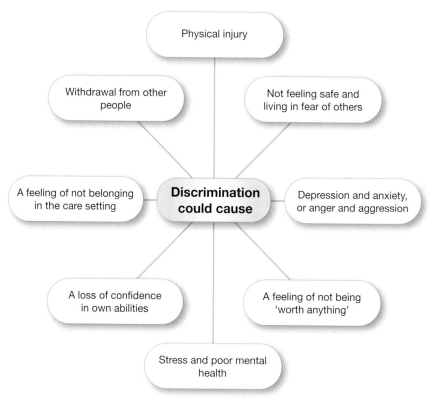

■ *Some effects of discrimination on people in care settings*

Sometimes people communicate in a way that does not show equal respect and value for all others. A person may not want to sit next to someone that they have a prejudice about. People may use different body language when they have a prejudice towards someone. Discrimination is not always obvious in the way it comes about. Very often carers might simply make assumptions that everyone does, or should, think like they do – this may come out in conversation.

Real Life Care

We treat everyone the same!

Many years ago, a manager of a care home explained that they provided a very good service because everybody was treated the same. Everyone was spoken to in the same way; everybody ate the same meals and so on. When asked about vegetarians, the manager explained, 'Well, they don't have to eat the meat – we tell them to leave it if they don't want it.'

1 How might a person who had religious reasons for not eating meat feel if they were given a meat meal and just told to leave it if they did not want it? ✓

2 Explain why 'treating everybody the same' might result in discrimination. ✓✓

3 Explain some of the possible consequences for service users if they are not treated as individuals and are discriminated against. ✓✓✓

Political factors affecting diversity and equality

There are many laws in the United Kingdom that help create a fairer society, so that people are not discriminated against.

Legislation

The main Acts of Parliament to do with discrimination are:

- the Equal Pay Act 1970 (amended 1983)
- the Sex Discrimination Act 1975 (amended 1986)
- the Race Relations Act 1976 (amended 2000)
- the Disability Discrimination Act 1995 and the Disability Rights Commission Act 1999
- the Equality Act 2006

These laws directly influence the quality standards that are used to inspect health and care services. Every health and care service will have equal opportunities policies designed to make sure that people's legal rights – created by these Acts of Parliament – are respected.

Over to you

Look at the titles of these Acts. What do you think they mean?

The Equal Pay Act 1970

This Act made it unlawful for employers to discriminate between men and women in terms of their pay and conditions of work. Before this law was passed, it was possible for an employer to pay men more than women, even though the women were doing the same job.

Equal pay legislation was updated in 1975 and 1983 to make it possible to claim equal pay for work that was considered to be of 'equal value'.

The Sex Discrimination Act 1975

This Act made it unlawful to discriminate between men and women in respect of employment, goods and facilities. The Act also made it illegal to discriminate on the grounds of marital status. The Act identified two forms of discrimination:

- direct discrimination
- indirect discrimination.

The law was updated in 1986 so that it also applied to small businesses.

The Race Relations Act 1976

This Act makes it unlawful to discriminate on 'racial grounds', in employment, housing or services. Racial grounds means colour, race, nationality, ethnic or national origins. The Act makes it an offence to incite or encourage racial hatred. As in the law against sex discrimination, both direct and indirect discrimination are made unlawful.

The Race Relations Act was strengthened and widened in 2000 in order to prevent discrimination in any public situation.

The Disability Discrimination Act 1995

This Act is designed to prevent discrimination against people with disabilities, in employment, access to education and transport, housing and obtaining goods and services, including access to health and social care services. Employers and landlords must not treat a person with disabilities less favourably than a non-disabled person. New transport must meet the needs of disabled people, and colleges, shops and other services must ensure that disabled people can use their services.

The Equality Act 2006

This act of Parliament further strengthens the law on gender equality, with new duties for public bodies to ensure gender equality when formulating policies or providing services. The act also makes discrimination on the grounds of religion or sexuality illegal.

The Equality and Human Rights Commission

Before the Equality Act there was an **Equal Opportunities Commission** to prevent discrimination on the basis of gender, a **Commission for Racial Equality** to prevent discrimination on the basis of race, and a **Disability Rights Commission** to prevent discrimination on the basis of disability. The Equality Act created a new **Commission for Equality and Human Rights** which will take over the work of these previous commissions and also seek to protect people from discrimination associated with religion or belief, sexual orientation and age. This new commission will also promote human rights issues. The **Equality and Human Rights Commission** started work on the 1st October 2007.

■ *Care workers have to work to National Minimum Standards and they have to work within the law*

Policies

The welfare state was first set up in 1948. Before then, people had to pay money to see a doctor or get treatment. The development of the National Health Service (NHS) and social services meant that people could get free treatment when they needed help, because the welfare state services were funded by taxation.

Today, the NHS, local authority social services and private and voluntary organisations provide health and care services. Since 1997, the government has set out to improve health and care services. It introduced the Care Standards Act 2000 in order to improve the quality of social care. (For more information on the way in which health and care services work, see Units 2 and 3.)

National Minimum Standards of Care

The Care Standards Act 2000 resulted in a set of regulations and National Minimum Standards that care services must achieve. There are different sets of standards for different care services. The aim of the standards is to provide detailed guidance for providing good services. Care services are now inspected by the Commission for Social Care Inspection (CSCI) to make sure that services meet National Minimum Standards.

The NHS plan

In 2000 the government introduced the NHS plan with the aim of providing greater choice for people and improving services by providing more money, better inspection of services and better staff training and equipment.

The NHS plan was updated in 2004 and emphasised the importance of 'personalised services'. Since then government policy papers such as *'Our health our care our say: a new direction for community services (2006)'* have emphasised the importance of choice and personalisation.

Personalisation

Government policy is that people should not only have a choice of what hospital they might go to, or what GP they might register with, but also that people should be able to 'shape their own lives and the services they receive in all care settings'.

Individual budgets

Personalisation might lead to some service users receiving an individual budget so that they can choose what support or services they would like to buy. The government is currently undertaking research to explore how individual budgets might work for different service users.

Practice for Assessment

Carrying out this activity will allow you to provide evidence for P3.

You need to be able to identify the factors that contribute to diversity and influence the equality of individuals in society.

Design a poster to celebrate diversity and show value for the equality of diverse groups of people.

At merit grade

To achieve M2, you will need to be able to describe the effects of at least six factors on the equality of individuals in society. Develop your work on celebrating diversity by writing about the risks of discrimination that at least six categories of people might face.

The care value base

The care value base in health and social care work

The idea of a value base came from early National Vocational Qualifications (NVQs) in Care. The value base explained how a care worker must 'value' the service users that they worked with. Nowadays, these qualifications still require that care workers demonstrate values, but care values are now defined by the General Social Care Council (GSCC) code of practice.

Key point

The GSCC code of practice sets out the rights of service users and the values that care workers must work with.

Over to you

Why are values important? Imagine that you went abroad and then became seriously ill. Imagine that you could not communicate easily with the people who were looking after you. Now imagine that your carers did not seem to like you, or respect you. Imagine that you were watched all the time and had no privacy, even when going to the toilet. Imagine that the staff talked about your details and your illness without asking your permission. How would this make you feel?

Most people would probably feel threatened. Care values and the code of practice are designed to try to help service users to feel safe – and valued.

Below is a summary of the GSCC code of practice for social care workers.

According to the code you must:

- **Protect the rights and promote the interests of service users and carers**
  Includes: respecting individuality and supporting service users to control their own lives; respecting and maintaining equal opportunities, diversity, dignity and privacy.

- **Establish and maintain the trust and confidence of service users**
  Includes: maintaining confidentiality; using effective communication; honouring commitments and agreements; declaring conflicts of interest and keeping to policies about accepting gifts.

- **Uphold public trust and confidence in social care services**
  Includes: care workers must not abuse, neglect or exploit service users or colleagues, or form inappropriate personal relationships; discriminate or condone discrimination; place self or others at

unnecessary risk; behave in a way that raises suitability issues; abuse the trust of others in relation to confidentiality.

- **Promote the independence of service users while protecting them from danger or harm**
Includes: maintaining rights; challenging and reporting dangerous, abusive, discriminatory or exploitative behaviour; following safe practice; reporting resource problems; reporting unsafe practice of colleagues; following health and safety regulations; helping service users to make complaints and using power responsibly.

- **Respect the rights of service users while seeking to ensure that their behaviour does not allow them to harm themselves or other people**
Includes: recognising the right to take risks; following risk assessment policies; minimising risks; ensuring others are informed about risk assessments.

- **Be accountable for the quality of your work and take responsibility for maintaining and improving your knowledge and skills**
Includes: meeting standards, maintaining appropriate records and informing employer of personal difficulties; seeking assistance and cooperating with colleagues; recognising responsibility for delegated work; respecting the roles of others, and undertaking relevant training.

Other codes of practice, charters and policies

Over to you

Try to visit a care setting and ask the care workers about the ways in which they protect the privacy and dignity of service users and maintain confidentiality of information.

Nurses follow a code of professional conduct published by the Nursing and Midwifery Council (NMC). The code has similar principles to the GSCC code for social care. Its key principles are listed below.

You must:

- respect the patient or client as an individual
- obtain consent before you give any treatment or care
- cooperate with others in the team
- protect confidential information
- maintain your professional knowledge and competence
- be trustworthy
- act to identify and minimise risk to patients and clients.

Another source of policies that define the values and principles of caring are charters. Many health services, such as GPs' surgeries, may have a charter that lays down the quality of service that a patient might expect. Originally, the idea for these charters may have come from the Patient's Charter, launched by the government in 1992. This charter was replaced in 2001 by a lengthy publication called 'Your Guide to the NHS: Getting the Most from Your National Health Service'.

Individual rights

Service users have a range of rights that are established in codes of practice and legislation, as shown in the diagram below.

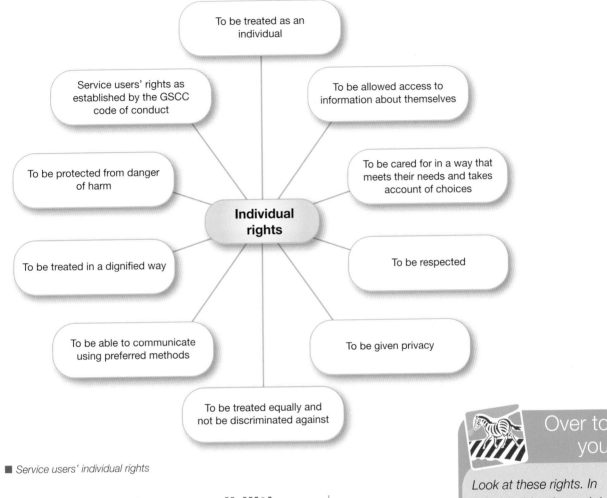

- *Service users' individual rights*

Care workers' responsibilities

As a care worker, you will be expected to work with service users in a way that demonstrates the values set out in the relevant codes of practice. This includes respecting the individual rights of service users. In order to do this, you will need to provide active support to service users to enable them to communicate their needs, views and preferences.

Active support

Some service users may not feel confident in expressing their thoughts and feelings. To help them, you will need to use the communication skills explained in this unit together with skills for overcoming barriers to communication. As well as using active listening skills, you will need to demonstrate respect and value for the people you work with. Without these, the kind of event illustrated in the following example could happen.

Over to you

Look at these rights. In pairs decide why each is important and feed this back to your group.

Real Life Care

Discriminatory practice

The following conversation took place at 7.30 am in a resident's bedroom in a care home.

Care worker: Morning, Mabel, let's have you up then, come on.

Service user: What time is it?

Care worker: It's 7.30 – time you were up and dressed for breakfast.

Service user: I want to stay in bed.

Care worker: Now come on, don't give me a hard time. I have to get you up, just like everyone else. They'll say I'm not doing my job if you stay here, and I'm not having that. *(Lifts service user to side of the bed)* Right now, what dress shall we have today? The blue one, that would look nice – let's help you into this.

Service user: What's for breakfast?

Care worker: Bacon and egg, same as always – something nice, eh. I wish someone would wait on me and get my breakfast.

Service user: I don't eat bacon!

Care worker: Well, you ought to be grateful – you don't have to eat it, you know. Here, you're not one of those nutty ones who don't eat meat, are you? I hate all those moaners, never pleased whatever you do for them, meat's too good for 'em, that's what I say.

Service user: Oh …

Care worker: Right now, I'll wash your face and hands, it will be quicker. I haven't got all day, you know. After that, I'll put you on the toilet while I help Rose downstairs. *(Shouts down the corridor)* I'm just putting this one on the toilet. I won't be a minute, Rose.

1 Describe how this conversation could have negative consequences for the service user. ✓

2 Identify some of the service user's rights that have been ignored. ✓✓

3 Explain how the conversation should go in order to meet the service user's rights. ✓✓✓

Compare your list of rights that have been ignored with the one below:

1 **Discrimination.** The service user may not like bacon because of her ethnic customs, religious or moral beliefs. People who do not like meat are labelled 'nutty ones' by the care worker. The care worker is discriminating against people who do not think the way they do. The worker is also forcing their opinions on a powerless person.

2 **Care.** The service user is not being cared for in a way that meets her needs or takes account of her choices; she is being given orders by the care worker. The conversation fails to value Mabel. In the end, the service user gives up and groans 'Oh …'.

3 **Respect for others**. There is no evidence of respect. The service user is accused of being 'nutty'. She is not allowed to stay in bed (although in the past she used to get up later). The service user's routine is not respected. Finally, the service user gets put on the toilet while the care worker helps Rose. The service user is treated like an object rather than a person.

4 **Choice and dignity.** The service user's rights are not respected; she is given no choice. She has no dignity and is ignored, e.g. by being pulled out of bed against her wishes. The service user is not given any independence and has to follow the care worker's routine. The

service user has no choice of what to wear or to eat for breakfast. Everyone gets bacon and egg!

5   **Privacy.** The service user has no right to privacy. The care worker shouts down the corridor that 'this one' is being put on the toilet. Going to the toilet is now a public event – the service user is denied any privacy for her personal body functions.

The conversation between Mabel and the care worker lasted only a few minutes, but in that time Mabel's rights were ignored. If this were to go on throughout the day, the service user would have a very poor quality of life. Some people might say that Mabel would have little to live for.

If care workers respect individual rights and work within a value base, a caring conversation might go like this:

Care worker: Good morning, Mabel. How are you feeling this morning?

Service user: What time is it?

Care worker: It's 7.30. Do you feel like getting up for breakfast yet?

Service user: No, I want to say in bed a bit longer.

Care worker: That's all right. Shall I come back in half an hour?

Service user: Mmm.

Care worker: See you later. (*Later*) Good morning, Mabel. It's 8 o'clock. Are you ready to get up now?

Service user: All right.

Care worker: What would you like to wear? There's the blue dress or the white one, or the yellow top and skirt. What do you think?

Service user: Don't know.

Care worker: Well, would the blue dress be good? It matches the colour of your eyes, you know.

Service user: (*Laughs*) Go on then … What's for breakfast?

Care worker: Well, there is bacon and egg.

Service user: I don't eat bacon.

Care worker: Oh, I'm sorry, I forgot you don't eat bacon. There's lots of things – you can have toast or cereal, or fruit, coffee, bread and marmalade. What would you like?

Service user: Don't know.

Care worker: Well, we'll go through the list when we get downstairs.

Service user: Toast.

Care worker: OK, toast. I'll make sure you get some toast. Would you like to wash now or later? Would you like me to help you? Do you use a flannel? Let me see if I can find it for you.

This time, the care worker enables the service user to communicate her needs. Communication is used effectively and in a way that values diversity and is non-discriminatory. The service user is respected and her needs are understood. Mabel's privacy is respected and she makes her own choices.

Tensions between rights and responsibilities

Service users have a right to choose their lifestyle and their beliefs, but a person's lifestyle and beliefs must not reduce the quality of other people's lives. Rights have to be balanced with responsibilities. People have a right to act as they wish, but not a right to cause problems for others. For example, people have a right to smoke, even though smoking causes serious illnesses, including heart disease and cancer. However, people do not have the right to make others breathe in their smoke and risk their health.

Over to you

Mia is a smoker who works in a health clinic and smoking is illegal within the building. Mia says that it is her right to smoke, but the law forces her to go outside the building, where it is sometimes cold and wet, in order to smoke. She says that the law is unfair – 'Why should the law discriminate against me just because I smoke?'

Is the law unfair? What rights and responsibilities are involved here?

Service users' rights and responsibilities	
People in care have a right to:	**People in care have a responsibility to:**
Control and independence in their own life	Help others to be independent and not try to control other people
Be valued and respected	Value and respect others
Maintain own beliefs and lifestyle	Respect the different beliefs and lifestyles of others
Make choices and take risks	Not interfere with others or put others at risk
Not be discriminated against	Not discriminate against others
Confidentiality	Respect the confidentiality of others

Real Life Care

Graham is a 38-year-old man with a learning disability. He gets great pleasure from eating and particularly enjoys sweet things such as honey and jam. Graham is overweight and care workers think that he should go on a diet for health reasons. Graham cannot understand their ideas and becomes angry if he cannot have his usual food.

1 Identify the rights and risks involved in Graham's situation. ✓

2 Describe the consequences that might follow from restricting Graham's independence and choice. ✓✓

3 Given the balance of rights and risks, does Graham have a right to eat sweet things and be overweight – even if this damages his health? ✓✓✓

The balance between rights and responsibility is often hard to decide. Sometimes it is important to involve an advocate for a service user and there is often a need for negotiation and problem-solving work.

Confidentiality

Confidentiality is an important right of all service users, as shown below.

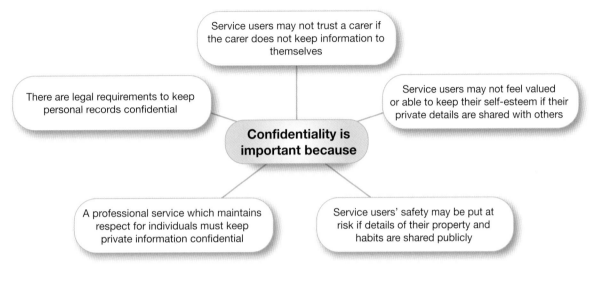

Service users may not trust a carer if the carer does not keep information to themselves

There are legal requirements to keep personal records confidential

Service users may not feel valued or able to keep their self-esteem if their private details are shared with others

Confidentiality is important because

A professional service which maintains respect for individuals must keep private information confidential

Service users' safety may be put at risk if details of their property and habits are shared publicly

■ *Importance of confidentiality in health and social care*

Trust
If a service user knows that their care worker will not pass information on, they may feel able to tell their care worker what they really think and feel.

Self-esteem
If a care worker promises the service user to keep things confidential, then it shows that they respect and value them; it may even show that the service user matters to them.

Safety
Care workers need to keep personal details confidential to protect service users' property and personal safety. For example, if a care worker lets slip that a particular service user keeps their money in a certain place in their home and that they are always out on a Tuesday, then that information might tempt someone to break into the service user's home.

Staying professional
Medical practitioners and lawyers have always kept strict confidentiality as part of their professional role. If service users are to receive a professional service, care workers must copy this example.

Over to you

You keep a diary, but you find out someone has been reading it. How do you feel?

Legal requirements – the Data Protection Act 1998

The Data Protection Act protects people's rights to confidentiality and covers both paper and electronic records. The Act provides you with a range of rights including:

- the right to know what information is held on you and to see and correct this information

- the right for you to refuse to provide information

- the right that data held on you should be accurate and up to date

- the right that data held on you should not be kept for longer than necessary

- the right to confidentiality – information about you should not be accessible to unauthorised people.

Confidentiality and disclosure

As a care worker, you should always ask a service user first if it is all right to let other people know things. It would be wrong even to pass on the date of a person's birthday without getting their permission. Whatever you know about a service user should be kept private unless they agree that it is all right to share the information. The exception to this rule is that information can be passed on when others have a right and a need to know it.

Some examples of people who may have a need to know about issues are:

- managers – they may need to make decisions that affect the service user

- other care workers – they may need to know important issues about a service user

- other professionals – they may need to be kept up to date with information.

Confidentiality *To keep secure and private information about service users. This is an important care value.*

When information is passed to other professionals, it should be passed on with the understanding that they preserve **confidentiality**. Relatives will often say that they have a right to know about service users. Sometimes care workers will ask relatives to discuss issues directly with a service user rather than giving out information, for example:

Relative: Has the doctor said anything more about my mother's illness?

Care worker: I expect your mother would like to talk to you directly. Shall I show you to her room?

Accurate recording

Because care work involves communicating with many people, it is vital that information is carefully checked and recorded. When phone calls or other messages are taken, it is vital that key details are written down, because it is easy to forget information.

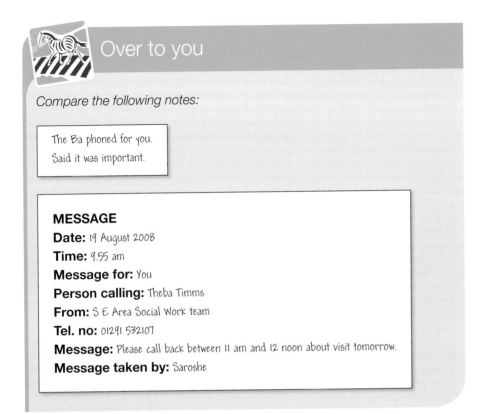

Over to you

Compare the following notes:

> The Ba phoned for you.
> Said it was important.

MESSAGE
Date: 19 August 2008
Time: 9.55 am
Message for: You
Person calling: Theba Timms
From: S E Area Social Work team
Tel. no: 01291 532107
Message: Please call back between 11 am and 12 noon about visit tomorrow.
Message taken by: Saroshe

The first note is inaccurate and contains little information. The second note follows a set of headings which helps the worker to take accurate information.

Storing and retrieving records

Personal records and information may be kept electronically on a computer, or manually in handwritten or printed files. Whichever way records are kept, there should be a range of security measures to make sure the information stays confidential and is not lost or inappropriately altered.

Manual records

- Records should be kept in a locked room or a locked cupboard where only authorised staff can get access to the files.

- Records should not be taken out of a secure room or area (to avoid the risk of loss) or left somewhere where others might see them.

- Records should be filed using a system, such as an alphabetical system, so that they can be found easily.

- There should be a policy as to who should update records or change details.

- When a person changes records they should initial the changes and add the date of any changes.

Electronic records

- There should be a back-up copy in case the computer system crashes and the originals are lost.

- Everyone should use a password to ensure that only authorised staff have access.

- There should be a policy on the printing of records (similar to manual records) so that hard copies do not get lost or are seen by unauthorised staff.

- There should be a policy about who is authorised to update or change records. The recording system must prevent information being altered or lost by accident.

- Faxed documents should be printed out in a secure area and the documents kept in a secure system to prevent unauthorised people having access to confidential material.

If records are not managed in accordance with the Data Protection Act, service users might suffer a range of damaging consequences, as shown below.

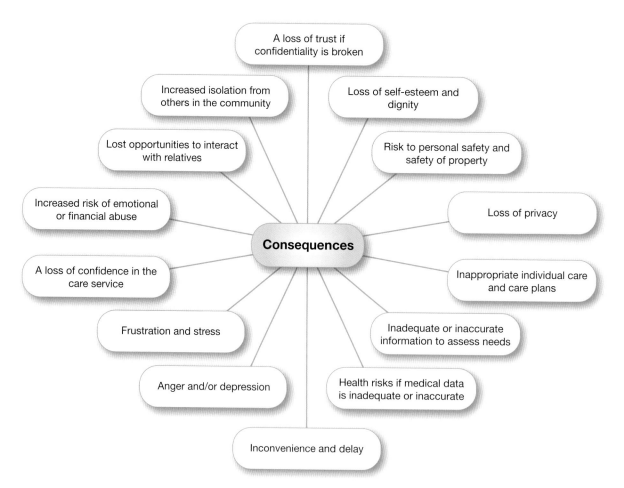

A loss of trust if confidentiality is broken

Increased isolation from others in the community

Loss of self-esteem and dignity

Lost opportunities to interact with relatives

Risk to personal safety and safety of property

Increased risk of emotional or financial abuse

Loss of privacy

Consequences

A loss of confidence in the care service

Inappropriate individual care and care plans

Frustration and stress

Inadequate or inaccurate information to assess needs

Anger and/or depression

Health risks if medical data is inadequate or inaccurate

Inconvenience and delay

■ Possible consequences of not maintaining records correctly

Practice for Assessment

Carrying out these activities will give you evidence for P4 and P5 for Unit 1.

1 You must describe the rights of patients/service users.

2 You must identify the principles of the care value base and care workers' responsibilities to patients/service users.

To help identify these issues, design an introductory leaflet for a care setting that you have visited, or that has been described in detail in class. Your leaflet should provide a list of the rights that users of the service might expect.

Your leaflet should also identify standards of behaviour that users of the service might expect from care workers. In this way, the leaflet could identify the principles of the care value base.

At merit grade

To achieve a merit grade for Unit 1, develop your work on the introductory leaflet to include examples that describe how care workers might respond to various situations. For example, explain how care staff can provide choices, how care workers can show respect towards service users, how care staff can treat people as individuals. Alternatively, provide examples of how the care value base works by discussing case studies and providing your answers to these studies.

At distinction grade

To achieve a distinction grade for Unit 1, you will need to explain how the principles of the care value base and care workers' responsibilities can be applied to promoting patients' and service users' rights.

If you have identified a list of care values and workers' responsibilities, you should go through your list and provide examples and explanations of how care workers can demonstrate each value or responsibility. If you are on placement in a health or care setting you can use examples from your placement for this distinction criterion. Make sure you maintain confidentiality.

Check your understanding

1. What does non-verbal communication mean?

2. Why is eye contact important during group communication?

3. What is the difference between active listening and just hearing what someone has said?

4. What is the communication cycle and why is it called a 'cycle'?

5. What is an advocate?

6. How could you try to communicate with people who have difficulty in hearing you?

7. What does stereotyping mean?

8. Why is it wrong for care workers to tell their friends about the personal details of service users that they work with?

9. Give three reasons why it is important to keep accurate records about service users.

10. Why is it wrong to discriminate against people who are different from you?

2 Individual Needs within the Health and Social Care Sectors

Introduction

Every individual has physical, intellectual, emotional and social needs. This unit looks at those needs and at the life choices that people make and how those choices can have a dramatic influence on their needs. You will have the opportunity to plan a healthy life style by developing a detailed understanding of the holistic needs of individuals. The unit also explores hazards in care settings and how legislation promotes the needs of service users.

How you will be assessed

This is an internally assessed unit.

In this unit you will learn about:

- the needs of individuals in society
- factors influencing the health and needs of individuals
- hazards in health and social care environments
- health and safety legislation and guidelines.

The needs of individuals in society

Maslow's hierarchy of needs

It is very hard to define what is meant by an individual's need. In fact, it is not possible to see a need until it is not met. When our needs are not satisfied, we become hungry, tired, cold, bored and even lonely. The **psychologist** Abraham Maslow suggested that it is possible to group needs in order of importance.

Psychologist *A person who studies human behaviour.*

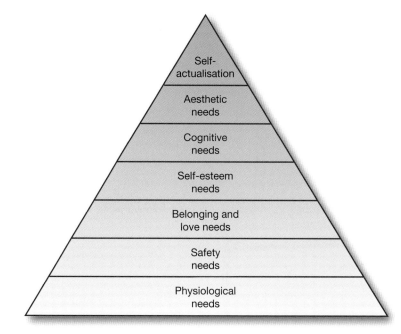

Maslow's hierarchy of needs
- Self-actualisation
- Aesthetic needs
- Cognitive needs
- Self-esteem needs
- Belonging and love needs
- Safety needs
- Physiological needs

■ *Maslow's hierarchy of needs*

Maslow believed that basic physical needs such as food, drink, air, sleep and warmth must be met first before individuals can grow and develop. If a person is hungry and cold, they cannot think about anything else until these basic needs are satisfied. Once basic physical needs are met, we can then consider personal safety and security. It is important that we feel safe and secure in our environment. We naturally try to avoid things that make us anxious, and usually feel safest when we can predict what is going to happen. It is not until we feel safe that we can begin to think about any other needs we may have. Self-esteem is how we feel about ourselves. People need to feel that they are respected and valued and that they have a special and unique place within their own society. To Maslow, the most important stage is that of self-actualisation or self-fulfilment. Self-actualisation is the point in life when all other needs have been met, and we can now meet our true full potential, achieving our personal goals and challenges. Some people will never reach self-actualisation as they spend their lives trying to satisfy basic physical and emotional needs.

Real Life Care

Sleeping rough

Greg left school at 16 and started full-time work at the local supermarket as a shelf filler. When he was 17 years old, Greg's parents divorced and he left home because he felt nobody wanted him. As he had nowhere to live, he started to sleep on a bench in a park and soon lost his job at the supermarket.

Aged 18, Greg was given his own room in a hostel. The staff were very supportive and he made some good friends. He was able to find work filling boxes in a local packing factory. Shortly after starting work he met Debbie.

Greg is now 28. He is the supervisor of the packing factory, and a respected member of staff. He is married to Debbie and they have a baby daughter. Greg is also going to college to study Business Skills. He is very happy and contented with his life.

1 Describe which of Greg's needs are not being met and where he is on Maslow's hierarchy at the age of 17. ✓

2 Now describe where Greg is on Maslow's hierarchy of needs at the age of 18. What has changed? ✓✓

3 At 28, have all of Greg's needs been met and has he reached self-actualisation? If not, explain why. ✓✓✓

Physical needs

These needs are things such as food, drink, warmth, shelter and security. Throughout our lives our physical needs change. As a young child, you relied on others to provide your physical needs – babies cannot feed themselves; the infant needs warmth and protection. As we become adults, we begin to take over the responsibility of supplying our own physical needs, for example buying food to feed ourselves and taking on a mortgage or paying rent to provide a home in which to shelter. Old age may once again result in the need for others to help provide and maintain our physical needs.

Social needs

Social needs are met through relationships with other people. By forming relationships with others, we achieve a sense of belonging and acceptance. Within our daily lives, we form many social relationships, for example as a friend, colleague, voluntary worker or member of a sports team. Happiness often comes from achieving a sense of belonging and being needed by someone else, but relationships can go wrong. When relationships become difficult or collapse and social needs are not met, people can become lonely and depressed. Consider the teenager who is bullied by her friends. If she has nobody to turn to for comfort and support, then her life may become very lonely and difficult.

■ *Where social needs are not met, a person can become lonely*

Real Life Care

Bullied!

Susie is 14 years old. She is being bullied at school and feels she has nobody to turn to. She is shy and has few friends.

1 Identify how Susie's social needs are not being met.

2 How could Susie improve her social needs?

3 Where would Susie be on Maslow's hierarchy of needs?

Over to you

Think about an ordinary day in your life. Now write a list of the number of daily social relationships that you have. Put them in an order that is most important to you. Describe how you would feel if one of these people no longer wanted to be with you.

Emotional needs

Everybody needs to be liked and even loved. A newborn baby needs love from its parents. Emotional needs change as we grow and develop. Children begin to test the boundaries that relationships provide, experiencing many different emotions for the first time. As adolescence takes over, we begin to find fulfilment from developing a close bond with one person with whom we share an emotional attachment.

Intellectual needs

Try to learn something new every day! Intellectual needs are about keeping the brain stimulated and interested in new and challenging activities. This has nothing to do with getting qualifications and doing exams; it is to do with finding hobbies and interests that stop us from getting bored. Children meet their intellectual needs constantly by exploring and questioning the world around them. You may be getting your intellectual needs met by learning about health and social care. As people grow older, physical needs decline, and intellectual needs become even more important to ensure that healthy development continues.

Practice for Assessment

This could contribute to P1.

Try to list all the needs you have in a day. Now place them in an order that you feel is important to you.

Do you agree with Maslow?

In what way will your needs change as you get older?

Factors influencing the health and needs of individuals

Key point

If the egg from your mother had been fertilised by a different sperm, you would not be here!

Over to you

We all have inherited characteristics from our parents. Which characteristics do you think you have inherited? Which do you like? Which would you give back if you could?

Physical factors

Biological inheritance

There are many factors that make us all unique individuals. Probably the most important are the genes that we inherited from our mother and father. During fertilisation a sperm penetrates the egg (ovum) which begins the long process of making another human being. The sperm and egg each carry 23 chromosomes – one set from each parent. Chromosomes carry strands of DNA which carry genes. Every single cell in the body has the same chromosomes, but it is the genes that tell the cell what it is to do, for example be a blood cell or a nerve cell.

Genes do not all have the same effect; some are dominant and some are recessive. For example, think about eye colour. What colour eyes would a child have if one parent had brown eyes and the other parent had blue eyes? The child would have a 1 in 4 chance of having blue eyes, and a 3 in 4 chance of having brown eyes. Remember that each child receives a chromosome from each parent, making a pair. Brown eyes is a dominant gene (B) and blue eyes is a recessive gene (b). To have blue eyes, the child must receive two recessive genes, one from each parent. If one or both genes are dominant, then the child will have brown eyes, as dominant genes overpower recessive genes. Look at the diagram below.

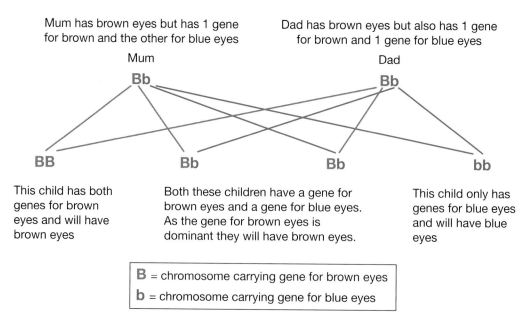

Mum has brown eyes but has 1 gene for brown and the other for blue eyes

Dad has brown eyes but also has 1 gene for brown and 1 gene for blue eyes

Mum

Dad

Bb

Bb

BB

Bb

Bb

bb

This child has both genes for brown eyes and will have brown eyes

Both these children have a gene for brown eyes and a gene for blue eyes. As the gene for brown eyes is dominant they will have brown eyes.

This child only has genes for blue eyes and will have blue eyes

B = chromosome carrying gene for brown eyes
b = chromosome carrying gene for blue eyes

■ *The genetic inheritance of eye colour*

Sometimes the genes we receive from our parents are faulty. Abnormal genes are responsible for many conditions such as breast cancers, Huntington's disease, deafness and cystic fibrosis. Sickle cell anaemia is found mainly in people of African and Caribbean origin. The genes for sickle cell anaemia cause red blood cells to be crescent-shaped instead of round. These abnormal blood cells cannot carry as much oxygen as normal blood cells, and they get stuck in small blood vessels, preventing blood from reaching the body's organs. Blockage of a blood vessel causes an attack known as a crisis. The treatment for sickle cell anaemia is oxygen and injected pain killers until the crisis stops. Diseases such as haemophilia are linked to gender and only occur in boys but can be carried by the female.

Scientists have now been able to identify all the genes on a strand of DNA. It has taken scientists from all over the world many years to identify all genes. This project is known as the Human Genome Project and the consequences of its findings are enormous. One day scientists will be able to select genes in a growing foetus and change or remove them all together. This is known as genetic modification.

Environment

What does the environment mean to you? When I wake up each morning, the first thing I do is look out of the window at the weather. The weather makes up part of my environment. My environment is all that is around me, the air I breathe, the water I drink and the ground I walk on. Without thinking, we assume that our environment is safe for us to live in, but this is not always true.

People can put themselves at risk in many different ways. Sometimes the chemicals we put into our bodies affect us; at other times the air we breathe can seriously affect our health. Environmental factors are those that are outside our bodies. This section considers radiation from the sun and mobile phones and discusses the harm that can be caused by overexposure to harmful rays. There are many other environmental factors that may also be considered important, as shown in the diagram.

Over to you

Look up haemophilia on the Internet or in a medical reference book. How is it passed from one generation to another?

Talking point

View 1: Genetic modification can be used to prevent hereditary diseases from occurring.

View 2: Genetic modification could be used to select normal genes over less desirable genes.

Real Life Care

Sickle cell crisis

Desmond is 17 years old and has sickle cell anaemia. He is admitted to hospital in sickle cell crisis after playing football. The sickle cells are blocking blood vessels and stopping oxygen reaching his kidneys.

1 Describe what symptoms Desmond may be experiencing. ✓

2 What risks does Desmond's hereditary condition present to him?

3 Describe the communication skills you would use to reassure Desmond.

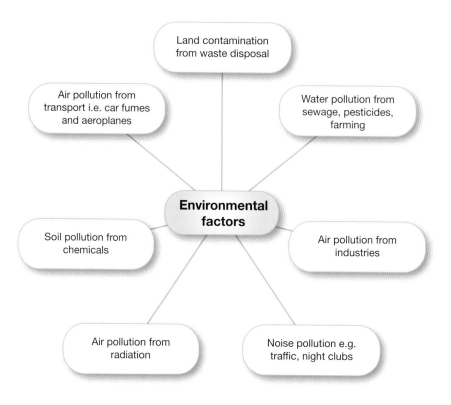

■ *Possible environmental factors that could affect health*

Air pollution

When people think about air pollution, they usually think about smog, acid rain, CFCs, and other forms of outdoor air pollution. But did you know that air pollution can also exist inside homes and other buildings? Every year, the health of many people is affected by chemical substances present in the air within buildings. Air supplies us with oxygen which we need to breathe. Air is about 99% nitrogen, oxygen, water and other safe gases. Fumes from human activities such as transport,industry and burning fuels can release substances into the air that may cause problems for humans, plants and animals.

Examples of short-term effects of air pollution include irritation to the eyes, nose and throat, and respiratory conditions such as bronchitis and pneumonia. Air pollution can also aggravate medical conditions such as asthma and emphysema. Long-term effects may include lung cancer and heart disease.

Skin

The feel of the sun on our skin often makes us happy and contented. Without it, some people begin to feel tired and depressed. In fact, we need the sun on our skin to make vitamin D, which the body uses in forming healthy bones and teeth. However, too much exposure to the sun can have serious consequences for our health.

One of the most dangerous environmental hazards is the sun. Rates of skin cancer in the UK are increasing faster than any other type of cancer, especially in women. Ultraviolet (UV) rays from the sun damage the skin and can cause malignant melanoma – a fast-growing cancer that spreads in the bloodstream and the lymph and travels to other parts of the body. In the UK more than 7,300 people a year are diagnosed with malignant melanoma; about 1,700 people a year will die as a result. Women are more likely to get the disease than men even though they may be aware of the damage that the sun can do to their health. Why does the incidence of malignant melanoma among women still continue to rise? Women use more sun screen than men, but they are using it in order to stay out in the sun for longer periods of time. Women seek a sun tan by many means – a few extra sessions on the sun bed, or an extra hour's sunbathing. Whatever means they choose, overexposure to the destructive rays of the sun will increase the risk of permanent skin damage, premature ageing, and even death.

Reproduced with the kind permission of Cancer Research UK

■ *Health campaigns such as SunSmart have helped to make people aware of the dangers of exposure to the sun*

A clean environment

It is very difficult to achieve a clean, safe environment. As there are more and more people on our planet, they produce increasing amounts of waste. They make more noise, and demand more computerised technology and mobile phones.

Socio-economic factors

Employment

Employment is one of the easiest ways to improve or change lifestyle choices. An increase in income can help a person to improve their housing and maybe family relationships as well as health prospects. A good job,

> **Socio-economic** *Socio-economic factors are those that affect how we live and work. Factors include poverty, employment, class and housing.*

which is well paid, and where the staff feel valued and appreciated, will help raise an individual's self-esteem, self-worth and confidence. When people are happy at work, they are often better able to cope in difficult situations and are more willing to try and maintain a healthier lifestyle.

However, employment can also have negative effects on health. Lone parents may find it hard to find work that will allow them to balance work life with family commitments. Part-time work, based around school hours, is often low paid and under-valued. Combining working hours with child care is expensive, and stressful, and may lead to lone parents neglecting their own health in favour of providing for their family.

People with disabilities may suffer from discrimination and may find it hard to get suitable work, which results in them relying on state benefits to meet their everyday needs. If people with disabilities are not encouraged to find employment, then society as a whole will lose a valuable workforce. By employing people with disabilities, employers are showing that they value people for their individuality and unique capabilities.

Over to you

What does class mean to you? Do you consider yourself as part of a social class or are we all equal?

Social class

Social class is a term used to group people together depending on their wealth, income and job (see Unit 4 Cultural Diversity in Health and Social Care, page 149, for more information on social class). In 1980, the Black Report found that there were differences in health between the classes. The lower a person's social class, the more likely they are to die at an earlier age compared to people in a higher social class. This may be due to lifestyle choices that lower-class people choose or are forced to make.

People of a lower social class are more likely to smoke and drink alcohol than people in the higher classes. One of the reasons for this may be that people of a lower class have greater stresses on their lives due to lower wages. An increase in stress may result in the use of cigarettes and alcohol as a release from everyday difficulties. A lack of understanding of the harm caused by smoking and alcohol will also result in their continual use.

Quality of diet may also be linked to class. Poor quality, mass-produced food costs much less than good quality food. Junk food and take-aways can be a cheap, quick meal for a family on a low income where the adults work long, unsocial hours. Lack of education about how to prepare food and the nutritional value of foods may result in families simply being unaware of the importance of diet and its effect on health.

Exercise is an important factor in remaining healthy, but exercising costs money and takes up time. Exercising may be beyond the reach of some low-income families, as the cost of gym and club memberships and sports equipment may prevent them from taking part. Exercise also takes time and commitment. People who have lower incomes may need to work more hours and have less time available for sport or exercise.

People of a lower social class may have more stress due to a low income, poor housing, poor working conditions and poverty. An increase in stress may result in making lifestyle choices that can harm health, such as smoking, drugs and alcohol.

People of a higher social class may earn higher salaries which will result in more money left at the end of the month for non-essential items. This is known as disposable income. With more disposable income, people can choose the quality of the food they buy and can afford to shop around rather than going to the nearest food shop. More money allows people to take part in sports and join clubs, and to buy the equipment necessary for sport as well as having more spare time to enjoy exercise.

Real Life Care

Shona's lifestyle

Shona is 30 years old and married with two children. She works part time as a teacher and her husband works as a banker in London. Shona visits her local gym twice a week and plays netball every weekend. She is very aware of her family's health and only buys organic foods produced in the UK. She will drive several miles to ensure she buys quality food for her family. Neither Shona nor her husband smoke, but they enjoy drinking wine with their friends at the weekend.

1 Can you decide which social class Shona **might** belong to?

2 Discuss what she is doing to ensure good health for her family.

3 Analyse how Shona's children will view health in the future.

Real Life Care

Shena's lifestyle

Shena is 30 years old and married with two children. She works full time as a classroom assistant and as a cleaner in the evenings. Her husband works as a bus driver in London. Shena has no time for herself and does no exercise. She is aware of her family's health, but due to lack of income she buys cheap food from the local supermarket, stocking up on food when it is on promotion or reduced in price. Shena, her 16-year-old daughter and her husband all smoke a packet of cigarettes each a day. On Shena's two nights off, she and her husband visit the local pub.

1 Can you decide which social class Shena **might** belong to?

2 Discuss what she is doing to ensure good health for her family.

3 Analyse how Shena's children will view health in the future.

Housing

Each one of us has our own idea of what our 'ideal' home would be like. Our home is somewhere we should feel safe and secure, somewhere we can make our own and stamp our own personality. Several families may live in the same row of terraced houses, but no two houses will be the same – each family will have made their house their own, and painted, decorated and furnished it differently from their neighbours' houses.

Housing can affect health in many ways. Poorly maintained housing will be cold and damp, causing conditions such as asthma, arthritis and chest complaints. Too many people crowded together in the same house may result in accidents, the spread of infections, increased stress and sleeplessness. When people are unhappy with where they live or the state of their housing, their health will suffer. Poor and inadequate housing may result in emotional stress, a feeling of uselessness and helplessness.

■ *Poor housing conditions can have serious effects on a person's health*

Income

Income is the money that people receive – this can be from work, state benefits, savings or pensions. Everyone has to pay for the essentials in life such as food, housing, heating bills and clothing. Once essentials are paid for, any extra money can be used for things people want rather than need. Sometimes it is difficult to decide what is a want or a need. The poorest people in the country are women, children, the elderly and people from ethnic minorities. Wealth is not shared evenly in the UK – 23 per cent of wealth is owned by 1 per cent of the population; the wealthiest 50 per cent of the population own 94 per cent of wealth (Economic and Social Research Council).

■ *Restricted income can cause many risks to health*

Education

By law, everyone between the ages of 5 and 16 years old must receive an education, either in a school or at home. The amount and quality of education you receive will affect your health. The benefits of education are enormous – it has been found in Third World countries that if women are educated, their children are healthier and live longer. Education is placed highly on Maslow's triangle, as it increases social standing, makes people feel good about themselves and gives a sense of achievement. Alternatively, education gives a wider choice of better paid jobs.

Accessibility to services

The NHS has been a free health service since 1948. It was set up so that everyone had the same access to health care provisions despite their wealth, age, gender or ethnic background. Everyone should be able to see a GP when they are ill, visit a pharmacy for a prescription, call an ambulance or receive a hospital referral. Unfortunately, this is not always the case. Access to health facilities may be prevented for many reasons.

Culture can prevent people getting the facilities that they need. For example, if you do not speak the same language as your health care provider, it may be difficult to explain what is wrong and what type of

Talking point

View 1: There are many things I need: chocolates, nights out, new clothes, a boyfriend, a car, cigarettes and lots of sleep.

View 2: Really? I want chocolates, nights out, new clothes, a car, cigarettes and lots of sleep but I don't *need* all of it.

Real Life Care

Andrew is 18 years old. He is at college doing a health care course with a view to becoming a nurse in the future. He enjoyed school and got good grades in his GCSEs. His parents have always supported him with his education, by getting involved in school activities and helping him with his homework.

Drew is 18 years old. He is not at college; he is working in his local corner shop. Drew wanted to go to college and then become a nurse. He did not do very well in his GCSEs as he hated school and did not attend very often. Drew's parents do not think that nursing is for

boys, and encouraged him to get a job instead of an education.

1 Is education due to personal choice or influenced by other factors?

2 If Drew managed to go to college, what factors might prevent him from doing as well as Andrew? ✓✓✓

Talking point

View 1: Men don't go to the doctor as much as women because they are embarrassed to go.

View 2: Men don't go to the doctor as much as women do because they don't want to take the time off work.

help you need. Different cultures may also have different expectations of how they should be treated. For example, some cultures will not allow women to be cared for by men, and some older men feel uncomfortable being treated by women.

Where you live and how much you earn will also affect how you use a service. If you live a long way from your GP, then you may visit them less often as you cannot afford the bus or taxi fare. Some health care treatments are not free, such as infertility treatment; therefore, accessing that service will be dependent on how much you earn. For more details, read about barriers to accessing health in Unit 8 Health and Social Care Services, page 332.

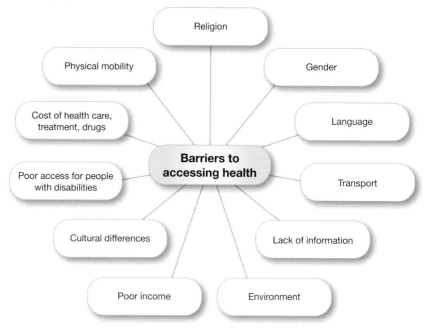

■ Barriers to accessing health services

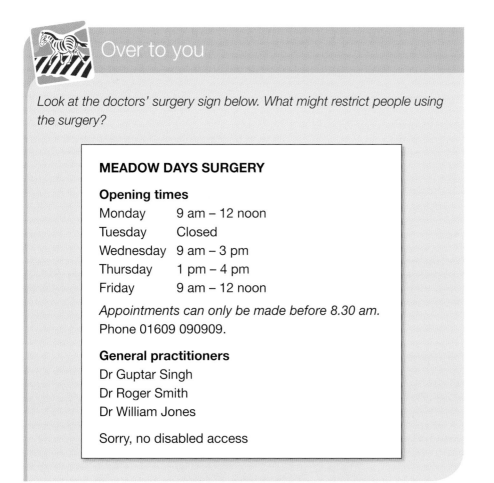

Look at the doctors' surgery sign below. What might restrict people using the surgery?

MEADOW DAYS SURGERY

Opening times

Monday	9 am – 12 noon
Tuesday	Closed
Wednesday	9 am – 3 pm
Thursday	1 pm – 4 pm
Friday	9 am – 12 noon

Appointments can only be made before 8.30 am.
Phone 01609 090909.

General practitioners

Dr Guptar Singh
Dr Roger Smith
Dr William Jones

Sorry, no disabled access

Media

The media can affect every aspect of our life. The media includes newspapers, magazines, television, radio and advertisements. For many years people have argued about how much the media affect the way we live our lives. Some people believe that it has no effect and that we are all individuals who can think independently and decide what we want to do without being influenced by what we read or watch. But is this really true? Television adverts influence children who then 'pester' their parents to buy them fast food, sweets and fizzy drinks. Smokers were once encouraged to change their brand, or even take up smoking, by glamorous celebrities and sports advertising. One of the most controversial effects of the media is in relation to body image. Body image can be affected by how we see other people around us. If everyone in magazines and on the television is thin, then we may believe that this is the only acceptable way to look.

Anorexia nervosa

Anorexia nervosa is an eating disorder affecting mainly young girls and women. Sufferers choose not to eat because they have a distorted image of how their body looks to others and so they set out to lose weight through diet and over-exercise in order to achieve an image

Talking point

View 1: People make up their own mind about their choices in life.

View 2: TV adverts help influence the choices people make.

they feel is expected of them. Anorexia results in a severe deterioration in health due to weight loss. This may result in malnutrition, infertility, organ failure and, if suffered for a very long period, death. The causes of anorexia are varied, but constant images of extremely thin models, pop stars and celebrities can only add fuel to a very serious disease. Some girls as young as 9 or 10 years old believe that the way to be liked by their friends and to become rich and famous is by being thin and dieting.

■ *Images of thin models encourage young people to believe thin is best*

Over to you

Have a close look at the adverts in a fashion magazine. Can you find anyone overweight in any of the pictures? How does this make you feel?

Gender

Whether you are male or female will have an effect on your health. Females are more likely to diet and less likely to participate in sports. There are many reasons for this. Perhaps women are more influenced by social and media pressures and more concerned about fitting in with an image that they feel is acceptable. Men are less likely to seek help from their doctor as it may seem a weakness to admit they are ill or need help.

Culture and religion

Culture and religion are very important issues when considering the needs of individuals. All religions have their own beliefs, traditions and

Over to you

Talk to someone you know who goes to a slimming club. How many men go compared to the number of women?

ceremonies, often linked to a variety of foods and music. Culture affects individuals in many different ways and can even influence how they access health and the care they receive in health care settings. For more information on the many factors that arise in different and diverse cultures, see Unit 4 Cultural Diversity in Health and Social Care.

Lifestyle factors

Personal hygiene

One of the few lifestyle choices that we have total control over is that of personal hygiene. It is important that we keep our bodies and clothing clean, as dirt provides a home for bacteria which spreads disease. When caring for others, it is often necessary to get physically close to them to offer support. If you have offensive body odour from poor personal hygiene, it becomes uncomfortable for good communication to take place.

Touch is a valuable tool, often offering compassion and understanding where words are not enough. In a profession of caring for people, it is necessary to touch others to offer physical contact in order to nurse, comfort and care for those who are vulnerable. It is through touch that infection is often spread, a silent but deadly killer. As a care worker, you must be constantly vigilant to ensure that bacteria and viruses have as little chance as possible to spread.

Skin

Skin is made up of two main layers, the outer epidermis and the inner dermis. There are many reasons why it is important to keep skin clean:

- The epidermis is constantly being shed and replaced with new skin cells.

- The skin contains cells that produce sweat, and which provides an environment in which bacteria can breed.

- The skin is exposed to dirt in the environment.

All of these factors combine to produce a warm, moist environment for bacteria to breed.

 Key point

Skin is the largest organ in the body, stretching 193 square metres.

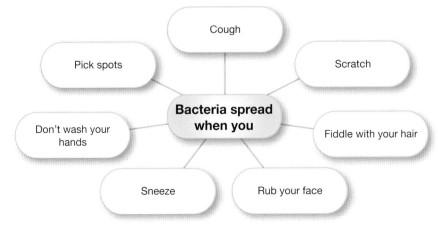

■ *How we pass on bacteria*

Preventing the spread of bacteria

Bacteria will grow in any environment that is warm, light and moist – in other words, almost anywhere. Good personal hygiene plays an important part in limiting the risks associated with bacteria.

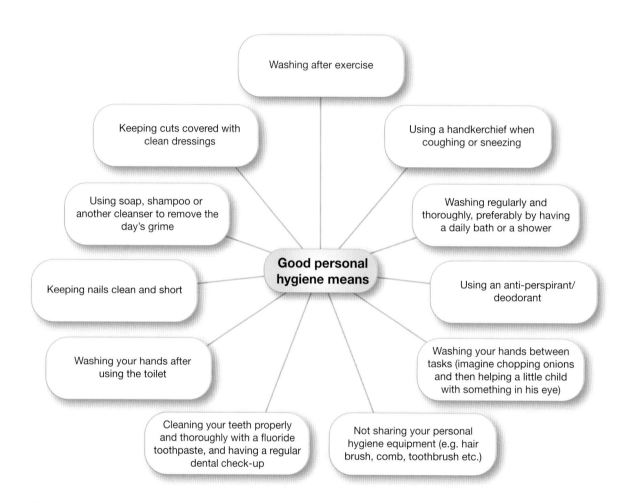

- Washing after exercise
- Keeping cuts covered with clean dressings
- Using a handkerchief when coughing or sneezing
- Using soap, shampoo or another cleanser to remove the day's grime
- Washing regularly and thoroughly, preferably by having a daily bath or a shower
- **Good personal hygiene means**
- Keeping nails clean and short
- Using an anti-perspirant/deodorant
- Washing your hands after using the toilet
- Washing your hands between tasks (imagine chopping onions and then helping a little child with something in his eye)
- Cleaning your teeth properly and thoroughly with a fluoride toothpaste, and having a regular dental check-up
- Not sharing your personal hygiene equipment (e.g. hair brush, comb, toothbrush etc.)

■ *Good personal hygiene is essential*

Over to you

Think carefully about your day so far. List everything you have touched since you got up, e.g. your pillow and bedding, clothing, toothbrush, soap, doors, handles, toilet, bus seat, bus ticket, even this textbook. Now look at your list and underline all the things that other people might have touched as well as you, e.g. soap, door handles.

What can you conclude from your findings?

Diet

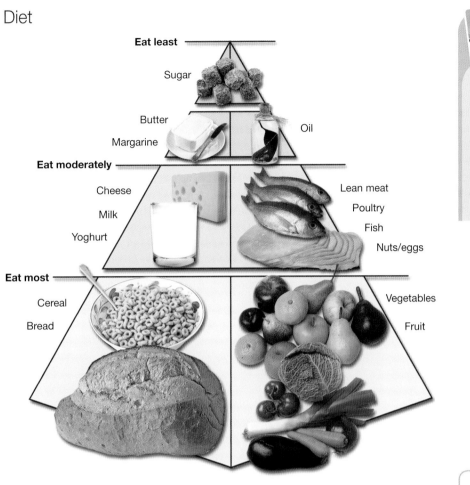

Eat least — Sugar

Butter
Margarine   Oil

Eat moderately —

Cheese   Lean meat
Milk   Poultry
Yoghurt   Fish
    Nuts/eggs

Eat most —

Cereal   Vegetables
Bread   Fruit

■ *The nutrient triangle*

In 1998, an independent government inquiry showed that diet can be closely related to social class. The inquiry demonstrated that people from lower social classes eat less fruit and vegetables as they cannot afford good quality food and rely heavily on cheap processed junk food to feed their families. Consequently, it was suggested that manufacturers should reduce the amount of salt in bread and junk food to help improve the nutritional value of foods eaten by people from lower social classes. A lack of fresh fruit and vegetables in the diet is linked to the possible development of certain cancers and heart disease. The normal development of a child depends greatly on their diet. A poor diet during pregnancy might affect the growth and development of the baby. Unit 9 looks at the health risks associated with a poor diet.

Over to you

Keep a diary of your weekly intake of food. Compare your results with the nutrient triangle. Are you getting the right amount of each of the food groups?

Talking point

View 1: Poorer people lack the money to buy healthy food, so eat more junk food.

View 2: Richer people are better educated and understand the importance of a healthy diet.

Physical exercise

Regular exercise is important to help our bodies remain healthy.

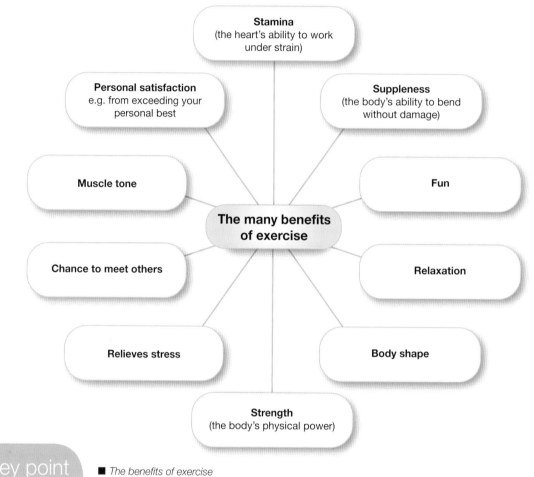

Stamina
(the heart's ability to work under strain)

Personal satisfaction
e.g. from exceeding your personal best

Suppleness
(the body's ability to bend without damage)

Muscle tone

Fun

The many benefits of exercise

Chance to meet others

Relaxation

Relieves stress

Body shape

Strength
(the body's physical power)

■ *The benefits of exercise*

Key point

Exercise can be:

■ aerobic exercise, which requires oxygen to be breathed in in large amounts causing the heart and respiration rate to increase, e.g. running, cycling, swimming.

■ anaerobic exercise, which causes muscles to use up oxygen faster than your body can replace it, so that they have to get their energy from glycogen stored in the liver, e.g. sprinting, weight lifting.

Over to you

Try out this simple exercise. Find your pulse, either in your wrist or in your neck. Count how many beats you can feel in one minute – it should be 60–80 beats. Now run up two flights of stairs or a quick 100-metre dash. Check your pulse again – it will be much faster and you will probably be out of breath.

Why not try and build some form of regular exercise into your life? Check out your local gym, join a sports club or try running from home, building up the distances each time you go.

After a month of regular exercise, try the pulse test again. If you have been exercising regularly, your pulse rate should be slower, indicating that you are getting fitter.

Childhood obesity

■ *Obesity in children is becoming an increasing problem*

In the UK, 22 per cent of girls and 20 per cent of boys aged 2–15 years old are overweight, even obese. Obesity in children is leading to an increase in diabetes, joint problems, high blood pressure, and low self-esteem.

■ *Reasons for increase in childhood obesity*

The benefits of being active as a child include:

- healthy growth and development of bones and muscles
- high energy levels
- reducing the risks of heart disease and high blood pressure in later life
- opportunities to meet new people
- a sense of achievement
- mental well-being
- helping to improve concentration
- the reduced likelihood of smoking, or drug or alcohol abuse.

Practice for Assessment

Carrying out this activity will give you underpinning knowedge for P1, P3 and M1.

Jacob and his friend Raj are both 9 years old. For his birthday Jacob received a Wii. His parents are pleased as he seems to be getting fitter from all the interactive sport he now plays through his console. Raj received a football. His parents are pleased as he seems to be getting fitter from all the football he is playing with his friends at the local park.

Identify the benefits of increasing activity in your daily life.

Explain what social and psychological benefits can be gained from sport activities besides increasing your exercise levels.

Discuss some issues behind why children can become obese and how obesity can be prevented.

Substance abuse

Illegal and legal drugs

The use of illegal drugs and the misuse of prescription drugs is increasingly becoming a risk to health. The misuse of these drugs results in physical, emotional, social and psychological problems, with the user becoming dependent on them and then possibly resorting to crime to pay for their addiction.

Adults over the age of 18 can buy certain medicines such as paracetamol over the counter in a supermarket, shop or pharmacy. Drugs like paracetamol and ibuprofen are sold in small quantities (and, depending on the type of medicine, in a low strength) to prevent misuse. Your GP may prescribe medicines that you cannot buy over the counter in order to treat you when you are ill. Some prescription-only medicines are classified as controlled drugs, for example the painkiller pethidine. The law places drugs into three categories – Class A, B and C. Class A drugs are thought to be the most harmful, with Class C not quite as harmful. The illegal use of controlled drugs may cause dangerous side-effects and lead to addiction.

Over to you

Before reading this section, find out the differences between the three different classes of drugs. The NHS Direct website may help you. To access this website, go to www.heinemann.co.uk/hotlinks and enter the express code 3322P.

Real Life Care

Diana's dilemma

Diana is 16 years old and is a regular user of cannabis, which she smokes instead of cigarettes. Her supplier of cannabis has suggested that she tries something stronger such as cocaine. Diana desperately wants to give up drugs, but she also wants to be accepted by her friends and is tempted to try cocaine.

1 What effects do cannabis and cocaine have on the user? ✔

2 What advice could you give Diana to help her give up drugs? ✔✔

3 Analyse the external influences that will affect Diana's ability to give up drugs. ✔✔✔

Alcohol and binge drinking

Alcohol helps people lose their inhibitions and talk openly. In moderation, it is enjoyed by many cultures around the world as a means of gathering people together for celebrations and to renew and build friendships.

In recent years, there has been a growing concern about the way British people drink – 40 per cent of all male drinking occasions are now binge drinking sessions. It is difficult to define exactly what a binge-drinking session is; recent research suggests ten or more drinks in one session, or over half the recommended number of units for a week in one session.

Key point

It takes as few as eight paracetamol to cause permanent liver damage, organ failure, and even death.

■ *Binge drinking in women aged 16–24 has risen dramatically in the last three years*

Effects of some commonly misused drugs

Drug	Type of drug	Appearance and use	Effects	Risk to health
Cannabis – blow, hash, draw, dope, grass, smoke, pot, weed	Class C drug	Looks like dried grass, brown resin. Smoked or eaten	Hallucinogenic, feeling relaxed, increased appetite, increased pulse, dry mouth, blood-shot eyes	Respiratory problems, lung damage, increased pulse rate, loss of memory, mental illness. Smoking-related cancers
Cocaine – coke, snow, crack, freebase, rock, Charlie	Class A drug	Fine white powder or white chips. Sniffed or injected. Heated and inhaled	Sense of well-being, confidence, alertness. After initial 'high', sleepiness, hunger, thirst, depression	Insomnia, paranoia, increased blood pressure. If sniffed, may damage septum between nostrils. Injection may lead to thrombosis of injection site. Risk of HIV
Ecstasy – E, Adam, Eve, doves, X, burgers, echoes, hug drug	Class A drug	White or coloured tablets. Different shapes, often with pictures printed on them	Hallucinogenic, increased energy but remaining calm, empathy	Anxiety and panic attacks, brain damage, mood alterations, dehydration, poor temperature control leading to heat stroke
Ketamine – special K, K, green , blind, squid, keller, kat, Super C	Possession not illegal	Clear liquid or white powder. Sniffed, smoked or swallowed	Painkiller with hallucinogenic ability. Increasingly associated with 'date rape' as it causes the victim to become unconscious	Strong psychological dependency, weight loss. Death may result from vomiting when unconscious
Heroine – smack, H, brown, scag, horse	Class A drug	Brown/white powder, often mixed with other drugs. Smoked, sniffed, injected. Little effect if swallowed	Altered state between wakefulness and drowsiness, cloudy mental function	Liver disease, collapsed veins, infected heart lining, abscesses, pneumonia
Methodone – meth, phy	Class A drug	White tablets, ampules for injecting, linctus. Can be used as a replacement for heroine dependency	Used for severe pain and as a substitute for opiates	Breathing difficulties, irregular periods, risk of infection from injections, circulation problems
Solvents/glue, e.g. petrol, aerosols, Evo, paint thinners, propane gas, lighter refills	Possession not illegal, but may not be sold to under-18s	Sniffed	Euphoria, lowered inhibitions, disorientation, blurred vision, slurred speech	Fatal heart problems, nausea, vomiting, blackouts, brain damage, kidney and liver failure

The consequences of binge drinking may include:

- high blood pressure
- increased risk of heart disease
- casual sex
- sexually transmitted infections
- road accidents
- violent attacks on the drinker and by the drinker, e.g. assault, rape.

A glass of wine (125 ml) is equivalent to 1.5 units, as is an alcopop

$\frac{1}{2}$ pint of lager

one standard pub measure of sherry or port (50ml)

one small pub measure of spirits (25ml)

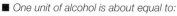 One unit of alcohol is about equal to:

Effects of alcohol abuse

Short-term effects: Alcohol affects the part of the brain that controls judgment, which results in a loss of inhibitions. Alcohol is a depresssant. It also affects coordination, causes blurred sight, loss of balance and blurred speech. Very large amounts of alcohol in one session may result in unconsciousness, coma, and even death.

Long-term effects: Alcohol is a dangerous drug. The misuse of alcohol over a long period will result in:

- damaged brain cells
- liver failure, known as cirrhosis

- bleeding stomach ulcers
- high blood pressure, causing strokes
- cancers of the mouth, liver, stomach
- heart failure.

Practice for Assessment

This could contribute to P1, M2 and D2.

Read the case study below and then answer the questions.

Terry is 40 years old and has been drinking heavily since he was 16. He has developed liver cirrhosis and is determined to cut down, then stop drinking altogether.

Describe the immediate and long-term actions Terry could take to cut down on his drinking.

Are there any factors that might prevent Terry from following your plan?

How would Terry's life change if he stopped drinking?

Smoking

Tobacco was introduced to Europe from America in the sixteenth century, but it took another 500 years before people understood the effects of smoking on the body. Today, over 12 million adults smoke cigarettes (ASH, 2005). Smoking is responsible for 114,000 deaths every year – almost half of regular smokers will be killed by their habit. Cigarette smoke contains over 4,000 different chemicals, many of which are highly poisonous, and more than 40 of them are known to cause cancer.

Effects of some of the chemicals contained in cigarettes	
Chemical	**Effects**
Nicotine	This is the addictive chemical in tobacco. It causes an increase in the heart rate and blood pressure, and tightens the small blood vessels under the skin causing wrinkles. In large quantities, it is very dangerous.
Tar	A thick, sticky, black substance that causes mouth, lung and throat cancers. It causes the yellowish-brown stains on the fingers, teeth and lungs of smokers. It also kills the fine hair-like fibres called cilia in the cells lining the airways which results in the smoker's cough.
Carbon monoxide	A poisonous gas that stops the blood taking up oxygen from the lungs. This means that the body gets less oxygen, depriving vital organs such as the heart from its oxygen supply. If a smoker is pregnant, her baby would not get sufficient oxygen for healthy growth.

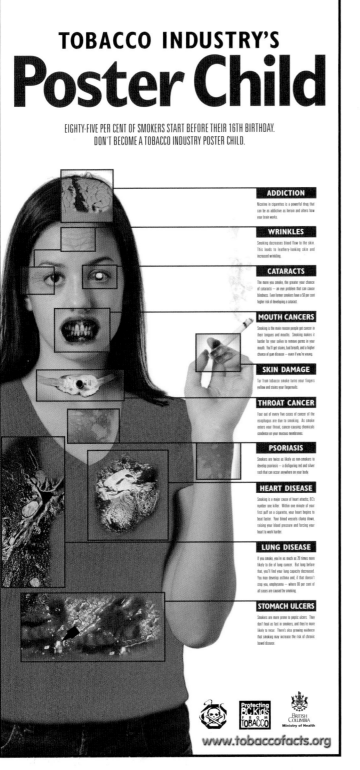

■ *The effects of smoking*

Many smokers would like to stop smoking. It is the most important thing a smoker can do to live a longer, healthier life. There is no quick and easy way to stop smoking. First, the smoker must want to stop – nothing else will make them stop.

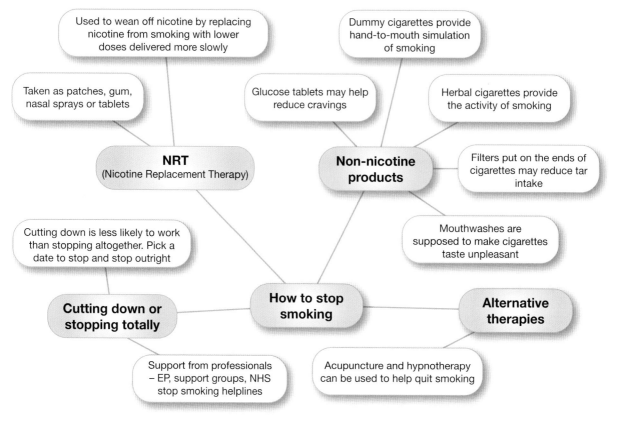

Used to wean off nicotine by replacing nicotine from smoking with lower doses delivered more slowly

Dummy cigarettes provide hand-to-mouth simulation of smoking

Taken as patches, gum, nasal sprays or tablets

Glucose tablets may help reduce cravings

Herbal cigarettes provide the activity of smoking

NRT
(Nicotine Replacement Therapy)

Non-nicotine products

Filters put on the ends of cigarettes may reduce tar intake

Cutting down is less likely to work than stopping altogether. Pick a date to stop and stop outright

Mouthwashes are supposed to make cigarettes taste unpleasant

Cutting down or stopping totally

How to stop smoking

Alternative therapies

Support from professionals – EP, support groups, NHS stop smoking helplines

Acupuncture and hypnotherapy can be used to help quit smoking

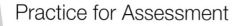

■ *Ways to stop smoking*

Practice for Assessment

Carrying out this activity could contribute to P3 and M2.

More than 80 per cent of smokers start smoking as teenagers. In the UK, about 450 children start smoking each day, even though it is illegal to smoke until they are 16 years old.

Describe some of the reasons why teenagers take up smoking.

Look back at the short- and long-term effects of smoking, then discuss why teenagers find it hard to give up smoking.

Suggest some methods that teenagers could use to give up smoking.

Stress

We all need a little stress in our lives to ensure that we get up in the morning, complete that assignment, or even run for the bus. Small amounts of stress can be good for us, but sometimes stress builds up and interferes with our health. When we are under stress, our bodies produce a hormone called adrenaline.

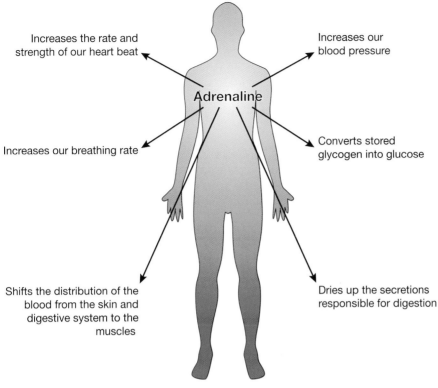

Increases the rate and strength of our heart beat

Increases our blood pressure

Adrenaline

Increases our breathing rate

Converts stored glycogen into glucose

Shifts the distribution of the blood from the skin and digestive system to the muscles

Dries up the secretions responsible for digestion

■ *The effect of adrenaline*

The sudden release of adrenaline into the bloodstream causes a number of short-term effects, including a fast heart beat, faster breathing, dry mouth, wide eyes, sweaty hands, the need to go to the toilet and a pale face. These signs of stress do not last long as they require energy. If a stressful situation does not improve, then the person may become ill. Long-term signs of stress include sleeplessness, ulcers, high blood pressure, headaches, indigestion, muscle ache, poor circulation, unhappiness, accidents and mental illness.

To reduce stress it is necessary to remove the thing that caused the stress, which is not always easy. Below are some ways to relieve stress:

- Change the situation to remove the thing that is causing the stress.

- Time management training might help to avoid stress caused by lack of time.

- Emotional expression – talk about or write down feelings, listing the positives and negatives.

- Assertiveness training may address source of problem.

- Relaxation techniques, e.g. water therapy, massage, hypnotherapy.

- Exercise.

- Drugs prescribed by a GP.

- Therapy to help organise thoughts to look at a situation differently.

- Role play – work out strategies to cope by practising them first.

Key point

The release of adrenaline into the bloodstream is known as the 'fright, flight or fight' response. To understand what happens in the body when adrenaline is released, see Unit 5 Anatomy and Physiology, page 191.

Real Life Care

Under stress

You are working as a carer in a residential home. Two members of staff are off sick. You have a new resident arriving in an hour and there is no room ready for her. The breakfasts are late. One resident has been reported missing from his room. The GP has arrived to visit one of her patients.

1 Describe the physical processes your body will be going through.

2 If the staffing levels do not improve and the situation does not get any better, what long-term effects might this have on your health?

3 Plan some coping strategies that you and other members of staff could use to ensure that your health is not affected.

Sexual practices

A sexual relationship is an intimate physical relationship between two people.

People are starting sexual relationships at an earlier age than ever before.

Sexual intercourse performed without the use of any form of **contraception** may result in an unwanted pregnancy or a sexually transmitted infection, or both.

Contraception *Ways of preventing a pregnancy.*

Many, if not all, of the sexually transmitted infections shown in the table on the next page are preventable by using protective contraception.

If a man uses a condom, he is protecting himself and his partner from an unwanted pregnancy and sexually transmitted disease. However, the majority of contraceptive methods that a woman uses only protect against pregnancy, not sexually transmitted infections.

Key point

Heterosexual – a person who is sexually attracted to people of the opposite gender.

Homosexual – a person who is sexually attracted to people of the same gender.

Bisexual – a person who is sexually attracted to people of the same and opposite gender.

Signs and symptoms of some sexually transmitted infections

Sexually transmitted infection	Signs and symptons	Effects	Treatment
Gonorrhea	Women: yellow/green discharge with strong smell. Men: discharge from penis; pain passing urine	Women: infertility, ectopic pregnancy. Men: inflamed testes	Antibiotics. Partners need to be tested
Syphillis	Genital sores, all over body rash; flu-like symptoms, genital warts, headaches, hair loss	If untreated, causes damage to brain, heart and nervous system causing death	Antibiotics. Partners need to be tested
HIV/Aids	No symptoms	HIV damages immune system; may develop Aids and death	No cure, but drugs can prevent the patient from becoming ill
Non-specific urethritis (NSU)	Uncomfortable, burning feeling when passing urine. White discharge from penis	Inflamed testes and prostate gland	Antibiotics. Partners need to be tested
Genital herpes	No symptoms or genital sores, flu-like symptoms, genitalia and anal itching	Serious problems are uncommon	Antiviral tablets
Pubic lice	Itching, visible white eggs and lice on pubic hair	No serious problems though easily passed to partner	Shampoos, creams, lotions from pharmacist
Chlamydia	Women: pain on passing urine, abdominal pain. Men: white discharge from penis, pain passing urine	Infertility in men and women. Long-term pelvic pain	Antibiotics. Partners need to be tested

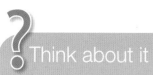

Methods of contraception

There are many different forms of contraception, each of them designed to work in different ways. Their main aim is to prevent a woman from getting pregnant, but some methods may also prevent the spread of a sexually transmitted infection.

Barrier methods

Barrier methods of contraception work by preventing the sperm from reaching the egg by creating a barrier between the two. Barrier methods include the following:

- Condoms – the male condom is a latex sheath which is placed over the penis; female condoms are similar in shape to male condoms but are inserted into the vagina with a flexible ring left on the outside to keep it in place. Both types of condom may protect against sexually transmitted diseases.

- Caps and diaphragms – these are dome-shaped discs which are inserted into the vagina and placed over the neck of the womb (the cervix).

Hormonal methods

This method of contraception affects the hormone levels in the woman's body to stop her from getting pregnant. Hormones can be injected into the arm, inserted into the vagina or swallowed in the form of a pill. They include the following:

- Injectables – the hormone progestin can be injected into the upper arm or thigh. Progestin interferes with the woman's natural menstrual cycle preventing her from getting pregnant. The injection lasts about three months, after which another injection will be needed.

- Implants – progestin contained in match-stick-sized implants can be inserted under the skin in the upper arm. These implants last about three to five years.

- Vaginal ring – the ring is about 5 centimetres in diameter. It is inserted in the vagina where it stays for three weeks. The ring contains very low doses of hormones similar to those contained in the oral pill.

- Oral pill – this prevents pregnancy by stopping the production and release of eggs from the ovaries.

Mechanical methods

The intrauterine device (IUD), also known as a coil, is inserted into the uterus by a doctor. It works by stopping the sperm from fertilising the egg and makes the womb unsuitable for the egg to implant.

Surgical methods

Sterilisation is a form of surgical contraception. It involves an operation, performed on either men or women, to make them infertile.

Emergency contraception

Emergency contraception can be used to prevent a pregnancy from happening after unprotected sex has taken place. The 'morning after' pill is a high dose of female hormones and should be taken within 24 hours of having unprotected sex.

Abuse

Abuse can be described as any situation in which someone suffers avoidable harm or is at risk of harm from another person. Below we consider both child abuse and the abuse of the elderly. Children and the elderly are both vulnerable groups of people who can become susceptible to abuse from family members and carers.

Child abuse

It is very difficult to guess how many children suffer abuse at the hands of adults. Many cases of abuse are never reported as the children involved are either too young, too scared or physically unable to report their injuries. The recent development of telephone helplines and child support agencies has gone some way to helping children to gain access to people who can help them.

Signs of physical abuse

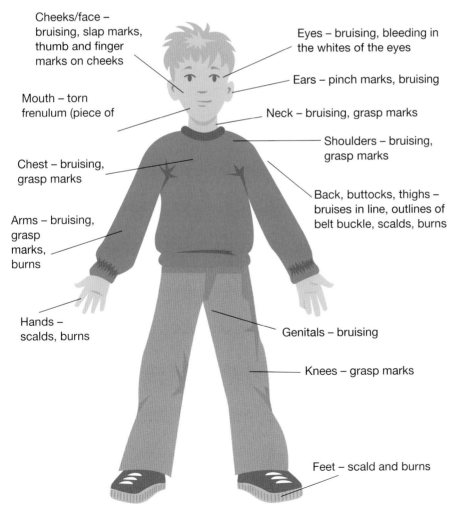

Cheeks/face – bruising, slap marks, thumb and finger marks on cheeks

Mouth – torn frenulum (piece of

Chest – bruising, grasp marks

Arms – bruising, grasp marks, burns

Hands – scalds, burns

Eyes – bruising, bleeding in the whites of the eyes

Ears – pinch marks, bruising

Neck – bruising, grasp marks

Shoulders – bruising, grasp marks

Back, buttocks, thighs – bruises in line, outlines of belt buckle, scalds, burns

Genitals – bruising

Knees – grasp marks

Feet – scald and burns

■ *Signs of physical abuse in children*

Real Life Care

Is Jack being abused?

Jack is 5 years old. You have been asked to look after him while his mother goes shopping. It is a very hot day and Jack wants to play in his paddling pool in the garden. It is then that you notice that he has hand-shaped bruises on his upper arms. He begins to tell you that his mummy holds him tight when he is naughty.

1 How do you react to Jack? What are your feelings towards Jack and his mother? ✔

2 What could the reasons be for Jack's mother holding him tightly? ✔✔

3 What are you going to do about this situation? ✔✔✔

Over to you

Confidentiality is an issue you have considered in Unit 1. What issues would apply here?

The ways in which you should have reacted to Jack are outlined below.

Listen

It is very important that you listen carefully to Jack. Remember, you may be the first person he has ever talked to about it. Allow him time to tell you how he feels; do not rush him. Do not ask leading questions, such as 'Where else does your mummy hit you?'. If possible, write down anything Jack tells you. Do not promise Jack that you will keep his secret, but reassure him that you will find someone to help him and his mother.

Believe

Believe Jack – not being believed can make the abuse worse. Don't laugh or make light of the situation – to Jack it is important that an adult understands him. It is up to someone else to find out the facts of the story; whether you believe him or not is not the issue.

Report

Do not assume someone else will report it. You have the responsibility to ensure that the information is passed on. Make a note of what has happened – when and where and if anyone else was present. Report your findings to social services or the police – your call will be treated in confidence. If you are working in a care situation, report any suspected abuse to a supervisor or manager. It is very unlikely that a child will be taken from his family. Social services will work with the parents and children to resolve the problems that resulted in the abuse occurring. Where possible, they will aim to keep the family together.

Elder abuse

The charity, Action on Elder Abuse, defines abuse as 'a single or repeated act or lack of appropriate action occurring within any relationship where there is an expectation of trust, which causes harm or distress to an older person'. It is only in recent years that abuse of the elderly has been recognised. Many of its causes are not yet fully understood. Abuse can occur to both men and women, in their own homes, hospitals, nursing or residential homes – in fact, anywhere you find old people.

Kinds of abuse

- Physical abuse – unexplained falls or injuries, small bruises on the chest from poking, bruising in unusual places, burns, restraint marks on wrists and ankles, ulcers, rashes from wet clothing, finger marks.

- Psychological abuse.

- Financial abuse.

- Sexual abuse.

- Neglect.

Who abuses?

Abusers are usually well known to the elderly person. They may be a partner, child or relative, friend or neighbour, any visitor to the home such as volunteer carers, health visitors and social workers, or any other professional. Old people may even be abused by the people who care for them.

Why does abuse occur?

There are many reasons why abuse occurs. At home, abuse may occur because carers are unable to offer the level of care necessary for an elderly person with physical or mental problems. In care settings, some staff may be poorly trained, lack adequate supervision and have no support from their managers.

Report

Where an elderly person is in immediate danger, elder abuse should be reported to the police. There are many organisations such as Help the Aged, Age Concern and Action on Elder Abuse that can offer help and advice to people suffering from abuse or people who are concerned about someone in danger.

Harm

Friends, family and even professionals are often so distressed when someone deliberately harms themselves that they do not know how to help them, leaving the sufferer to feel helpless, ashamed and alone. Self-harm takes many forms, from cutting, poisoning and burning to scalding, banging and hair pulling. Above all, self-harming is a way of expressing very strong emotions. When crying or shouting does not help, turning to self-harm can be a way of turning aggression inwards to get desperately needed relief. Self-harm is not attention seeking, but a form of communicating distress. People who self-harm may hide the problem for many years, choosing to injure areas of their body that nobody will see. As they harm themselves more often, they become less aware of the pain, so they have to inflict more severe damage to get the same relief.

Over to you

Write a list of how you reduce your stress and show your anxieties. Do any of the ideas on your list involve inflicting pain on yourself, such as punching a wall, exercising until it hurts, or pinching yourself? Is this self-harm?

People who self-harm may use the following techniques to reduce the risk of injury:

■ Count down slowly from ten.

■ Point out five things, one for each sense, in their surroundings.

■ Breathe slowly.

■ Use a red felt pen instead of cutting.

■ Punch a bag instead.

■ Plunge a hand into a bowl of ice cubes (but not for too long).

■ Rub ice where the person would have cut.

Methods of helping someone who self-harms

Remember you cannot necessarily change your friend or relative's life or coping mechanisms.

■ Be caring, willing to listen and allow the self-harmer to keep their dignity and express their feelings without being judged.

■ It may be hard, but do not try to explain why they may have self-harmed, or take control – above all, don't panic.

■ Try to become part of the self-harmer's support network – this is a step towards helping them develop other methods of coping.

■ Be patient – your support will make a big difference even though it may not seem like it.

Action plan

When producing an action plan to help reduce risks to health, it is necessary to get the full cooperation of the service user. Action plans can be used to support a wish to change some aspect of health, but they require the service user to have willpower and a determination to succeed. Action plans must have real obtainable goals that can be measured and adapted as situations change. They should be designed to meet the needs of the individual and should be frequently reviewed and updated. Above all, they should consider the service user **holistically** and consider all physical, intellectual, emotional and social needs.

An example of an action plan for someone who wants to give up smoking follows on the next page.

Holistically *Treating the whole person and looking at all apects of their health: physical, intellectual, social and emotional.*

Example of an action plan for a 26-year-old woman who wants to give up smoking

Type of plan	Objectives/goals	Methods	Strengths	Weaknesses
Short term (0–3 months)	To cut down the number of cigarettes smoked to 10 a day	Pick a day to stop Inform friends and family of decision Talk to GP Contact NHS helplines Use nicotine replacements Keep a diary of when cigarette is needed and plan other activities instead Avoid places where service user may be tempted, e.g. pubs and clubs	Body will begin to heal Breath will smell fresher Clothing will smell fresher Lungs will begin to recover Pulse rate will slow down Food will taste better More money to spend Will be able to go to areas previously barred to smokers Meet new people	May find it difficult to break smoking-related habits, e.g. cigarette breaks with friends/colleagues May become stressed May start to eat more to replace hand-to-mouth habit May be persuaded to start again by other smokers May not have access to support groups or Internet Nicotine replacements are expensive if not prescribed by GP
Medium term (3–6 months)	To cut down the number of cigarettes smoked to 3–5 a day	Continue to seek support of GP Start to cut back on nicotine replacements Use support chat rooms on Internet Talk to other ex-smokers	Health improves, will feel fitter, less breathless Continue to save money Meet new friends and ex-smokers	May lose friends as service user may not want to socialise with smokers Cost of nicotine replacement May put on weight
Long term (1 year +)	To stop smoking completely	Use support of friends and family	As a non-smoker, service user will feel healthier Reduced risks of heart disease Reduced risk of lung cancers Physical health improves Money saved Sense of achievement	May find it hard to see herself as a non-smoker May battle against friends and family who are all smokers May not be able to afford other interests to replace smoking

Hazards in health and social care environments

Over to you

Think carefully about the room you are sitting in. Make a list of all the hazards you can see. Remember to include exits, furnishings, books, waste bins, electrical equipment and wires, etc.

Hazards

There are hazards all around you all the time, for example the chair you are sitting on, the flooring you walk on, the water you wash your hands in are all hazards. Hazards are anything that can cause injury.

What is the difference between a hazard and a risk?

A hazard is the object that could potentially hurt someone, for example a wet floor, and the risk is the harm it could do, for example someone could slip and hurt themselves. When hazards have been identified, the next step is to consider the risks they present. These risks may be low, medium or high, depending on the severity.

Risk assessment

You perform a risk assessment every time you cross the road! Is it safe to cross? Are there any cars coming? How fast are they travelling? Should I cross somewhere safer? You have made a risk assessment – now you cross the road or not.

Risk assessment simply involves carefully examining something that could cause harm and then deciding whether enough precautions have been taken to prevent injury.

How to assess risks in the workplace

The Health & Safety Executive suggests the following five-point process:

1   *Look for hazards.* Look carefully at your work environment and consider what could be a hazard. Make a note of your findings.
2   *Decide who might be at harm, and how.* Consider clients, staff, relatives, visitors and the general public.
3   *Evaluate the risks arising from the hazards and decide whether more should be done.* After identifying hazards, think carefully what risk they pose. Is it possible to reduce the risk? Or is it necessary to control the risk? Risks cannot always be totally removed, only the severity reduced (low, medium or high). For example, in a nursery:

Hazard – adult-size tables
↓
Risk – children might hurt themselves on the corners
↓
Level of risk to children – high
↓
Minimise risk – buy small tables designed for children
↓
Risk – adults could hurt themselves on the corners
↓
Level of risk to adults – low

In the example above, the level of risk has been reduced but not eliminated. It is especially important to consider the risk to children, as children cannot control their environment and actions – they may put themselves at more risk. The adults in the nursery could step out of the way of a small table or receive a knock on the shin.

4   *Record your findings*. Workplaces should record their findings on a risk assessment form. This should show that:

- checks have been made

- hazards have been dealt with

- the number of people affected has been considered

- precautions have been taken to reduce the risk.

5   *Review your assessment from time to time and revise if necessary*. Hazards and associated risks do not go away once you have written them down on a form. Hazards need to be reassessed frequently especially as technology changes and new equipment is used.

Practice for Assessment

This could contribute to P4, M3 and D2.

Look carefully at the picture of hazards in a care setting.

Identify any potential hazards.

Describe how you could reduce the risks that the hazards present.

Minimising a risk sometimes creates more problems. Looking at the picture, analyse the strengths and weaknesses resulting from the reduction of each the risk.

■ *Hazards in a care setting*

Queen Elizabeth Day Unit, St Mary's Hospital

RISK ASSESSMENT

Hazard = task/activity with potential to cause harm	Type of injury that could result if harm occurs	Type of people and number affected	Risk level (low, medium, high)	Current control measures in place	Further control measures required	Person responsible for implementation of further measures required and date to implement	Date to review assessment (annual review unless task changes/alters)
Wheelchairs blocking fire exits	Unable to evacuate ward quickly – may result in people being trapped	All staff, clients and visitors to the Day Unit	H	Storage provided away from fire exits	Folding wheelchairs for safer storage	Health and safety officer; unit manager	
Meals kept aside on work surface for clients absent from ward	Food poisoning	Clients	H	All meals sent should be sent back to the kitchens and fresh meals prepared when clients return to the ward	Fridge needed to store food safely	Health and safety officer; unit manager	
Broken hoists	Lifting injuries	Staff	H		Maintenance book needed to ensure equipment is regularly checked	Staff in charge of each shift	

■ Example of a risk assessment

Toys

Play is not risk free but, with a little thought, it is possible to control most of the dangers children will be exposed to. All toys bought in the UK must conform to the Toy Safety Regulations 1995, but how they are used and their appropriateness for the age of the child are also important factors in preventing accidents. Toys are involved in over 40,000 accidents each year (Royal Society for the Prevention of Accidents, 2005). Accidents do not always occur because toys are unsafe but because they have been left in the wrong place and people trip over them. Accidents may also happen when a toy intended for an older child is given to a younger child, for example when babies are given toys to play with that are designed for children aged 3 and over.

Toy safety tips

- Only buy toys from recognised suppliers or shops.

- Ensure children are supervised at play.

- Make sure that the toy is suitable for the age of the child. Children less than 3 years old should never be allowed to play with toys that are marked as unsuitable.

- Check the toy for loose hair, small parts, and sharp edges.

- Check toys for signs of wear and throw away old and damaged toys.

- Keep the play area tidy.

- Follow any instructions or warnings that are supplied with the toy.

Control of infectious diseases

Hand washing

The most important way to prevent cross-infection is to wash your hands.

When to wash your hands:

- Before starting work and when finishing work.

- Before and after eating.

- After using the toilet.

- Before and after touching someone.

- After handling dirty laundry or emptying waste bins.

- After sneezing, coughing or blowing your nose.

Key point

Before buying a toy or giving a toy to a child, look for:

$C\epsilon$ the European Community (CE) symbol, which is the manufacturer's statement that the toy meets European Union safety standards

the Lion Mark, the British Toy & Hobby Association symbol of toy safety and quality

a symbol or wording which indicates that the toy is unsuitable for children under the age of 3.

A toy without any of the above symbols has not been checked for safety.

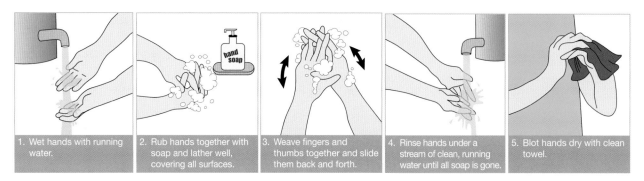

| 1. Wet hands with running water. | 2. Rub hands together with soap and lather well, covering all surfaces. | 3. Weave fingers and thumbs together and slide them back and forth. | 4. Rinse hands under a stream of clean, running water until all soap is gone. | 5. Blot hands dry with clean towel. |

■ *Steps to good hand washing*

Talking point

View 1: When caring for a patient, I never get time to wash my hands as I'm always too busy.

View 2: I always wash my hands whenever possible – people just have to wait a little while longer.

Wearing gloves

Wearing disposable gloves will also offer a protective barrier against infection.

Infection can travel in body products, especially blood. Cuts and grazes on hands that are not covered by gloves may allow someone else's blood to enter the body and cause an infection. Gloves must be worn when:

■ dealing with body products, e.g. blood, urine, mucus, sputum, vomit

■ changing soiled bed linen

■ clearing up spillages

■ dressing wounds and pressure sores

■ changing nappies.

Protective clothing

As well as protecting your hands, it may be necessary to protect your clothing and others from the bacteria you carry. Disposable aprons should be worn and disposed of immediately before going to attend another person. In some care situations, it is necessary to cover hair and shoes or to wear disposable gowns and masks. Protective clothing must be worn when:

■ coming into contact with bodily fluids or wastes

■ disposing of waste

■ caring for someone who is being treated for an infection

■ changing soiled linen.

Cleaning equipment

As well as keeping yourself clean and carrying out precautions to prevent the spread of infection, it is essential to ensure all equipment and work surfaces are clean. Many items are designed to be used only once and should be disposed of immediately after use. Large items such as mattresses and trolleys should be washed with antiseptic solutions and allowed to dry thoroughly before being used again. Smaller items such as instruments may come in packets and can be sterilised after use. Clean equipment before using on a new client, immediately after use and before putting it away.

Real Life Care

Suns and Moons day nursery

Suns and Moons day nursery, is a thriving, well-run nursery. Suzy is 3 years old and has been sent to nursery with a stomach ache. Suzy has a packed lunch that the nursery staff lay out for her at a table with five other children. Suzy is struggling to open her sandwiches, so a visiting parent helps her. Suzy does not like her tomatoes, so she gives them to her friend Ushma. After lunch, the cleaning staff quickly wipe down the tables before afternoon activities. The following day Suzy is not at nursery as she has diarrhoea and vomiting. Two days later, six children and three members of staff are also ill.

1 List the different ways that bacteria may have been spread from Suzy to other children and staff. ✓

2 How could this illness have been prevented? ✓✓

3 Evaluate the nursery's responsibility in ensuring infections are not spread. ✓✓✓

Responsibilities

Employers

UK laws put obligations on employers to ensure the health and safety of their employees. Employers must ensure:

- arrangements are made to ensure the health and safety of employees
- equipment is safe
- adequate health and safety training is provided
- the working environment does not put anyone at risk
- a written safety policy is in place
- the workplace is kept in good condition
- personal protective equipment, e.g. gloves, overalls, uniforms, is provided free of charge to employees
- the workplace does not emit toxic fumes or dust.

Employees

Employees also have responsibilities:

- To take care of themselves and others who may be affected by what they do and what they fail to do.
- To cooperate with their employer in implementing health and safety regulations.
- Not to interfere with or misuse any equipment provided to meet health and safety requirements.
- To report any dangerous situations to the manager.

Over to you

Think carefully about your part-time job or work experience. What responsibilities does your employer have to ensure you are protected at work? How much of what you do at work is your own responsibility and how much is your employer's? Make a list of your employer's responsibilities and a second list of employees' (your) responsibilities.

Health and safety legislation and guidelines

Many of the hazards present in the workplace are covered by health and safety legislation. The table below will help you identify which legislation is relevant to particular hazards.

Legislation covering particular hazards	
Hazard	**Relevant legislation**
Rooms and outdoor play areas that pose a risk	Health and Safety at Work Act 1974
Equipment in an unsafe condition	Health and Safety at Work Act 1974
Toys in an unsafe condition	Health and Safety at Work Act 1974
Incorrect storage of chemicals	Control of Substances Hazardous to Health (COSHH) Regulations 2002
Inadequate control of infectious diseases	Reporting of Injuries, Diseases and Dangerous Occurrences Regulations (RIDDOR) 1995
Fire	Fire Precautions (Workplace) Regulations 1997
Poor working conditions	Health and Safety at Work Act 1974
Unsafe furnishings	Health and Safety at Work Act 1974
Inappropriate furnishings for service users	Health and Safety at Work Act 1974
Inappropriate use of equipment	Health and Safety at Work Act 1974
Inadequate equipment maintenance	Health and Safety at Work Act 1974
Poor staff training	Health and Safety at Work Act 1974
Lack of security measures	Manual Handling Operations Regulations 1992
Inadequate building maintenance	Health and Safety at Work Act 1974
Inadequate personal safety precautions	Health and Safety at Work Act 1974
Close proximity to radio transmissions	Health and Safety at Work Act 1974
Pollution of air and/or water	Control of Substances Hazardous to Health (COSHH) Regulations 2002

Fire Precautions (Workplace) Regulations 1997

By law, all workplaces must have a fire risk assessment. There must be a fire and evacuation procedure, and at least one fire evacuation practice each year. Many workplaces opt for more frequent evacuation practices to ensure that every employee, trainee or temporary worker is aware of how to act in an emergency.

BUILDING EVACUATION PROCEDURES IN THE EVENT OF FIRE OR BOMB ALERT

The following procedure has been agreed and must be followed. Any staff member who does not comply is committing an infringement of (the college) disciplinary code. Whenever a fire occurs, the main consideration is to get everybody out of the building safely. Protection of personal (or college) property is incidental.

Raising the alarm

Anyone discovering fire must immediately raise the alarm by operating the nearest fire alarm and report to the controller the fire location.

On hearing the alarm the receptionist will immediately contact the emergency services and then evacuate the building.

In the event of a fire being discovered when the reception is unmanned, the premises officer on duty will contact the emergency services and assume control.

On hearing the alarm

All those in senior positions proceed to the control point, normally at a main entrance to the building – where one person must take control of the proceedings.

All other staff: close windows; switch off machinery and lights; and close doors on leaving the room.

Assist able colleagues, leave the building by the nearest marked route and proceed quickly to the appropriate assembly point. Staff must supervise their class.

Staff evacuating the building must check the locality is clear.

Assembly points

Everyone must remain at assembly points well away from buildings and clear of access roads.

Report to control in person or via two-way radios where allocated.

Everyone must remain at the assembly points until further instructions.

DO NOT re-enter the building until you are told it is safe to do so.

■ *An evacuation procedure*

Evacuation in a care setting has additional problems, including moving people with mobility problems due to age, disability, immaturity or medical treatment.

If you discover a fire …

- Get everyone out of the building as quickly and calmly as possible, closing fire doors behind you.
- Ensure a member of staff calls the fire service.
- Take with you any registers of patients/service users.
- If safe to do so, work in teams to evacuate wheelchair users and immobile service users.
- Use equipment provided to move service users.
- If unable to move a service user, leave them in a fire-free area, with all fire doors closed, and immediately inform fire fighters where the patient is.
- Never put yourself or others at risk.
- Never return to a burning building.

■ *Fire precautions*

Safety equipment

Fire extinguishers

Fire extinguishers are designed for different purposes. Using the wrong fire extinguisher can make a situation worse.

Water with additive	Foam	Powder	CO₂ gas

■ *Different types of fire extinguishers*

Fire blankets

Fire blankets are usually located in kitchens or where there is a risk of coming into contact with flames. Fire blankets are flame retardant and are designed to place over a fire to smother the flames. They must be used in a calm and controlled manner, as flapping a blanket about will cause the flames to spread.

Health and Safety at Work Act (HASWA) 1974

The Health and Safety at Work Act (HASWA) applies to all work situations. It covers everyone at work or anyone, such as the general public, who may be visiting a workplace. HASWA covers all health and safety legislation, providing a safe environment for all employees and employers.

> **Key point**
>
> If you cannot control a fire, leave it, close the door behind you, move to a safe area and call the fire service.

Employers' responsibilities	Shared responsibilities	Employees' responsibilities
Planning safety and security	Safety of individuals being cared for	Correct use of the systems and procedures
Providing information about safety and security	Safety of the working environment	Reporting flaws or gaps within the system or procedure when in use
Updating systems and procedures, with five or more employees		Taking reasonable care of themselves and other people affected by their work and cooperating with employers in the discharge of their obligations

■ *Health and safety responsibilities*

Employers must:

- provide a safe workplace
- ensure that there is safe access to and from the workplace
- provide adequate and accessible information on health and safety
- provide necessary health and safety training, e.g. manual handling
- undertake risk assessments for all hazards.

Employees must:

- be responsible for their own safety and that of others
- cooperate with employers regarding health and safety
- not intentionally damage any health and safety equipment or materials provided by the employer.

Over to you

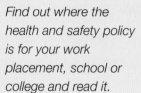

Find out where the health and safety policy is for your work placement, school or college and read it.

Manual Handling Operations Regulations 1992

Poor lifting techniques result in many thousands of lost working hours due to injury. As a result, the Health & Safety Executive (HSE) has set out guidelines to follow to avoid muscular and skeletal injury.

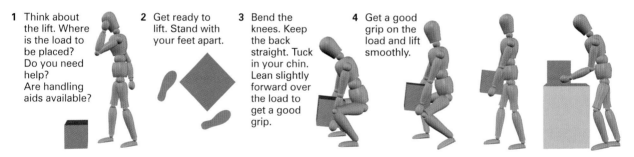

1 Think about the lift. Where is the load to be placed? Do you need help? Are handling aids available?

2 Get ready to lift. Stand with your feet apart.

3 Bend the knees. Keep the back straight. Tuck in your chin. Lean slightly forward over the load to get a good grip.

4 Get a good grip on the load and lift smoothly.

■ *Safe lifting procedures must be observed*

Key point

Always lift with a straight back and bent knees. Where possible, always seek help when lifting.

Caring for frail and vulnerable people may occasionally involve different forms of lifting. It is very important that when you lift a person you do not put yourself or them at risk. Before lifting, carefully consider if there is a safer alternative and what equipment is available to help you. Lifting should be the last option when moving a person.

Tips for safe lifting in a care environment

- Practise lifting in a safe, controlled environment.
- All members of staff should be trained in manual handling.
- Plan a lift carefully before starting.
- Inform the service user that you need to lift them.
- Where possible, lift with another person.
- Decide who is going to lead the lift.
- Where possible, get the service user to help move themselves.
- Use equipment that is available.
- Never hurry a lift.

Key point

You should never be asked to lift anyone whilst on your work placement.

Reporting of Injuries, Diseases and Dangerous Occurrences Regulations (RIDDOR) 1995

Employers must report accidents, diseases and dangerous occurrences and deaths to the HSE. The HSE can then use this information to perform risk assessments.

Every workplace should have an accident report form as correct documentation of an accident, incident or near-miss is important. The person completing the form should make a detailed note of dates, times, witnesses and the treatment necessary. With a clear description of the event it may be possible to ensure that measures are taken to reduce the risk of a similar incident occurring again.

Real Life Care

A near-miss

Sam and Jake are 4 years old and are identical twins. Jake is an asthmatic and occasionally uses an inhaler to help him breathe. Shara is a new member of staff at school. She has been told that one of the twins suffers from asthma. After sports day, she notices Sam looking breathless and rushes over to him with Jake's inhaler. She is stopped by the nursery manager before Sam takes the medication.

1 What action should the manager and Shara take to ensure that this near-miss does not happen again? ✓

2 If Sam had used the inhaler, would the manager's action have been different. If so, how? ✓✓

3 If this incident kept reoccurring as staff were unable to tell the boys apart, what further actions could the manager take? ✓✓✓

Beeches Residential Home
Report of an Accident, Dangerous Occurrence or Near Miss

Date of incident | 06/07/05 | **Time of incident** | 10:00

Location of accident, etc. | Dayroom

In the event of the casualty being absent from normal duties, please fill in the date of the first absence and date of return to work

Date off work | 07/07/05 | **Date return to work** | 08/08/05

Details of the person injured or involved in the accident, dangerous occurence or near miss

Full name, address and post code:
Daisy May
39 Draft Street
Portsmouth PO1 1XX

Age: 26

Sex (M or F): F

Occupation of injured person or status if not an employee (e.g. Resident, Visitor) | Staff Nurse

Nature of injury | Burn to hand

Management of injury
(Please tick appropriate box)

First aid only ✓   Advised to see doctor ☐

Casualty sent to hospital ✓   Admitted to hospital for more than 24 hours ☐

Account of accident, dangerous occurrence or near miss
Describe what happened and how. In the case of an accident, state what the injured person was doing at the time.

Daisy was handing out cups of tea to the residents when Mr Jones, who is blind, knocked in to her, causing her to spill tea on her left hand.

Witnesses
(Please give names, address and occupation)

Health Care Support Worker
Kate Hill, 17 Beenthere Street
Portsmouth PO2 3ZY

Remedial action taken
(**Note:** All accidents, other than minor incidents, will require an accident investigation form to be completed.)

Kate Hill immersed Daisy's hand in cold water for ten minutes, wrapped it up in a towel and took her to A&E.

Signature of person making report | Hill   K. Hill | **Date** | 06/07/05

Signature of Safety Co-ordinator | | **Date** |

On completion the residential home should retain a copy and send a copy to:
1. the Director of Environmental, Health and Safety Services (EHSS)
2. the Person(s) involved in the incidents

■ Accident report form

Control of Substances Hazardous to Health (COSHH) Regulations 2002

This law is designed to ensure that employers control exposure to hazardous substances in the workplace. In care settings hazardous substances include cleaning materials, acids, disinfectants, as well as body products such as blood and urine.

Every workplace should have a member of staff who is responsible for implementing the guidelines set down by the Control of Substances Hazardous to Health (COSHH) Regulations. These cover the following:

- Correct storage of chemicals:
  - All substances should be stored in a safe place.
  - Where there are children present, the storage area should be locked and out of reach.
  - Chemicals must be kept in the appropriate containers supplied by the manufacturer.
  - Where appropriate, containers must have safety lids and caps. (Some drugs are not stored in safety containers as they are needed for emergency use.)

- Labelling:
  - Hazardous substances should be labelled with an appropriate symbol indicating the associated danger.
  - The contents of the container should match the name on the outside. Never reuse a container designed for a different substance.
  - The container should display a use-by date.
  - Instructions on how to use the substance safely should be supplied with the chemical.
  - There should also be instructions on what to do in the case of a spillage.
  - The length of storage time from opening should be given.

| Dust | Toxic | Flammable | Irritant | Corrosive | Oxidising agent |

■ *Hazardous substances symbols*

Disposal of hazardous waste

It is important that hazardous waste is disposed of correctly to ensure a safe working environment. The following table describes the method of disposal for each type of waste.

Over to you

You are working in a residential care home when a relative hands you a bottle of drugs that belongs to his mother. What do you check the bottle and label for?

Methods of disposal of waste	
Type of waste	**Method of disposal**
Clinical waste, e.g. used wound dressings, bandages, nappies, sanitary dressings, soiled gloves	Yellow bag – when the bag is full, carefully seal and tag it indicating where the waste has come from, e.g. labour ward, paediatrics, accident and emergency. This waste is burnt in an incinerator.
Sharps, e.g. needles, glass, syringes	Yellow sharps box – when the box is full, seal and tag it indicating location of box.
Body fluids, e.g. vomit, urine, faeces, blood, sputum	Wash down the sluice drain, and disinfect.
Dirty and soiled sheets and linen	Red bag – seal and send to the laundry (the bag will disintegrate in the wash).
Recyclable instruments and equipment for sterilisation	Blue bag – seal and return to central sterilisation services department (CSSD) for cleaning, sterilising and repackaging.
Waste paper	Black bag – seal and tag for incineration or shredding of confidential information.

Practice for Assessment

This could contribute to P5 and M4.

Read the case study below and then answer the questions.

You are a health care support worker working in a busy medical ward. One morning, you are asked to help wash 90-year-old Mrs Needham, who has been urine incontinent during the night. You and a new member of staff must help Mrs Needham to wash and dress, then you will need to change her bedding and incontinence dressings.

Describe how you would protect yourselves and Mrs Needham from cross-infection.

Describe all the methods of waste disposal you would use to perform your duties to maintain health and safety requirements.

Explain which two pieces of health and safety legislation cover what you are doing and how their implementation will protect you, the new member of staff and Mrs Needham.

Check your understanding

1. List six needs that you would find on Maslow's triangle.
2. Identify three environmental pollutants.
3. Name four factors that could affect the health of an elderly person.
4. Name two support groups that could help people change a lifestyle factor.
5. What is the difference between a risk and a hazard?
6. Why is it necessary to record accidents?
7. What should you do if you think a client is being abused?
8. Which regulations are concerned with the storage of chemicals hazardous to health?
9. Describe four things that you would check for on a bottle of prescription pills.
10. What colour extinguisher would be used to put out an electrical fire?

3 Vocational Experience in a Health or Social Care Setting

Introduction

This unit is designed to complement the 60 hours of work experience that you will need to do in order to successfully complete Unit 3. It explains how to apply for a work placement as well as giving you the opportunity to practise interview skills. The unit will also enable you to gain an insight into the health and social care workplace and show you how to develop your chosen career path. Using the interpersonal communication skills outlined in Unit 1, you should have the guidance necessary to successfully complete any internally set assessment that fulfils the requirements of Unit 3.

How you will be assessed

This is an internally assessed unit.

In this unit you will learn about:

■ the application process
■ work experience
■ the use of interpersonal skills
■ describing a period of work experience.

The application process

Applying for a job needs a lot of care and thought. This section shows you how to apply for the job you want as well as outlining the importance of interview skills in starting out on the first rung of your career ladder.

Personal information and methods

Application procedures

Did you know that 60–70 per cent of jobs are not advertised? So how do you find the right job for you?

Speculative approach

To apply for a job speculatively means to approach an employer even if they are not advertising a vacancy. You will need to research the company you are interested in and know what job roles might be available. By researching what jobs are available, you may discover a job that you had not considered before and so increase the variety of jobs open to you.

The speculative approach lets you take the initiative in job hunting and will help you to get the vacancy you want. It also means that you are up against fewer applicants. The first step is to find an organisation you want to work for.

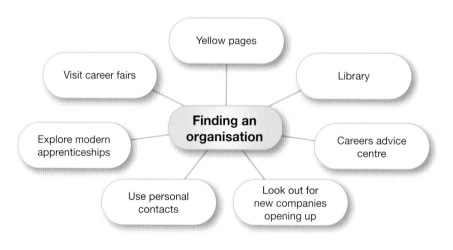

■ *Finding the right organisation*

Newspapers

Try looking in daily and weekly newspapers covering the area you wish to work in. Many newspapers have their own websites with job pages.

Specialist magazines

Magazines such as the *Nursing Times*, *Nursing Standard*, *Nursery Nurse* and *Community Care* advertise jobs specific to their area of interest. The adverts will reach many people and the applicants may come from all over the country.

Recruitment agencies

Specialist recruitment agencies employ staff to fulfil particular jobs, for example care workers, administration staff and temporary staff. You can find out what types of jobs recruitment agencies advertise by looking at their websites or in the *Yellow Pages*. To register with an agency, it is best to go in and meet with a consultant who may interview you straightaway or ask you to come back later, so have your CV to hand, and be presentable. (For information on how to prepare your CV, see below.)

Online recruitment sites

Online recruitment is the fastest method of hiring new staff. Many websites will give you the opportunity to post your CV on their website.

Online recruitment agencies will often help you to produce a CV, which they will then send with your application details to many different health and social care providers. This approach increases the number of jobs open to you, as your CV may be sent to providers that you were not aware existed and who would not otherwise have seen your application. Some health and social care providers only use recruitment agencies to find their staff and do not reply to personal applications that are not received via the recruitment service.

There are problems with recruiting online. Sometimes you will be charged for sending your CV to a health provider, and you may have no control over who receives your application. You may be sent details of jobs that are unsuitable or located in areas that are too far away for you to travel to.

JobCentres

JobCentres usually deal with vacancies for 18-year-olds and above, but they may be able to tell you about vacancies in other areas. JobCentres are run by the government and offer a wide range of services. Job seekers can get advice about their entitlement to benefits as well as training and advice about interview techniques.

JobCentres also offer specialist help for people with disabilities. People with disabilities are allocated a disability employment adviser (DEA), who can help them prepare for work, assess their employment needs as well as organise two-week trials in jobs that may be suitable.

Television and radio

Listen out for local radio 'job spots'. On the TV, Teletext and digital channels may advertise local and national jobs.

Over to you

Look through local newspapers and specialist magazines for job adverts. Then create a notice board for your classroom that advertises vacancies relevant to the health and social care sector.

Over to you

Think about a job that interests you in health and social care. Try searching online websites to find a suitable vacancy in your area. To access some job search websites, go to www.heinemann.co.uk/hotlinks and enter the express code 3322P.

■ *A JobCentre*

Notice boards

Employers may advertise vacancies on their customer notice boards in shop windows or reception areas. It is always worth going in and asking!

Curriculum vitae (CV)

Curriculum vitae (CV) means 'the course of one's life'. It is a brief description of you, your education, employment, experiences, skills and hobbies. A CV outlines all your relevant facts for a prospective employer or trainer. You should use a CV when applying for a new job or perhaps speculatively (see above) when a vacancy has not been advertised but you would like to be considered if one becomes available.

Your CV should create a good impression of you even before meeting a new employer. It needs to be interesting, up to date and well presented. It should be word processed and cover no more than two sides of A4 paper. Make sure your CV is relevant to the job you are applying for.

The following are CV dos and don'ts:

Do:
Keep your CV clear and concise.
Present it neatly.
Make sure that all information is relevant.
Make sure all information is up to date.

Don't:
Leave time gaps in your CV. If you were not employed, say so. Don't leave this information out.
Lie and make up details.
Waffle.
Include information that is not relevant. An employer does not need to know about a swimming certificate that you got at the age of 10, for example!
Look at the examples of a good and poor CV on pages 105 and 106.

Over to you

Think about the things that you do such as a part-time job, baby sitting, voluntary work, Duke of Edinburgh award, etc. and list the skills you have gained.

Personal profile

Name:	Sarah Smith	Telephone number:	0110 390189
Address:	20 Pickle Street,	DOB:	9 November 1991
	Smallville,	Mobile:	0797 8695949
	Hampshire	Age:	17 years
	PO2 2OP		

Friendly, good humoured, quick to learn, with good listening and communication skills. Experience in customer services and dealing with customer complaints. Hard working with a good college attendance record.

Qualifications

2008   BTEC First Diploma in Health and Social Care (equivalent to 4 GCSEs A-C) including communication and individual rights, individual needs, vocational experience, anatomy and physiology, cultural diversity and life span development
Key Skills, Communication, Application of Number and IT all at level 2.
First Aid at Work Certificate

2007   3 GCSE passes in English, Science, History

Occupational Skills

Customer services: Welcoming and serving customers while maintaining a friendly, appropriate manner in the ' Fit for life leisure centre'. Taking bookings, planning children's activities and dealing with customer complaints.

Child care: Collecting two 6-year-old children from school, preparing them a meal and supervising play and coordinating their after school activities.

Organising child activities: Extensive experience helping to organise Saturday clubs, after school fun days and Brownie revels

Employment and work experience

2007 to date   Receptionist at 'Fit for life leisure centre' (part time)

2008 January   Two weeks' work experience at Neverland day nursery for pre-school children

2008 March   Two weeks' work experience at Rainbow centre for children with disabilities

2006 to date   Baby sitting twins for Mr and Mrs Bold. After-school care

Education

2007–2008   South Downs College, Portsmouth

2003–2007   Westergate Community School, Bognor Regis

Interests and other skills

I have been a helper at a Brownie unit for 3 years and have taken the Brownies on several pack holidays, as well as organising weekly activities for them. I am also a keen reptile keeper and have developed a successful breeding programme for snakes.

Referees

Mr D. Ruby, Course manager, BTEC First Diploma in Health and Care, South Downs College, Portsmouth PO3 1ZZ

Ms F. Itness, Manager 'Fit for life leisure centre', Smallville, Hampshire PO2 3PP

■ *Example of a good CV*

Personal profile

Name:	Sarah Smith
Address:	20 Pickle Street, Smallville, Hampshire, PO2 2OP
Telephone number:	0110 390189 Mobile: 0797 8695949
D.O.B.	9th November 1991 Age 17 years

Qualifications.

2008   BTEC First Diploma in Health and Social Care. Did not complete
as dropped out of college.
        First Aid at Work Certificate.

2007   3 GCSE's English, Science, History.

Occupational Skills.

Work on the reception desk at 'Fit for life leisure centre'. I take the
bookings and money and sometimes sort our lost property when asked.

I look after my twin cousins after school and watch TV with them, until
mum gets home.

I sometimes help with the Saturday club at the leisure centre. I might help
with the holiday club if they are short handed.

Employment and Work experience.

2007 to date   Receptionist at 'Fit for life leisure centre', P/T
2008 January   Work experience at Neverland day nursery.
2008 March   Work experience at Rainbow centre.
2006 to date   Baby sitting.

Education

2007 – 2008   South Downs College
2003 – 2007   Westergate community school

Interests and Other Skills.

I don t have many interests other than smoking, going out with my friends
and playing SIMS on my Playstation. My dad keeps snakes and I help him
look after them

Referees.

BTEC First Diploma in Health and Care, Course manager,
'Fit for life leisure centre, Hampshire.

Over to you

Compare the two CVs. Write a list of the differences you have noted. If you did not know that they referred to the same person, who would you employ and why?

■ *Example of a poor CV*

Your CV will need to include the following information:

- Personal details – name, address, telephone number, date of birth and nationality.
- Unique selling points – emphasise your top three achievements or skills.
- Qualifications – starting with the most recent, list all your exam results.
- Education, employment and work experience – the name of your secondary school and/or college; jobs and work experience, which should include a brief description of your responsibilities.
- Other information and skills – other skills or qualifications you may have such as IT, first aid, food hygiene certificates, life-saving awards.
- Interests – try to make this section interesting by listing hobbies, sports or voluntary activities.
- Referees – names and addresses of two people, usually one from college or school and one from work. Don't forget to ask them first!

Key point

You should update your CV regularly emphasising your personal development.

Application forms

The purpose of completing an application form is to convince the employer that you are worth inviting to an interview because you are a suitable candidate for the job and the kind of person the organisation would like to employ.

---

application form for employment (please print in black pen)

| Job title | Health Care Support Worker | Location | Mayflower Nursing Home |

part 1 - personal details

Title: Mr/Mrs/Miss/Ms	Miss	Date of birth	08 · 08 · 1991
Surname/Family name	JAY	National insurance number	NP480911A
First name(s)	SALLY	Home telephone number	01329 697976
Address	29 Sunny Dale Close	Mobile number	7918247479
	Fareham	Work telephone number / May we phone you at work:	Yes ☐ No ✓
	Hampshire Postcode PO14 2AJ	Do you hold a current full driving licence?	Yes ☐ No ✓
Email address	sjay @ yahoo.net	Do you have use of a car?	Yes ☐ No ✓

| Professional qualifications | Membership of professional bodies |

| Do you require a work permit? Yes ☐ No ✓ | Approximate absences due to illness in the last year = O days |

Briefly describe any health problems which could be relevant to the position applied for

Asthma which is well control, I have had no attacks in the last three months.

---

part 4 - previous employment history

From	To	Name & address of employer	Job title & main responsibilities	Reason for leaving
Jan 2008	June 2008	Happy Days Nursing Home Blackpool	Week-end health Care support worker. Responsible for daily care of elderly residents	Moved away from Area

part 5 - other details

Briefly explain why you feel you are suitable for this vacancy, and what qualities you will bring to the post

I have had experience in caring for elderly people with a range of physical and emotional difficulties. I am a cheerful and confident person who is able to cope in stressful situations. I consider myself professional, a good time keeper, smart and polite. I work well with elderly people and their families. I enjoy working as a member of a team and am quick to learn new techniques and adapt to change.

Give details of leisure activities or pursuits that you feel could be relevant to your employment

I am a young leader for guides and have recently been involved in organising a community Arts Project for the elderly. I also help on Sunday making tea and coffee at my local church.

■ *A completed application form*

Points to consider

■ Find out as much information as you can about the organisation before filling in the form. Look at its website or contact the organisation for further details. You may need to visit a careers centre or large library to find out more information.

■ Read the whole form through carefully before filling in any of the sections. It's a good idea to make a photocopy of the blank form and use this to practise your answers on.

■ Once you have filled in the form, complete the checklist below. You should be able to put ticks in all the columns.

Application form checklist		
	Yes	No
I have read the whole form through carefully.		
I have followed all the questions carefully.		
I looked at the amount of space allocated to each question. When there was more space, I gave more detail.		
I completed all the questions.		
Any questions that were not relevant I wrote N/A (not applicable).		
I did not leave any gaps in my record of employment.		
I pointed out the voluntary work that I have done.		
I have not written more than space allowed.		
I was concise, positive and I did not waffle.		
All my writing is easy to read.		
There are no spelling mistakes.		
My points are all relevant and interesting.		
I have applied skills I learnt from my last job to this application.		
I have used the 'any other information' section to draw attention to activities not covered anywhere else.		
I checked with my referees before giving their names.		
My referees are from school/college or someone I have worked for.		
I have kept a copy of the form before sending it.		

Letter of application

Letters are the first impression an employer has of you, so they are very important. It is your opportunity to select and emphasise your good points for employers to see and convince them that they must interview you!

Plan your letter

Writing a letter of application requires time and preparation. This is your chance to sell yourself. Your letter will show your suitability for the job, so make sure you are happy with it, and that it displays your good qualities. A letter usually accompanies your CV when you apply for a job. Most of the information the employer wants is already in your CV or application form, so your letter is the chance to introduce yourself in a positive personal way, and to add quality to the dry details of your CV.

Over to you

Write a paragraph about yourself emphasising your positive aspects.

Make it relevant

Make sure the information in the letter is relevant to your application. There is no point talking about your 1000-metre swimming certificate if you are applying for a job working with the elderly. Your CV will include all your qualifications, so the accompanying letter needs to highlight the skills and qualities that you could bring to the job. Think about your activities and achievements and tell the reader what they want to know about, not what you want to tell them.

Be positive

Be positive about your successes; try to avoid negative words. Emphasise the good things about you. For example:

Instead of: **Try:**

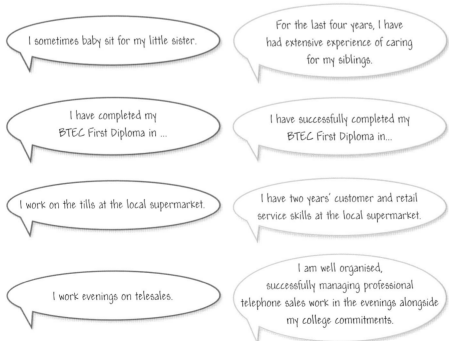

I sometimes baby sit for my little sister.

For the last four years, I have had extensive experience of caring for my siblings.

I have completed my BTEC First Diploma in ...

I have successfully completed my BTEC First Diploma in...

I work on the tills at the local supermarket.

I have two years' customer and retail service skills at the local supermarket.

I work evenings on telesales.

I am well organised, successfully managing professional telephone sales work in the evenings alongside my college commitments.

Over to you

Try rewording these phrases to make them more positive:
'I like listening to music.'
'I work as a lifeguard.'
'When I have finished my studies I might become a nurse.'
'Once a week I visit my gran.'

Below are some useful active words:

- achieved
- developed
- managed
- coordinated
- led
- promoted
- initiated

- created
- supervised
- monitored
- produced
- directed
- designed
- organised

Tips for successful letter writing

- Your letter only needs to be one side of an A4 sheet of paper.
- Word process and spellcheck your letter. Then proofread it carefully for any mistakes that the spellchecker did not pick up.
- Write your letter to a named person. If you don't know a name, then ring up the organisation and find out who you should address the letter to.
- Write your letter in rough first.
- Write in full sentences, in clear 'everyday' English, not text language.
- Avoid lists of activities as they don't say much about you.
- Don't repeat yourself.

What your application letter should cover
Employers will usually want to know the following in order to consider your application:

- The reason why you are writing a letter.
- What you are doing or studying at the moment.
- Work experience and personal skills that relate to your application.
- Personal qualities that are relevant to the job, e.g. good timekeeping, organisational skills.
- Your knowledge of the organisation and why you would like to work there.
- Complete the letter by saying that you enclose your CV and look forward to hearing from them.

Emily Clarke,
Toosmiley Way,
Sunny Park,
Southampton
SO22 007

31 January 2008

Mrs S McAdams
Care Manager
Happy Days Residential Home
Sunny Park Road
Southampton
Hampshire SO22 009

Dear Mrs McAdams

I am writing to enquire whether you have opportunities at Happy Days
Residential Home for a health care support worker.

I am currently studying a BTEC First Diploma in Health and Social Care at
Westown College. This is a one-year course equivalent to 4 GCSEs, covering
all aspects of care, meeting the health needs of all individuals in care settings.

I have also had several different placements during the course, working with
the elderly and children in different care settings. I particularly enjoyed
working with the elderly at St Christopher's Day Centre, where I helped at
outings and social events arranged for the day visitors. As part of my work
experience I was able to accompany several clients to outpatient appointments,
and watched physiotherapy and occupational therapy sessions.

In addition to my course I have a part-time voluntary job as a shop assistant at
the Age Concern charity shop in Southampton. I enjoy working in a team
especially with the elderly volunteers. I enjoy serving the customers and
rearranging the shop, so as to encourage people to buy and therefore help
Age Concern.

I would appreciate any advice on gaining work within a residential home. I am
very keen to work at Happy Days Residential Home as many of the elderly
people I work with have friends who live with you and have always told me of
the kind and supportive care they receive.

I enclose my CV outlining my qualifications and experience to date. Thank
you for taking the time to read this application.

Yours sincerely

Emily Clarke

■ *Letter of application*

Practice for Assessment

Carrying out this activity will give you underpinning knowledge for P1.

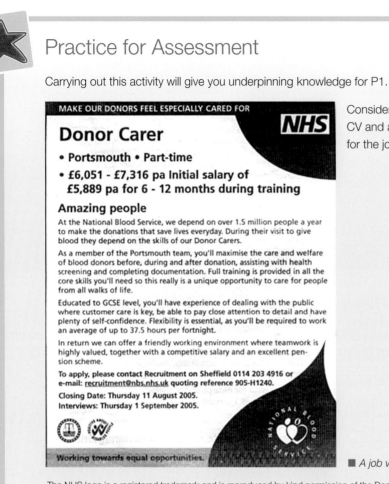

MAKE OUR DONORS FEEL ESPECIALLY CARED FOR

NHS

Donor Carer

- **Portsmouth** • **Part-time**
- **£6,051 - £7,316 pa Initial salary of £5,889 pa for 6 - 12 months during training**

Amazing people

At the National Blood Service, we depend on over 1.5 million people a year to make the donations that save lives everyday. During their visit to give blood they depend on the skills of our Donor Carers.

As a member of the Portsmouth team, you'll maximise the care and welfare of blood donors before, during and after donation, assisting with health screening and completing documentation. Full training is provided in all the core skills you'll need so this really is a unique opportunity to care for people from all walks of life.

Educated to GCSE level, you'll have experience of dealing with the public where customer care is key, be able to pay close attention to detail and have plenty of self-confidence. Flexibility is essential, as you'll be required to work an average of up to 37.5 hours per fortnight.

In return we can offer a friendly working environment where teamwork is highly valued, together with a competitive salary and an excellent pension scheme.

To apply, please contact Recruitment on Sheffield 0114 203 4916 or e-mail: recruitment@nbs.nhs.uk quoting reference 905-H1240.

Closing Date: Thursday 11 August 2005.
Interviews: Thursday 1 September 2005.

Working towards equal opportunities.

Consider this job vancancy. Produce a CV and a letter of application to apply for the job.

■ *A job vacancy for the National Blood Service*

The NHS logo is a registered trademark and is reproduced by kind permission of the Department of Health

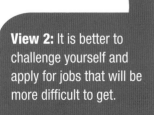

Talking point

View 1: You should only go for jobs that you know you stand a good chance of getting.

View 2: It is better to challenge yourself and apply for jobs that will be more difficult to get.

Letters of acceptance/decline

If you are offered the job, it is polite to write a letter of acceptance, saying how much you are looking forward to working with the organisation. If you had an interview but did not get the job, do not get disheartened. Remember, you got an interview which means you must have had some of the qualities the employer was looking for. Now, you have a little more experience than you did before, which may help you get the next job you apply for. Keep in contact with the organisation you really want to work for. To do this, write a letter thanking them for considering you and saying you hope that they will consider you for any other positions that may arise. The next one may be better than the first! Don't give up, be confident and keep trying.

If you decide not to accept a job (for whatever reason), always write a polite letter of decline.

Interview skills

Congratulations! You have been offered an interview. Think carefully about the impression you want to make on the interviewer.

What to do at the interview

- Before entering the interview room, take a few seconds to stand tall, pull back your shoulders and lift your head. This will help you talk more clearly and show that you are confident.

- As you enter the interview room, smile and make eye contact with the interviewer(s) – but don't overdo it.

- Shake hands with the interviewer(s) and say, 'Hello, very nice to meet you.'

- Sit down when invited.

- Sit well back in your chair, with your feet together and hands in your lap. Good posture will help you feel alert and confident.

- Keep eye contact.

- As you relax, allow your personality to shine through, but don't get too carried away and start waffling or going off the point. Keep your answers concise and answer what you were asked, not what you wanted to be asked.

- If you start to feel nervous, take a deep breath and relax your shoulders.

- Be alert, don't talk too much, and look out for signs that the interview is coming to an end.

- As you leave, keep smiling, shake hands with the interviewer(s) and thank them for seeing you.

- The interview is not over until you leave the building. Remember, the people you may work with will also be watching. Impressions last so make them good ones!

■ *Relaxing in an interview allows your personality to shine*

Real Life Care

The interview

Steve is 16 years old. He is out shopping with his friends when he remembers that he has a job interview in an hour. On arriving for the interview, he is out of breath because he missed the bus and is hot and flustered. As he is late, Steve is taken straight to the interview room. During the interview, he lounges in the chair, with his arms resting over the back of the seat, and does not make eye contact with the interviewer. Steve talks constantly and in a casual, informal manner. When the interview is over, he says, 'Cheers, thanks a lot', and ambles out of the room.

Rab is also 16 years old and out shopping with Steve. He leaves Steve early to get ready for his interview. He catches his bus on time, arrives 10 minutes early for the interview, giving himself time to relax, breathe calmly and concentrate on his prepared questions. On entering the room, he greets everyone politely and makes eye contact as necessary. He sits upright in the chair with his arms in his lap. During the interview, Rab is careful to answer questions thoughtfully and ask questions as appropriate. As he is relaxed, he is able to add a little humour to his answers. On leaving, he shakes hands with the interviewers and thanks them for their time.

1 Which interviewee do you think would get the job? Explain your reasons.

2 Discuss the different communication skills used by both boys.

3 In what ways does Steve need to improve his interview technique?

Practice for Assessment

Carrying out this assignment will give you underpinning knowledge for P2.

You are going for an interview as a ward receptionist at the local hospital. With a partner, practise your interview skills and decide if you would have got the job. Carefully consider which skills you would need to improve.

Answering questions

As a school or college leaver, you will not have much work experience and you will not have developed many skills, so you may feel at a disadvantage at an interview. The solution is to make the most of the experience you do have. It does not matter if your experience is gained in a different sort of workplace from the one you are hoping to work in. All that matters is that you have the skills required and that you can demonstrate when you have used them.

For example, if the interviewer asks, 'How do you get on with other people?', they are trying to find out if you are able to mix with and work with people from all backgrounds and ages. They may be concerned that you have only ever associated with people of your own age. Use an experience from your life to demonstrate when you have worked with people of different ages. This could be as a shop assistant, Brownie helper, volunteer or sports coach.

If they ask, 'Why do you think you would like this type of work?', you will need to have read the job description well. Then you can compare what you know they are looking for with examples from work you may have done. This will show where your work interest has developed from. For example, if you work Saturdays in a hairdressing salon, you could answer that talking to customers about their interests and problems has helped you to realise that you would like to do a job where communication is important.

Over to you

Think of a job in health and social care that you would apply for. The job adverts at the beginning of this unit may give you some ideas. Then look carefully at the list of interview questions below and suggest appropiate answers. Remember to relate your answers to your chosen job.

- *Why did you choose the BTEC First Diploma?*
- *What are your favourite subjects?*
- *What have you learnt that would be useful here?*
- *How do you feel about routine work?*
- *What are your greatest strengths?*

Asking questions

It is a good idea to have some questions prepared that you could ask at the end of the interview, as this will show that you are interested in the job and the organisation. Areas you might want to ask questions about could include the following.

The job itself
Avoid asking anything that you would be expected to know from reading the job description. Think about what responsibilities might be expected of you, and whether there are any future changes planned that might affect the job.

Possible questions you could ask:

- 'What are the main responsibilities of the job?'
- 'Why has the job become available?'

The organisation
This could be your opportunity to check that you understand the role of the organisation. It also shows that you are interested in it.

Possible questions you could ask:

- 'Will the organisation be developing any new centres?'
- 'Do you care for children from all ethnic backgrounds?'

Opportunities

You might find it helpful to know what opportunities for development within the organisation are available to you. For example, you might be asked to work in several centres depending on staffing levels. There could be the opportunity to take further courses or add to your responsibilities and progress your career.

Possible questions you could ask:

- 'What would my career prospects be within the organisation?'
- 'Will I have the opportunity to study for my NVQ3?'

Finally, if you have the courage, you could ask:

- When can I expect to hear from you?
- How will you inform me of your decision?

Preparation for interview

There are many things you can do before an interview to improve your chances of success. The person interviewing you will have prepared for the meeting, so you should do the same. The point of an interview is to:

- meet the job applicant
- find out whether they will fit in well with the organisation
- check the applicant's CV to make sure they have the relevant skills
- complete the picture of the applicant as presented in their CV.

Telephone skills

Talking on the telephone is now second nature to most people; in fact, many people carry a mobile phone with them most of the time. Nevertheless, it is important to think carefully about the impression you give over the phone. When asking about an interview or phoning an organisation you hope to work for, you will need to consider many things:

- Have a pen and paper ready. There is no point asking for directions, then saying 'Hang on a minute while I find a pen.'
- Plan what you are going to say before dialling.
- Don't make a call if you are stressed, harassed or short of time. Relax, take a breath and put a smile in your voice.
- Speak clearly and in full sentences. 'Yah, right, see ya, ta' does not give a very professional image.
- Say who you are and what you want. Don't expect the person on the other end to know who you are; they will need clues, e.g. 'Hello, I am Sandra May and I am enquiring about the job for a … advertised in this week's *Herald* newspaper.' Finally, thank the person you speak to for their help.

Over to you

Work in groups of three. Two of you need to have mobile phones and the other (the observer) needs a pen and paper. The two with phones are going to have two conversations. The first is about a party last Saturday. The second conversation involves a care worker answering the phone in a nursing home to someone enquiring about an advertised job vacancy. The observer should write notes about the language used in both conversations, the tone, speed and volume of the voice.

Planning for an interview

There are six steps to planning for your interview:

Step 1: Find out as much as you can about the job and the organisation. This knowledge will help you ask suitable questions at the end of the interview, and will also show the interviewer that you are interested in the organisation.

Step 2: Find out how to get to the interview. Check how long it will take to get there and give yourself plenty of time so as not to arrive flustered, hot and stressed. If travelling by bus, perhaps get off a stop earlier to give yourself time to relax and compose yourself. Arriving suddenly on the doorstep means you have to be prepared straightaway, but make sure you get there in plenty of time. Punctuality is important – the interviewer will get a bad first impression if you rush in ten minutes late. If walking to an interview, wear appropriate but smart footwear, as hobbling in with blisters from new shoes will not make a good impression. Take the telephone number of the organisation with you in case you get lost or are held up.

Over to you

You are going for an interview at your local hospital. Plan how you might get there.

Step 3: Think hard about what the employer is looking for. Consider how you could show them that you have the skills and experience they are looking for. Most jobs in the health and social care profession require staff to be:

- friendly, outgoing and approachable
- a good listener
- helpful and willing
- good at dealing with and helping people
- a good communicator with excellent interpersonal skills
- courteous and tactful
- calm under pressure.

Over to you

List some of the skills that you would need to be an effective carer.

Step 4: Decide what your best selling points are and what you would like the interviewer to learn about you.

Step 5: Think about what you want to take with you to the interview, e.g. certificates, examples of work, something to write with or a notepad with some prepared questions to ask. As the interview is finishing, you may be asked whether you have any questions – this is your chance to show you are interested in the job and the organisation.

Step 6: Overall impressions count for a lot at an interview. Decide what to wear beforehand, and look clean, smart and tidy. Interviewers notice things like clean fingernails, washed and combed hair, even polished shoes. Pay attention to little details, and show that you have made an effort to 'dress to impress'.

Dress code and appearance

Talking point

View 1: Interviewers should take me for who I am, and not expect me to dress differently for an interview.

View 2: First impressions are important and you should make an effort to impress the interviewer.

Things to avoid when going for a interview	
For women	**For men**
Extreme hair styles	Straggly beards
Untidy or dirty hair	Untidy or dirty hair Extreme hair styles
Body odour	Body odour
Smelling of alcohol	Smelling of alcohol
Perfume – even a little can seem overpowering, especially if the interviewer does not like your choice of scent	Aftershave – the interviewer may not like your choice
Smelling of cigarettes or stained fingers	Smelling of cigarettes or stained fingers
Jeans and casual clothing	Jeans and casual clothing Pens in shirt pockets
High-heeled shoes, boots, bare legs, sandals, brightly coloured shoes	Pointed shoes, large heels, boots
Low-cut or see-through tops, bare midriff, wearing no bra, tight clothes, short skirts	Shirts undone to chest Tight clothing
Too much jewellery, dangly earrings	Too much jewellery
	Joke socks or joke ties

Over to you

You are the manager of a day centre for adults with learning difficulties. You are looking to employ someone who can work with your clients to show them how to live independently and how to find suitable employment. The person you employ will need to be confident, presentable and responsible for approaching possible employers on behalf of your clients. On first impressions, which of the two people below would you employ, and why?

Work experience

Organisations providing care

This section considers how care is delivered. Not all health and social care is provided by the National Health Service (NHS) and social services. It can be a mixture of help from volunteers, private organisations, even a person's family and neighbours.

Who provides health and social care?

Statutory services
Statutory services are funded and provided for by the government. All UK citizens have a legal right to receive statutory services such as maternity care, access to a general practitioner (GP) and to hospital accident and emergency departments.

Private care
Private organisations providing care are run as businesses which need to make a profit to survive. Examples include residential homes and private hospitals.

Voluntary care
Voluntary organisations are non-profit-making organisations such as the 24-hour children's helpline, ChildLine, and some hospices caring for the terminally ill.

Informal care
Informal care is provided free by family members, friends and neighbours.

Over to you

Write a list of as many health and social care organisations as you can think of. Try to find out which are statutory, private, voluntary or informal.

Real Life Care

Maggie's accident

Maggie is 86 years old. She is a very active member of her community, helping run her local charity shop two days a week. Last February, she slipped on some ice whilst on her way to work. An ambulance was called to take her to the nearest hospital twenty miles away. Maggie was diagnosed with a broken femur and required hip surgery and a long stay in hospital to recover. Maggie received good care at the hospital but was aware of the high risk of getting MRSA in her wound. Maggie decided to pay for care in a small private hospital nearer her home until she was well enough to go home. Once home, Maggie found she was having difficulty looking after herself and required domiciliary care and meals on wheels. With the help of her friends and two daughters Maggie is making a good recovery.

1 Identify the types of care Maggie received.

2 How much of Maggie's care was the NHS expected to provide as a statutory requirement? ✓✓

3 Do you think that the NHS should provide all care? Or is it good that people can choose to pay for their care? ✓✓✓

The statutory sector

The original NHS came into being in 1948, with the aim of being 'free at the time of use' and available to all. It was to be financed through taxes, with hospitals run by the government. A Ministry for Health was set up to ensure:

■ a high standard of health care was maintained throughout the country

■ all services could be planned and coordinated.

The NHS was an instant success and demand for services rapidly increased. Social workers were employed to care for the social needs of the community. Children's departments were introduced and childcare officers appointed. As the NHS developed, it became obvious that it was a victim of its own success. The NHS was struggling to supply the population with all its care needs. Something needed to be done.

In 1980, in order to reduce the pressure on hospitals, the government decided to promote care in the community. The aim was to transfer back into the community people who were in long-term hospital care. They included people with learning difficulties, those with long-term mental illnesses and the elderly. For care in the community to be successful, more help would be required from voluntary and private organisations, such as private dentists and opticians, and relatives would need to be more involved in the caring process.

The private sector

Private health organisations are commercial businesses that are operated to make a profit for their shareholders. Access to private health care is determined purely by the ability to pay, and is therefore only accessible to those with larger incomes or health insurance. Patients can gain access to private care through self-referrals and referrals from health care practitioners (see page 332 for more information on referrals).

The private sector has grown in recent years, and includes a wide range of specialist health care practitioners, such as counsellors, dentists and physiotherapists. Private hospitals can offer services similar to the NHS but often with reduced waiting times. Private residential care homes offer an increase in choice of care for the elderly. As public health demands outstrip NHS resources, more and more care may be offered on a private basis. The diagram on the next page highlights the wide range of services offered by private health care providers such as BUPA.

Talking point

View 1: Everyone should have all their health needs provided for by the NHS.

View 2: The NHS should limit what it provides to those who have the greatest need.

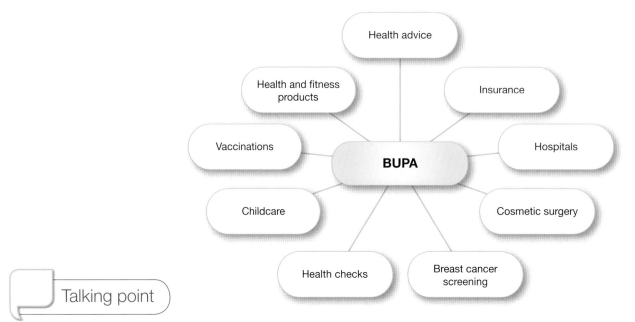

■ *Services offered by private health care providers*

The voluntary sector

Over the past 30 years there has been major growth of the voluntary sector. The reasons for this could be that people have more disposable income, and, since the reorganisation of the NHS in the 1980s forced cutbacks to be made, there has been an increase in the number of donations to charitable organisations.

Volunteering involves giving your time and energy to a worthwhile cause, but in return, you will get the opportunity to work with others less fortunate than yourself, helping people to build their self-confidence and skills and to raise their self-esteem and feelings of self-worth. Volunteering strengthens communities and helps people learn about the wider world. Your CV and employability will benefit too!

There is a wide range of voluntary organisations including support phone lines, such as the Samaritans, ChildLine and the National Drugs helpline, and support groups that help people with conditions such as arthritis, cancer, anorexia nervosa, head injuries and alcoholism.

Over to you

Think of a physical, social or emotional condition that someone might need help with. Now visit the website of Self Help UK, a free database of more than 1000 self-help organisations and support groups, to see if you can find a voluntary organisation that can help. To access the site, go to www.heinemann.co.uk/hotlinks and enter the express code 3322P.

Real Life Care

The volunteer

Daisy is 70 years old. She gets great pleasure from doing voluntary work for the WRVS (Women's Royal Voluntary Service), a voluntary organisation that delivers 8.5 million meals a year to people who are no longer able to carry their shopping or cook for themselves. Daisy helps deliver meals to people's homes two days a week. She also helps run the local hospital's shop, selling snacks, drinks, sweets, cards and newspapers. She enjoys staying active and helping other older people.

1 If there were no volunteers, who would run services such as hospital shops and meals delivery? ✔

2 Find out information about volunteers, e.g. who volunteers the most, men or women? To access a useful site, go to www.heinemann.co.uk/hotlinks and enter the express code 3322P. Discuss the reasons for your findings. ✔✔

3 Discuss the implications for a society where there are no volunteers. ✔✔✔

Many voluntary organisations, such as Age Concern, Scope, Oxfam, Help the Aged and Barnardos, are active at national, regional and local levels, and have become familiar shops in every high street. These organisations are often involved with helping the government to develop policies and procedures to help their users. For example, Age Concern has helped improve the status of the elderly within society. It has also been instrumental in addressing issues such as 'elder abuse' in care establishments. Age Concern acts regionally to improve the quality of care received by the elderly, and locally to provide facilities such as holidays, day centres and even gardening.

HELP THE AGED WE WILL

Can You Claim It?

Claiming pension credit and other benefits

Advice for older people

The informal sector

There are approximately 7 million carers in the UK. Informal care often goes unnoticed. A child might be caring for a chronically ill parent, or a parent might be caring for a child with physical and mental disabilities. Informal care often comes from a family member, friend or neighbour. The government has begun to recognise the importance of informal care and is putting into place support to help carers carry out their role.

Informal carers have an invaluable role to play, for example:

- They help the person wash, bathe or shower.
- They help them dress.
- They help with toileting.
- They give out medicines.
- They prepare meals.

Over to you

Do you know anyone who could be described as an informal carer?

Real Life Care

The carers

Clare is 6 years old. She suffers from severe cerebal palsy, and consequently needs total care. She lives at home with her parents and 10-year-old brother, Daniel. Clare's mother and father look after her daily needs which include washing her and helping her to eat and play. Clare is taken to school by the parents of her friend Jessica. Daniel is a happy boy who enjoys helping care for his sister when he gets home from school. Occasionally, Clare's grandparents look after her for the weekend so that Daniel and his parents can have some time together.

1 Identify all the informal carers responsible for looking after Clare. ✓

2 Discuss the importance of informal care in the overall picture of health and social care provision. ✓✓

3 Research the help that is available to carers. Who provides support for carers? ✓✓✓

Which organisations/placements would be suitable for you?

There are many areas of health and social care that you will be able to experience as a BTEC First student or in paid employment. There are some areas of the health care profession, for example the ambulance service, midwifery and paediatric nursing, that you will not be able to observe until you are aged 18 years. The following table shows the areas of care that are open to you now, but most of them will require you to take more qualifications to further your career.

Examples of areas of work experience			
Age group	**Job**	**Provider**	
Children	Nursery assistant	Statutory/private	Helps in nurseries with educational activities and care needs
	Au pair	Private	Works within a family setting in the home
	Care worker	Statutory/private	Assists with everyday care and activities
Adults	Health care support worker	Statutory/private	Assists hospital nursing staff
	Medical receptionist	Statutory/private	Administrator and clerk for a hospital ward or outpatient department
	Dental assistant	Statutory/private	Assists dentist
	Hospital visitor	Voluntary	Visits patients in hospital to offer companionship
People with disabilities	Care worker	Statutory/private/voluntary	Assists with everyday health care and activities
	Domestic helper	Statutory/private	Cleans care settings
Older people	Domiciliary	Statutory/voluntary	Cares for elderly people in their own homes, helps with shopping, transport and cleaning
	Care worker	Statutory/private	Cares for elderly in residential homes
	Domestic help	Statutory/private	Cleans care facilities
	Meals delivery service	Voluntary	Delivers hot meals to people in their own homes

Practice for Assessment

Carrying out this activity will contribute to P3 and D1. Now that you have looked at several areas in the health and social care sector, arrange to complete a period of work experience in a setting of your choice. Remember to consider areas of voluntary work, such as helping children read in an infant school, going on residential trips with children with disabilities or becoming a volunteer at a hospital.

Before you go think about: how you feel (scared or excited?), why you feel like this? After your visit reflect on: how you feel now, was it worse or better than expected, what have you learnt about yourself, how did the placement benefit from your work?

The use of interpersonal skills

The use of interpersonal skills is covered in detail in Unit 1. If you have not already done so, turn back to Unit 1 and read it carefully so you understand what is meant by interpersonal skills and the communication cycle.

Practice for Assessment

Carrying out this activity will give evidence towards P4 and M1.

Greta is doing her work experience in a residential home for the elderly. She notices that Peggy spends all day sitting in a dark corner of the day room talking to nobody. Greta kneels beside Peggy and touches her lightly on the arm to indicate that she is there and begins to talk to her. Speaking softly and gently, but in a clear and concise manner, Greta spends some time getting to know Peggy. After their chat Greta informs the Sister in charge that Peggy is feeling ignored as she cannot see well enough to make out the faces of the staff and residents, especially in the dark corner. She can also not hear very well and would like to sit nearer her friends at the other end of the room.

Describe a situation in your placement where communication had been difficult. Why were there problems? What communication skills did you use to overcome them?

Describe the strengths and weaknesses of your own interpersonal skills that you demonstrated in your example. How could you have improved?

Describing a period of work experience

Organisations

Funding

Funding the NHS is very complex. Money is taken from workers' wages in the form of taxes and allocated to health care services. In the 1980s the government believed that instead of simply pouring money into the NHS, money should be given to health authorities and later GP fundholders instead. The GP fundholders could then 'buy' the best care for their patients. The idea was to encourage the providers of health care to improve their quality of care to ensure that GPs would send their patients to them. Health care providers such as hospitals now had to be run like businesses, carefully budgeting their money to ensure no waste. GPs would be able to choose where they sent their patients, selecting health care providers that had the best success rates.

In 1997, the newly elected Labour government decided to limit the power held by GPs and end health care providers competing for patients, so it once again took control of spending, getting rid of GP fundholders. (For more information on the development of the NHS since 1997, see Unit 8 Working in the Health and Social Care Sectors, page 324.)

Current government policy is working towards giving service users a greater choice in health care providers. By 2006, all service users will be able to choose from at least five hospitals where to have their treatment, including one independent provider.

However, it is still felt that people should be encouraged to look at other care choices rather than relying totally on statutory health care providers. Care should be shared between families and private and voluntary organisations, with the individual showing more responsibility for their own health. This shared care is known as a mixed economy of care and outlines the following:

- The range of social services is to be reduced (e.g. home meals service, residential care homes) and alternatives such as private and voluntary organisations should be used.

- There should be more importance placed on 'informal' care such as care from friends and family.

- People should be more personally responsible for their own health.

Talking point

View 1: People who do not work and do not pay taxes should not receive free health care.

View 2: Care should be available for everyone – those who can afford it should pay for those that can't.

Real Life Care

Making a choice

Mrs Jones is 24 weeks pregnant, and is discussing with the midwife where to have her second baby. She had an quick, uncomplicated first labour. The midwife offers Mrs Jones a choice of four places for the birth:

1   St Anne's hospital serves the local town and is approximately 10 miles away. It has four very busy, understaffed maternity wards and a very good special care baby unit.

2   Queen Elizabeth's general hospital is 20 miles away. It is quiet and has a well-staffed maternity unit, but it has no special care baby unit.

3   The Granwell is the local cottage hospital one mile away. It is run by midwives and has a birthing pool. There are six beds and each has a private bathroom. In an emergency, women are transferred by ambulance to St Anne's, which takes 15 minutes.

4   She could give birth at home with two midwives present.

Mrs Jones is a heavy smoker and there is a risk that the baby will be born small for its age.

1 What factors should Mrs Jones consider when making her choice?

2 Does the information that Mrs Jones is a smoker affect her choice? If so, why?

3 Do we really have a choice in the care we receive?

Resources

Funding is important as it ensures that the necessary resources are provided in health and social care settings. Resources are things that are needed to run a setting efficiently, for example books, wheelchairs, bandages, drugs, operating tables, thermometers, children's coat hooks – the list is endless. The managers of care settings must decide which resources are important to their individual settings and which are not. As the allocation of money is tight, staff must prioritise which resources they need the most and which they can do without or save for. For example, new technology such as scanners may help doctors make quicker diagnoses that might ultimately save lives, but the money put towards a new scanner will have to be taken out of funds allocated to something else. Private and charitable fundraising often helps buy resources that care settings would not otherwise be able to afford.

Over to you

You are the manager of a nursing home with a limited budget. Put the following list of resources in order of importance:

wheelchairs	*TV for each resident's room*	
bed sheets	*walking sticks*	*cups and saucers*
jigsaws	*staff training courses*	*flower vases*
new lounge chairs	*day out for residents*	*commodes.*

If you only have enough money to buy nine of the above items, which would you leave out? Explain your answer.

Policies and procedures

All care settings will have policies and procedures in place to protect service users and staff and ensure that a high quality of service is maintained. Throughout this book, there are many examples of policies and procedures which you should be familiar with. Most policies and procedures will differ from placement to placement but several will be the same wherever you go. For example:

- fire safety
- health and safety
- storage of harmful chemicals
- confidentiality
- data protection.

It is up to you to ensure that you know what policies and procedures are in place in each placement where you work.

Health and safety

Health and safety is covered in Unit 2 Individual Needs within the Health and Social Care Sectors, but as well as maintaining safety in the workplace, it is also important to consider how staff ensure that they maintain their own personal safety.

■ *Staff need to be aware of their own personal safety*

To maintain safety and security, staff are usually given identity cards that help identify them from visitors and clients. Identity cards usually display a photograph of the individual and show their name and place of work. Personal identification helps to limit access to strangers who should not be in the care setting.

Staff may also be identified by a uniform that indicates they work for the organisation. Remember, uniforms can be stolen, so do not assume that a man in a white coat is a doctor; he could have bought it from a workwear shop in the high street.

Many health care settings have security procedures to stop unauthorised people from entering the building. Staff enter a code on a keypad to open the door, while members of the general public use an intercom system where they have to identify themselves before gaining admission. Once inside, visitors may be asked to sign a register, which they sign again when they leave. With uniforms, identification cards, security locks and registers, it should be difficult for strangers to enter a care setting uninvited.

Personal safety should not stop there. People who work in health and social care settings often work shifts and do night duty. As care is offered 24 hours a day, staff may arrive at all times, sometimes even in the middle of the night. It is for these reasons that some establishments give their staff personal alarms or ensure that they are escorted to their cars. Staff may need to walk through dark alleyways and car parks, so it is important that these areas are well lit.

Multicultural factors

Unit 4 looks in detail at multicultural factors (see page 149).

Over to you

What would you do if you saw someone in a restricted area who did not have an identity badge?

Staff

This section looks in detail at the role of the midwife and also briefly discusses other health care occupations. This will help you to develop an understanding of job roles and responsibilities, personal skills/attributes, induction processes, terms and conditions of employment, ways of monitoring performance and professional development.

Staffing levels

Health care sectors are very often understaffed. Caring for vulnerable people places a lot of pressure on staff, which may result in staff illness and staff shortages. Nevertheless, all areas will have an ideal 'staff-to-client' ratio. This means having the right balance of staff for the number of service users. For example, in maternity units it would be ideal if every woman in labour could have her own midwife with her, and two if she chooses to deliver at home.

In care settings that care for pre-school children, staff-to-child ratios are as follows:

0–1 years: 1 member of staff to every 3 children

1–3 years: 1 member of staff to every 4 children

3–5 years: 1 member of staff to every 8 children.

Real Life Care

The right ratio

Little School nursery has 18 children. This morning, the staff are taking all the children for a walk in their local park. There are three members of staff accompanying them. Daisy, aged 4, asks one carer if she will take her to the toilet. This will leave 17 children with two members of staff.

1 How will the carer avoid leaving too many children with too few carers? ✓

2 As the manager, how could you avoid this situation arising? ✓✓

3 What might be the reasons why you cannot employ more staff? ✓✓✓

There are no set staffing levels when caring for the elderly. The qualifications of the staff on duty must be appropriate to the needs of the clients. For example, it would be inappropriate to have no trained nursing staff on duty in a nursing home that cares for people with severe disabilities. The skills mix of the staff employed to care for the elderly must be carefully matched to the needs of the service provided. All staff responsible for looking after a client's personal hygiene must be over 18 years old, and anyone left in charge of elderly clients must be over 21 years old.

Job role

Unit 8 covers many job roles and responsibilities that are found in the health and social care sector. One of these jobs is that of the midwife.

Midwifery has been around as long as women have had babies. Women have always helped other women to give birth. In the past, it was normal for a woman in labour to be attended at home by an untrained neighbour or self-elected village midwife. More recently, midwifery has become a highly trained profession, with most births now taking place in hospital. Today's midwife must also be able to care for the woman, her family and baby in any situation, from home to birthing centre to hospital.

Talking point

View 1: Staff-to-client ratios are only an ideal and do not work in a busy health care setting.

View 2: For health and saftey reasons there should always be the right staff-to-client ratio, even if this means being unable to offer some services because of short staffing.

Real Life Care

A staffing problem

Teresa is in charge of Mayflower nursing home for elderly people who need nursing care. She organises which staff work which shifts, and usually has at least one trained member of staff and three health care support workers working each shift. It is August and several members of staff are away on holiday. One of the trained nurses, Uzma, is on maternity leave and Dan, another trained member of staff, is off sick. Teresa decides to put four health care workers on together as she has no trained staff available to work.

1 How should Teresa have solved her staffing problem?

2 Discuss why it is important to have the right skills mix working together.

3 Consider the implications of maintaining a high standard of care if staff are not trained.

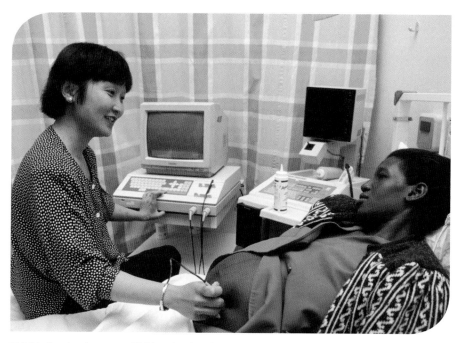

■ *Midwifery has become a highly trained profession*

Antenatal *Before the birth of a baby.*

Postnatal *After the birth of a baby.*

A midwife is involved in the care of the woman and her family during and after pregnancy. She needs to be able to support the woman and her partner as well as helping at the birth of their baby. Her care continues from the confirmation of the pregnancy until 28 days after the birth of the baby. She needs many different skills to deal with many varied situations. A midwife cares for the woman **antenatally**, during birth, and **postnatally**. She must also be prepared to help in emergencies when things are not going well and in the event of the death of a mother or baby.

■ *Skills required by a midwife*

To become a midwife, you need at least five GCSEs and must have studied A levels or BTEC Nationals. Then you must also attend university to study for a diploma or degree in Midwifery. Some midwives start their training after first becoming a registered nurse – this method of entry requires a further one and a half years of study.

Responsibilities

Every job will have a set of responsibilities that are specific to that job and the area where the job is being practised. The responsibilities of a midwife are vast and cover more than just delivering the baby.

A midwife must be able to deliver a high quality of care to the mother and her baby, which includes the following:

■ It is her responsibility to monitor the mother and baby and report any abnormalities to a doctor.

■ She must be able to work unsupervised and be responsible for her own actions.

■ She must be able to deliver parenting classes.

■ She should be able to work alone as well as with all other members of the maternity team.

■ She is responsible for her own professional development and must ensure that she is up to date with medical developments.

■ She must work with student midwives and help orientate new members of staff.

■ She must maintain a high level of record keeping.

■ She needs to have excellent personal skills and attributes.

Over to you

List all the characteristics you would associate with someone in the caring profession.

Personal skills and attributes

What is a skill?

A skill is something someone can do. A skill can be learnt and practised until it can be done well. For example, when a nurse or midwife gives an injection for the first time, she doesn't just grab a syringe and needle and stick it in some poor client's arm; she must learn the skill first.

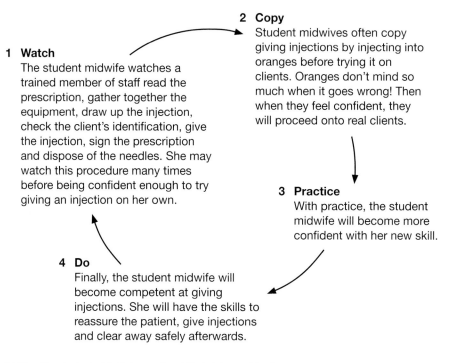

1 Watch
The student midwife watches a trained member of staff read the prescription, gather together the equipment, draw up the injection, check the client's identification, give the injection, sign the prescription and dispose of the needles. She may watch this procedure many times before being confident enough to try giving an injection on her own.

2 Copy
Student midwives often copy giving injections by injecting into oranges before trying it on clients. Oranges don't mind so much when it goes wrong! Then when they feel confident, they will proceed onto real clients.

3 Practice
With practice, the student midwife will become more confident with her new skill.

4 Do
Finally, the student midwife will become competent at giving injections. She will have the skills to reassure the patient, give injections and clear away safely afterwards.

■ *How the student midwife learns the skill of giving an injection*

Learning how to give an injection is a specialist skill that is required by some health care professionals but not all. General skills required by all care workers include:

■ Practical skills:
  – help with dressing, personal hygiene, feeding, mobility
  – domestic duties
  – prevention of spread of infection.

■ Interpersonal skills:
  – one-to-one communication
  – communicating in groups
  – building relationships
  – team work
  – working with other health care disciplines.

■ Scientific skills:
  – handing out medicines
  – using technical equipment

– monitoring health signs.

- Communication skills:
  - listening
  - record keeping
  - using computers.

During your studies, you will be given the opportunity to work in different care settings. You will probably already have views about which type of placement you would like to experience. At this stage in your career, it is important that you work with different client groups because you will develop different skills with each group. You may feel that because you have experience with children that you only want to work in care settings that cater for children. You may have a job in a care home and therefore only want to work with the elderly, but remember that there are many skills shared by both these areas of care.

What attributes are needed in the caring professions?
It is often assumed that someone in the caring profession has a caring personality. This, therefore, assumes that carers are understanding, sensitive and compassionate towards people, but these are not the only qualities needed to be an effective carer. These qualities show that someone has the ability to empathise with others, but they must also show many other skills, attributes and qualities. Essential caring attributes include:

- good interpersonal skills
- understanding of the care value base
- understanding of users' rights
- non-discriminatory practice
- up-to-date knowledge of care issues
- empathy.

Over to you

Think of a skill you learnt as a child and have not used for a long time. Do you think you could still do it?

Talking point

View 1: Only people who have caring qualities should work in a health care setting.

View 2: Qualifications and experience are more important than good caring qualities.

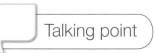

Real Life Care

Feeding your client

Using 'feeding' as an example of a practical skill, think about the skills you would need to help an elderly blind person with Parkinsons disease to eat, compared to a teenage boy who has broken his right arm and finds it difficult to use his left. Remember, in both situations you are trying to help maintain a level of independence and don't want to take over the task of feeding them, but allow them to do as much themselves as possible.

1 Which skills are common to both situations?

2 Which skills are different?

3 Describe how you have managed to maintain independence in both situations.

Qualities and attributes are part of our own uniqueness. Perhaps we have inherited them through our genes from our parents, or perhaps we have developed them by watching others and copying qualities we admire. To work as a care worker, each individual needs a set of qualities that will help them show compassion to others and confidence to continue when faced with difficulties.

Over to you

For each of the following situations, list the qualities the carer would need:

- *Greeting a new resident to a care home.*
- *Telling a mother her baby is ill.*
- *Filling in paperwork.*
- *Explaining to a 4-year-old how to use a toothbrush.*
- *Helping a teenage boy to use the toilet.*

Key point

A good induction to a workplace helps staff to feel valued and wanted.

The induction process

When starting a new job, it is important that a new member of staff undergoes an induction process. Induction processes are unique to each job and each care setting. In a maternity unit, the new midwife will need several days of preparation before she can begin her job.

In-service training

Each care setting will have its own in-service training. This training will prepare the new member of staff with the skills necessary to work safely and effectively.

Training needs

- Resuscitation – a midwife will update her knowledge of giving life support to adults, pregnant women and newborn babies. This training will need to be updated on a yearly basis.

- Manual handling – to ensure that the midwife does not injure herself or a client, she will need to undertake a manual handling course.

Orientation

During the first few months of a new job, a new member of staff should be paired with a mentor, who will be an experienced member of staff responsible for:

- introducing her to other members of the team
- showing her around the care setting
- showing her staff facilities
- instructing her on record keeping and using the ward computer system
- informing her of appropriate policies and codes of conduct
- familiarising her with equipment and resources.

Qualities:	How they could help when providing care
Patience	Care workers who are patient are less likely to get angry if a person asks the same question over and over again. They will understand that some people need time to make up their minds before they are able to make a decision, e.g. about when to have treatment, what to wear, and what they would like to eat.
Understanding	Understanding enables care workers to see things from another person's point of view or perspective, e.g. a service user who is upset because their pet has died should not be told 'well you knew it was going to happen soon'. Instead the care worker should listen and respond in a way that shows that they can identify with the pain that the service user is feeling. They might say, for example, 'Well Joan, think about some of the happy times you and Sam had together. Do you remember when he stole the meat from Betty's plate? He was so pleased with himself, he looked as though he was grinning at the time!' This approach is likely to help establish good relationships between the care worker and service user.
Empathy	To be able to empathise with the service users means to see and feel things in the same way as them. Care workers are able to put themselves in the same position as service users. Service users will recognise this by the way a care worker speaks to them and the words that they use.
Respect	Care workers who show respect value service users for who they are, not what they think they should be. They find out what the service users prefer to be called instead of calling them 'love' or 'dear'. They listen to what they have to say and do not walk away in the middle of a sentence.
Willingness	Care workers who are willing to be helpful are always appreciated by both staff and service users. Such care workers do not mumble and complain about the tasks they are given and often offer to do something without waiting to be asked. Service users appreciate such an attitude and are likely to trust and value the person with this quality.
Sense of humour	Care workers who have a sense of humour are always appreciated. They can often see the funny side of a difficult or embarrassing situation, e.g. a service user told a care worker that he had taken cat worming tablets by mistake when he should have taken a headache tablet. The care worker replied, 'Well at least you'll be ready for a night on the tiles!' The situation was lightened by the care worker's reply.
Cheerfulness	Cheerful care workers are easily recognised. They usually have a friendly approach which is conveyed by tone of voice. They greet service users in a manner that shows that they are pleased to see them and are genuinely interested in them. Care workers who are cheerful are much more likely to have a more positive experience with service users.

■ Qualities can enhance the care you give

Health checks

Before starting a new job, it is often necessary to undergo a medical examination. A new member of staff's medical history will be checked to ensure that there are no reasons why they will not be able to work effectively. It may also be necessary for a new member of staff to have a series of vaccinations to protect them from diseases that they may come into contact with, such as Hepatitis B.

Police checks

Any person coming into contact with vulnerable people, such as children or the elderly, will need to be checked by the police for criminal convictions. If there are disclosures on a police check, the person may be prevented from working in certain areas of care. It is important to remember convictions remain on record forever. Care settings must be informed of disclosures on members of staff.

View 1: Police checks are important as they protect vulnerable people. Nobody should be allowed to work in the caring professions without one.

View 2: Police checks are costly and take too long to complete. People should be allowed to work while they are waiting to be checked.

Monitoring performance

Performance can be monitored in many ways, for example through appraisal, peer assessment and client assessment.

Appraisal

Each member of staff should have a yearly appraisal conducted by a senior member of staff. The senior member of staff will discuss the staff member's progress, development, areas of concern or anticipated areas of difficulty. This appraisal gives the staff member the opportunity to look at their role within the establishment and how they see their career progressing.

Peer assessment

One of the easiest ways to find out how you are doing is to ask someone. By asking another member of staff about your work, you should be able to discover where you need to improve as well as your areas of success.

Client assessment

One of the most truthful methods of performance monitoring is to ask the service user you are caring for. If you ask a 3-year-old whether they like the way you tell stories, they might say that you are too quiet, or that your stories are exciting to listen to. If you ask an elderly person whether they like the way you help them to walk around the grounds, they might say that you walk too quickly or that you have a steady arm to hold on to. If you do not ask, you will never know or be able to change.

Over to you

Ask a friend to say one positive and one negative thing about your listening skills. How will the answers you receive help you improve the way you listen to people?

Real Life Care

Starting your work experience

You are starting your work experience in your local health centre. Working at the health centre are six GPs, two midwives, two practice nurses and one health visitor, plus visiting physiotherapists, occupational therapists, audiologists and ear, nose and throat specialists. You will be required to:

■ help the nurses and midwives set up for their clinics

■ organise and file client records

■ prepare rooms for visiting specialists

■ shadow various members of staff.

1 Outline the induction processes you feel you would need in order to feel happy in your work experience. ✓

2 If, after two days, you feel unhappy at the health centre, what should you do? ✓✓

3 Plan an induction programme for a student doing their work experience in the centre. ✓✓✓

PART A: Appraisee's Self-Evaluation

The Job
Please attach your up-to-date job description.

What you have done
What do you see as the main purpose of your job?

Does your job description need to be revised? If so what changes would you like to see?

How well did you achieve last year's objectives?

Overall, what do you feel have been your main achievements in the last year?

What new skills, knowledge, and experience have you acquired?

How you did it
What do you do well? What aspects of the job do you find most rewarding?

What aspects of your job do you find the most difficult? What have been the frustrations?

What would/could help (including any help/support from your line-manager or any training and development)?

How effective was any development or training you received?

What next?
How do you see yourself or your role developing in the next year?

Are there any development and training implications for the coming year?

■ *Example of an appraisal form*

Continuing professional development

In most health care jobs it is necessary to continually improve your knowledge. Once you have started working in the health care sector, your professional development does not stop. A midwife, for example, will need to attend regular training sessions to ensure that she is up to date with changes in practice as well as changes in technology. She might decide to specialise in one area of care, such as community midwifery, neonatal special care or as an operating theatre midwife, and will need to undergo further training to develop the skills she will need for her new job. The spider diagram below looks at the different areas of professional development that are available to a nurse once qualified as an adult nurse specialist.

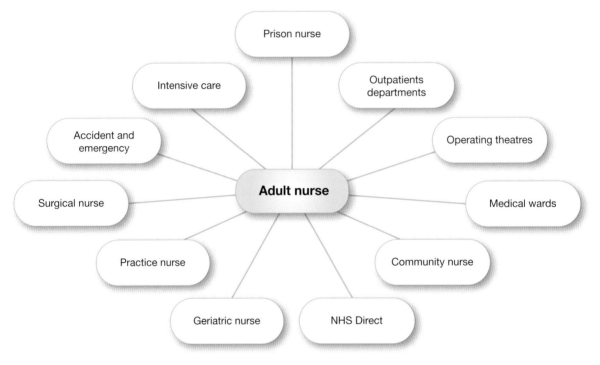

■ *Career opportunities available to an adult nurse specialist*

Over to you

Produce a spider diagram similar to the one above based on a children's nurse.

Career options working with the elderly include:

■ residential care worker
■ voluntary worker
■ domiciliary care
■ further training to become a nurse
■ geriatric health care support worker.

Professional development is a continuous process throughout a person's working life. When someone moves from one job to another, it is expected that as well as a CV there should also be a professional development portfolio. This portfolio could contain a CV, certificates of qualifications, information about training undertaken, letters of recommendation, previous job descriptions and contracts. Professional development adds depth and experience to a career.

Your own performance

Personal achievements

It is often difficult to think about our own personal achievements. All of us achieve something every day. Today, for example, I got to work on time, I set the video correctly to record my favourite programme and I managed not to eat that bar of chocolate in the fridge. These might sound trivial achievements, but try looking at them in another way – I have shown that I am punctual, know how to use modern technology and have self-discipline, not bad for one day!

Achievements come in many different guises. Some will be presented as certificates showing courses attended and achieved such as GCSEs and hopefully a BTEC First in Health and Social Care. Other achievements are not so obvious, for example getting to lessons on time or talking to someone different in class. Just because an achievement does not have a piece of paper attached to it does not make it less important.

Timekeeping

Timekeeping is very important in all jobs, but no more so than in the health and social care profession where team work is often the centre of care planning. A team may not be able to proceed if one member is not there or is late arriving. The late team member will be holding up the care of clients and causing other people extra pressure in their busy work routine. Poor timekeeping can cause resentment among staff members and might ultimately result in disciplinary action.

To avoid being late for a placement, it is important to plan your time carefully. Try to arrive a few minutes early for work – anticipate traffic holding you up or buses and trains being late. Aim to take an earlier bus or to set off ten minutes earlier than you would think necessary. If you

Over to you

What would you put into your own professional development portfolio?

Over to you

What have you achieved today?

Real Life Care

Josie's achievements

Josie is 18 years old and has four GCSEs, a First Aid certificate and a Food Hygiene certificate. In her spare time she helps out at the local youth club where she runs regular pool and dance mat competitions. She regularly attends college where she is working for a BTEC First Diploma in Health and Social Care. She has joined the college netball team. She has done two lots of work experience – one with the elderly and one with children with learning difficulties.

1 List the evidence Josie would have to show her achievements. ✔

2 What else has Josie achieved? ✔✔

3 At an interview for a job working with children, Josie is asked what are her most important achievements. What could she answer? ✔✔✔

have been celebrating a special occasion the night before work, you are more likely to wake up late for work. Set your alarm clock earlier. Continually being late will severely affect your placement report and career prospects. Members of staff will soon get fed up hearing about the late bus or your nights out. Being on time for work shows your professionalism and commitment to the placement and the health and social care profession.

Real Life Care

Always late!

Shamina is 16 years old and has been placed with Silver Birches residential home to do her two-week work experience. She lives about five miles from the home and catches the number 63 bus which arrives at 7.20 am outside the home. Shamina is expected to start work at 7.30 am in time for staff handover. She has arrived late the last four days, as she has missed the 7.20 am bus, catching the one that arrives 20 minutes later. As the nurse responsible for looking after Shamina during her placement, you have been asked to talk to Shamina about her timekeeping.

1 How could you help Shamina to plan her timekeeping better?

2 How do you think the other members of the team feel about Shamina's lateness?

3 If she does not improve, what action could be taken?

Confidence and initiative

Personal confidence is an important quality when caring for vulnerable people. As a care worker, you may come across situations or people that you personally find it difficult to look at or nurse. For example, as a children's nurse you might be asked to care for a child that has been abused by its parents. You will need confidence to care for the child, deal with the family and authorities such as social services or the police. If you lack confidence, you will not be able to work within the team responsible for the child's care.

As you progress in a career in health and social care, you will need to use more and more of your own initiative. When staffing levels are low and there is nobody to supervise your work, you may need to make decisions without first asking someone else. To be able to use your own initiative, you must first be confident in your own caring ability. You must never attempt to do something that you feel unhappy about or that you have not been trained to do.

Real Life Care

Showing initiative

You are a cleaner at St George's hospital. It is a busy day on the surgical ward – there is a staff shortage and everyone appears extremely busy. You have been given a long list of cleaning jobs to do and are already behind with your work. In one of the side rooms at the end of the ward, you notice that an elderly man has fallen out of bed.

1 What should you do?

2 Explain how you would feel if you could not find anyone to help.

3 Explain how helping the man back to bed would not be using your initiative.

Real Life Care

Developing confidence and initiative

Marina is 16 years old and is on her first work experience based in a children's nursery. She has been working with the children for two weeks. All the staff are busy working with the children in groups to produce decorations for the Christmas show. One of the children is demanding a lot of attention from one of the staff, preventing her from working with the other children in her group. Marina is sitting on a chair in the corner doing nothing.

1 What could Marina be doing?

2 After two weeks of work experience, is it still the staff's job to keep allocating Marina jobs to do?

3 As Marina's supervisor, how could you work with Marina to help her develop her confidence and initiative?

Following instructions

All staff must be able to follow instructions. This may seem obvious, but as a care worker, you should never take shortcuts when following instructions, nor should you decide that you know better. When instructions are not carried out correctly, mistakes are made and people can be harmed or lives put in danger.

Activities undertaken

There are a great number of different activities that you may be asked to do in your working day. Each job will have its own special requirements that should be pointed out to you when you first start a job.

Real Life Care

Taking a shortcut

Ray is a newly qualified nurse. A senior nurse has asked him to give some prescribed drugs to Mrs Baker. On his way to Mrs Baker, he meets her husband. To save time, Ray asks Mr Baker to give the pills to Mrs Baker instead.

1 Why is it important that Ray gives the pills to Mrs Baker himself as he was asked? ✓

2 What could be the consequences of Ray's actions? ✓✓

3 How could the ward manager ensure that this does not happen again? ✓✓✓

Over to you

Think carefully about a receptionist on a hospital ward. In small groups, list all the different activities that they may be asked to do in their working day. Now think about the role of receptionist in the local secondary school. List the activities that they would do in their day. How do the two lists differ?

Own strengths and weaknesses

It is very difficult to look at our own behaviour and consider what our own strengths and weaknesses are. It takes courage to admit that we are not good at some things and may need help to improve our performance. After completing a period of work experience, take the time to consider what you gained from the experience and what aspects of it you could use again. To help you, look at your strengths and weaknesses, then write a SWOT analysis. SWOT stands for Strengths, Weaknesses, Opportunities and Threats. A SWOT analysis can be a useful tool in helping you to improve your work performance.

Strengths

■ What are you good at?

■ What do you do well?

■ What do other people see as your strengths?

Consider your strengths from your own point of view and also from the point of view of the people you dealt with. Be realistic; if you are unable to list your strengths, try writing a list of your characteristics, and hopefully some of these will be strengths.

Weaknesses

■ What could you improve?

■ What do you do badly?

■ What should you avoid?

Think about your weaknesses as you see them but also as others might see them. Do people see weaknesses in you that you thought was a strength, for example always speaking your mind? Are other people in your class doing better than you? If so, why? Facing unpleasant truths about ourselves is never easy, but it is often the best way to help us make changes so we can improve.

Opportunities

- What new challenges were you able to experience?

Opportunities can come from changes in technology, changes in policies, local events, training or changes in lifestyle.

Threats

- What obstacles do you face?
- What is your competition doing?
- Could your weaknesses threaten your career?

Looking at the factors that might threaten your work will help you to identify the changes you could make to improve your working experiences.

Overleaf is an example of a SWOT analysis for a 16-year-old student who has just completed a two-week work experience in a residential home for the elderly.

Key point

After looking at your personal strengths and weaknesses, it is good practice to reflect on how well you did and how you could do better.

Practice for Assessment

Carrying out this activity will contribute to P5.

Keep a logbook or diary of your work experience. This can be used at a later date to evaluate your own performance.

Reflection

As we move through our lives and careers, we often forget to look back at what we have done. By thinking about how we have changed and developed over a period of time, we can begin to understand what we enjoy and what works for us and what we do not enjoy. Reflection is a very important part of developing a career plan. Sometimes we think we are enjoying an area of work when we really are not; we get enjoyment mixed up with routine and habit. Just because you keep going to your Saturday job every week, and you like the staff and the hours, are you really enjoying the work itself? Reflection helps us highlight the skills we have developed and also those we need to develop further.

Career development plans

Hopefully, by the end of your BTEC First in Health and Social Care course you will have decided if you want to work in the health and social care sector. There are many different areas of work, ranging from caring for children to care of the elderly. It is very important that you are honest with yourself; only you will really know which area and which level suits you best. Be realistic with your choices. If you are not very

Over to you

After you have written a SWOT reflect on your own Weaknesses, how will they prevent you from working more effectively? How will your Threats make you less employable?

SWOT analysis

Strengths	I was always cheerful even when asked to do things I did not like.
	I have good communication skills when talking to elderly people.
	I was always smartly dressed.
	I work well in a team.
	I learn new technical terms quickly.
	I smile a lot.
Weaknesses	I am often late for work.
	I don't like caring for people who have had a stroke.
	I don't speak up when asked to do something I am unsure of.
	I get bored easily doing repetitive tasks.
	I tend to gossip about patients with other staff.
Opportunities	I was able to go to outpatient appointments with clients and see other roles in the NHS.
	I was taught how to use a hoist.
	I attended a manual handling course.
	I was asked if I would like to apply for a Saturday job as a domestic helper.
Threats	My lateness meant I often missed staff handover.
	Other students on work experience were given more opportunities.
	As I cannot use a computer well, I will not be able to progress with my career.
	As I don't have English GCSE, I may not get onto a nursing course.

Practice for Assessment

Carrying out this activity will provide underpinning evidence for M2 and D2.

Before you start your next work experience, answer the following questions.

- What are you looking forward to the most?
- What are you worried about most?
- What skills do you think you will need the most?
- What skills do you think you are lacking in?

After the work experience, look at your answers. Do you still agree with what you have written?

Write a detailed description of your own performance during your placement.

How do you think you did in your placement? Describe the skills and attributes you have. Give examples and explain how you used them in a health and social care setting.

good at exams and studying at a high level, you may never be a doctor, nurse or midwife, but if you are very good at practical work and have good communication skills, you may be an excellent carer and do well on more practical-based courses such as S/NVQs.

Plan your career carefully, and if necessary, seek career guidance from a career counsellor. They will be able to help you choose the most appropriate route for you to take at this particular time in your life. The decisions you make now are not for life. As you get more experience and confidence, you will be able to develop a career that suits your abilities and that grows and changes as you do.

Progression opportunities

There are many progression opportunities within the health and social care sector, several of which have been discussed earlier in this unit. If you decide that you wish to progress in the field of health and social care, then you will need to research the training and qualifications you will need to develop your career further. Developing your career may mean continuing with your further education by taking a BTEC National qualification or A levels, then possibly going to university. You may decide to take the S/NVQ route and mix studying with work experience. Whichever route you decide is best for you, a career in health and social care is rewarding, fulfilling and continually challenging.

Over to you

Write a list of all the jobs you think you would like to do in the health and social care sector. Now research them and find out what you need to do to get in. Rewrite your list and decide where you are going to start on your career ladder.

Check your understanding

1. Name four different places where jobs may be advertised.
2. What four things would you *not* write on your CV?
3. What would you *not* wear for an interview?
4. Name four voluntary services?
5. What is the difference between the NHS and the private sector?
6. How is the NHS funded?
7. What are the safe staffing levels when working with children aged 2 years old?
8. What does empathy mean?
9. Name four different job opportunities for an adult nurse.
10. Why is it important to be on time for work?

4 Cultural Diversity in Health and Social Care

Introduction

This unit explores the enormous social and political diversity in British society. It will help you to understand the ways in which we are all different; this includes social and political factors and religious beliefs. You will discover how people are treated and should be treated according to their beliefs and values. You will also learn about the legislation that is in place to prevent people being mistreated, and investigate different policies and codes of practice that are specific for use in particular care settings.

It is important to remember that discrimination and the unfair treatment of people because they are different (from you) is wrong and against the law.

How you will be assessed

This is an internally assessed unit.

In this unit you will learn about:

- the diversity of individuals in society
- practices in different religious or secular beliefs
- factors influencing the equality of opportunity for individuals
- the rights of individuals in health and social care environments.

The diversity of individuals in society

Social and political diversity

> **Diversity** *The ways in which people are different from one another. Key differences include: gender, age, ethnicity, class, religion and sexuality.*

> **Multicultural** *Multi means many. Multicultural means many different cultures and groups in one area.*

In the past, Britain was classified as being 'white', meaning that the majority of people who lived in Britain were white. Although people's skin colour was predominantly 'white', the social backgrounds of individuals were very different. People could trace their origins back to many different peoples and cultures, including the Romans, Germans, Anglo-Saxons and Danes. This shows that even hundreds of years ago people of different origins moved from their homeland to settle in other countries such as Britain.

We now live in a modern society where the term multicultural is more appropriate. **Multicultural** means that many different peoples of various origins, cultures and religions live together in one society. We are very lucky to be able to be a part of a society where we can learn about a variety of ways of living from other people.

Over to you

Research into the origins of your surname. You could use a family tree or search on the Internet for its meaning. Compare your findings with a partner, or present your results to the rest of the class.

■ *We live in a multicultural society*

A multicultural Britain means much more than the colour of people's skin or their religion. There are many ways in which we are all different from each other, as the following spider diagram shows.

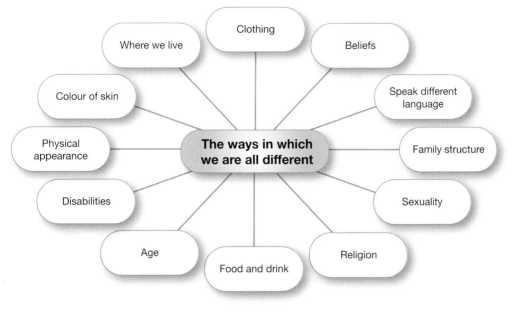

■ *How we are different from each other*

The groups we belong to can influence the way we think about other groups, and the way we act and behave towards others. People behave differently when in their different groups. For example, teenagers behave differently with their friends from how they behave with their family. It is important not to let these groups influence the way you behave towards other groups or individuals. **Carers** and service providers need to understand that everyone is different, and in some cases it may be important to learn what these differences are.

Ethnicity

Ethnicity defines individuals or groups who consider themselves, or are considered by others, to have some characteristics in common with others in their group but which differentiate them from other major groups in society.

People are grouped together and put into ethnic groups through cultural characteristics such as religion, language, dress, politics and so on. New ethnic groups are being formed all the time as people move to different countries. In Britain, for example, people from the Indian subcontinent constitute an ethnic group.

Social class

Social class refers to the status that an individual has in society. This may be based on the amount of money and wealth an individual has or on their occupation, or both. In Britain, social class is determined by the type of job an individual has, the status that comes with the job and the money (income) that they earn. Since there are many different jobs and occupations requiring various skills and paying varying amounts, social class in Britain has for a long time been divided into the social strata of working class, middle class and upper class.

Carer *Someone who provides care for another person or people.*

Key point

Ethnicity describes a group of people who have certain background characteristics, for example language, culture or religion, in common, which makes that group distinctive in society.

Social class *A group of people who share a common position in society. Social class is linked with occupation, income, wealth, beliefs and lifestyle.*

Think of the three classes in the shape of a pyramid. Upper-class people are at the top of the pyramid because they tend to have more power, influence and status than middle-class people and there are also fewer upper-class people. Similarly, middle-class people have more power, influence and status than working-class people and there are more working-class people than in either of the other groups.

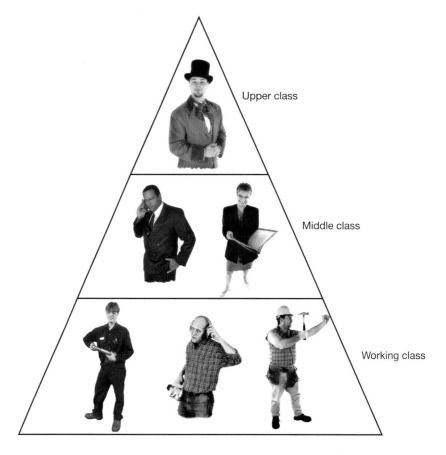

■ *Social classes pyramid*

Until 2001, people in the UK were classified using Census data into five groups or classes. This classification system was known as Social Class based on Occupation, formerly the Registrar General's Social Class. Each of the classes brought together people with similar levels of occupational skill, as shown below.

I	Professional, e.g. doctor, engineer
II	Managerial/technical, e.g. manager, teacher
IIIN	Non-manual skilled, e.g. clerk, cashier
IIIM	Non-manual unskilled, e.g. carpenter, van driver
IV	Partly skilled, e.g. warehouse worker, security guard
V	Unskilled, e.g. labourer

■ *Social Class based on Occupation*

After the 2001 Census, it became apparent that the social class classification was inadequate to deal with the ever-increasing variety of professions. A new classification system, the National Statistics Socio-economic Classification, was introduced – see below. It contains eight classes that are much more detailed than the previous five.

---

1. Higher managerial and professional occupations
    1.1 Large employers and higher managerial occupations, e.g. chief executives
    1.2 Higher professional occupations, e.g. doctor, lawyer
2. Lower managerial and professional occupations, e.g. actor, nurse, teacher
3. Intermediate occupations, e.g. secretaries, cabin crew, fireman
4. Small employers and own account workers, e.g. self employed builder, hairdresser
5. Lower supervisory and technical occupations, e.g. train drivers, plumbers, electricians
6. Semi-routine occupations, e.g. shop assistants, postman, security guard, care assistant
7. Routine occupations, e.g. cleaner, waitress
8. Never worked and long-term unemployed

■ *National Statistics Socio-economic Classification*

One problem with classifying people by social class is that it can give false information. For example, teachers are included in socio-economic class 2, which relates to high middle class. This can be true of head teachers or senior teachers or lecturers, but perhaps not so true of newly qualified teachers who are paid considerably less than those who have been in the job a long time.

Social class also affects health and well-being as a person in a lower class is unlikely to have the same opportunities and life chances as those in a higher class. People in the lower classes find it hard to progress significantly in their careers and may be unemployed and living in a poor environment due to their low income.

Gender

Until recently, people used to say that a woman's place was in the home. In 1918, men over the age of 21 years were given the right to vote in elections. Women had to wait another 10 years before receiving this right. Even so, women were generally not perceived to be equal to men in society. A wife was expected to stay at home and look after the children, do the housework, cleaning and cook dinner, while her husband went out to work to earn money (the family breadwinner) and carried out the administrative and manual jobs that women were believed to be incapable of doing.

Talking point

View 1: I don't know why working-class families want their children to have a university education. They cannot afford to send them to college or university to get a good job.

View 2: Just because an individual is working class does not mean that they are going to become a cleaner or a refuse collector.

Key point

The word gender is often confused with the term sex. A person's sex refers to the biological differences between a male and female, whereas gender refers to the socially constructed behaviour for each sex, for example masculinity and femininity.

Real Life Care

Social class

Brian is a surgeon at the local hospital and has recently bought a five-bedroom, two-bathroom house in a well-off area in Surrey. He owns a top of the range people carrier and a sports car. He is a member of the local theatre company and enjoys luxury holidays with his family two or three times a year. Brian's two children are doing well at school and have recently received glowing school reports about their academic abilities.

Kelly is a catering assistant at the same hospital as Brian. Unlike Brian, Kelly lives on a run-down social housing estate. She has three children, but her flat only has two bedrooms so the children have to share. The flat is damp and the children often have colds and are ill.

Kelly does not own a car and has to use public transport to get to work. The family has never been on holiday and receives essentials such as new underwear and school shoes for their birthdays and Christmas presents.

1 Identify which classes, based on the Socio-Economic Classification, you think Kelly and Brian would appear in. Explain your answer.

2 Analyse why Brian has a much better lifestyle than Kelly's. Describe the career prospects that Kelly has.

3 Evaluate what future Kelly's children have compared to Brian's. Explain your answer.

Key point

In 1960, women averaged 110 minutes of housework a day compared to men, who averaged 10 minutes a day.

In 2000, women in paid employment averaged 90 minutes of housework a day compared to men who averaged 50 minutes a day.

The gender pay gap between men and women for hourly pay was 12.6 per cent in favour of men.

Since 1945, changes have occurred to make men and women more equal. Women started to go out to work, and divorce (legalised in 1923) became more common. Both of these helped to make women more independent. The Sex Discrimination Act 1975 made it illegal to discriminate against either gender in education and employment, so there is now a legal obligation for women to be treated equally.

However, some women still find that they are treated unfairly at work due to their gender. Women generally hold fewer top jobs and seem to gain less out of promotion (if they get promoted at all). There are more women than men working in nursing and primary school teaching; neither of these professions is highly paid. Even in these areas, which are dominated by women, men still seem to have the most senior and, therefore, the most well-paid jobs. For example, in hospitals, surgeons and specialist doctors are generally men, and in schools, the head teachers are often men.

Key point

Women account for 23 per cent of the civil service top management and 29 per cent of health service chief executives.

Just 7 per cent of the senior judiciary, 7 per cent of senior police officers, less than 10 per cent of top business leaders and 9 per cent of national newspaper editors are women.

Over to you

Design a questionnaire to give to two older members of society (over 65) such as your grandparents. If possible, ask a male and a female. On the questionnaire, include questions that ask what jobs they did, whether a woman was expected to work or stay at home, how many women worked in their offices or in similar jobs and whether they were paid the same.

As more women go out to work than ever before, men have started to do the household chores. However, some sociologists suggest that many women are worse off now than they were 80 years ago, as they are expected to be successful in their careers, excellent parents and partners, while also running the household efficiently and providing emotional support for the family, although this is arguable.

Mr Smith at work Mrs Smith at work

■ *The roles of the twenty-first century man and woman?*

Over to you

In 2000, 60 per cent of men claimed to do more housework than their father had, while 75 per cent of women claimed to do less housework than their mother.

Discuss the implications of these statistics. What type of housework do you think men are doing? Is it the same as women or are they doing different jobs in the home?

Talking point

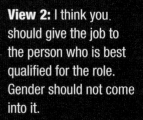

View 1: I am not giving that woman the job as a medical consultant. The male candidate would do a much better job.

View 2: I think you should give the job to the person who is best qualified for the role. Gender should not come into it.

Over to you

Discuss in class what jobs members of your family do. Are they typical of the gender differences described above? How many of the class have a mother who goes out to work?

Talking point

View 1: I've just found out that my son's Scout leader is homosexual. That does not bother me one bit as he does a fantastic job.

View 2: I think he should be asked to leave. If he is homosexual, he might fancy the young boys.

Key point

People often fear that homosexual people of the same sex as them are going to 'fancy' them. This suggests that heterosexual individuals should be attracted to every member of the opposite sex, which is not the case.

Key point

In 2003, 16 per cent of the population were over 65 years of age and 20 per cent were under 16 years old.

Sexuality

Sexuality refers to a person's sexual behaviour and choice of partner. The majority of people are heterosexual, a minority are homosexual and some people are bisexual.

Many individuals who are homosexual have found it very hard to admit their sexuality to themselves and to their friends and family because of the prejudices that exist in society towards homosexuality. Individuals can become confused and sometimes even afraid as they accept their sexuality. It can be very hard to be positive towards yourself when people are making negative comments about you. Sometimes the term homosexual confuses people and they think it can mean other things. Just because someone is homosexual does not mean that they are paedophiles or stalkers, etc.

Some individuals are homophobic because they are influenced by their culture and society. This negative attitude towards homosexual individuals is often learnt from older generations and peers. Since society has only recently started to accept homosexual behaviour, changing this belief is a challenge.

The Civil Partnership Act 2004, which came into force in December 2005, gives equal treatment to civil partners and married couples over tax, employment benefits, income-related benefits, tax credits and child support, child maintenance, parental responsibility of their partner's child, access to compensation if the civil partner dies and protection from domestic violence, as well as many others.

Age

Demography is the study of the population – the way it grows and declines. Two hundred years ago, if you lived beyond the age of 50, you were considered to be old and to have lived a long life. One hundred years ago, the life expectancy of a newborn child was 55 years. Today's life expectancy is around 75 years. Since more people are living longer and fewer people are dying younger – because of the advances in medicine and a greater awareness of health risks – the population in the UK has increased.

Family structure

A family is a social group made up of people who are related to each other by marriage, birth or adoption. They are called a family so that other members of society can recognise that these people are connected and related. The structure and culture of the family can vary, but in the UK, when we think of a family, generally speaking, it consists of adults with their children. However, it can also include aunts, uncles, grandparents, single parents and so on.

Sociologists have identified four main types of family structure:

■ nuclear

■ extended

■ lone-parent

■ reconstituted.

Nuclear family

During the middle and towards the end of the twentieth century, the **nuclear family** was the most common. It comprised a mother and father and their children. Traditionally, the father would go to work and the mother would stay at home, look after the children, do the housework and cook. This type of family is nicknamed the 'Cornflake Packet Family', as television adverts for cereals and other items always portrayed the family form to look like this.

Nowadays, the structure of the nuclear family has changed, with the mother often going out to work to provide a second income. This means that the role of the mother within the home is changing too, as she is no longer able to look after her children full time. As a consequence, there has been a dramatic increase in registered childminders and nannies in the UK. With an increasing number of women working outside the home, men are now expected to contribute equally to the household chores, although research suggests that women are still doing 70 per cent of the tasks.

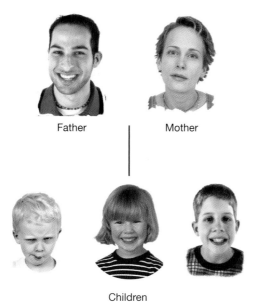

Father   Mother

Children

■ *A nuclear family structure*

Extended family

The **extended family** comprises parents, children and grandparents and may also include uncles and aunts. This type of family used to be the most common family form in the UK, but now there are not as many

Over to you

What is a family? Write down a brief definition of what you think a family is.

Nuclear family *A family consisting of two parents and their children who share a home and co-operate economically and socially.*

Extended family *A family that consists of parents, their children, and other relatives such as grandparents and/or uncles and aunts.*

of this type. A major benefit of the extended family is the support it can give to family members. For example, grandparents may help to provide childcare so that parents can go out to work; younger family members often give care and support to older members or those who are ill.

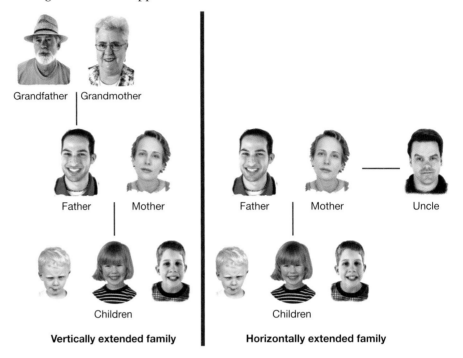

Vertically extended family | **Horizontally extended family**

■ *Families may be vertically or horizontally extended*

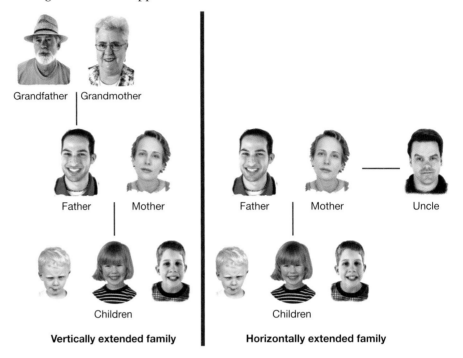

Over to you

Suggest some other reasons why families move to different parts of the country or abroad. What types of families do you think are the most likely to move away from the rest of their family? Why?

A number of families are starting to move considerable distances from the rest of the extended family, either abroad or to a different part of the country. This could be for several reasons such as a new job in a different area or promotion within a company to a different town. Other reasons include the need for a cheaper lifestyle or the wish to retire to a warmer climate. The extended family breaks up as parts of the family move away.

Lone-parent family

This type of family consists of one parent and a child or children. Until recently, this family form was uncommon, but as separation and divorce have become socially acceptable, the number of lone-parent families has increased. **Lone-parent families** also sometimes result from the death of a parent.

To give a true perspective on the change in family structure, studies and surveys have been carried out to determine the number of lone-parent families. They have found that approximately a quarter of families with dependent children are lone-parent families. Around 90 per cent of lone-parent families are headed by the mother.

Lone-parent families *A family consisting of one parent and their children.*

Some children in lone-parent families find that they become closer to their parents once they have separated or divorced. Other children feel that because their parents have divorced or separated, it must mean that their parents do not love them or care for them. This is rarely the case.

Most couples separate and divorce for reasons that have nothing to do with their children. Some nuclear families have only stayed together so as not to hurt the children, but in some cases this can be more damaging as the children overhear their parents arguing.

Some celebrities and very well-off members of society are now finding it fashionable to be lone-parent families. One way to become a single parent is to adopt children.

Reconstituted families

Husbands and wives are now far more likely to separate and divorce than they were 20 years ago. Approximately one in three marriages ends in divorce, with the most common reason given that a partner has had an affair; the second most common reason is constant arguing.

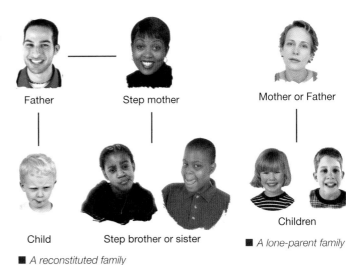

Father   Step mother   Mother or Father

Child   Step brother or sister   Children

■ *A reconstituted family*   ■ *A lone-parent family*

To avoid divorce, and the complications that can arise, many couples are now co-habiting, often deciding to have children outside marriage. Other couples sign a pre-nuptial agreement which states what each individual will receive if they ever get divorced. Evidence suggests that even couples with pre-nuptial agreements are separating.

The nuclear family is still seen as the 'desirable' family structure, so many people remarry to form another family. A reconstituted family consists of one parent who has separated from their partner and has now remarried or is co-habiting with another partner. This person may or may not have children; they may also not have been married. Over a third of marriages that take place each year are re-marriages and about one million children live with a step-parent and step-families.

The family type in which an individual lives can change a number of times throughout their life as they grow up and build their own life and family.

Key point

■ The number of people living in nuclear families has fallen from 52 per cent in 1971 to 37 per cent in 2007.

■ Nine out of ten lone-parent families are headed by lone mothers.

■ Two in five marriages in 2005 were second marriages.

■ Twenty-seven per cent of reconstituted families have three or more dependent children compared with 18 per cent of non-step-families.

Over to you

Carry out a survey in your class, school or college. Find out what family structure students live in, and which is the most common. You could even ask what family type they would like to live in and why. Some sample questions you could ask are:

■ *What type of family do you live in?*

■ *What is the most common type of family in your class?*

■ *What family structure did your parents and grandparents live in?*

Disabilities

Physical disability

This refers to any part of the human body that is not functioning properly and which prevents a person doing something physical such as walking or picking up a pair of scissors and cutting some paper.

Real Life Care

Physical disabilities

Stuart was born without his lower left leg. He has an artificial leg, which he uses to be able to walk and be mobile. Stuart has not let his disability get in his way. He is a manager in a children's home and enjoys his job. He is also a keen swimmer.

Stuart has swum since he was 6 years old, and he enjoys it very much. When he is in the water, he does not notice his disability, which makes him feel fully able. Stuart has swum for his county and region, and he has just been selected to represent Britain in international events.

1 Identify the type of disability Stuart has.

2 Describe how Stuart has coped with his disability.

3 Explain how Stuart's job and swimming has impacted on his health and well-being. What would his life be like without his job and swimming?

Mental disability

Mental disability is a disorder of the brain that results in a disruption in a person's thinking, feeling, moods, their ability to relate to others and competence to carry out everyday tasks. It can refer to extreme illnesses such as schizophrenia or dementia, whereas some people have a mental disability through inheriting a defective gene, or may have suffered from brain damage or illness. Mental illness can be caused by a variety of issues, diseases and injury. What causes one person to have a mental illness might not have the same effect on another. Learning difficulties such as dyslexia or dyspraxia can be classed as a mental disability.

Sensory disability

Human beings have five senses – sight, hearing, touch, taste and smell. A sensory disability occurs when one or more of the senses is lost. The most common senses that people lose are their hearing and sight, both of which may occur as people grow older.

Even though we celebrate diversity and are proud to live in a multicultural society, there are individuals in the community who do not feel the same way. They may try to treat people differently and unfairly based on their social, political and religious differences. This is called discrimination and is looked at more closely in the section on factors that influence the equality of opportunity.

Key point

When working in a care environment, you will need to understand that there are different levels of disability. Someone who cannot walk would be at a different level of physical disability compared with an individual who can walk but for only short periods of time.

Real Life Care

Tina and Dafydd

Tina lives in a residential home and occasionally has difficulty with her short-term memory. Sometimes she wakes up in the morning and forgets where she is, but it does not take her long to remember her surroundings. At other times, she will forget the names of the other residents and staff and repeat herself on several occasions. Tina likes to involve herself in the day-to-day activities of the residential home such as playing games and bingo. She has a very good long-term memory and likes to tell stories about her life to staff and residents.

Dafydd has Alzheimer's disease and thinks that the members of staff are some of his family and children. Dafydd does not know where he is and believes he is living in the first house that he owned, so he is often found wandering around the residential home looking for the kitchen or bathroom. Dafydd still thinks he is independent and wants to look after himself – he wants to be able to make a cup a tea and cook dinner.

1 Identify the types of disabilities that Tina and Daffyd have.

2 Describe what kind of care you would give Tina and Daffyd. Would it be the same or different?

3 Explain the levels of care that you would provide for Tina and Daffyd.

Practices in different religious and secular beliefs

One of the main differences within our society is in the beliefs that we hold. If you were to ask someone whether they had any beliefs, you would get a different answer from if you asked whether they considered themselves to be religious. Religion is a set of beliefs, symbols and practices (such as praying), which is based on the idea of a sacred and very important being. **Secular** beliefs are beliefs that have no connection to religion or church, but are beliefs of other natures instead.

Secular *Something that has no connection with any religion or church.*

The range of religious groups and secular beliefs

There is a wide range of religions and beliefs in the world, and new cults, sects and religious groups are forming all the time. It is, therefore, impossible to know exactly what a person's beliefs are, but this section focuses on some of the main religions and their beliefs.

Buddhism

Buddhists follow the teachings of Siddhartha Gautama who lived around 580 BCE in Nepal. He meditated on life, death and suffering and eventually found enlightenment. Siddhartha is known as the Buddha, which means 'Awakened One'.

Buddhism is different from other religions because the Buddha was not a god; he was simply another human like you and me. However, because he was able to achieve enlightenment, and then taught others the path to enlightenment, people continue to honour the Buddha.

Some Buddhists believe in reincarnation, that after death a person's soul is reborn in a new body. They see life as one big cycle – the samsara – which consists of birth, life, death and rebirth. The only way to end this cycle is to reach enlightenment. Breaking the cycle is nirvana, the state of enlightenment and the end of greed, hatred, suffering and ignorance – everything that is not perfect. Buddhists try to reach nirvana through meditation – this teaches them to empty the mind of all thoughts. It is only then that they can realise what is really important.

The most important Buddhist festival – Wesak (or Buddha Day) – is held on the day of the full moon in May or June. It is said that on this day the Buddha was born, gained enlightenment and passed away, but all in different years! Buddhists celebrate the day by giving and receiving presents, sharing a meal together and going to a temple or monastery for services or teaching. They will often meditate as well.

Because Buddhists are opposed to causing harm to any living creature, their diet is vegetarian.

 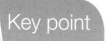
Key point

Enlightenment is a special understanding and realisation of the truths about the way things are. Think about turning on a light to see things more clearly.

■ *A Buddhist monk*

Key point

There are different types of Buddhists, each following an alternative path to enlightenment. Not all Buddhists celebrate the same festivals. Some celebrate them at different times because they are in different countries, and celebrations may be different in each country. Festivals are times when Buddhists remember and celebrate the Buddha's teaching.

Christianity, Judaism and Islam

Christianity, Judaism and Islam are all monotheistic, that is, they believe in one God. They have been grouped together here to provide a broad understanding of their similarities and differences.

Origins

Christianity arose in the Middle East about 2000 years ago from the teachings of Jesus Christ. There are many strands of Christianity, but Christians all have one fundamental belief – that Jesus Christ lived a humble and selfless life, helping poor and oppressed people, but had such charisma and strength that he inspired others to follow him; he died to save humankind and took the sins of humanity with him. Some forms of Christianity include Protestantism, Roman Catholicism, Orthodox and Pentecostal, to name a few.

Islam originated in the Middle East around 1400 years ago when the Prophet Muhammad first heard the word of God (Allah). Muslims believe in one God and that Allah is eternal.

Judaism began in the Middle East around 3800 years ago. Jews, like Christians, believe that God created the world and everything in it. They also believe that God spoke to Moses through the burning bush giving him the responsibility of saving the Jewish people from slavery in Egypt.

Beliefs

Christians worship one God. They see God as a trinity – Father, Jesus (the Son of God) and the Holy Spirit (or Holy Ghost), who can enter believers and inspire them. Muslims worship Allah, and believe that the Prophet Muhammad was the last prophet of God. Jews believe that there is only one God.

Key point

Jesus was an example of self-sacrifice and suffering.

Key point

Followers of Islam are called Muslims.

Christians believe that they only have one life and that after death they will join God in the kingdom of heaven. Some Christians think that non-believers and people who do not repent of their sins will go to Hell and enter an eternity of pain and suffering.

The story of Jesus's life, death and resurrection, together with his teachings, can be found in the Bible, which is the Christian holy book. For Christians, the Bible is a guide to their worship, beliefs, practices and values. It is divided into two parts – the Old Testament and the New Testament. The Old Testament teaches about life before Jesus and other holy people such as Abraham and Moses; the New Testament tells of Jesus's life and experiences of the early Christians.

The Jewish Bible comprises the Torah (Five Books of Moses), the books of the Prophets and holy writings. Together they are known as the Tenakh. The Torah (meaning instruction) tells Jews who they are, and the laws and moral teachings of the Torah tell Jews how to live and fulfil God's will.

The Muslim holy book is the Qur'an. It contains the words of Allah as revealed to the Prophet Muhammad in the seventh century CE. Muslims believe that the Prophet Muhammad was the last messenger sent by God for the guidance of humanity until the Day of Judgement. The Qur'an sets out the basic beliefs of Islam, and for Muslims is the only source of guidance from God. It is divided into 114 surahs or chapters.

In order to live their lives according to Islam, Muslims have five main duties to perform. These are known as the Five Pillars of Islam, but they have to follow many other rules too to become a good Muslim. At midday each Friday they go to the mosque to worship with other

Key point

Religious Jews pray three times a day. The Jewish prayer book, the siddur, contains special morning, afternoon and evening services for this purpose. For Jews, prayer enables them to have a personal and individual relationship with God.

Key point

Muslims treat the Qur'an with much respect and Muslims wash their hands and feet before touching or reading the Qur'an. They do not eat, drink or speak when it is being read, and it is usually placed upon a stool. It is NEVER allowed to touch the ground and, when it is put away, it is placed on the highest shelf and wrapped in a special cloth. Nothing is allowed to be stacked on top of it.

■ *The Muslim holy book is the Qur'an*

Muslims. They must remove their shoes and wash themselves in a special way. Inside the mosque, they use prayer mats and they must face in the direction of Makkah wherever they are in the world.

Christians and Jews follow the Ten Commandments, which they believe were written by God onto stone tablets and given by God to Moses. The Commandments are ten rules that are said to be the way that the entire human race should live, as they define right and wrong principles and actions which guide people through life.

Food

There is no special diet that Christians follow, although some have their own beliefs about eating meat. During Lent (the 40 days that lead up to Easter) some Christians fast or give up something they enjoy. For Roman Catholics, Ash Wednesday (the day after Shrove Tuesday) and Good Friday are required days of fasting.

In contrast, the Jewish Bible contains many rules about foods that Jewish people are permitted to eat – kosher foods – and those that are prohibited. Kosher foods include fruit, vegetables, eggs, cheese, beef, lamb, poultry and some fish. Meat must be killed and prepared (koshered) in a special way, so Jewish people buy their meat and other foods from specialist kosher shops and butchers. Prohibited foods include pork, rabbit and shellfish. Meat and milk foods are never prepared or eaten together. Jewish homes will have two sets of utensils, one for meat and one for milk.

Similarly, the Qur'an recommends pure and good foods and prohibits certain meats such as pork. Foods that are fit to eat are called Halal, and include vegetables, fruit, milk, lamb, beef, poultry and nuts. Meat must be killed according to the Islamic way, and Muslims buy their meat from specialist Halal butchers. This also means that some biscuits, cakes and cheese that have animal fat in them have to be prepared with Halal fat or vegetable oil.

Festivals and holy days

Christians celebrate many festivals, although less strict Christians do not celebrate all of them. The main festival is Christmas, which is celebrated on 25th December. The festival reminds Christians of the birth of Jesus. On this day, Christians give gifts and presents and eat a meal together.

Easter is another major festival, which takes place in Spring, and represents the death and resurrection of Jesus. Christians believe he rose from the dead on Easter day and is still alive today. Chocolate eggs are given at this time because eggs symbolise new life.

The main holy day for Christians is Sunday, which is seen as a day of rest. Many Christians will attend a communal service in church, which is taken by a vicar or priest, and involves praying and singing as well as teaching.

Key point

Muslims pray five times a day. All prayers are said in Arabic.

Key point

To be kosher, an animal must be killed in a special way that allows the blood to drain away completely – the Jewish Bible commands Jews not to eat blood. Then the meat is soaked and salted to complete the koshering process.

Key point

Did you know that Christmas Day was not actually the day that Jesus was born? Nobody knows the exact day on which Jesus was born.

Key point

The symbol of Christianity is the cross or the crucifix, as Jesus died on the cross. Some Christians wear a small cross around their necks. Most churches are in the shape of a cross.

Talking point

A Jehovah's Witness: The Bible tells us to 'abstain from blood'. I think that means we should stay away from blood, and not have blood transfusions.

A Christian: Being Christian, I think it means not to kill or harm anybody.

Key point

The Qur'an forbids Muslims to drink alcohol.

Judaism also has a number of festivals and holy days, including Pesach (Passover), which is a Spring festival and lasts eight days. It reminds Jews that their ancestors were once slaves in Egypt and that God helped them to flee from slavery. The story is retold during a special festive meal – the Seder – which includes special foods with symbolic meanings to remind Jews of the first Passover. Other important holy days include Rosh Hashanah, the Jewish New Year, and Yom Kippur, the Day of Atonement.

Hannukah is the Jewish festival of lights. It takes place in midwinter and celebrates a miracle that took place around 2200 years ago. Each night Jews light a candle to remind them of the miracle.

Shabbat (Sabbath) is the weekly holy day. It lasts for 25 hours from sunset on Friday evening to Saturday night. Jewish families eat a meal together on Friday night to celebrate it. Before starting the meal, a blessing is made over a cup of wine and some special bread called challah. The challah is made in the shape of a plait and there are always two loaves on the table for the family to share. Jewish families attend a Shabbat morning service in the synagogue, the Jewish place of worship.

There are only two Muslim festivals laid down by Islamic law – Eid-ul-Fitr and Eid-ul-Adha – but Muslims celebrate other special days too. Eid-ul-Fitr marks the end of a month of fasting called Ramadan. During this month, Muslims do not eat or drink during the hours of daylight. At the end of Ramadan, Muslims celebrate with special services in the mosque and enjoy a special meal during daylight hours.

■ A Jewish family celebrates Hannukah by lighting candles – one for each day of the festival

Eid-ul-Adha means the festival of sacrifice. It is a solemn festival and marks the end of Hajj, the annual pilgrimage to Makkah. Even Muslims who do not perform Hajj celebrate this festival, which commemorates the time when Ibrahim was about to sacrifice his son to Allah. At Eid-ul-Adha each family offers an animal for sacrifice.

Devout Muslim men sometimes wear a small, embroidered cap. At prayers and in the mosque, the head should be covered. Men are expected to cover themselves from their waist to their knees. Traditionally, women cover their heads and bodies and avoid contact with unrelated males. In schools, strict Muslim girls are expected to keep covered at all times, even when playing sport.

Hinduism

Hinduism is a very old religion. No one knows when or how it began, but people estimate that it pre-dates 3000 BCE.

Hindus believe in one ultimate power and source of being, which is called Brahman. They believe Brahman is in everything and can be seen in everything, and that Brahman's power can be seen in different gods and goddesses.

Hindus also believe in reincarnation and think that everything living has a soul – atman. When a person dies, the atman moves into another living body. This could be a plant, animal or person. The only way this can be broken is when someone becomes good enough to become part of Brahman.

Hindu women wear a sari, but there are no strict requirements for men.

Key point

Hajj and fasting during Ramadan are both one of the Five Pillars of Wisdom.

Over to you

Research into the different strands of Christianity. Put your findings into a newspaper article.

Key point

Hindus call Hinduism Sanatan Dharma, which means 'eternal truths'.

Real Life Care

Celebrating religious festivals

Alison is a primary school teacher. In her class, she has a Jewish child, a Muslim child and a Christian child. Alison would like to explain these religions to the other children in the class but does not know how to go about doing this. She did think about celebrating some religious festivals, but she does not know enough about each religion to decide what to do.

Can you help Alison to improve her knowledge about the religious festivals?

1 Describe the different religious festivals that Muslims, Christians and Jews celebrate. ✓

2 Explain how each religion celebrates its festivals. ✓✓

3 Compare and contrast each festival with one from another religion. ✓✓✓

Most Hindus are vegetarian, and the few Hindus who eat meat do not eat beef because cows are considered to be sacred. Also many will not eat pork, fish or food that contains eggs. Hindus do not drink alcohol or smoke.

Hindus worship in a temple or at a shrine and read their holy books, the Vedas. The best known Hindu festival is Divali (Diwali) – the festival of lights – which celebrates the New Year and the victory of good over evil. Divali takes place at the end of October or early November. At Divali, homes, shops and public places are decorated with lights, and people give each other presents and share meals with their families. They also have fireworks, as the loud bangs and noises are said to scare away evil.

Sikhism

Sikhism is one of the youngest of the major world religions, having only been in existence for about 500 years. Some of the central beliefs of Sikhism are that there is only one God and that everyone can have direct access to God. Sikhs look for God within themselves and in the world around them. They are encouraged to lead moral lives, earn their living through hard work and share their earnings charitably.

Sikhism was formed in the Punjab district of modern-day India and Pakistan. It follows the teaching of ten Gurus. They teach the unity of God, equality of men and women, belief in reincarnation (the cycle of birth, death and rebirth) and meditation, leading to their union with God.

Being a member of the Khalsa is shown by wearing the 5Ks of Sikhism. The 5Ks are:

- Kesh (uncut bodily hair – men tie their hair up in a turban)
- Kangha (a small wooden comb worn in the hair)
- Kara (a steel bracelet worn on the wrist)
- Kaccha (cotton shorts, worn underneath clothes)
- Kirpan (a ceremonial steel sword).

Together the 5Ks symbolise a Sikh's devotion to the Guru.

Women often grow their hair long and wear it in a plait for convenience. They wear either a sari or shalwar.

Officially to be classed a Sikh you must follow the teaching of the Eternal Guru. You must have taken the Amrit (holy water) and have vowed never to touch, cook or eat any kind of meat, fish or eggs. However there are some individuals, who consider themselves Sikh, but are less strict. Some of these followers may choose to eat meat (although may still avoid beef and/or pork) as long as it has not been killed in a Jewish or Muslim way.

There are many Sikh festivals, which are celebrated throughout the year. Some of the main festivals are:

- Vaisakhi – this is the New Year festival and is one of the most important dates in the Sikh calendar (April).

- Guru Nanak's birthday – this is celebrated all over the world by thousands of Sikhs in November. It celebrates the beginning of the faith and there are processions that are led by five people who represent the first people to join the Khalsa.

- Divali (Diwali) – the festival of light is celebrated by both Hindus and Sikhs but for different reasons. Sikhs celebrate it because it is the anniversary of the release from imprisonment of the sixth Guru. It is therefore important as a symbol of freedom.

Over to you

Investigate the different ways Sikhs and Hindus celebrate Divali (Diwali). Examine the reasons why they celebrate it and the ways in which they carry out their celebrations.

Real Life Care

Sanjay

Sanjay is a strict follower of Sikhism and a member of the Khalsa. Sanjay works as a builder and is often required to wear a safety hat. However, because Sanjay is a Sikh, he wears a turban and refuses to wear his safety hat, as he says his turban provides enough protection. Sanjay gets paid for the amount of hours it takes to do a job. Some of Sanjay's friends purposely take longer to do a building job so that they can get paid more, but Sanjay does not like doing this as he feels it is wrong and he works as efficiently as he can.

1 Describe why Sanjay wears a turban as a Sikh. ✔

2 Explain why Sanjay does not agree with his friends about the time they take on a building job. ✔✔

3 Analyse the effect that Sanjay's behaviour of not wearing a safety hat and being efficient and quick in his building job will have on Sanjay's relationships with his work colleagues. ✔✔✔

Rastafari

This is a movement of black people and was formed in the 1930s in Jamaica. Rastafarians (also known as Rastas) worship a single God and their prime beliefs are that Africa is the birthplace for humankind and that the Emperor Haile Selassie is a living God. They also believe that black people are the chosen people of God, but that they have been suppressed through slavery. Their general aims are to educate the young so that they may work to improve conditions for black people everywhere, to free Africa from foreign rulers and to promote African culture. They consider Ethiopia to be their homeland and believe that one day they will return there to live in freedom.

Some Rastas believe that Selassie is a reincarnation of Jesus, that Rastafarians are the true Israelites, and that one day they will return to their homeland. Rastas sometimes classify their religion as Ethiopian Orthodox Christianity, Protestant Christianity or Judaism.

Over to you

Research into a religious festival of your choice (choose one that you do not know much about) and plan a celebration of this festival for your class or for a client group on your work experience. You need to take into account when the celebrations are, as you cannot celebrate Christmas in the middle of June! You should also plan what food and drink you will need, the type of clothing you will wear and the style of decorations you need (if any).

Key point

The lion is the symbol of Rastafari. The lion represents Haile Selassie.

■ *Bob Marley was a Rastafarian icon and made reggae music*

Rastas do not have any specific dress code, but girls sometimes keep their hair covered by a scarf and boys can wear a hat (called a tam). Strict Rastas do not cut or comb their hair but wear it as dreadlocks.

Rastas do not have a specific building for religious worship. They meet in people's homes or community centres, usually once a week, for Reasoning sessions. The meetings include chanting, singing and prayers. Sometimes at these sessions marijuana, which Rastas refer to as the wisdom weed, is smoked in order to produce visions of a religious and calming nature.

Reggae music plays a very important role in Rastafari, as it contains words of protest and celebrates the beliefs of Rastas.

Rastas have a deep respect for nature and therefore Rastas are mostly vegetarian, but fish is acceptable, except for shellfish. They do not drink milk, coffee or alcohol.

Paganism

Paganism includes several spiritual movements that are based on a respect for nature, many of which predate the major religions. Most Pagans feel that the preservation of the environment is important and their beliefs stem from this. There are many strands and traditions – including those who practise witchcraft and the Druids.

Pagans have no public buildings and most ceremonies take place outdoors. Their view is that the finest places of worship are those not built by human hands. Pagans worship their gods and goddesses and celebrate the different seasons. They worship in many different ways but generally hold rituals that involve the recognition of the four elements – fire, water, earth and wind – in a circle of chanting, singing, dancing, and so on. Pagans feel that if what they do does not cause any harm to anyone or anything, then they may do it. Their ultimate aim is to make contact with the 'divine world' that surrounds them. The 'divine' can be found in lots of things such as nature or humanity. Because of this most Pagans are eco-friendly, and try to live in such a way as not to harm the environment. They also emphasise the equality of both sexes.

Pagans do not have any special requirements with regard to diet, medicine, dress, and so on. As there are many different strands within Paganism, individuals follow the beliefs and influences of their particular faith, so some Pagans are vegetarian, others will take herbal medicines.

Humanism and atheism

Humanists are non-religious people who live by moral principles based on reason and respect for others. Humanist beliefs have only been recognised for about the last 100 years. Humanists think that this world and this life are all we have – they do not believe in an afterlife. They accept the theory of evolution. Because Humanists believe that people only have one life, they believe it should be as happy as possible. This, in turn, will benefit others to help them to have a happy lifestyle.

Humanists do not believe in God and can be classed as atheists, which means 'without God'. They feel that major religions require believing in something that contradicts knowledge and common sense, and is like taking a leap of faith. However, Humanists are very anti-discriminatory and believe that everyone has a right to believe what they want and that no society should be geared towards a particular religion.

Atheism is generally understood as not believing in God, but atheists say that it is more than that. Atheists have come to the conclusion that God does not or cannot exist because of their knowledge and understanding of the world and the different religions. Atheism is not classed as a religion but as a secular belief.

Humanists and atheists celebrate important occasions such as weddings, or the birth of a child, but do not always follow a particular religion in the celebrations. They adapt the ceremony to centre more on the people included.

Key point

Pagans are not evil witches. They do not worship the devil, nor do they practise black magic.

They do not follow any dress codes, have any special rules on diet, but many have their own beliefs on the world and some choose to follow certain diets such as vegetarianism.

Every ten years the government conducts a survey in the UK by sending out a questionnaire for every household to fill in. This is called the Census. This survey finds out all kinds of information, and everyone must answer all the questions apart from one question, which is optional. This question asks you which religion you follow and provides options such as: Christianity, Islam, Judaism, Sikhism, Buddhism, etc. There is an 'other' category for people to fill in if their option is not there. The last survey was conducted in 2001 and over 10,000 people completed the 'other' option with the answer 'Jedi' from the cult film Star Wars in the hope that it would be made a religion!

Think about it

As well as the Census form, the question about religion is sometimes asked in job applications and surveys. How helpful do you think it is to know what people's religion is?

Practice for Assessment

This could contribute to P1.

Make a poster that identifies and describes the social and political factors that make people different from each other. You could include pictures from magazines to illustrate it.

(The next section explores religious and secular beliefs, which could also contribute to P1. You could therefore do this assessment after completing the next section.)

Practice for Assessment

This could contribute to P1 and P2.

Choose two different religions or secular beliefs systems that contrast with each other in terms of their beliefs. Research each religion or secular belief and produce a fact sheet or a poster on each one showing similarities and differences between the two. (P2)

Make a booklet for a year-nine student that lists and explains ways that we are different from each other. You should include social and political factors from the first section of this unit as well as different religious and secular beliefs. (P1)

Factors influencing the equality of opportunity for individuals

Earlier in the unit, we learnt that we are fortunate enough to live in a multicultural society, which means that people have their own beliefs and ideas which might be different from ours. We discovered that these differences could be in a whole range of areas such as religion, beliefs, sexuality, language, food, family structure, age, culture, festivals, etc. This part of the unit looks at how people are treated unfairly because of their differences.

Discriminatory practice

Most of us want others to treat us fairly and with respect. We want to be given the same chances as others and get help when needed. People have a right to be treated fairly no matter what the colour of their skin, their physical appearance, their background, culture, religion, and so on. Not respecting these rights is called discrimination.

Discrimination

Discrimination can be described as telling things apart, and seeing the differences in particular things. It is fine to discriminate between a chocolate bar that you like and one that you don't. However, if you make comparisons of this kind with people, it is not simply about telling people apart. It is very important to understand that we are all different.

People can be discriminated against in a number of ways. They could be turned down for jobs, refused entry into shops, bars, or clubs, be given poor service in shops and spoken to rudely by people.

There are two different types of discrimination:

- **Direct** discrimination. This means treating people differently and unfairly because they fall into a particular category. In the past, many employers refused to employ black people, women and ethnic minorities because of their differences. In the USA, there were signs in shops saying 'No Blacks', and on public transport, white people had priority over black people – black people had to give up their seats to white people if there were no seats left on the bus. All this has changed and there are now laws that prohibit this behaviour.

- **Indirect** discrimination. This means that one person is treated exactly the same as another, but this treatment has an impact on people's beliefs. This type of discrimination makes the point that treating everyone fairly does not necessarily mean treating everyone the same. For example, 14-year-old Samina, who is a Muslim, was asked not to wear her head scarf to school as it was not part of the uniform dress code. The school was trying to treat

Think about it

The only thing we have in common is that we are all unique (different).

Key point

Discrimination involves a behaviour or action resulting in an individual or a group of people being treated unfairly.

Talking point

View 1: All types of discrimination are wrong as people are treated unfairly.

View 2: Direct discrimination is acceptable in certain situations, e.g. men not being allowed to work in a refuge for women that have been assaulted by men.

Over to you

Look back over the social and political factors in the first section of this unit. Discuss which factors you think cause most discrimination. In what circumstances and situations are people discriminated against? Why?

everyone the same – pupils should wear the correct uniform, but this indirectly discriminated against Samina as it impacted on her religious beliefs.

There are many reasons why people are discriminated against. The first two sections in this unit focused on the different social and political factors as well as on the variety of religious and secular beliefs. These are all reasons why people are discriminated against. (For more information on discrimination, see the section on Diversity and equality in society in Unit 1 Communication and Individual Rights within the Health and Social Care Sectors, pages 21–34.)

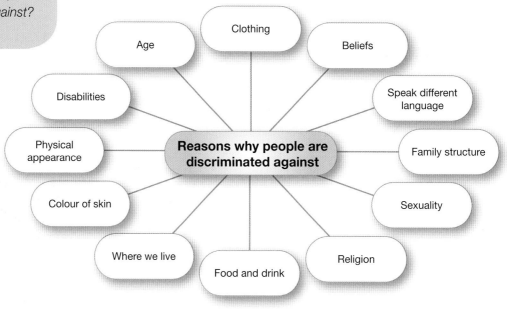

■ *Common reasons why people are discriminated against*

Real Life Care

Discrimination in action

Anish is 36 years old and works in a supermarket. He has worked in this job for the past four years and is considered to be experienced in the job. Anish wears a turban to work and is fluent in two languages. However, Anish has applied for promotion on several occasions and not got the post. When Anish asked his supervisor why he had not received the promotion despite his qualifications and experience, his supervisor replied, 'You should think yourself lucky that someone like you even has got a job at all.'

1 Why do you think Anish is struggling to achieve his promotion? ✔

2 Why has Anish not said anything earlier? ✔✔

3 What impact on his emotional health and well-being will this have? ✔✔✔

Stereotyping and labelling

Discrimination can occur because of the assumptions that we make about people. We have all met people who think that all women drivers are bad or that all male ballet dancers are homosexual. This is called stereotyping. Making assumptions about people based on types can lead to people discriminating against others. (For more information on stereotyping, see Unit 1 Communication and Individual Rights within the Health and Social Care Sectors, page 25).

Key point

A stereotype is a fixed idea or assumption about an individual or group of people.

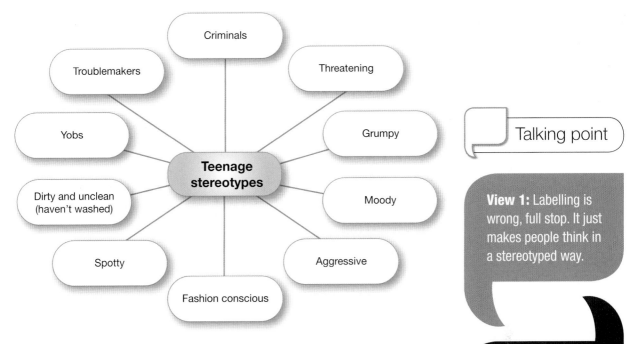

■ *Typical teenager stereotypes*

Labelling is another way of discriminating against people and is similar to stereotyping. Labels are short and easy to remember as the person is 'labelled' with one word that sums them up.

Talking point

View 1: Labelling is wrong, full stop. It just makes people think in a stereotyped way.

View 2: It's ok to label people if the label is positive.

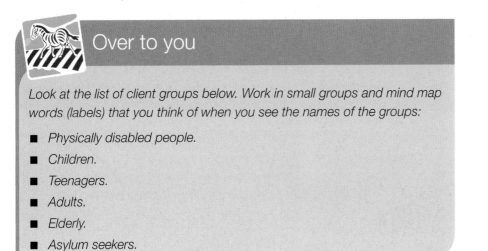

Over to you

Look at the list of client groups below. Work in small groups and mind map words (labels) that you think of when you see the names of the groups:

- *Physically disabled people.*
- *Children.*
- *Teenagers.*
- *Adults.*
- *Elderly.*
- *Asylum seekers.*

Labels group people together and claim that they are all the same. When people are labelled, the individual can feel that they have lost their identity and individuality. Some even go as far as to think 'If I have been labelled this, I might as well act like it.' This is called a **self-fulfilling prophecy**. (For more information on labelling, see Unit 1 Communication and Individual Rights within the Health and Social Care Sectors, page 26).

> **Self-fulfilling prophecy** *This term refers to the process of labelling. When you are labelled the label itself becomes embedded so that you end up becoming what the label suggests.*

Prejudice

Prejudice is an attitude that we have about others that new information is unable to change. For a full discussion of prejudice, see Unit 1 Communication and Individual Rights within the Health and Social Care Sectors, page 27.

Real Life Care

Labelled for life?

Glen and Kieran are in the same class in year 10 at Dovern Park Comprehensive and walk to school together. Glen's ethnic origin is White British while Kieran's is African Caribbean. On the way they discuss school. Glen says he likes going to school. He is popular, not just with other pupils, but with staff as well. The teachers describe Glen as 'gifted', 'intelligent' and 'well-behaved' and he is predicted to get good GCSE results.

On the other hand, Kieran says he is always in trouble at school. The teachers say that he hangs around with 'troublemakers' and that he is very 'aggressive' in class. Kieran feels that no matter what he does, even when he is trying to be good, it always has a negative

impact in class. He has been sent out of the classroom so many times that he has lost count. Glen agrees and says that he was talking in class but was not sent out of the lesson, but Kieran had been sent out the day before for doing the same thing.

1 What labels have Glen and Kieran been given? Are they positive or negative? What other labels can you think of? ✓

2 Explain how the teachers could avoid this discriminatory practice. ✓✓

3 Analyse how this discriminatory behaviour might affect Glen and Kieran. ✓✓✓

Over to you

What prejudices do you have? Be honest!

In pairs or small groups, choose a life stage. What stereotypes can you think of for each life stage? (Remember that a stereotype can be positive or negative.)

Effects of discrimination

Discrimination can affect people in a variety of ways. Carers have to be very careful not to discriminate against service users as it could have a negative effect on their health and well-being. As a carer, you will need to make sure that prejudices, stereotypes and labels do not interfere with the care you provide. For a full discussion of the effects of discrimination on service users, see Unit 1 Communication and Individual Rights within the Health and Social Care Sectors, page 28.

Over to you

Have you ever been discriminated against? Why? How did it make you feel?

The effects of being discriminated against can last throughout a person's life. In particular they may:

- *be unable to fulfil their potential, because they feel unvalued by others*
- *find it hard to form relationships because of the lack of self-worth or self-esteem*
- *start to believe the labels that they have been given*
- *feel ashamed about their own culture*
- *feel that they are to blame for the treatment they have received.*

Discrimination also removes the service user's rights. It can make it very hard for a service user to voice their opinion. Therefore, it can devalue them and make them feel unwanted and useless.

Over to you

Look back at the Real Life Care of Glen and Kieran. What do you think the possible effects of labelling are on Glen's and Kieran's physical, intellectual, social and emotional health and well-being?

The role of the media

When we talk about the media, we are referring to newspapers, television, radio, magazines, the Internet, and so on. The media are a very good way of communicating and passing on information to the world. They are very powerful when it comes to portraying images of particular groups. They can influence the public to like or dislike certain celebrities, ethnic groups, and so on, by reporting and capturing pictures of people in society in a positive or negative way.

Over to you

In how many different ways can the media convey their message to us?

Newspapers

The most powerful section of the media is the newspapers. The various newspapers report on a variety of stories in different ways. The tabloids pride themselves on covering celebrity lifestyles and gossip, while the broadsheets focus on the more political aspects of society. Millions of people read newspapers every day as they provide a detailed account of events happening not just in the UK but in the world too. Newspapers can influence us, even just the headlines and the pictures they use. The actual article confirms the headline and strengthens the opinion of the paper.

Over to you

Look at the two newspaper headlines below. Both papers are discussing the subject of asylum seekers. How do the newspapers make you feel about asylum seekers? Why do they have this effect on you?

SOFT TOUCH Numbers seeking asylum soar in Britain – and fall in Europe

Source: Daily Mail, 26 September 1995

New law 'to split' family denied refugee status

Source: Guardian, 3 August 2005

 Over to you

Have a look at some national (broadsheets and tabloids) and local newspapers. Look at the headlines, articles and pictures. Are they positive or negative towards the subject? How does it make you feel?

Collect any health and social care articles and compare them with articles that other people have found in your class. Do they try to influence the way you think about a subject? How do they do this?

Television

The television is another excellent way of communicating with people around the UK as nearly all households have a television. Some channels have regular news bulletins where they update the nation on world events. Sometimes when something important happens, a special news bulletin will be broadcast between programmes. Television news tries to give a non-biased view of the stories covered and leaves it to viewers to make up their own mind. However, other programmes on television can stereotype groups positively and negatively and provide a biased image of these people.

Other forms of biased and non-biased media coverage

There are other ways that the media can spread their messages. Biased forms of media are magazines and books as they give the author's or editor's opinions. The most popular types of magazines include feature stories about celebrities, for example what they are wearing, what religion they follow and what diet they are on. More serious magazines cover current economic and political issues. Books cover a wide range of issues, both fiction and non-fiction.

A non-biased form of media is the information leaflet. Such leaflets try to provide purely factual information about health issues, groups in society, and so on.

The Internet provides information in different forms, such as articles, reviews, pictures, games, and from different sources, for instance a national newspaper or television company website.

Examples of non-discriminatory practice

To stop discriminatory practice from happening in the workplace (and in society), organisations try to promote equality of opportunity. Equality of opportunity does not mean treating everyone the same, as this would not help those who needed to use special equipment or who required extra help with different tasks. One way organisations try to be anti-discriminatory is to have relevant policies and procedures in place.

Materials

The materials that you use when working with groups should be varied to accommodate all preferences. For example, toys and books should include positive images of gender and race, such as a picture of a woman mechanic, or perhaps something as simple as putting chopsticks in the home corner.

Visual displays in schools and day centres that show off the work of the service users must avoid stereotypes and could perhaps provide positive images of individuals or groups in society. This also applies to residential homes that display paintings done by the residents.

Activities could be focused on or around different religious festivals, so the service users could celebrate their own and other people's festivals. Other activities might involve eating foods from around the world or having a day where everyone has to think of an activity to do from another culture.

Using materials that are negative can add towards discrimination, as service users do not learn any other way. For example, a series of books that show white people as police officers and black people as criminals reinforces stereotypes that white people are good and black people are bad. Therefore, it is important to use materials and activities in a positive way so that everyone is treated equally.

Key point

Anyone can have a website, so not all information on the Internet is either correct or unbiased. Before using a website, it is important to check where the information has come from.

Over to you

Discuss as a class what websites would be good to use for information, and which websites and chat rooms you should be wary of (might be used by paedophiles).

Key point

Equality of opportunity means having the same chance of gaining access to or the use of something.

Practice for Assessment

This could contribute to P1 and M1.

Draw a comic strip or write a story that identifies and describes the factors that may influence equality of opportunity for individuals. Act these to your class and discuss the factors that you identified. (P1)

Give different examples of how health and social care services can promote equality of opportunity. Explain why different services use different methods. (M1)

Over to you

Reflecting on what you have learnt so far, in small groups consider what your responsibilities are in the workplace.

Individual worker responsibilities

It is important that care workers adopt the policy and approach of their workplace. Most organisations issue new staff with a handbook that gives a detailed account of the policies that they follow and the way they expect staff to behave. Care workers are expected to meet the individual needs of the client as opposed to treating everyone the same. Carers therefore need to be aware of:

- the correct form of communication (such as language) so as not to cause offence
- the different forms of prejudice that people have
- the different types of discrimination that can occur
- the social and ethnic backgrounds of the service users.

Real Life Care

Nicki and James

James is a nurse at the local hospital. Nicki is sister on the same ward and is therefore in charge of James. James is the only male nurse on the ward and Nicki often treats him differently from the female nurses. She asks him to wash and move the patients from ward to ward more often than the female nurses, and this makes him feel that he is not seen as a proper nurse because of his gender. Some of the other nurses have noticed Nicki's treatment of James and want to help him but they do not know what to do.

1 How would you help James? ✔

2 Explain what you would suggest to Nicki so that she does not discriminate against James. ✔✔

3 Evaluate how Nicki's behaviour towards James makes him feel. ✔✔✔

Institutional responsibilities

It is the responsibility of the institution or organisation to make service users and staff feel safe and comfortable. This means they must ensure that staff and other service users do not discriminate against each other. They do this by ensuring that staff follow policies, procedures and codes of practice that have been created to protect every one (see page 188).

Working with colleagues

Working with others can be fun – shared experiences can often lead to friendship. However, sometimes working with others is not always easy and enjoyable. Carers have a duty to challenge any discriminatory behaviour that they see.

Real Life Care

Alex and Dawn

Alex has just started work as a care worker in Mason Dieu residential home. She has worked at a day care centre before but not in a residential home, and is shocked by the amount of responsibility she has as an individual. She has been issued with a handbook, which states that she is expected to meet the individual needs of the clients.

Dawn has worked at Mason Dieu for a long time and has been asked by the manager of the home to train Alex and help her settle in. Dawn tells Alex that she cooks all the residents the same meal and if they do not eat it because of their beliefs, then that's up to them. Dawn explains that she has not got the time to find out what each individual eats and then to cook it

because she has also to change the beds and tidy up. Dawn often uses offensive language when talking to staff if they do something wrong or not quickly enough.

Alex is worried about working with Dawn as she is sure that this kind of practice is not appropriate, but she does not know what to do or what her responsibilities are as a new member of staff.

1 Identify and describe how Dawn is being irresponsible to the residents and other members of staff in the home. ✔

2 Explain how Dawn should be responsible. ✔✔

3 Evaluate what Alex should do to deal with the situation. ✔✔✔

Some carers discriminate against service users without being aware that they are doing it, and a simple chat with them is all that is required to solve the problem. Unfortunately, this is not always the case and if you witness discriminatory practice, you should tell your manager or employer.

The General Social Care Council (GSCC) code of practice for social care workers requires workers to tell their employer of any bad practice that may lead to poor quality care, including discriminatory practice. It also says that employers must have policies and procedures that employees can follow should they wish to report another carer. Employers are expected to deal with any complaints quickly and efficiently. If the complaint is valid and is cause for serious concern, or a repeat offence, then the GSCC has the power to caution, suspend or remove the carer from the service.

Working with patients/service users

It is important not to discriminate against the people you work with. A carer must take responsibility and learn to work with service users without discriminating against them. There are several ways to help avoid discriminatory practice:

- Allow service users to state a preference.
- Provide translation or interpretation facilities.
- Ensure food meets religious and other dietary requirements.
- Be understanding of circumstances and treat people equally, not the same.

Practice for Assessment

This could contribute to P4, M2 and D1. Read about Sally and Ishbel, and then answer the questions below.

Ishbel is a resident at Seven Trees Residential Care Home for the over-65s. She has lived there for two years after becoming physically disabled and unable to walk up the stairs in her own home. Ishbel is a strict vegetarian and likes to have her own independence around the care home.

Sally is a new carer. She has never worked in the care industry before and thinks that it will be really easy – just dress, wash and feed the residents.

Ishbel does not like Sally because the last few times Sally has been on duty Ishbel thinks that Sally did not treat her properly. Sally did not understand that Ishbel was a vegetarian and only made meals with meat in them for the residents. Sally also took everybody on a trip into town, but left Ishbel behind because she found it difficult to push Ishbel in her wheelchair. She also said that all physically disabled people would have to stay in their rooms all day and watch television while the 'normal' people played bingo and snakes and ladders. Sally does not think that physically disabled people are able to play these games.

How could understanding diversity have helped Sally to promote Ishbel's rights? (P4)

In what ways did Sally discriminate against Ishbel? Suggest ways in which Sally could have achieved this discriminatory practice. (M2)

How would Sally's discriminatory behaviour towards Ishbel affect Ishbel's health and well-being? Explain the effects on the physical, intellectual, emotional and social well-being of Ishbel. (D1)

Rights of individuals

Every individual in the UK has a right to do particular things and live their life in the manner that they wish. In order to do this, there are rules that people have to follow individually at home, at work and as an organisation or work force. This section looks at the legislation that protects the rights of the individual, the responsibilities that employers and employees have, and the organisations that supervise the maintenance of the rules.

Individual rights

We all have rights when receiving health and social care, and these rights determine the way we are treated. We deserve to be treated with respect, without being discriminated against, in a dignified manner with our privacy protected. The rights we have as individuals are covered in greater detail in Unit 1 Communication and Individual Rights within the Health and Social Care Sectors, page 37.

In recent years, our rights as individuals have become more apparent and they are now protected by laws and policies that care settings must follow.

The role and impact of conventions, legislation and regulations

To help the UK and the world to become a happier place to live, where there is equality of opportunity, certain rules have been laid down to make life run more smoothly and to ensure that everyone is doing the same thing. When the UK government implements such rules, they are called **legislation** or Acts of Parliament. Organisations make policies or codes of practice for their staff to abide by. An agreement between countries to obey the same law is known as a convention. The conventions and legislation described below are all important for the health and social care environment.

European Convention on Human Rights and Fundamental Freedoms 1950 and the Human Rights Act 1998

The European Convention on Human Rights provided the backbone for the Human Rights Act. Before 2000, UK law only covered three areas of discrimination: disability, race and sex. In 2000, the Human Rights Act was updated to incorporate the Convention on Human Rights to make UK legislation more effective. The main points of the Act are as follows:

- Respect for human rights.
- Life is protected by law.

> **Legislation** *Laws, made by the government, which cover many different areas, including disability, race, human rights and so on.*

> **?**
> **Think about it**
>
> *What do you think life would be like if the Human Rights Act did not exist? Think about each of the main points of the Act and how it would affect you if it were not there.*

- No one shall be tortured, held in slavery or forced to work.
- Right to a fair trial.
- Freedom of thought, religion and speech.
- Right to marry and have a family.

The Race Relations Act 1976 and the Race Relations (Amendment) Act 2000

The Race Relations Act was passed in 1976 as it was felt that there was no real definition of what discrimination is. The Act therefore defines discrimination (see page 32) and lays down circumstances where discrimination is lawful or unlawful (where you can and cannot discriminate).

The law protects people who have been discriminated against because of their race, skin colour, nationality or ethnic background. It also protects those who are victimised for making a complaint of racial discrimination or for supporting another complaint made by someone else. The Act protects people at work, at school, college or university, when looking for a job or applying for benefits, finding somewhere to live and receiving medical treatment.

The Act was updated in 2000 to strengthen and extend its scope.

Mental Health Act 1983 and the Mental Capacity Act 2005

The Mental Health Act 1983 is designed to protect individuals suffering from mental health problems and also to protect society from individuals behaving dangerously as a result of their mental health problems. This means that individuals can be detained in a hospital against their wishes if they are considered to be ill, or in prison if they have committed a criminal offence. This is a severe restriction of an individual's freedom and there is a right of appeal to a special court if the individual wishes. However, it is easy to see the dilemma that could exist between an individual's right to freedom and the community's right to be safe.

The Mental Capacity Act updates current law where decisions need to be made on behalf of others. The Act will govern decision making on behalf of adults who have lost mental capacity (e.g. dementia) or where incapacity has existed from birth. This replaces Part 7 of the Mental Health Act.

Convention on the Rights of the Child 1989

In 1989, world leaders thought that children needed a special convention because children often need care and protection that adults do not need. Adults have rights, so why not children? The rights apply to all children and young people aged under 18. They are the same for children living in different settings, such as at home or away, in foster care, boarding schools, etc.

The convention was based around four main principles:

- The child's best interests should be at the heart of making decisions affecting them.
- The child should not be discriminated against.
- The child should be free to express themselves (freedom of speech).
- The child has a right to survive and develop.

The Children Act 1989

This Act is important as it provides children with the right to be protected from 'significant harm'. Social service departments will be notified that a child is being harmed and will inform the court who decides if it is 'significant harm'. The parents could inflict this harm.

The Act also ensures that minimum standards and regular inspections are in place for nurseries and residential schools, and ensures that they are following the correct rules and not abusing children. It gives rights to children who have been cared for by social service departments to be supported and assisted to become independent and to have access to information concerning their personal histories. The rights of the children are considered to be paramount.

The Children Act 2004

This builds on the Children Act 1989 by setting out a new framework focused around the needs of the child. The National Society for the Protection of Children (NSPCC) campaigned for a number of changes, many of which were taken into account in this new Act. One idea was to organise agencies and departments so that they can all work together in a more efficient way that would benefit the children. Another was that education for those in care should be promoted just as much as education for children living in their own families.

 Real Life Care

Ewan's pre-school

Ewan has been running a pre-school for the past ten years. It is very popular and always full. Parents of children book well in advance to make sure their child has a place at the pre-school. The school is regularly inspected and always receives a glowing report.

Ewan treats each child equally and fairly, by meeting their individual needs. He makes sure that every child is comfortable in the environment and that they are free to express themselves in an appropriate manner. Ewan takes children that are in care as well children living in their own families.

1 Suggest why it is important that the pre-school is regularly inspected.

2 Analyse the way Ewan treats the children. Is there anything he could do differently?

3 Evaluate what the pre-school would be like if there were no regulations that it had to follow, or inspections.

Data Protection Act 1998

The Data Protection Act is very important as it covers how information about any living person is used. All organisations, companies, care settings, and so on, must comply with this Act as it protects both staff and service users. It does this by limiting how long information may be kept, who is allowed access to the information and by obtaining only the information that is relevant.

Nursing and Residential Care Homes Regulations 1984

This is also known as the Registered Homes Act and it controls the setting up and running of care homes. It informs homes of the procedures that they must follow to provide a safe environment for residents. This involves having a list of rules that the homes must follow, for example the type of information that must be kept. Each home must also be registered with the local authority. Residential and nursing homes are subject to inspection from time to time to make sure that they are correctly following procedures.

Residential and nursing homes must produce, when asked, a list of all their service users, including name, address, doctor and date of birth. They also have to keep other information such as details of all the staff that work in the home.

According to the Act, homes must make sure that enough people work there to cater for the number of service users, that the service users have access to bathroom facilities and have their own personal space (their own room) and privacy.

The Act is very important as it offers residential and nursing homes valuable guidance on how to run the home.

Disability Discrimination Act 1995 and 2005

The Disability Discrimination Act is designed to provide the rights of people with disabilities in terms of employment, access to education and transport, housing, goods and services.

 Key point

One part of the Act requires that all service providers ensure that disabled people are not discriminated against. Therefore, they all have to provide access for disabled people by making 'reasonable adjustments' to the way in which they provide their service, for example by providing a ramp or lift as well as stairs or a leaflet in Braille.

Disability is defined as a condition that makes it difficult for a person to carry out normal day-to-day activities.
It can be physical, sensory or mental disability, and it must be substantial and have a long-term effect (at least twelve months).

The Disability Discrimination Act of 2005 has mainly amended the DDA 1995 in areas of transport and public authorities. However it has also amended the definition of disability in respect of people with a mental illness, multiple sclerosis, HIV infection or cancer to be disabled.

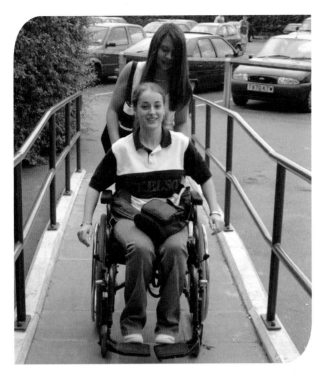

■ *The Disability Discrimination Act has helped to remove barriers for individuals*

Real Life Care

Cerys' after-school club

Cerys is the owner of an after-school club. She has just had the building refurbished and adjusted to cater for the needs of all her service users, and to make it fully accessible to everyone no matter what their disability. Cerys had to turn away wheelchair users before as the only access to the after-school club was up some stairs. To comply with the Disability Discrimination Act 1995, Cerys has put in a ramp next to the stairs, but she has still to make changes to the doors which, at present, have to be pushed or pulled, supply free water and provide information about the service in locally used languages.

1 Suggest how Cerys can comply with the Disability Discrimination Act by changing the doors, supplying free water and providing information about the service in locally used languages. ✓

2 Explain why Cerys has to change these facilities. ✓✓

3 Analyse the effects this will have on the business of the after-school club. ✓✓✓

Care Standards Act 2000

The Care Standards Act 2000 replaced part of the Registered Homes Act 1984 and some areas of the Children Act 1989 that dealt with the regulation of voluntary and registered children's homes. The new Act largely updates the earlier legislation so that it better suits twenty-first century society. The Act created the following bodies:

- General Social Care Council (GSCC) for England
- Care Council for Wales
- Scottish Social Services Council
- Northern Ireland Social Care Council.

The councils supervise the training of carers and social workers in their area. They provide codes of conduct for employers and employees to make sure that everyone follows the same rules and works in a similar way.

The care councils set out the standards expected of social care workers in two codes of practice: for social care workers and employers of social care workers. For a summary of the GSCC code of practice for social care workers, see Unit 1 Communication and Individual Rights within the Health and Social Care Sectors, page 35. Each country has a slightly different variation of the codes of practice and delivers and monitors the rules in their own ways. However, they all seek to protect both service users and staff.

Responsibilities

Employers and employees

In any industry or organisation, including health and social care settings such as hospitals or day care centres, it is important that employers and employees follow certain rules. As we saw above, the social care councils of England, Wales, Scotland and Northern Ireland each produce codes of practice for employers and for employees.

It is also the responsibility of the employer and the organisation to provide policies and procedures for employees to follow. This is to minimise hazards, dangers and discrimination in the workplace. These policies would be in line with the legislation mentioned earlier and it is the employer's job to make sure that employees obey these rules.

Codes of practice and charters

All care settings have guidelines which tell both care practitioners and their clients about the quality of care that is expected and how it will be provided. You will need to understand the differences between guidelines, charters, policies, procedures and codes of practice.

Procedures

A **procedure** is a particular way that a task must be done. It is a list of steps that must be followed in the correct order to complete the task properly. A good example of a procedure would be changing a dressing on a wound. This will be written down so that a nurse could change the

---

? Think about it

How useful do you think each of the Acts is in protecting individual rights? If you were the prime minister, would you introduce any more legislation to protect the rights of service users and staff?

Procedure *A set way for carrying out a task.*

dressing by providing minimal risk of infection to the wound and to the rest of the hospital.

Codes of practice

A code of practice is a list of rules that helps to guide workers on what is expected of them. It can help staff when dealing with specific situations as it sets down what they should do. All care professions have codes of practice as they aim to reflect and set a standard for good practice in care settings.

Policies

It is easy to get policies and codes of practice confused as they are similar. A policy is set for an individual care setting in a particular place and it tells care workers how to do things in a certain way. For example, a policy for all registered doctors applies to all doctors in any care setting, but a doctor working in a hospital will have a different policy and a way of dealing with things from a general practitioner.

Over to you

Norval is a manger of a newly built day care centre for mentally disabled children. He is employing new staff to help run the centre and needs to create a policy for his staff to follow. He has no idea what should be in the policy. Can you help? Write a policy for Norval to use in the day care centre.

Charters

A charter is set out by the government and informs people of their rights and what they can expect from statutory services that the government provides. The NHS has a charter called 'Your Guide to the NHS', which was published in 2001. It informs service users of the treatments they can have, how to be referred for this treatment, how long it will take to receive the treatment and what to do if they do not receive the level of care they were expecting.

Many health centres, colleges and other organisations are now producing charters to inform their service users of when they can collect test results, how to complain, when they are open, and so on.

Practice for Assessment

This could cover the evidence to contribute to P5, M3 and D2.

Choose one piece of legislation and one code of practice or charter that aims to support the rights of the individual. Make a leaflet for each one describing them in a chosen health and social care environment. (P5)

Explain in your leaflets how each supports the rights of the individuals within health and social care environments. (M3)

Evaluate your chosen legislation and code of practice or charter by explaining how effective it is in valuing diversity, promoting equality and supporting the rights of individuals in health and social care environments. (D2)

Check your understanding

1 Give three examples of social and political diversity.

2 Name the three religions that are monotheistic.

3 Describe the three types of sexuality.

4 Give an example of each type of disability.

5 Which religious or secular beliefs ask people to follow a mainly vegetarian diet?

6 Describe the two different types of discrimination.

7 Explain the concept of labelling.

8 Which piece of legislation was amended in 2000, and protects individuals from being discriminated because of the colour of their skin and religion?

9 Which legislation created the General and Social Care Council?

10 Give examples of the type of diet that Jews follow.

5 Anatomy and Physiology for Health and Social Care

Introduction

This unit will enable you to develop a knowledge and understanding of the way the body works, the systems within the body and the processes that are necessary to keep us alive. It also provides an introduction to the organisation of the body and the major organ systems, and how the systems work together. You will learn about routine measurements that health care workers carry out, hazards and risks, and the potential malfunction of body systems and the care service users receive when this occurs.

How you will be assessed

This is an internally assessed unit.

In this unit you will learn about:

- the organisation of the human body
- the structure, function and interrelationship of major body systems
- routine measurements and observations
- malfunctions in body systems.

The organisation of the human body

Cells

The human body is made up of millions of tiny cells that can only be seen under a microscope. They vary in size and shape and have different functions, but all animal cells have three features in common:

- the cell membrane, which is the outer covering of the cell
- the nucleus, which controls the cell's activities
- the cytoplasm, a fluid-like material.

The nucleus of the cell contains chromosomes which contain DNA (deoxyribonucleic acid). This is the genetic coding material which determines the different characteristics that an individual has. The cytoplasm contains many different structures known as organelles, which carry out different functions within the cell. A mitochondrion (*plural* mitochondria) is one very important organelle. It releases energy from food, which gives human beings the energy they need to function. The number of mitochondria in a cell will depend on the amount of energy it needs to perform its functions. A muscle cell for example will have many mitochondria as it needs a lot of energy.

Permeable *Allowing gases or liquids to pass through.*

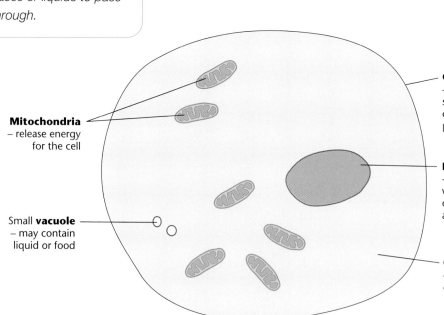

Mitochondria – release energy for the cell

Small vacuole – may contain liquid or food

Cell membrane – controls the movement of substances into and out of the cell. Often described as partially **permeable**

Nucleus – contains the instructions for the work, growth and maintenance of the cell. These instructions are on the chromosomes

Cytoplasm – contains organelles that carry out the 'work' of the cell

■ *The structure of a cell*

During the development of the foetus in the uterus, cells will take on different characteristics depending on what part of the body they will eventually become and what functions they will perform. For example, some will become muscle cells and others will become nerve cells. This means that they will look and act very differently.

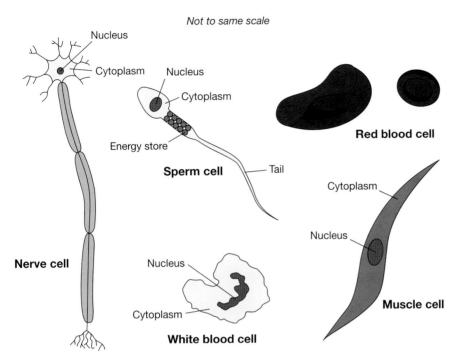

■ *Specialised human body cells*

 Over to you

As a group, research the structure and function of different body cells. You could each research one different type of cell. The diagrams above should help to start you off. Make sure that you include in your research as many of the cells' structures as you can. When you have gathered all the information, pool your research results and create a poster or booklet with diagrams as a quick reference guide.

Tissues

A tissue is a group of cells of the same structure that perform the same function. Cells cannot function by themselves, so in order for them to function efficiently, they group together to form tissues. There are four main types of tissue in the body:

■ epithelial

■ connective

- muscular
- nervous.

The epithelial tissue is formed of sheets of cells that cover internal and external surfaces of the body. The skin is epithelial tissue, and epithelial tissue is also used to line blood vessels and the respiratory, digestive and urinary tracts. Connective tissue makes up the main supporting structure of the body.

Muscles are obviously made up of muscle tissue, although the heart is made up of a more specialised type of muscle tissue. This will be explained further in the section on the cardiovascular system. Nervous tissue makes up nerves, the spinal cord and the brain.

Organs

Organs are made up of different tissues that work together to carry out a particular function. An example of this is the heart, which is made up of different types of tissue, such as cardiac muscle, nervous tissue and epithelial tissue.

Systems

A system is made up of different tissues and organs working together to perform a specific function in the body. Some systems are relatively small, such as the renal system where the main organs are two kidneys, two ureters, a urinary bladder and a urethra. Other systems involve many more organs such as the digestive system, which includes among others the oesophagus, stomach, liver, pancreas, large and small intestines. Some of the organ systems work together to help the body to work efficiently. This will be covered later in the unit.

Practice for Assessment

Carrying out this activity will give you underpinning knowledge for P1.

Organise your organs! You will need:

- flip chart paper
- felt pens
- paper or card
- Blu-Tack or sticky tape
- scissors.

Use a sheet of flip chart paper to draw an outline of the human body. Draw and cut out shapes of the different organs. You may need more than one set of these if you are in a large group.

Divide into teams and, with each member of the team taking it in turns, stick the organs onto the body shape in the right places. When all the organs are stuck onto the body, compare them to see how accurate you are in locating organs in the body.

Location of organs in the body

Organ	System and location
Skin	Excretory system. Covers the whole of the external surface of the body.
Heart	Cardiovascular or circulatory system. Located in the thoracic or chest cavity within a bony cage consisting of the sternum, the rib cage and the vertebral column. The heart is about the size of an adult fist and lies in the middle of the chest between the two lungs. It lies slightly diagonally with the top or apex towards the right and the base towards the left.
Lungs	Respiratory system. Two lungs are situated in the thoracic cavity either side of the heart. They extend from under the clavicle or collar bone to the diaphragm, the muscular sheet that separates the thoracic and abdominal cavities.
Brain	Nervous system. Situated inside the skull, which is made up of several bones fused together.
Eyes	Nervous system. There are two eyes either side of the front of the skull. They lie in the orbits – bony sockets that protect the eyes from damage.
Ears	Nervous system. There are two ears that are situated either side of the skull. The outer ear or pinna is the only part of the ear that is externally visible. The middle and inner ears are situated within the skull.
Stomach	Digestive system. Situated in the upper part of the abdominal cavity just below the diaphragm.
Pancreas	Digestive and endocrine systems. The pancreas is situated on the left side of the abdominal cavity just below the stomach.
Intestines	Digestive system. The intestines are made up of the small and large intestine. They are situated in the lower part of the abdominal cavity below the stomach. The small intestine runs from the lower end of the stomach to the large intestine. The large intestine surrounds the small intestine in an 'n' shape. It ends at the anus.
Liver	Digestive system. Situated on the right side of the abdominal cavity next to the stomach.
Kidneys	Excretory or renal system. There are two kidneys lying either side of the vertebral column in the loin area of the body.
Bladder	Excretory or renal system. The urinary bladder is situated in the pelvis behind the pubic bone, which protects it from damage.
Ovaries and testes	Reproductive system. The ovaries are situated in the pelvic cavity either side of the uterus at the end of each fallopian tube in the female. There are two testes, which are situated in the scrotum behind the penis in the male.
Uterus	Reproductive system. The uterus is suspended centrally in the pelvic cavity between the urinary bladder in front of it and the large intestine behind it in the female.

Major body systems

The cardiovascular system

The cardiovascular or circulatory system's main functions are to help in the maintenance of the oxygen supply to the body and to transport and supply materials to the cells.

The cardiovascular system consists of:

- the heart – a double pump that pushes the blood round the body
- blood – a fluid that transports oxygen and other materials to the cells
- blood vessels – a network of tubes that carry the blood to all parts of the body.

The heart

The heart is about the size of an adult fist. It is known as a double pump because each side of the heart works separately – the left side pumps blood from the heart to the lungs and the right side pumps blood from the heart to the rest of the body. The two sides of the heart are separated by the septum.

The heart is made up of cardiac muscle, a specialised type of muscle tissue. Because the heart pumps throughout life, it needs to be made up of tissue that can maintain its efficiency throughout a person's lifespan. This tissue is supplied with blood by the coronary vessels.

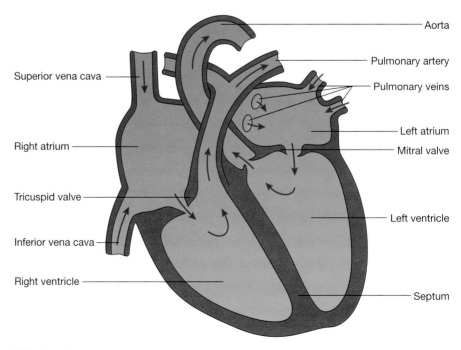

Aorta
Pulmonary artery
Pulmonary veins
Superior vena cava
Left atrium
Mitral valve
Right atrium
Tricuspid valve
Left ventricle
Inferior vena cava
Right ventricle
Septum

■ The heart

The heart is made up of four chambers – each side of the heart contains the upper atrium and lower ventricle. Of these, the left ventricle has the thickest muscular wall as this is the chamber that pumps blood from the heart to the rest of the body. There are valves between the atrium and ventricle on both sides.

Electrical conduction

In order for the heart to continue to beat at a regular rate, the timing of the heart beat is controlled by a small area in the top of the right atrium called the sino-atrial node or pacemaker. From here, the electrical impulses are conducted to the rest of the heart.

Blood circulation

Not only does the heart have a double pump, but the circulatory system also has a double circulation. This means that the blood passes through the heart twice during one circulation of the body.

Key point

In some people, the electrical conduction of the heart does not work properly, and the heart beats too slowly, too fast or very irregularly. This can reduce the quality of someone's life or may even be life-threatening. In such cases a battery-operated, artificial pacemaker can be inserted under the skin of the patient. It is about the size of a matchbox and is set to maintain the heart beat at a regular rate. Around 10,000 people in the UK have pacemakers fitted every year.

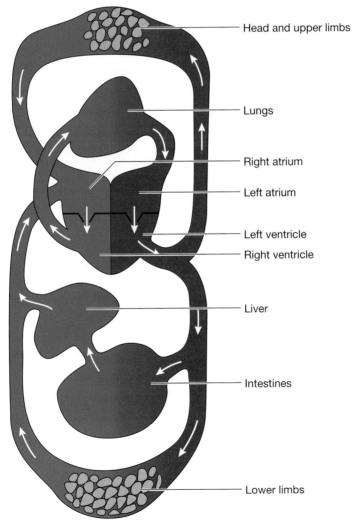

Head and upper limbs

Lungs

Right atrium

Left atrium

Left ventricle

Right ventricle

Liver

Intestines

Lower limbs

■ *The circulatory system*

Deoxygenated blood arrives in the right atrium from the vena cava, the largest vein in the body. The atrium contracts, forcing blood into the right ventricle. The ventricle then contracts and pushes blood into the pulmonary artery. From here, the blood flows to the lungs where gas exchange takes place. Carbon dioxide leaves the blood and moves into the lungs to be expelled, and oxygen leaves the lungs and moves into the blood to be transported to the body's cells. The blood is now oxygenated and travels to the left atrium via the pulmonary veins. The left atrium fills and forces blood into the left ventricle. The ventricle then contracts and forces blood into the aorta, the main artery, which then branches into other arteries and takes the blood to all parts of the body. In the capillaries gas exchange takes place. The oxygen is delivered to the cells and carbon dioxide is collected from the cells and taken back to the heart for the whole process to start again. This part of the circulation is known as the systemic circulation as it transports the blood to all parts of the body. The circulation of the blood between the heart and the lungs is known as pulmonary circulation.

Over to you

Explain the journey one red blood cell takes from arriving at the entrance to the right atrium and completing a whole circuit of the body.

The blood

An average adult has about 5–6 litres of blood. The blood is made up of 55 per cent plasma, which is the liquid part of the blood, and 45 per cent blood cells.

Plasma is a straw-coloured fluid that is made up of 90 per cent water. The remaining 10 per cent consists of dissolved food and waste, minerals such as potassium, sodium and chloride, blood clotting factors, hormones and antibodies.

Different types of blood cells are suspended in the plasma:

■ Red blood cells or erythrocytes are bi-concave discs which, when mature, do not contain a nucleus. They contain haemoglobin, a protein that carries oxygen and makes the cells red.

■ White blood cells or leucocytes are cells that help to fight infection. There are three different types:
  – monocytes and neutrophils are phagocytes – they engulf foreign matter in the blood
  – lymphocytes – B lymphocytes that produce antibodies and T lymphocytes that destroy infected cells.

■ Platelets or thrombocytes are fragments of blood cells that produce enzymes that help with blood clotting.

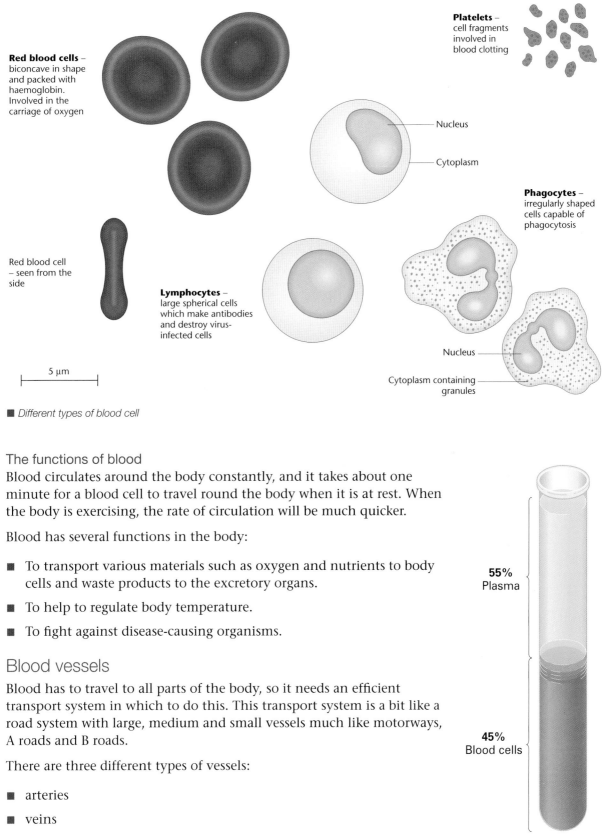

Red blood cells – biconcave in shape and packed with haemoglobin. Involved in the carriage of oxygen

Red blood cell – seen from the side

Lymphocytes – large spherical cells which make antibodies and destroy virus-infected cells

Nucleus

Cytoplasm

Platelets – cell fragments involved in blood clotting

Phagocytes – irregularly shaped cells capable of phagocytosis

Nucleus

Cytoplasm containing granules

5 µm

■ *Different types of blood cell*

The functions of blood

Blood circulates around the body constantly, and it takes about one minute for a blood cell to travel round the body when it is at rest. When the body is exercising, the rate of circulation will be much quicker.

Blood has several functions in the body:

■ To transport various materials such as oxygen and nutrients to body cells and waste products to the excretory organs.

■ To help to regulate body temperature.

■ To fight against disease-causing organisms.

Blood vessels

Blood has to travel to all parts of the body, so it needs an efficient transport system in which to do this. This transport system is a bit like a road system with large, medium and small vessels much like motorways, A roads and B roads.

There are three different types of vessels:

■ arteries

■ veins

■ capillaries.

55% Plasma

45% Blood cells

■ *The composition of blood*

Over to you

Carry out some research to find out which materials are transported in the blood and how they are used.

Arteries are the vessels that carry oxygenated blood away from the heart, except for the pulmonary artery which carries deoxygenated blood from the heart to the lungs. Arteries vary in diameter and smaller ones are known as arterioles.

Veins carry deoxygenated blood to the heart except for the pulmonary vein, which carries oxygenated blood from the lungs to the heart. Smaller veins are known as venules.

Differences between arteries and veins

Arteries	Veins
Carry blood away from the heart	Carry blood towards the heart
Carry blood with a high oxygen content (except pulmonary artery)	Carry blood with a low oxygen content (except pulmonary vein)
Walls are thick, muscular and elastic	Walls are thin (little muscle)
Valves are absent (except at the base of large arteries leaving the heart)	Valves are present
Blood flows rapidly under high pressure	Blood flows slowly under low pressure
Blood flows in pulses	Blood flows smoothly
Tend to lie deeper in the body	Tend to lie near the body's surface

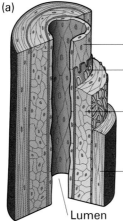
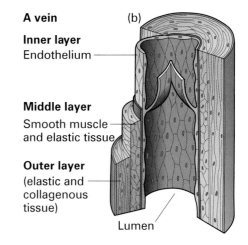

(a) An artery — Inner layer Endothelium, Elastic tissue; Middle layer Smooth muscle and elastic tissue; Outer layer (elastic and collagenous tissue); Lumen. A vein (b) — Inner layer Endothelium; Middle layer Smooth muscle and elastic tissue; Outer layer (elastic and collagenous tissue); Lumen.

■ *The structure of an artery and a vein*

Capillaries are tiny blood vessels that lie in the tissues of the body. Their walls are only one cell thick and they are so small in diameter that only one red blood cell at a time can pass through them. The thinness of the walls means that it is easy for oxygen and nutrients to move out of them and waste products such as carbon dioxide to move into them. The capillaries are the connecting network between the arterioles and venules.

The respiratory system

The respiratory system's main function is to maintain the supply of oxygen and to remove carbon dioxide from the body.

Air is breathed in through the mouth and nose where it is warmed and moistened. The nose is lined with cilia – small hair-like structures that help to filter the air and prevent the entry of dust and debris into the respiratory organs. The air passes down the throat and through the larynx and trachea. The trachea branches into two bronchi, and one bronchus goes to each lung, branching into bronchioles, which are smaller air passageways. The bronchioles end in sacs called alveoli.

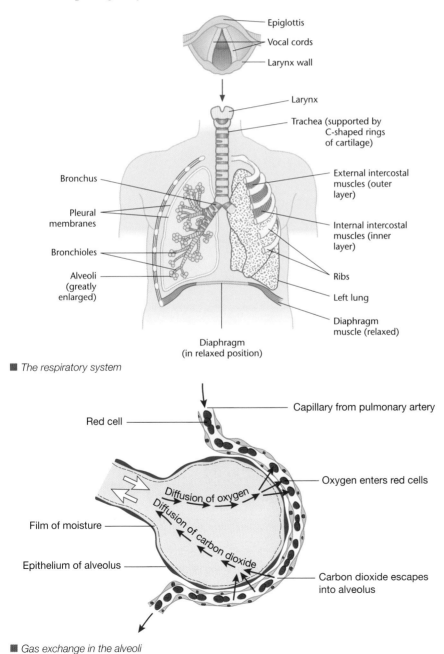

■ *The respiratory system*

■ *Gas exchange in the alveoli*

Gaseous exchange takes place by a process of diffusion. In the alveoli there is a high concentration of oxygen and a low concentration of carbon dioxide. In the capillaries there is a high concentration of carbon dioxide and a low concentration of oxygen. The process of diffusion allows the oxygen to move out of the alveoli and into the capillaries and the carbon dioxide to move out of the capillaries into the alveoli. In addition, the lungs work as organs of excretion, as water vapour is also expired with the carbon dioxide.

The nervous system

The nervous system is responsible for receiving information from the environment. It then coordinates actions in response to the information that it receives. It is made up of the brain, the spinal cord and nerves.

The brain

The brain is the control centre for the body. It receives impulses from sense receptors in the body and interprets them, and sends impulses to cause muscles and glands to work.

The brain coordinates the body's movements, so allowing it to function efficiently. It controls feeding, sleeping, temperature regulation and salt and water balance in the body. It stores information in the memory and deals with emotional and intellectual processes.

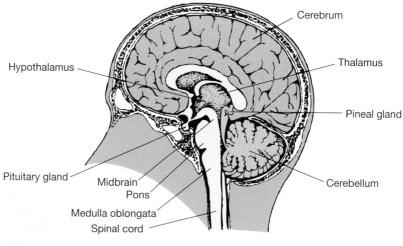

■ The brain

There are four main parts of the brain:

- The brain stem or medulla oblongata controls involuntary reflex actions.

- The cerebellum maintains posture and coordinates movement. It receives messages from the cerebrum and muscles and joints.

- The diencephalon controls homeostatic mechanisms and the autonomic nervous system. It contains the thalamus and the hypothalamus.

- The cerebrum is the largest part of the brain and a major part of the forebrain. It is divided into three areas that control movement, interpret sensory impulses and control thought, memory, emotions and personality traits.

The spinal cord

The spinal cord is a long, cylindrical organ that lies in the spinal canal inside the vertebrae. The spinal canal has a central cavity containing cerebrospinal fluid. Thirty-one pairs of nerves branch off the cord to provide the nerve supply to the whole of the body.

Nerves

Nerves are made up of nerve cells or neurones. They vary in structure according to where they are or what they do. All cells have a cell body containing the nucleus, which is usually located in the brain or spinal cord.

Neurones have:

- a cell body with a nucleus
- an axon – a fibre taking an impulse away from the cell body
- a dendron – a fibre taking an impulse towards the cell body.

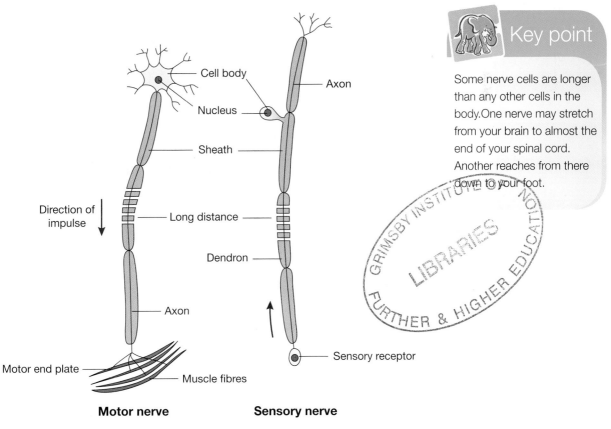

■ *Different types of nerve*

Key point

Some nerve cells are longer than any other cells in the body. One nerve may stretch from your brain to almost the end of your spinal cord. Another reaches from there down to your foot.

Sensory neurones carry nerve impulses to the brain or spinal cord from other parts of the body. At the end of the long fibre there is a sensory receptor that can detect a stimulus, for example touching the skin.

Motor neurones carry nerve impulses from the brain or spinal cord to parts of the body – a muscle or gland will be stimulated to act by the impulses. There are motor nerve endings in the muscle or gland. The brain and/or spinal cord link impulses coming from the sensory nerve cells with relevant motor nerve cells. The body then takes necessary action in response to the signal from the sensory neurones.

Groups of nerve fibres running to the same parts of the body are grouped together in bundles and held together by connective tissues. These are nerves – they make up the peripheral nervous system, brain, spinal cord and the central nervous system.

 Key point

Ouch! Think about what happens when you burn yourself on a hot dish from the oven or prick your finger with a pin. What happens? You drop the hot dish or pull your hand away very quickly. How is your nervous system working to make this happen?

When you burn or prick yourself, receptors in the skin send messages to a sensory neurone, which takes a message to the spinal cord. Here the message is passed to a motor neurone, and it travels down it to a muscle in the hand. This causes you to pull your hand away from the danger. This is called the reflex arc and is a reflex action. You do not use your brain because your reaction is completely automatic.

The autonomic nervous system

The autonomic nervous system is part of the peripheral nervous system and works without us being aware of it. It is responsible for many processes that happen all the time such as maintaining the stability of the body (homeostasis) and blood pressure, which are described later in the unit. There are two parts to the autonomic nervous system – the sympathetic and parasympathetic nervous systems. In an emergency, the sympathetic nervous system takes over, influenced by the action of the hormone adrenaline. The result of this is raised heartbeat and breathing, sweating and a dry mouth. This is known as the 'fright, flight or fight' response.

The parasympathetic nervous system

The parasympathetic nervous system is the system that is in control most of the time when we are relaxed. It slows heart rate and breathing and helps us to digest food after a meal.

The endocrine system

The endocrine system is a system that produces chemical messengers called hormones. When there is a change in a function or structure of

the body, hormones are released by glands directly into the bloodstream
to counteract the change.

Functions of the endocrine system		
GLAND/ORGAN	**HORMONE**	**PROCESS**
Pituitary gland	Trophic hormones Somatotrophic hormone (growth hormone or GH) Prolactin Luteinising hormone (LH) Follicle stimulating hormone (FSH)	Stimulates production of hormones from other glands Growth of bones Milk production Controls menstrual cycle, triggers ovulation, controls sex hormones from testes and assists in sperm production
Hypothalamus	Hormone releasing factors Anti-diuretic hormones (ADH) stored in the pituitary gland Oxytocin (stored in the pituitary gland)	Stimulates pituitary gland to produce hormones Control of water balance Helps uterine contraction in childbirth and stimulates the let-down reflex for breastfeeding
Thyroid	Thyroxine	Controls rate of body processes and heat production and energy production from food, controls the growth and development of the nervous system
Parathyroid glands	Parathormone or parathyroid hormone	Controls the amount of calcium in blood and hormones
Pancreas	Insulin	Controls blood sugar
Adrenal glands	Adrenaline Cortisol Aldosterone Androgens	Controls emergency action, response to stress Stress control. Conversion of fats, proteins and carbohydrates to glucose Acts on the kidneys to control salt and water balance Stimulate male sex hormones and characteristics (beard growth, deepening of voice, muscle development)
Testes	Testosterone	Control of sperm, growth and development of male features at puberty, beard growth
Ovaries	Progesterone Oestrogen Placental hormones (pregnancy only)	Helps control normal progress of pregnancy. Interacts with FSH and LH and oestrogen to control the menstrual cycle Controls the development of female features at puberty. Interacts with FSH and LH and progesterone to control menstrual cycle Controls normal process of pregnancy. Oestrogen and progesterone start milk production
Stomach wall	Gastrin	Starts acid production by stomach
Small intestine	Enterogastrine Secretin	Turns off acid production by stomach Triggers release of digestive enzymes from pancreas

The pituitary gland is sometimes called the master gland because it controls the functions of the other glands that produce hormones, as well as producing its own hormones. The hypothalamus receives messages about changes in the body. It transmits the messages to the pituitary gland, which then sends messages to the relevant gland to secrete a hormone to counteract the change and bring it back to normal. An example of this is blood sugar control by the pancreas, which is explained later in the unit.

Adrenaline – the 'fright, fight or flight' hormone

Adrenaline is a hormone that is secreted by the adrenal glands situated above the kidneys in times of emergency or stress. It prepares the body for action. People often experience 'butterflies in their tummy' when adrenaline is secreted. Other symptoms include a dry mouth, pale face, a rapid heart rate and clammy hands. Adrenaline produces the following specific reactions in the body:

- Stored glycogen in the liver is converted into glucose to provide energy.
- The rate and depth of breathing increases.
- Blood is diverted from the blood vessels to the brain and muscles.
- The heart rate increases.

Once the emergency is over, adrenaline stops being secreted and the body returns to normal.

The digestive system

The digestive system begins at the mouth and ends at the anus, and is made up of several organs that are involved in the digestion and absorption of food.

The process of digestion includes the following processes:

- Ingestion – the taking in of food via the mouth.
- Digestion – the mechanical and chemical break down of food by chewing and enzymes.
- Absorption – food passes through the intestinal wall into the blood system.
- Elimination – the removal of undigested waste.

Ingestion

Food is taken in by the mouth where it is chewed and mixed with saliva, which moistens the food and starts the process of digesting starch. The saliva contains amylase, the enzyme that breaks carbohydrates down into glucose. The teeth cut and grind the food into small enough particles that can be swallowed.

Over to you

Produce a poster of the human body showing the position of the endocrine glands and which hormones they secrete. Make sure that you include the hypothalamus and its functions on your poster.

Over to you

Carry out some research into the mouth and teeth to find out what structures are used in the digestion of food. You should be able to identify and describe the teeth, salivary glands and taste buds.

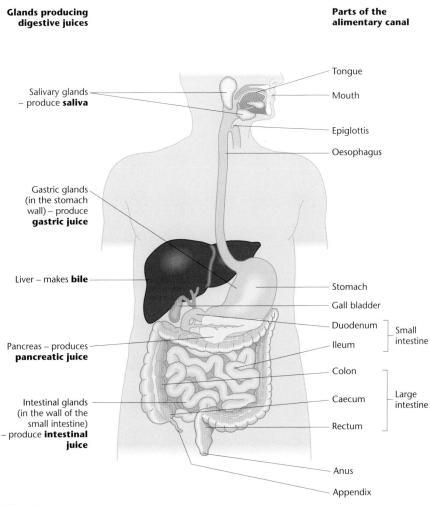

Glands producing digestive juices

Salivary glands – produce **saliva**

Gastric glands (in the stomach wall) – produce **gastric juice**

Liver – makes **bile**

Pancreas – produces **pancreatic juice**

Intestinal glands (in the wall of the small intestine) – produce **intestinal juice**

Parts of the alimentary canal

Tongue

Mouth

Epiglottis

Oesophagus

Stomach

Gall bladder

Duodenum ⎫
Ileum ⎬ Small intestine

Colon ⎫
Caecum ⎬ Large intestine
Rectum ⎭

Anus

Appendix

■ *The digestive system*

As the food moves to the back of the mouth, it is swallowed and moves down the oesophagus to the stomach. The oesophagus is a tube about 30 cm long which transports the food to the stomach. This does not just happen as a result of gravity. The muscular walls along the whole length of the alimentary canal or digestive tract contract and relax, pushing the food onwards. This is known as peristalsis and it happens automatically all the time.

Digestion

When the food particles reach the stomach, further digestion takes place chemically. The walls of the stomach produce hydrochloric acid and gastric juice. Food stays in the stomach for about five hours and then the mixture of food and enzymes, known as chyme, moves into the small intestine where further digestion takes place. The walls of the small intestine secrete more enzymes to break down the food and pancreatic juice from the pancreas also flows into the small intestine. This, too, is made up of digestive enzymes.

Enzymes used in the digestion of food		
	Enzyme	**What it does**
Mouth	Salivary amylase	Starts to break down carbohydrates
Stomach	Hydrochloric acid	Kills bacteria and converts pepinogen to pepsin
	Pepsin	Begins digestion of protein
	Rennin	Curdles milk
	Intrinsic factor	Helps body to absorb vitamin B12
Small intestine	*Pancreatic juice:*	
	Amylase	Converts starch to maltose
	Lipase	Converts fats to fatty acids
	Trypsin and chymotrypsin	Converts proteins to peptides
	Intestinal juice:	
	Maltase	Converts maltose to glucose
	Sucrase	Converts sucrose into glucose and fructose
	Lactase	Converts lactose into glucose and galactose
	Peptidases	Converts peptides into amino acids
From the liver	Bile	Emulsifies fats

As you can see from the table above, there are many enzymes that are used in the digestion of food. Ultimately, carbohydrates are broken down into glucose, proteins into amino acids and fats are **emulsified**.

Emulsify *To disperse the particles of one liquid evenly in another.*

Absorption and elimination

At this stage, the molecules are small enough to be absorbed through the gut wall and into the blood. Fats are absorbed into the lymphatic system and then into the blood. The process of digestion in the small intestine takes about four hours. After about seven to nine hours, the food that has not been digested moves into the large intestine. Water is absorbed into the body at this stage leaving behind faeces, a semi-solid mass that is eventually eliminated at the end of the digestive tract, the anus.

The excretory system

The body carries out chemical processes known as metabolism. During metabolism, waste is produced. This cannot be used and may be harmful to the body.

The waste consists of:

Over to you

Explain how a cheese sandwich made with wholemeal bread is digested and absorbed in the digestive tract. Make sure that you state which enzymes act on which foods to break them down.

- carbon dioxide – a product of respiration
- water – a product of respiration
- urea – a waste product of the break down of amino acids by the liver.

The excretory system is also known as the renal system. This is the system that is used to filter waste products from the blood. It consists of:

■ two kidneys – bean-shaped structures that lie either side of the vertebral column – which are about the size of a fist

■ two ureters – tubes about 3 mm in diameter and 25–30 cm long that carry urine from the kidneys to the bladder

■ a bladder – a muscular bag that collects urine

■ an urethra – a tube leading from the bladder to the outside of the body through which urine is expelled.

Each kidney is supplied with blood by a renal artery, which branches off the aorta, the main artery of the body. Filtered blood is returned to the vena cava, the main vein of the body via a renal vein.

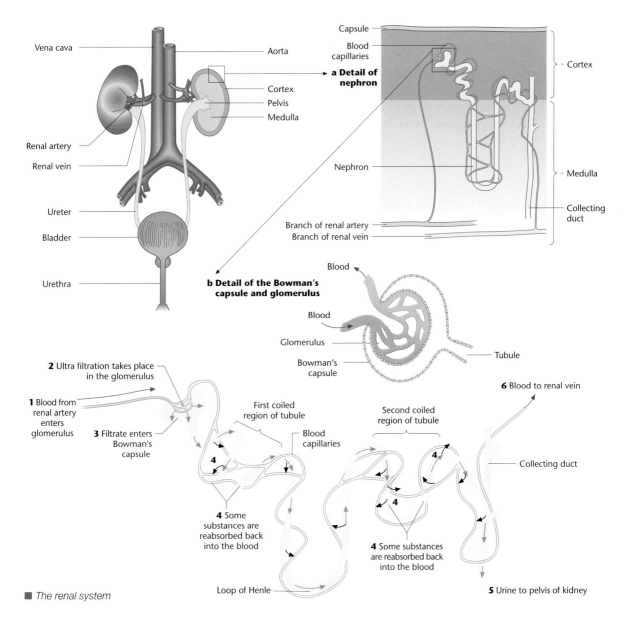

■ *The renal system*

The kidneys

The kidneys regulate:

- the water content of body fluids
- the chemical composition of body fluid (e.g. sodium chloride, potassium and calcium)
- the acid balance of the body.

They consist of three parts:

- the cortex
- the medulla
- the pelvis.

The cortex and medulla make the urine, which collects in the pelvis from where it flows into the ureters and onto the bladder.

The part of the kidney that filters and produces waste products is the nephron, and there are about one million of these in each kidney. Nephrons work by filtering the blood, reabsorbing the useful materials such as glucose, amino acids, salts and water and getting rid of the waste products such as urea, which is the waste product of the break down of proteins.

The water content of the body is controlled by antidiuretic hormone (ADH). If the blood is too concentrated and there is not enough water in the body, ADH is secreted, which stops the water being excreted. If the body is well hydrated and the blood is not too concentrated, then ADH is not secreted and excess water is excreted in the urine.

About 150–180 litres of fluid are processed by the kidneys every day and about 1.5 litres of urine are manufactured.

The reproductive system

Reproduction involves the manufacture of specialised sex cells called ova (*singular* ovum) in the female and sperm in the male. These cells are known as gametes, and when one of each join together, a cell called a zygote is formed. It contains a full set of chromosomes – half each from the mother and father. After 40 weeks of pregnancy, this zygote eventually becomes a baby.

The male reproductive system

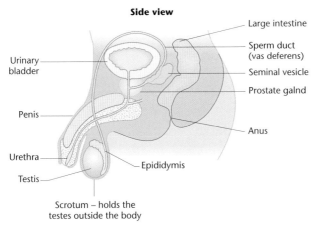

■ *The male reproductive system*

The male reproductive system is made up of the penis and the scrotum in which two testes are suspended. The testes produce sperm and testosterone, and the penis deposits the sperm inside the female's reproductive system. The testes are suspended in the scrotum, a sac that is outside the body because the best temperature for sperm production is slightly lower than human body temperature of 37°C. Nutrients are supplied to the sperm by the prostate gland and the seminal vesicles for use after the sperm have been released inside the female.

The seminiferous tubules are tiny tubes in which the sperm are formed. They are then stored in the epididymis, another tube, until they are used. If they are not used they are broken down.

During sexual arousal, the penis fills with blood and becomes erect. At the point of ejaculation, the epididymis, the vas deferens or sperm duct and the muscles at the base of the penis contract strongly and semen, a fluid containing the sperm, is released from the tip of the penis into the female's vagina. Men can continue to produce sperm well into old age.

The female reproductive system

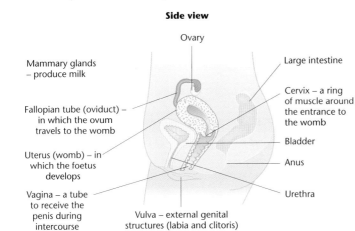

■ *The female reproductive system*

The female reproductive system is made up of two fallopian tubes and two ovaries, the uterus and cervix (neck of the uterus), and the vagina. The ovaries are suspended at the end of each fallopian tube and produce ova.

The fallopian tubes transport the released egg (ovum) to the uterus, and it is usually in these tubes that the egg is fertilised. The uterus is a small muscular sac that is situated behind the pubic bone, but in pregnancy it enlarges greatly to accommodate the baby being carried and nourished inside.

Whereas men are able to continue producing sperm during their lifetime, when a baby girl is born she already has all the eggs that she will produce. At puberty, when menstruation begins at the age of about 13, one egg will be produced every month until the menopause, which usually occurs around the age of 50 and is the end of a woman's ability to reproduce.

Characteristics of sperm and ova	
Sperm	**Ova (eggs)**
Very small – $\frac{1}{500}$ mm	Very large – $\frac{1}{10}$ mm
Nucleus contains half of the male's chromosomes	Nucleus contains half of the female's chromosomes
Cytoplasm contains lots of mitochondria to provide energy	Cytoplasm contains lots of nutrients for embryo development
Can move on their own	Cannot move on their own
Several hundred million produced every day from puberty onwards	Present at birth and produced about every four weeks from puberty to menopause
Each ejaculate contains 200–400 million	Only one released every four weeks

The menstrual cycle

The menstrual cycle is controlled by hormones, and is designed to prepare the uterus for a possible pregnancy. During the first five days or so of the cycle, a woman has a period. This is the shedding of the lining of the uterus. At the same time, hormone levels are changing. Follicle-stimulating hormone (FSH) is secreted by the pituitary gland and this stimulates the maturation of an egg in the ovary. Oestrogen is also secreted and this stimulates the uterus to start rebuilding its lining. High levels of oestrogen stop the production of FSH.

Over to you

Find out what oestrogen and progesterone are, why they are produced and what they do.

Luteinising hormone (LH) is also secreted due to the high levels of oestrogen, and this causes ovulation or the production of an egg in the ovary and the development of a corpus luteum (yellow body). The corpus luteum produces small amounts of oestrogen and larger amounts of progesterone. This is a message to the uterus that an egg or ovum is about to be released from the ovary. Progesterone also stops the production of FSH. If a fertilised egg has not arrived at the uterus by day 24 of the cycle, the corpus luteum starts to deteriorate, and oestrogen and progesterone production stops. Because they are no longer being produced, the lining of the uterus breaks down on about day 29 and the uterus lining is shed. The cycle then starts again with the production of FSH.

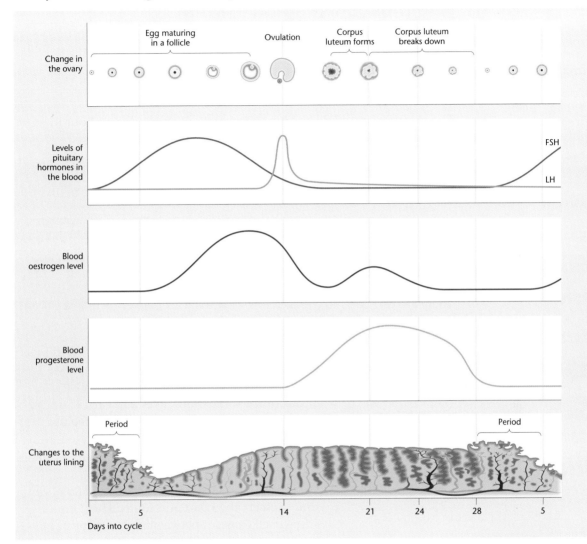

■ *Changes during the menstrual cycle*

What happens if the egg is fertilised?

If the egg is fertilised, the corpus luteum remains active for about three months, producing oestrogen and progesterone. By this stage of the pregnancy, the placenta has formed and starts to produce both hormones for the remainder of the pregnancy as well as nourishment to the embryo. The hormones ensure that the lining of the uterus continues to develop and stops production of FSH so that no more eggs are produced. High hormone levels also stimulate the development of breast tissue in preparation for milk production.

Over to you

Produce a table of hormones that are secreted during the menstrual cycle. Explain when in the cycle each is produced and what effects they have on the female reproductive system.

Just before birth, the pituitary gland is stimulated to produce prolactin and oxytocin, two more hormones. Prolactin triggers the production of breast milk and oxytocin triggers labour.

The musculoskeletal system

The musculoskeletal system is the body system that controls movement. The human body contains 206 bones and over 600 muscles.

The skeleton

The skeleton provides the bony framework of the body. Without it, humans would not have a shape. It has the following functions:

- To allow the body to move in conjunction with the muscles.
- To protect some of the vital organs of the body such as the brain and heart.
- To produce new blood cells in the bone marrow of some bones.
- To produce calcium, which helps with blood clotting and muscle contraction.

There are two parts to the skeleton – the axial and appendicular skeletons.

Axial skeleton
The axial skeleton consists of the skull, vertebrae and ribcage. The skull consists of 22 separate bones which are fused together to provide protection for the brain, eyes and ears. It sits on the vertebrae or backbone. The 33 vertebrae protect the spinal cord. They are separated from each other by pads of cartilage which act as shock absorbers. The back muscles attach to the vertebrae. The ribcage consists of 12 pairs of ribs and protects the heart and lungs. There are intercostal muscles between each rib and these are involved in breathing.

Appendicular skeleton
The appendicular skeleton consists of the bones of the arms and legs, the pectoral girdle that attaches the arms to the vertebrae and the pelvic girdle that connect the legs to the vertebrae. The pelvic girdle helps to protect the reproductive organs in the lower abdomen, and is strong enough to support the body's weight.

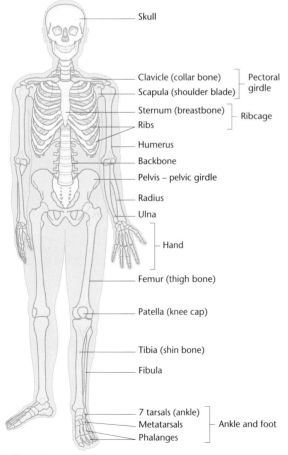

■ *The skeleton*

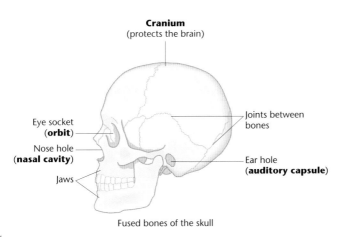

■ *The skull*

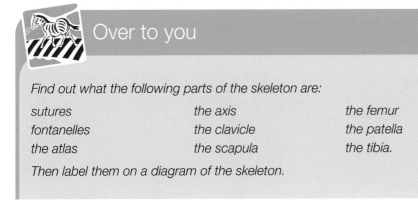

Over to you

Find out what the following parts of the skeleton are:

sutures	*the axis*	*the femur*
fontanelles	*the clavicle*	*the patella*
the atlas	*the scapula*	*the tibia.*

Then label them on a diagram of the skeleton.

Joints and ligaments

Joints are where two bones meet. There are three types of joint:

■ immoveable, which are fixed, such as the skull bones

■ slightly moveable such as the vertebrae of the spine

■ freely moveable such as the hip and knee joints.

Ligaments are strong elastic structures made of a protein substance. They hold bones together at a joint.

Bones cannot move by themselves. They need the action of muscles to allow movement.

Muscles

As well as different types of joints, the body contains different types of muscle. Cardiac muscle is specialised tissue found only in the heart (see the cardiovascular system on page 196), and smooth muscle is found in the intestines, uterus and blood vessels. The muscle tissue that is involved in the movement of the body is striped or striated muscle. This tissue is so-called because, when viewed under a microscope, it looks striped.

Over to you

Move different parts of your body and identify as many joints as you can. Then carry out some research to find out what types of joint they are and how they move.

Over to you

Describe with diagrams the structure of cardiac, smooth and skeletal muscle.

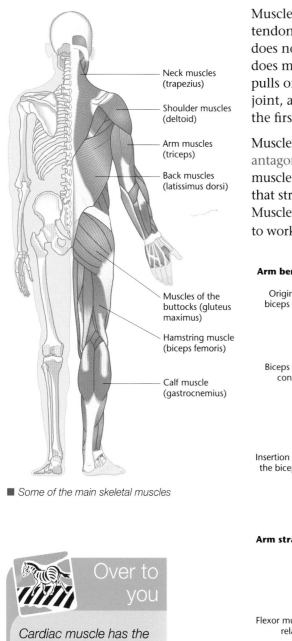

■ *Some of the main skeletal muscles*

Muscles are attached to bones by fibrous tissue called tendons. One end of the muscle is attached to a bone that does not move. The other end is attached to the bone that does move near the joint. When the muscle contracts, it pulls on the bone and moves the joint. To straighten the joint, another muscle on the other side of the bone contracts, the first muscle relaxes and the joint straightens again.

Muscles always work in pairs and they are known as antagonistic pairs because they work against each other. The muscle that bends the joint is the flexor muscle and the muscle that straightens it again is known as the extensor muscle. Muscles can only work by contracting, which is why they need to work in pairs. The diagram below shows how this works.

Arm bent (flexed)

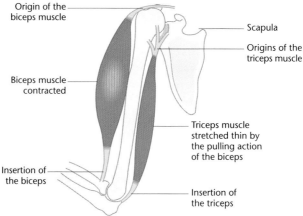

Arm straight (extended)

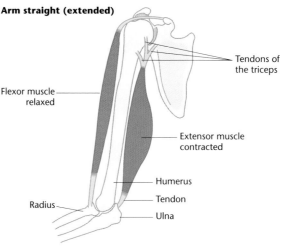

■ *The antagonistic movement of the arm muscles*

Over to you

Cardiac muscle has the property of myogenicity. Find out what this means.

Over to you

Identify the antagonistic pairs of muscles in the upper arm and thigh.

Muscles are always slightly contracted so that they are ready for movement. This is known as muscle tone.

Interrelationships between body systems

The cardiovascular system works with the respiratory system to ensure that all living cells receive a constant supply of oxygen – the cardiovascular system pumps the oxygen around the body and the respiratory system allows oxygen to enter the blood from the inhaled air.

The musculo-skeletal system works with the nervous system to allow movement of the body at the joints.

The cardiovasculor system works with the digestive system to ensure that all living cells are supplied with nutrients.

The digestive system works with the hormones insulin and glucagon from the endocrine system to maintain the supply of blood sugar to the living cells.

Homeostasis

Homeostasis is the process by which the body maintains a stable environment in which cells can function. Chemical processes in the body are controlled by enzymes. If there is a change in the body, these processes can stop or slow down. Homeostatic mechanisms make sure that this does not happen. Different body systems will work together to make sure that the body functions efficiently.

What is maintained by homeostatic mechanisms?

There are many activities that take place in the body that are controlled by homeostatic mechanisms. Some of these include:

- body temperature
- blood pressure
- oxygen supply
- blood glucose levels.

There are two types of feedback that take place in the body – negative feedback and positive feedback.

Negative feedback

Negative feedback is the mechanism used to detect and correct changes in the body:

1   Receptors in the nervous system detect a change in the body.
2   Impulses are sent to the control centre, often in the brain.
3   Impulses are sent from the effector to counteract the change.

Monitoring takes place to ensure that the change does not go too far and that the status quo is maintained.

Negative feedback works rather like the central heating system in your home. You set the thermostat to the desired temperature. If the temperature falls below this, the thermostat will detect it and send a

message to the boiler to switch on. The heating comes on and your home warms up. When the temperature set by the thermostat is reached, the heating switches off. The heating will switch on again when the temperature falls once more, and the whole process starts again.

Positive feedback

This is rare in humans because it pushes any change onwards and does not bring it back to a normal level. This eventually results in a 'bust' situation. An example of this is childbirth where the stimulation of uterine muscles continues and results in 'bust' – the birth of a baby. This is a relatively short-term mechanism.

Temperature control

Homeostatic control of temperature works rather like the central heating system described above.

Humans are able to maintain body temperature regardless of external temperatures. It is important that this happens because the core body temperature needs to be kept constant. This will happen at the expense of **peripheral** areas such as the skin and limbs.

In warm conditions, heat is lost to keep the core cool.

In cold conditions, heat is retained to keep the core warm.

> **Peripheral** *On the outer limits.*

Blood pressure control

Blood pressure is measured in millimetres of mercury (mm/Hg). A newborn baby's blood pressure is about 80/50 mmHg. During growth, the blood pressure rises steadily and a young adult's blood pressure will average about 120/80 mmHg. A normal blood pressure should be below 140/85mmHg. The higher figure (140) shows the systolic pressure, that is, the pressure in the vessels when the heart is beating. The lower figure (85) shows diastolic pressure, that is, the pressure in the vessels when the heart is at rest.

Certain factors can change blood pressure, and a rise in blood pressure is often due to stress. Baroreceptors or pressure receptors in major arteries such as the aorta and carotid arteries in the neck detect a rise in blood pressure and send a message to the medulla in the brain. Messages are sent out to slow the heart rate and widen the arteries, which lowers the blood pressure.

Oxygen control

The medulla of the brain contains clusters of neurones that represent the respiratory centre. One cluster is responsible for inspiration and one for expiration.

In normal breathing, the inspiratory centre is active for two seconds and the expiratory for three.

Over to you

How do you feel when you are in a warm room and wearing lots of clothing? What do you do?

How do you feel when you are in a cold room with insufficient clothing on? What do you do?

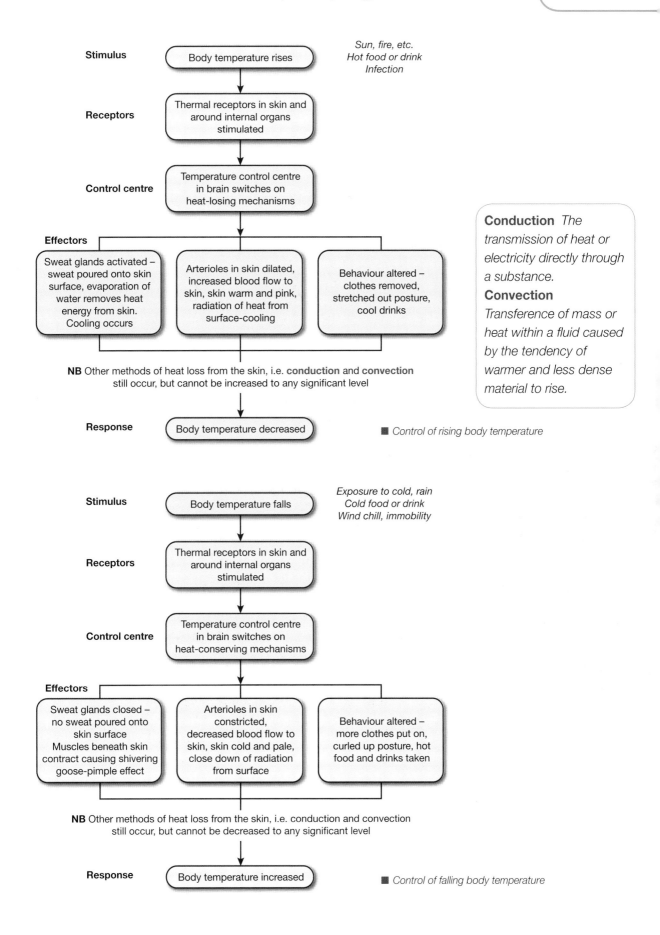

Stimulus   Body temperature rises   *Sun, fire, etc.*
Hot food or drink
Infection

Receptors   Thermal receptors in skin and
around internal organs
stimulated

Control centre   Temperature control centre
in brain switches on
heat-losing mechanisms

Effectors

Sweat glands activated –
sweat poured onto skin
surface, evaporation of
water removes heat
energy from skin.
Cooling occurs

Arterioles in skin dilated,
increased blood flow to
skin, skin warm and pink,
radiation of heat from
surface-cooling

Behaviour altered –
clothes removed,
stretched out posture,
cool drinks

Conduction *The
transmission of heat or
electricity directly through
a substance.*
Convection
*Transference of mass or
heat within a fluid caused
by the tendency of
warmer and less dense
material to rise.*

NB Other methods of heat loss from the skin, i.e. **conduction** and **convection**
still occur, but cannot be increased to any significant level

Response   Body temperature decreased   ■ *Control of rising body temperature*

Stimulus   Body temperature falls   *Exposure to cold, rain*
Cold food or drink
Wind chill, immobility

Receptors   Thermal receptors in skin and
around internal organs
stimulated

Control centre   Temperature control centre
in brain switches on
heat-conserving mechanisms

Effectors

Sweat glands closed –
no sweat poured onto
skin surface
Muscles beneath skin
contract causing shivering
goose-pimple effect

Arterioles in skin
constricted,
decreased blood flow to
skin, skin cold and pale,
close down of radiation
from surface

Behaviour altered –
more clothes put on,
curled up posture, hot
food and drinks taken

NB Other methods of heat loss from the skin, i.e. conduction and convection
still occur, but cannot be decreased to any significant level

Response   Body temperature increased   ■ *Control of falling body temperature*

Mechanism of respiration

This is the drawing in of oxygen – inspiration – and the pushing out of carbon dioxide – exhalation:

- Inspiration – the lungs expand, the ribs move upwards and outwards and the diaphragm is lowered.
- Exhalation – the lungs deflate, the ribs move downwards and inwards and the diaphragm is raised.

Above the medulla, in a region of the brain called the pons, there are two other regions concerned with respiration. The apneustic centre sends impulses to the inspiratory centre to change the depth of breathing, while the pneumotaxic centre stimulates the rate of breathing.

There are also other influences on the control of breathing. Chemoreceptors in the aortic arch and the carotid arteries are sensitive to the chemical changes in the blood, especially oxygen and carbon dioxide levels. If they detect a rise in carbon dioxide, then they stimulate the inspiratory centre to increase the rate and depth of breathing. A rise in carbon dioxide causes the acidity level of the blood to lower. When carbon dioxide levels fall, the chemoreceptors are not stimulated and breathing returns to normal.

Blood sugar control

We normally eat three meals a day to provide energy, but the cells need to be supplied constantly with glucose to maintain the supply at a steady rate. Therefore, there is a mechanism to ensure that the supply remains constant.

When we eat a meal or a snack containing carbohydrates, they are broken down into glucose and absorbed into the bloodstream. This means that the level of glucose in the blood rises. The rise in blood sugar is detected and the pancreas receives a message to secrete insulin, which allows the glucose to enter the cells. Once the blood glucose levels return to normal, the insulin is no longer secreted.

If, however, blood glucose levels fall very low, different cells in the pancreas are stimulated to secrete a hormone called glucagon. The glucagon causes glycogen which is stored in the liver to be converted into glucose and enter the bloodstream. Once blood glucose levels have been raised to normal, this mechanism switches off.

Over to you

How do you feel in the following situations?

1. *You are very hungry.*
2. *You are very full.*
3. *You have just eaten a meal or snack high in sugar.*

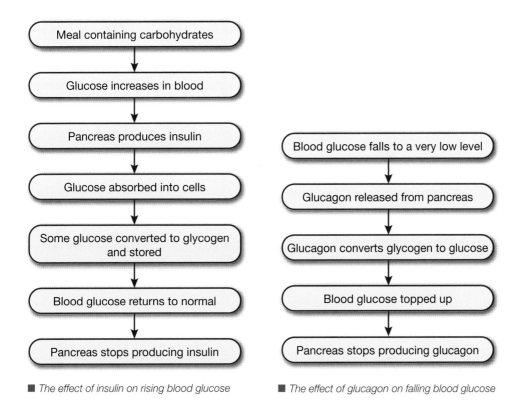

Meal containing carbohydrates

↓

Glucose increases in blood

↓

Pancreas produces insulin

↓

Glucose absorbed into cells

↓

Some glucose converted to glycogen and stored

↓

Blood glucose returns to normal

↓

Pancreas stops producing insulin

■ *The effect of insulin on rising blood glucose*

Blood glucose falls to a very low level

↓

Glucagon released from pancreas

↓

Glucagon converts glycogen to glucose

↓

Blood glucose topped up

↓

Pancreas stops producing glucagon

■ *The effect of glucagon on falling blood glucose*

Routine measurements and observations

Routine physiological measurements

Pulse rate

The pulse rate is a non-invasive measurement of the heart rate. It is often measured by medical or nursing staff as it can be a good indicator of how healthy you are. The rate, strength and rhythm are all important as they can also provide important information. The pulse is recorded in beats per minute (bpm).

Key point

The pulse can also be taken in the neck, in the groin, at the temple and the upper surface of the foot.

The pulse is usually taken where an artery crosses a bone, and the most common place to take the pulse is at the wrist just below the thumb. There are other places on the body where the pulse can be taken. A fast pulse rate can indicate fever, fright or bleeding, and a slow pulse rate can indicate heart problems, compression of the brain or the fact that a person is very fit and active.

Over to you

In pairs, practise taking each other's pulse. You will need to make sure that you find the right place on the wrist and that you use your middle finger to take it. Count the number of beats in 30 seconds and multiply your result by two to get the number of beats per minute.

Blood pressure

Key point

Yoga and massage can be used to help reduce high blood pressure.

Stroking pets such as cats and dogs have been proven to lower blood pressure.

Blood pressure is the pressure exerted by the blood on the walls of the blood vessels. The blood pressure is normally measured by a sphygmomanometer, which is battery or electrically operated. Sphygmomanometers used to contain mercury but EU regulations now state that these should be phased out as mercury is considered to be a dangerous substance. A cuff containing a rubber bladder is placed round the upper arm at the level of the heart and is inflated, which blocks off blood supply to the arm. A valve is then slowly released and the cuff deflates, allowing blood to flow again. Once the machine has recorded the data, the results are shown on a display screen. Often the pulse will be displayed as well.

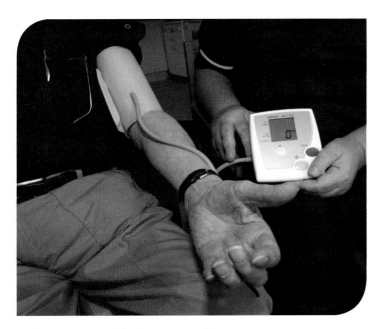

■ *A battery-operated blood pressure machine*

Real Life Care

Under pressure

Alan Johnston is 58 years old and is managing director of a large manufacturing company. He travels to the company's head office in the USA about once a month for meetings. He finds his job very stressful and says his wife often complains that he falls asleep in front of the television on the rare evenings that he is not sitting in front of his laptop. His days are very busy with many business lunches and he regularly eats three-course meals at lunchtime. These tend to be rich – high in fat, salt and sugar, and often include at least one whisky before and two to three glasses of wine with the meal. He says he has no time to take exercise due to his busy lifestyle and he smokes about 15–20 cigarettes a day and at least two cigars a week.

Last week, Alan went to see his GP for a general check-up and his blood pressure was 180/130 mmHg. His GP has put him on drugs to help bring this down and has told him that he has to take steps to change his lifestyle.

1 Identify the factors that may have contributed to Alan's high blood pressure.

2 Even though you do not have much medical experience, what do you think Alan could do to change his lifestyle to help him bring down his blood pressure?

3 Why is having high blood pressure bad for you?

Breathing rate

The simplest and most non-invasive method of measuring breathing rate is to watch a service user's chest rise and fall and count the number of times it happens in a minute, or half a minute and double it. This can be done at the same time as the pulse is being taken as the service user is usually unaware and does not change their breathing rate. If they are aware of what you are doing, the breathing rate can change. As with the pulse, staff should observe the type and rhythm of breathing, as this can often indicate an underlying problem.

Peak flow

Peak flow measurement is a method of measuring lung function. It measures the speed of an exhalation and gives an indication of the width of the bronchial tubes. It is used to monitor lung function, particularly in asthmatics.

Body temperature

Body temperature needs to be kept within quite narrow limits to enable the body to function properly. However, during the day people can experience variations in temperature, and women experience a rise in temperature during ovulation. Temperature is taken with a thermometer. Like sphygmomanometers, clinical thermometers used to contain mercury, but this type is now being phased out.

There are several different types of thermometer:

- Ear thermometers take a temperature measurement by an infra-red beam in the ear canal but are not always very accurate.

- LCD strip thermometers can be placed on the forehead and the liquid crystal display strip will show the temperature. These thermometers are not very accurate but will show a rise in temperature.

- Electronic digital thermometers work the same way as mercury thermometers, but they have a digital readout to display the temperature. These are probably the most accurate but will vary according to the manufacturer.

Blood glucose levels

Non-invasive *Not involving the introduction of instruments or other objects into the body.*

Blood glucose levels are most important for diabetics. Diabetes is a condition in which the pancreas does not produce enough insulin, or the body is resistant to the insulin that is produced and cannot use it efficiently. Most diabetics have their own blood glucose monitor and record their results themselves. A finger stick test is used whereby a strip is placed in the machine and a drop of blood is dripped onto it. The machine then displays the result. The latest machines allow blood glucose results to be taken without needing to pierce the skin, which makes the procedure **non-invasive**.

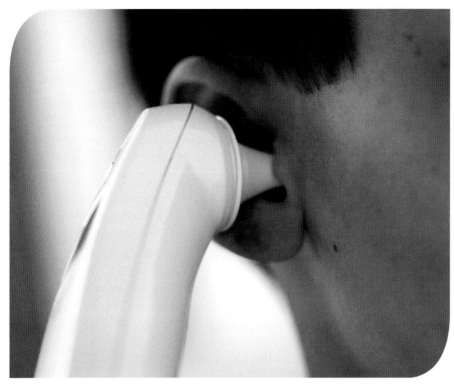

■ *An ear thermometer*

Over to you

Obtain some different types of thermometer and try them out with a partner. Try using them after you have had hot and cold drinks to see if there is a difference. Which type of thermometer do you think was easiest to use and the most accurate?

Points to consider

Reasons for measuring and monitoring

When people are feeling ill or are admitted to a hospital or care establishment, it may not always be clear what is wrong with them. Taking a full medical history, including a range of measurements, will help doctors to diagnose and treat any condition that is present. The measurements taken will help to establish which are within normal ranges and which are higher or lower than those expected. Taking a set of baseline observations, as they are called, will also help to establish the normal

Expected range of measurements	
Physiological measurement	**Range of measurement**
Pulse	60–80 beats per minute
Blood pressure	110/75 mmHg (young person); 140/90 mmHg (older person)
Breathing rate	8–17 breaths per minute
Peak flow	500–700 litres per minute (men); 380–500 litres per minute (women)
Body temperature	36.5–37.2°C
Blood glucose level	5–8 mmol glucose per litre of blood

measurements for an individual. This is important because what is normal for one person may not be normal for another. Doctors can use the results to decide the most suitable form of treatment for the individual.

Over to you

Discuss why it is important to ensure accuracy when taking measurements. What could be the consequences of inaccuracy?

Importance of accuracy

It is very important that all measurements are taken accurately. The equipment used must be in good working order and maintained regularly. Batteries should be checked to ensure that they have not run down. Inaccurate data could lead to delays in correct diagnosis and treatment for the service user.

Results must also be recorded accurately on the correct paperwork so that any member of the team treating a service user can quickly and easily see the person's condition and any improvement or deterioration.

Repeated measurements

Some measurements may have to be repeated at regular intervals to ensure that no problems are developing. For example, it is normal practice to take the service user's temperature hourly while they are having a blood transfusion because a raised temperature is often one of the first signs of a reaction to the blood being given.

It is also usual for a peak flow measurement to be taken three times and the average taken of the three readings. As far as possible, the same equipment should be used because there may be differences in the results that different pieces of equipment give.

Reasons why measurements may be inaccurate

There are several reasons why measurements may be inaccurate, including the use of different equipment to take measurements from one person, malfunctioning of equipment and human error, such as counting breathing rate or pulse incorrectly. Different types of equipment can produce varying degrees of accuracy, for example an LCD strip thermometer will not be as accurate as a digital thermometer.

There could be several other reasons why measurements may not be accurate. If a client has had a hot or cold drink immediately before a temperature is taken, this may provide a false reading. Taking a pulse after a heavy meal may not be the most appropriate time as this can cause the pulse rate to increase. It is advisable to leave a client to sit quietly for a few minutes before taking their blood pressure because some people find having their blood pressure taken to be quite stressful, and this can cause the blood pressure to rise further.

Observations

One very important aspect of care work is observation. A lot of information can be gained by simply observing a service user. This can be very important and is of relevance if a care worker regularly works with the same service users. The better you get to know your clients, the better able you will be to observe small changes in their condition.

Skin colour and texture

The colour and texture of skin can provide care workers with a lot of information, as shown in the table below.

What skin colour and texture can show	
Symptom	**Possible reason**
Pale clammy skin	Shock or haemorrhage
A blue tinge especially round the lips or the finger nails	Lack of oxygen, possible heart problems
Flushed pink skin	Fever
Dry, flaky, itchy skin	Eczema, dermatitis
Reddened skin with silvery, scaly patches	Psoriasis
Congested skin with spots and blackheads	Acne

Abnormal breathing rates and rhythms

Many medical conditions that affect the blood or the lungs can increase the breathing rate and may cause breathlessness. It is important to listen and observe as you take other routine measurements, as you may hear wheezing, bubbling, gasping or grunting.

Examples of conditions that may produce abnormal breathing rates are:

- anaemia
- asthma
- damage to the brain
- fractured ribs
- heart problems
- pneumonia
- bronchitis
- emphysema.

Coughing and the expulsion of sputum

The two basic types of cough are chesty and dry. Chesty coughs usually produce phlegm or sputum. A dry cough is irritating but does not produce sputum. Coughing is a method of removing sputum from the respiratory system. Chesty coughs can be productive or non-productive. In both, mucous or sputum is present, but a person with a productive cough will be able to move some of it whereas in a person with a non-productive cough the sputum will not be moved.

Coughing can be a symptom of different disorders or diseases. Some coughs are temporary and accompany a cold, but others are longer lasting and may produce sputum.

Over to you

Find out the symptoms of the following:

- *vitiligo*
- *melanoma*
- *basal cell carcinoma.*

Over to you

Research the diseases and disorders listed above and find out their signs and symptoms, especially how they affect breathing rate and rhythm. Make a table of your findings.

Thick green or yellowish sputum is often a sign of a chest infection such as bronchitis or pneumonia.

Blood in the sputum can indicate tuberculosis.

Health and safety

Hazards, risk, correct use of equipment and infection control

If the equipment being used is electrically operated, care should be taken to ensure the safety of clients. Care workers must check all monitoring devices for faulty wires, malfunction and loose or faulty plugs and sockets. If a piece of equipment is faulty, it should be labelled, reported immediately, both verbally and in writing – some establishments may have special forms or a book for this. It must be taken out of use and repaired by the appropriate people. Most pieces of equipment have instruction booklets and these should be used only for that specific piece of equipment.

Clinical thermometers must be sterilised in an antiseptic solution before use. Thermometers should never be washed in hot water as this can cause them to break. Ear thermometers should always be used with disposable probe covers to prevent the risk of infection.

Peak flow meters should be replaced approximately every two years to ensure accuracy of measurement. Ideally, clients should have their own meter to use, but if not, the mouthpieces should be disinfected after use or disposable mouthpieces should be used.

There are a few risks associated with measuring body functions – the main direct risk to service users other than those mentioned above is when taking peak flow. Forced exhalations into the meter may cause some clients to experience an asthmatic attack.

Hand washing is one of the most important and easy ways to minimise the possibility of cross-infection. An explanation of how to wash hands and when particularly to wash them is given in Unit 2 Individual Needs within the Health and Social Care Sectors, page 87.

Legislation and regulations

In the UK, the Health & Safety Executive (HSE) is the government body responsible for enforcing legislation and providing guidance on health and safety in the workplace.

Health and Safety at Work Act 1974

The Health and Safety at Work Act 1974 is the main piece of legislation that provides the legal framework for maintaining health and safety in workplaces. It is like an umbrella under which there are many other regulations designed to cover particular areas of risk.

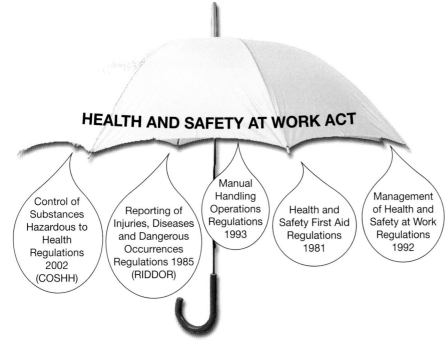

HEALTH AND SAFETY AT WORK ACT

Control of Substances Hazardous to Health Regulations 2002 (COSHH)

Reporting of Injuries, Diseases and Dangerous Occurrences Regulations 1985 (RIDDOR)

Manual Handling Operations Regulations 1993

Health and Safety First Aid Regulations 1981

Management of Health and Safety at Work Regulations 1992

■ *The Health and Safety at Work Act is like an umbrella*

The Act requires all workplaces where there are five workers or more to have a written health and safety policy. Employers and employees both have duties under the Act, as shown in the table below.

Employers' and employees' duties under the Health and Safety at Work Act	
Employers' duties	**Employees' duties**
Employers must ensure that their employees know about the following: ■ carrying out the job without risk and in a safe way ■ any risks that may affect the employee ■ how risks have been minimised ■ how to get first-aid treatment ■ action to be taken in an emergency Employers must provide the following free of charge: ■ protective clothing and equipment ■ safety training	Employees must: ■ protect themselves as much as possible ■ use equipment provided for its intended purpose ■ carry out tasks with proper training in a safe manner ■ report any safety hazards ■ cooperate with employers on safety issues ■ inform someone if an accident occurs

In a care setting, the Act would apply to:

■ infection control

■ correct lifting techniques

■ good hygiene in food preparation areas

■ observations and measurements

■ disposal of clinical waste

■ proper heating, lighting and ventilation.

Control of Substances Hazardous to Health Regulations (COSHH) (2002)

The COSHH Regulations cover all the substances used in your workplace. This includes everything from cleaning fluids to dangerous drugs. The regulations apply also to any caustic or corrosive substances and gases or substances that could potentially release dangerous fumes. (There is more about this in Unit 2 page 90.)

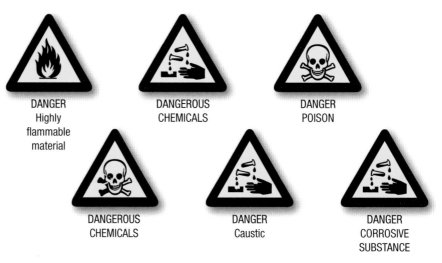

DANGER
Highly
flammable
material

DANGEROUS
CHEMICALS

DANGER
POISON

DANGEROUS
CHEMICALS

DANGER
Caustic

DANGER
CORROSIVE
SUBSTANCE

■ *The symbols that warn you of hazardous substances are always yellow*

Employers must meet basic requirements for hazardous substances used in the workplace. There must be a COSHH file listing all of the substances, which should:

■ identify what they are

■ say where each is kept

■ identify what the hazardous labels on the container mean

■ describe the effects of the substances

■ state the maximum amount of time it is safe to be exposed to them

■ describe how to deal with an emergency.

It is extremely important that all workers know where the COSHH file is kept in their work area and must follow any instructions given in it.

Management of Health and Safety at Work Regulations 1999

There are 30 regulations that relate to how the Health and Safety at Work Act must be interpreted and acted upon. The regulations include the following:

- Avoid risks and evaluate risks that cannot be avoided (carry out a risk assessment).

- Ensure that as far as possible risks do not exist.

- Adapt work to the individual and to the technical process.

- Replace dangerous items, processes, etc. with those that are less dangerous.

- Develop a **coherent**, overall prevention policy, covering technology, organisation of work, working conditions, etc.

- Give collective protective measures priority over individual protective measures.

- Give appropriate instructions to employees.

Coherent *Logical and consistent.*

Malfunctions in body systems

Sometimes body systems stop working as efficiently as they should and this could result in the onset of illnesses or diseases. In this section, you will learn about potential risk factors that could cause malfunctions, how people are cared for, and specific malfunctions and how care can be provided.

Potential risk factors

There are different risk factors that will contribute to how susceptible a person is to becoming ill. Risk factors that contribute to illness include:

- Lifestyle factors:
  - diet
  - exercise
  - stress
  - use of drugs
  - use of alcohol
  - smoking.

- Environmental factors:
  - quality of housing
  - air quality
  - water quality
  - noise pollution
  - employment
  - **socio-economic** status
  - safe neighbourhood.

- Inherited factors:
  - chromosome abnormalities such as Down's syndrome, haemophilia, cystic fibrosis, achondoplasia.

- Infections:
  - respiratory tract infections
  - pneumonia
  - urinary tract infections
  - influenza (flu).

Socio-economic
Relating to the interaction of social and economic factors.

Over to you

In four groups, investigate the four different types of risk factor outlined above. Find out what each is and how they could affect people's health. Make a poster of your findings.

Care needs

The care needs of a service user will vary according to what is wrong with them and how severe the illness is. The particular body systems involved in the illness also need to be considered.

Active support and encouragement

It is very important that service users are supported and encouraged to do as much as possible for themselves while they are ill. Maintaining independence and dignity can make a big difference to how quickly people recover from illness. It is generally of benefit to service users to be at least as fit as they were before their illness once they are better. Helping service users to maintain physical ability and encouraging them to be as independent as possible leads to feelings of high self-esteem and confidence.

Individual needs

Providing care to meet individual needs is an important part of the care process, and if a service user feels that their particular wishes are taken into account, it may well speed their recovery. Certain conditions such as diabetes require patients to have a diet that is high in complex carbohydrates such as potatoes, pasta and bread and not too much fat or simple sugars such as sweets and jams. If Crohn's disease is particularly troublesome, some people may find that they are helped by eating a low-fibre diet until the symptoms recede.

Monitoring the condition of someone who is ill will allow care workers to establish whether or not there is improvement. The importance of monitoring was discussed earlier in this unit.

Real Life Care

Fred's needs

Fred Johnson is 85 years old. His wife died two years ago. He lives in the three-bedroom house he and his wife bought when they married 55 years ago. He has three grown-up children and eight grandchildren. His elder son lives in Australia and only comes back to see him every two years. His younger son lives over 100 miles away and visits occasionally. His daughter Annie used to live about five miles away and tried to see him twice a week. However, six months ago, her husband was relocated to a new job 75 miles away and since then Annie has not been able to visit Fred more than once a month. Fred's GP has contacted Annie to say that Fred is not coping well with living alone. He is often

dirty, the house is cold and the GP suspects that he is not eating properly. He has developed a cough, which is not getting better, and the GP feels that he, the district nurse, Annie and Fred should get together to discuss possible options for Fred's care.

1 Make a list of Fred's needs, both short and long term.

2 How do you think the needs you have identified can be met?

3 Which health and social care professionals could be involved in meeting Fred's needs, and what could each do?

Over to you

Have you ever been in hospital or ill at home? Think about what was wrong with you and how you were looked after. In pairs, discuss what you think your needs were. Do you think that your needs were correctly identified and met? If not, how do you think they could have been met more fully or better? Do you think it would have made a difference to how quickly you got better?

Preventing hypothermia

Maintaining a warm environment will help to prevent hypothermia, particularly in babies, small children and elderly people. Babies lose a lot of heat from their heads, so it is recommended that they wear hats to prevent this. People aged 60 and over currently receive an annual Winter Fuel Payment to help them keep warm over the winter. Older people on a low income may also receive a Cold Weather Payment, which will help towards extra heating costs when the weather is particularly cold. There is further information on hypothermia later in the unit.

Preventing pressure sores

Pressure sores can easily occur in people who are not very active, and these can be very sore and difficult to heal. People who might be at risk, perhaps because they have had a severe stroke and are unable to move themselves, will need to be helped to move or turn over. This can be difficult if a service user is in pain and reluctant to move, but it will prevent further problems. There is no excuse for a service user to develop pressure sores if they are receiving good care.

Reducing the risk of thrombosis

A thrombosis is a clot that usually occurs in the deep veins of the legs. People who are especially at risk are those who are on prolonged bed rest or have had a long operation, most commonly on the legs or pelvic area. The blood flow slows down and causes a blood clot to form. Sometimes the clot can break off and travel to the lung and cause a pulmonary embolism, which is a very serious condition. A thrombosis can also occur in people who have taken long-haul flights, during pregnancy and in women who are on the contraceptive pill.

The importance of infection control

Infection control is a vital part of the care process because many people who are ill may already have weakened immune systems. All staff should observe Standard Precautions, which include frequent washing of hands, especially when working with more than one patient, the wearing of gloves and aprons to provide personal care and the correct disposal of waste and laundry. It is no good thinking you are helping service users to get better if you are not taking enough care to stop something else happening to them!

Malfunctions

Coronary heart disease (CHD)

The heart muscle needs a constant supply of oxygen, which is carried to it by the coronary arteries. In normal circumstances, the arteries are in good condition and the blood flows smoothly. However, if there is a build-up of fatty material known as plaque in the arteries, they become partially or eventually completely blocked. With partial blockage, people can suffer chest pains known as angina due to the lack of oxygen reaching the heart muscle. If a coronary artery becomes completely blocked, then the heart muscle beyond the blockage stops receiving oxygen and the heart muscle dies. This is known as a myocardial infarction or a heart attack.

Key point

'Coronary heart disease (CHD) is a preventable disease that kills more than 110,000 people in England every year. More than 1.4 million people suffer from angina and 275,000 people have a heart attack annually. CHD is the biggest killer in Britain. The government is committed to reducing the death rate from coronary heart disease and stroke and related diseases in people under 75 by at least 40 per cent (to 83.8 deaths per 100,000 population) by 2010.' (Department of Health)

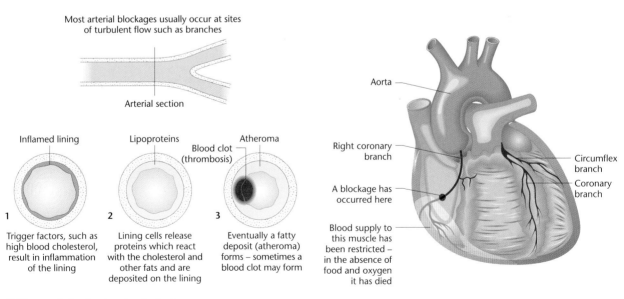

Most arterial blockages usually occur at sites of turbulent flow such as branches

Arterial section

Inflamed lining

1 Trigger factors, such as high blood cholesterol, result in inflammation of the lining

Lipoproteins

2 Lining cells release proteins which react with the cholesterol and other fats and are deposited on the lining

Blood clot (thrombosis)

Atheroma

3 Eventually a fatty deposit (atheroma) forms – sometimes a blood clot may form

Aorta

Right coronary branch

Circumflex branch

Coronary branch

A blockage has occurred here

Blood supply to this muscle has been restricted – in the absence of food and oxygen it has died

■ *The events leading to a heart attack*

Susceptibility *The ability to be influenced by something.*

Risk factors that will affect a person's **susceptibility** to heart disease include hereditary factors and lifestyle. Increasing age will have an effect, as will gender. Men are more likely to suffer from heart disease than women, although the risk to women increases after the menopause. If members of your family suffer or have suffered from heart disease, you will be more likely to suffer too. Diabetics are more at risk, as are some ethnic groups. Lack of exercise, being overweight or obese, high blood pressure, eating too many foods high in saturated fat, smoking and a high level of stress in everyday life all contribute to coronary heart disease. However, people who drink alcohol in moderation may be less at risk.

People who suffer from angina or have had a heart attack are advised to make changes to their lifestyle. Recommendations are to eat a healthy diet, including at least two to three oily fish meals per week, to prevent or reduce high blood pressure and cholesterol, and to maintain a healthy weight. Stopping smoking is also important, as is taking exercise. It is difficult to be precise about how much exercise should be taken and this should be advised by the patient's GP. Reduction of stress is also important.

Support and encouragement are important during the recovery period as people can often feel depressed about the changes to their lifestyle. If the person who has suffered the heart attack is young and has a young family, then a family approach to adopting a healthy lifestyle may help. In more severe cases of heart disease, people may require drugs, angioplasty (a procedure that clears the arteries of blockages) or even bypass surgery to replace coronary arteries with leg veins.

 Talking point

View 1: People who suffer from coronary heart disease caused by a poor diet and lifelong smoking should not be offered open heart surgery.

View 2: It does not matter how you became ill, you have a right to treatment – you have paid tax and national insurance all your working life.

Key point

The most common symptoms of heart disease are:

- chest pain or chest discomfort (angina), or pain in one or both arms, the left shoulder, neck, jaw or back
- shortness of breath.

The severity of symptoms varies widely. Symptoms may become more severe as the coronary arteries become narrower due to the build-up of fatty deposits (plaque).

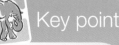 Key point

Every year over 150,000 people in the UK have a stroke, which is one person every three minutes (Stroke Association).

Stroke

A stroke is similar to a heart attack in that it can occur when a blood vessel in the brain becomes blocked or bursts. The part of the brain beyond the affected vessel cannot receive oxygen and dies. Depending on where in the brain this occurs, sufferers can experience loss of movement in the limbs and speech difficulties.

Risk factors include high blood pressure, smoking, heart disease and diabetes. People who have had a stroke or wish to avoid having one can make changes to reduce the risks. High blood pressure can be controlled by eating a healthy diet and particularly by reducing the amount of salt in the diet. Current recommendations are that the diet should contain no more than 6 grams of salt per day. Checking food labels carefully can help service users to reduce their salt intake. Smoking must be stopped and heart disease should be managed with help from medical practitioners. Stroke can be a complication of diabetes, so this should also be managed.

Transient ischaemic attacks are small strokes that can last for a short time. These should be treated as they may be an indication of the possibility of a severe stroke occurring.

People who have suffered a stroke may feel confused and frightened by what has happened to them, particularly if the stroke has affected their ability to communicate and be understood. They should be encouraged to remain positive and should have speech or physiotherapy to help them regain speech and movement. This can be intensive and people may find it difficult to keep motivated, so it is vitally important to help maintain good morale during the recovery period. Treatment may also include drug therapy and removal of blood clots and blockages in arteries or in the brain.

Real Life Care

Angelique

Angelique Matthews is 72 and has always led a very active life. Five days ago, she experienced numbness in the right side of her body and became unable to speak. Luckily, her neighbour called in to see her just after it had happened and was able to call an ambulance immediately. Angelique is making good progress in hospital but is likely to remain there for another three to four weeks. She is slowly regaining some use in her right arm and leg, although she still has difficulty making herself understood when she tries to speak. The medical staff expect her to make a full recovery and live independently when she is well enough to be discharged, although she will need care and support in the community for a while. Angelique experiences some mood swings, and becomes particularly agitated when people do not understand what she is saying. Only last night for supper she asked for cauliflower cheese, but was given chicken soup. She could not feed herself and by the time the staff noticed, the soup was cold and she no longer wanted it.

1 Visit the website of the Stroke Association (for a link to this site, visit www.heinemann.co.uk/hotlinks and enter the express code 3322P) and download a copy of the leaflet 'When a stroke happens'. ✔

2 Considering the extent of the disabilities that Angelique has experienced, and referring to the leaflet, what care and treatment do you think would be suitable to assist her to regain movement and speech while she is still in hospital? ✔✔

3 Visit the website for Nottingham Rehab Supplies (to access this site, visit www.heinemann.co.uk/hotlinks and enter the express code 3322P) and look at the aids that the company produces for people with disabilities. Make a list of six aids that could be useful for Angelique when she goes home, and state why they might be useful. ✔✔✔

Key point

Common symptoms of stroke are:

- sudden numbness or weakness of the face, arm or leg, especially on one side of the body
- confusion with trouble speaking or understanding
- difficulty in seeing in one or both eyes
- dizziness, loss of balance or coordination
- sudden, severe headache with no known cause.

Key point

About 5.2 million adults and more than 1.1 million children in the UK suffer from asthma.

Over to you

Find out how many people in your group suffer from asthma, what the triggers and symptoms are for them and what they do to relieve it.

Asthma

Asthma is a condition that affects the airways of the lungs. It usually happens because of an allergy and this causes the airways to become narrower as the muscles around their walls tighten. It is hard to breathe and sticky phlegm is produced. Symptoms can include coughing, wheezing, shortness of breath and tightness in the chest.

Infections and environmental factors are the main risk factors relating to asthma. Common triggers include infections, allergies to pollen, animals, house dust mites, irritants such as tobacco smoke, fumes and cold air and exercise.

Asthma treatment includes relievers and preventers. Relievers are used to relieve symptoms and relax the muscles surrounding the airways, which makes it easier to breathe. These inhalers are usually blue in colour. If asthma symptoms occur very often, for example daily or three to four times in a week in children, a preventer may also be prescribed. Preventers are used to help to control swelling and inflammation in the airways, and stop them from being so sensitive to triggers. Preventers generally build up over time, so it is important to take them regularly as prescribed. Preventers are usually brown, red or orange. The difference in colour between relievers and preventers helps to prevent confusion about which one to use.

Emphysema

Emphysema is a chronic lung condition which causes difficulty in breathing. It is caused by gradual damage to the lung structure. The alveoli gradually lose their elasticity and it becomes very difficult to exhale. The body does not receive enough oxygen and the sufferer is unable to breathe out carbon dioxide. Sufferers are constantly battling to breathe and get tired very quickly.

Risk factors for emphysema are cigarette smoking and living in an environment of high air pollution. It is therefore more common in urban than rural areas and among people who work in dusty environments. Most commonly, sufferers are men between the ages of 50 and 70.

Emphysema sufferers should stop smoking and may need to use oxygen frequently to help with their breathing. Infections, especially of the respiratory system, should be treated promptly with antibiotics to prevent the additional problem of bronchitis.

Chronic bronchitis

Bronchitis is the inflammation of the bronchioles of the lungs. Bronchitis can be acute and gets better relatively quickly, but chronic bronchitis will not get better although some of the symptoms can be relieved. Continued coughing will produce mucous or phlegm and eventually the bronchioles will become scarred, which makes them floppy and narrower. This results in shortness of breath and difficulty walking or taking any physical activity. Additional symptoms may include frequent infections of the respiratory tract, swelling of the ankles, feet and legs and blue tinged lips from lack of oxygen. Chronic bronchitis and emphysema can occur together.

The risk factors associated with chronic bronchitis are smoking and long-term exposure to smoke, air pollution and some occupations like coal mining and textiles manufacture. Allergies can also cause chronic bronchitis.

Sufferers should be advised to stop smoking immediately and drugs to help widen the airways can be prescribed. If the cause is infection, antibiotics should also be prescribed. Weight loss can be beneficial as people who are overweight or obese are making their lungs do extra work. Gentle exercise to increase the muscle power of the diaphragm, chest muscles, arms and legs may help to relieve symptoms.

As with many long-term illnesses, both emphysema and chronic bronchitis can cause depression, as people are much less able to carry on with the activities of daily living due to shortness of breath. It is therefore important to try to ensure that they remain as active as possible and perhaps to help them to find alternative activities that do not require a lot of physical activity. However, they should always be encouraged to be as active as possible when they feel physically able to.

Key point

An acute illness is usually short lasting and curable.

A chronic illness is usually long lasting and may be progressive or incurable.

Motor neurone disease (MND)

Motor neurone disease (MND) is a term used to describe a group of diseases that affect the motor neurones in the brain. The motor neurones are the nerve cells that transmit messages to the muscles. If the motor neurones start to lose function, the muscles start to weaken and waste. Often this starts in the limbs, but some people experience difficulty in speaking and swallowing. It is a progressive disease, and the cause is currently unknown. It normally affects people aged 50–70 years old and affects people differently. It does not cause deterioration in mental function. There is currently no cure for this disease, although there are treatments available to help relieve symptoms.

Key point

About two in 100,000 people in the UK develop MND each year. There are about 6000 people in the UK with MND.

Key point

Probably the most famous MND sufferer in the UK is Professor Stephen Hawking, a very eminent scientist at Cambridge University, who wrote *A Brief History of Time*. Although he is almost completely paralysed and no longer able to talk, with the use of computer technology he continues to research, write and give lectures around the world. For more information about him, visit his website (you can access this site by going to www.heinemann.co.uk/hotlinks and entering the express code 3322P).

A team approach to help relieve the symptoms is important, with input from neurologists, specialist nurses, physiotherapists, occupational therapists, speech therapists and dieticians and counsellors. As with other progressive diseases, sufferers will need to be supported to help them to come to terms with increasing disability and there are various support groups that can help with this. The Motor Neurone Disease Association provides support and direct care to sufferers.

Hypothermia

Hypothermia occurs in cold conditions where the body temperature drops below 35°C. Although the body will try to conserve heat by shivering, restricting blood flow to the skin and releasing hormones to generate heat, in extreme weather conditions these mechanisms will not produce enough heat. If a person suffering from hypothermia is not treated, he or she will lose consciousness and may die.

The main risk factors are environmental, and people most likely to be affected are babies, small children and older people, who are less able to control their body temperature. People who are exposed to extreme weather conditions, such as mountaineers, are at risk. Older people may suffer from hypothermia due to their socio-economic status. If they are afraid that they will not be able to meet household bills, they may decide not to put on their heating in order to save money.

Key point

The symptoms of hypothermia:

- Mild hypothermia – shivering, grogginess and muddled thinking; breathing and pulse are normal.
- Moderate hypothermia – violent shivering or shivering which suddenly stops, inability to think and pay attention, slow, shallow breathing and slow, weak pulse.
- Severe hypothermia – shivering stops, loss of consciousness, little or no breathing, weak, irregular or non-existent pulse.

Diabetes

Diabetes mellitus is a condition in which the amount of glucose in the blood is too high because the body cannot use it properly.

Insulin is a hormone secreted by the pancreas that allows glucose to enter the cells to form energy. Undiagnosed or untreated diabetics suffer from excess thirst, frequent urination, extreme tiredness and weight loss, among other symptoms. Long-term there may be problems with kidneys, eyesight and blood vessels, which can cause problems with circulation to the legs and feet.

There are two main types of diabetes – Type 1 and Type 2. Type 1 diabetes is thought to be triggered by a virus, although there may be a genetic component. Type 2 diabetes is more likely to occur in people who are overweight and tends to run in families. It is also more common in people of Asian or African-Caribbean origin. The table below shows the main differences between the two types.

Differences between Type 1 and Type 2 diabetes	
Type 1 diabetes	**Type 2 diabetes**
Insulin dependent (IDDM) – injections of insulin needed	Non-insulin dependent (NIDDM) – usually treated by diet and exercise
Juvenile onset – first appears during childhood	Adult or mature onset, although children as young as 9 years have been diagnosed
No insulin at all is produced	Reduced level of insulin produced or sufferer resistant to insulin produced

As long as people manage their diabetes well, they should be able to lead normal lives. Maintaining optimum weight and regulating the amount of fat and sugar in the diet will help sufferers to remain healthy. Daily exercise can be an important factor also. Type 1 diabetics will always need to check their blood glucose levels daily and calculate their insulin needs accordingly. Some Type 2 diabetics can regulate their condition by diet alone, but others may need to take tablets or insulin. Some young people may need extra support to encourage them to manage the condition – it can be difficult for them to adjust to a change in lifestyle that makes them different from their friends. Diabetes UK is a charity that can help to support diabetics.

Over to you

Contact your local hospital and find out if a diabetic specialist nurse would be available to come and talk to your group about diabetes. Make sure that you prepare some questions in advance and take notes during the talk.

Using a variety of sources, produce an information booklet about diabetes, including both Type 1 and Type 2, which is aimed at providing information to young people. Before you start, think about the information you might like to know if you were a newly diagnosed sufferer. You must make sure that you include:

- *statistics about the number of people suffering from both types*
- *an explanation of why its incidence is increasing in the UK*
- *signs and symptoms*
- *a short case study about a young person suffering from Type 2 diabetes, indicating how they have needed to change their lifestyle since diagnosis and how they are coping*
- *treatment*
- *possible complications from not treating the condition.*

The use of IT to produce your leaflet will enable you to produce an eyecatching leaflet to appeal to young people.

Crohn's disease

Crohn's disease is a chronic disease that can affect the whole of the digestive tract. Its cause is unknown, but there is thought to be a hereditary link. Infections such as gastro-enteritis and an inefficient immune system may also be causes. Most commonly, it affects the ileum, the lowest part of the small intestine and the large intestine. It affects the full thickness of the bowel, and symptoms include abdominal pain, bleeding from the rectum and abscesses in the anal area. Sufferers can be entirely symptom-free between flare-ups. Children can suffer from this disease and may experience delay in their development.

Certain foods can make Crohn's disease worse and sufferers may find that they have to avoid foods that cause the symptoms to flare up.

Crohn's disease is known as a relapsing remitting disease, which means that sometimes sufferers are symptom-free, but at other times the symptoms can be quite severe. Drugs can be used to relieve them, but some people have surgery to remove the affected part of the bowel. Most people are able to lead full lives, but in some young people, repeated bouts of illness can affect their education and future prospects. Support groups are available to help people to deal with the illness.

Key point

'It is believed that Crohn's disease severely affects up to 80,000 people in the UK. It is thought that there are 4,000–8,000 new cases every year.' (Action Medical Research)

Renal failure

The function of the kidneys is to filter waste from the blood to prevent a build-up of toxins in the body. Renal failure can be acute or chronic.

Acute renal failure can occur for several reasons – reduced blood supply to the kidneys, a falling blood pressure, severe dehydration or lack of salt. It can generally be treated and cured, although a sufferer may need to have kidney dialysis until full renal function returns. Occasionally, a transplant may be required.

Chronic renal failure can occur as a complication of diabetes mellitus, blockage to kidney drainage or some inherited conditions. It often occurs with high blood pressure. It is not usually curable and sufferers may need to be on long-term dialysis until they are able to receive a new kidney.

Over to you

Find out what dietary restrictions there might be for someone who is suffering from renal failure.

Rheumatoid arthritis

Rheumatoid arthritis is thought to be a disease of the immune system that causes inflammation of the joints, which become painful and hot to the touch. Sufferers also experience stiffness, especially in the morning or after periods of activity. Any joint can be affected and long-term inflammation will cause damage to the joints. It is not the same as osteoarthritis which is caused by wear and tear. There is no cure, but treatment includes rest, taking painkillers and anti-inflammatory drugs.

Malignancies

Malignancies are more commonly known as cancers. They can occur almost anywhere in the body and they produce different signs and symptoms. Treatment has to be tailored to the type of cancer that needs to be treated. If diagnosed and treated early, some people will be completely cured, but success rates vary and some cancers are very aggressive and can cause death relatively quickly. Often treatment will involve removal of the tumour and radiotherapy and chemotherapy together or separately.

People who develop malignancies may have difficulty dealing with the emotional consequences, especially if the cancer is advanced and the prognosis is not good. Extensive counselling for the sufferer and their carers and family is essential. It is important to encourage people to be as positive and self-caring as possible. Although in the later stages of a malignant disease, people may be too ill to do much for themselves and may require round-the-clock care, it is important to ensure that carers do not take over all aspects of care.

Real Life Care

Emma's dilemma

Emma is 52 years old and lives with her husband and children on a housing estate on the outskirts of a small market town. Her youngest child still lives at home, but the two older children are away at university and come home most weekends. The family all enjoy eating a lot of meat and a Sunday dinner of roast beef is a particular favourite. However, none of the family enjoys eating vegetables or fruit, and Emma hardly buys any nowadays because she ends up throwing it in the bin. Over the last two months, Emma has noticed that she has lost about a stone in weight and frequently has diarrhoea. Occasionally, she has pains in her abdomen

and yesterday noticed that when she went to the toilet, there was blood in her faeces. Emma is embarrassed about this and is worried about going to see her GP. She knows that you, her next-door neighbour, work as a health care assistant on a surgical ward at the local hospital. She asks you what she should do.

1 What might be wrong with Emma? ✔

2 What would you advise Emma to do? ✔✔

3 How hopeful would you be that Emma could make a full recovery? ✔✔✔

Real Life Care

The pensioner

Harry is 85 years old and lives alone. He has a small pension and worries that he does not have enough money to live on. He only puts his heating on for two hours a day in the winter to try to save money on his heating bills. One day a neighbour cannot get an answer when she knocks at the door and so calls an ambulance. The paramedics find Harry semi-conscious and his hands and legs are blue.

1 What would you suspect Harry is suffering from? ✔

2 How should Harry be treated? ✔✔

3 What advice should Harry be given when he is better to prevent this happening again? ✔✔✔

Real Life Care

The college lecturer

Ushma is 40 years old and leads a busy life as a college lecturer. She is married with two teenage children. She has been feeling tired for about five years and often falls asleep during the day. She has recently been very thirsty and needs to go to the toilet much more often than normal. Sometimes her eyes feel gritty and uncomfortable.

1 What do you think Ushma might be suffering from? ✓

2 What might have caused this malfunction in a body system? ✓✓

3 What advice might a doctor and dietician give her? ✓✓✓

Practice for Assessment

This could contribute to P2, P3, M1, M2, D1 and D2.

Describe the structure and functions of two of the body systems you have studied in this unit. Describe what routine measurements and observations are used to monitor both systems. (P2 and P3)

How does the structure of the two body systems relate to the way that they function? (M1)

Explain how routine measurements and observations taken of the two body systems that you have studied can indicate that there is a malfunction. (M2)

Explain how two body systems work together to perform a specific function. (D1)

Explain how health care workers can use routine measurements and observations to indicate health or ill-health. (D2)

Practice for Assessment

This could contribute to P4, P5, P6 and M3.

1 Choose two malfunctions of body systems to research in greater detail. You should identify the signs and symptoms, the risk factors and describe the care and treatment that could be given to patients. (P4, P5 and P6)

2 Explain how the malfunction of the two body systems you have chosen link to the care patients receive. (M3)

Check your understanding

1 What does a mitochondrion do?
2 Find out how electrical conduction takes place in the heart.
3 Explain what diffusion is.
4 What are the differences between the sympathetic and parasympathetic nervous systems?
5 Explain the action of adrenaline in an emergency situation.
6 How do antagonistic muscles work?
7 Explain the process of negative feedback.
8 Identify reasons why measurements may be inaccurate.
9 What are the Regulations that are covered under the Health and Safety at Work Act 1974?
10 What are Standard Precautions?

6 Human Lifespan Development

Introduction

The seven life stages – from conception to the final stage of life – are explored in this unit. Human development includes the study of physical growth and also the study of intellectual development, emotional development and social development. The unit considers how positive and negative influences may impact on a person's life. It also focuses on the development of self-concept, exploring factors that may influence how we think about ourselves. Finally, the unit examines the way in which care needs may be understood at different life stages. Care workers should help service users to feel that they are special individuals and that they are valued. Care needs include the importance of helping people to develop independence and self-esteem.

How you will be assessed

This is an internally assessed unit.

In this unit you will learn about:

- life stages
- positive and negative influences on individuals
- self-concept
- care needs at different life stages.

Life stages

Human beings grow from a tiny fertilised egg to a baby in nine months. The time from birth to adulthood takes 18 years. The average life expectancy of a person at birth is now 74.2 years for boys and 79.6 years for girls, although some people live beyond 100 years.

People do not all grow and develop at exactly the same rate. Many things can influence how an individual develops. Each person is born with a pattern formed by their genes – 'a genetic pattern'. Genes control the sequence of human development, so that many abilities, like walking and talking, seem to unfold from within a growing child. This process of unfolding development is called maturation.

Our genetic inheritance provides the plan for building our physical body, but the world we live in provides the building materials and influences the way in which a person develops.

People develop from an interaction of genes and environment. Environment includes physical things such as air quality, food quality and risks to health; but environment also includes our social and emotional experiences. So a baby in the womb grows according to a genetic pattern, but this growth can be influenced by the diet and habits of the mother. For example, alcohol can damage the development of the baby's nervous system, smoking can harm the unborn baby and the mother's diet is important too. After a child is born, they will be affected by experiences. A child may not develop language normally if they are not spoken to. A child will not learn to walk if they are prevented from standing. The kind of support and encouragement a child receives will influence the development of their skills and abilities.

Although we all grow up following a similar pattern, we do not all grow up exactly the same. There is a pattern to human life stages, but each person will have a different experience caused by the interaction of their genetic plan and the influences of the environment that they live in.

■ *Different human life stages are reflected in this family group*

Conception

Human life begins with conception. A fertile woman usually produces one egg cell each month, roughly two weeks after her menstrual period. The egg cell travels from the ovary, along a tube (known as the fallopian tube) towards the uterus. If sexual intercourse takes place while the egg is in the fallopian tube, then there is a possibility that a new life will be started. Millions of sperm are ejaculated by a man during orgasm. Just one sperm may fertilise the egg. Fertilisation means that the genetic material in the sperm joins with the genetic material in the egg to form a genetic plan for a new human being.

Normally, each sperm and each egg contains 23 chromosomes. Chromosomes contain the genes that control our physical development. Human cells are made from 23 chromosomes from the mother and 23 chromosomes from the father, so each egg and each sperm contains half the genetic material needed to make the 'plan' for a human being.

Only about half of all fertilised eggs develop to become babies. Many eggs are lost without the woman knowing that fertilisation ever happened. One to one-and-a-half days after conception, the single egg cell begins to divide. After two or three days, there are enough new cells to make the fertilised egg the size of a pin head. This collection of cells travels to the wall of the uterus, where it attaches itself to the wall. The developing collection of cells is now called an embryo. Once the embryo is attached to the uterus wall, a chemical signal stops the woman from having another menstrual period. After eight weeks, the embryo may have grown to between 3 and 4 cm, has a recognisable heartbeat and the beginnings of eyes, ears, mouth, legs and arms. At this stage, the growing organism is called a foetus.

During the remaining seven months before birth, all the organs continue to develop. By 20 weeks, the foetus will have reached about half the length of the baby at birth. By 32 weeks, the foetus will be about half its birth weight.

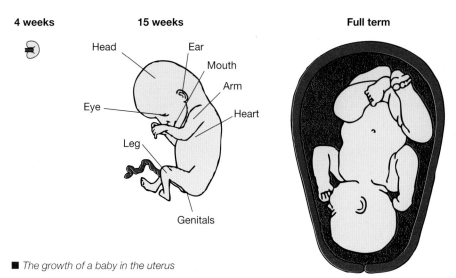

■ *The growth of a baby in the uterus*

Birth

At about nine months after conception the baby will be born.

Infancy (0–3 years)

Physical development

The newborn baby (or neonate) has to take easily digestible food such as mother's milk in order to grow. A newborn baby does not have a fully developed brain but can usually hear sounds, tell differences in the way things taste and identify the smell of their own mother or carer. Infants are born with various reflexes:

- A newborn baby will turn their head towards any touch on the cheek. This reflex is called the rooting reflex, and helps the baby to get the nipple into their mouth to feed.

- If you place your finger in the palm of a baby's hand, they will grasp your finger tightly. This is called the grasp reflex.

- If a baby is startled – perhaps by a loud noise – they will throw hands and arms outwards, arching the back and straightening the legs. This is the startle reflex.

- If a newborn baby is held upright with their feet touching the ground, they will make movements as if trying to walk.

Infants have the physical ability to recognise and interact with people. Babies prefer the sound of human voices to other sounds, and soon learn to recognise their mother's voice. Within a few weeks, babies show interest in human faces. It is as if babies come into the world ready to make relationships with their carers.

Babies are helpless when it comes to muscle coordination and control. Babies are unable to hold up their head, roll over, sit up or use their hands to move objects deliberately. The average age for some types of control over the body is shown in the table below.

Age at which types of body control start	
Body control	**Age**
Ability to lift head slightly	0–1 month
Ability to pass an object from one hand to another	6 months
Ability to roll over	6 months
Ability to crawl	9–10 months
Ability to stand alone	12 months

Intellectual development

During the first 18 months infants have to learn to coordinate their senses and their muscle behaviour. To begin with, a baby will rely on inbuilt patterns for behaviour such as sucking, crawling and watching. A baby will adapt this behaviour in order to explore a wider range of objects. Babies explore by sucking toys, fingers, cloth   and so on. In this way, they are slowly able to develop an understa   g of objects. According to the famous psychologist Jean Piaget (18   hinking is at first limited to memories of actions. The infant v   r grasping a toy. If given the toy, they may repeat th

Piaget's theory of stages of intellectual development		
Stage	**Age**	**Key issue**
Sensory motor period	1–2 years	Infants do not understand that objects exist when they are not in view.
Pre-logical thinking	2–7 years	Children do not think in a logical way.
Concrete logical thinking	7–11 years	Children can only think using limited logic.
Adult logical thinking	11 years +	Adolescents can solve problems in an adult way.

Piaget also believed that infants could not understand that objects existed on their own. For instance, if an infant's mother left the room, the infant would be afraid that she had gone forever. Piaget thought that an infant would not be able to understand that the mother still existed if they could not see, hear, smell or touch the mother. At the end of the first period (up to 2 years of age), Piaget thought that infants could at last understand that objects and people continue to exist, even if they could not sense them. Modern research suggests, however, that many 8-month-old infants can understand that people ill exist, even when out of view.

Social development

Infants soon learn to recognise their mother'   ell, and can probably recognise their mother's face by two   e. Infants try to attract attention. Many infants will smile ar   es to attract adults. Infants will often respond to the speech and smiles of their carers, and both infants and carers seem to have an inbuilt desire to make an emotional bond that ties them together.

At about 12 months   ge infants often develop a fear of strangers, and will protest if they ar   parated from their parents. After the first year of life, infants feel safe v   r family members if they have formed the necessary social

Some psychologis   this process of **bonding** is vital for future mental heal   eing. Infants who are rejected or who fail

Bonding *Forming an emotional attachment to a person. Infants usually make an attachment to carers during the first year of life.*

to make relationships during the first few years of life may face great difficulty in coping with relationships in later life. Infants who make safe and secure ties with their carers have a good foundation for future social development.

Emotional development

Infants aged 5–6 months seem to recognise emotions in their carers. As infants grow, they gradually learn that they can influence their carers. At about 2 years old, infants may develop the idea that they are persons with a fixed gender.

Childhood (3–10 years)

The word 'childhood' does not have a fixed meaning in terms of age. Here the word is used to cover 3–10 years of age, although exactly where childhood ends and adolescence begins is difficult to say.

Physical development

Children grow steadily at this time but less rapidly than during infancy. By the age of 6, a child's head will be almost adult size – even though the body still has a lot of growing to do.

Children's practical abilities continue to develop. At 2 years old children may be able to run and to climb stairs one step at a time. By 4 years, children may be able to kick and throw a large ball. By 6 or 7 years, a child may be able to skip and ride a bicycle.

Puberty often starts for girls between the ages of 11 and 13, although some girls may begin earlier.

Intellectual development

By the age of 2, children generally start to talk. By the age of 6, children can often use language as well as some adults. Language develops very rapidly between 2 and 6 years of age.

Between the age of 2 and 7 years, most children learn to count and to explain how much things weigh. Young children do not always fully understand the logic involved in counting and weighing things, however.

When faced with problems to solve, young children make decisions based on what things look like rather than the logic of counting; for example, they will say that there are more sweets in a long line than in a small heap, even though they can count the same number in each.

Over to you

What are your first memories of childhood? Can you remember stages in your physical, intellectual or language development?

Older children do not make the mistakes that younger children do. But 7–12-year-olds can often only understand logical problems if they can see what is involved. For example, you could ask a 9-year-old: 'Tanya is taller than Stephen, Tanya is shorter than Tolu. Who is the shortest out of these three people?' Although the answer is obviously Stephen, a 9-year-old might not be able to work this out without looking at pictures of the people.

Piaget called the period 7–12 years the 'concrete logical period', because older children can only work out logical problems if they can see 'concrete' examples to help them.

Language development

At around two years of age most children have started to speak, using two-word phrases such as 'Zoe sleep', meaning Zoe wants to go to sleep. As children grow, they start to use their own type of language pattern to communicate, such as 'I want drink', 'The cat goed' (the cat has gone out). Young children of 2 or 3 years do not use adult language, and it is probably best not to correct what they say. Children may go through stages of language development such as the stages listed below:

1 Two-word statements – 'Cat goed'.
2 Short phrases – 'I want drink'.
3 Being able to ask questions – 'What that?', 'Where is cat?'.
4 Using sentences – 'Jill come in and the doggy come in'.
5 Adult sentences – 'I would like a drink and a piece of cake'.

Children can use adult speech and have a reasonable knowledge of words by the age of 5 or 6 years. However, children continue to develop their knowledge of words and ability to understand and use speech throughout childhood.

■ *Language develops very rapidly in young children*

Over to you

If you know a young child who can count to seven, try getting the child to count out two lines of sweets with seven sweets in each line. Ask the child to say how many sweets there are in each line and they will say 'seven' in each line. Now pile one line into a heap and ask if there are more or less sweets in the heap than in the line.

The child may say that there are more sweets in the line because it is longer, even though there are seven sweets in both the line and the heap. Young children cannot always understand what 'seven' means – even though they can count to seven!

Social development

Young children still depend very much on their carers to look after them. They need secure emotional ties with their family. As children develop, they become more and more independent, but the family provides safety and a setting in which to learn social roles. Young children use imagination to play-act social roles. Children learn how to behave socially through the process of **socialisation** in the family (see Socialisation in the section Positive and negative influences in individuals further on in this unit – page 263).

> **Socialisation** *Learning the values and normal behaviour of a group; learning to become part of a group or culture.*

Emotional development

As children develop language skills, they can understand and explain who they are in greater detail. Children develop from being aware of themselves at 2 years of age to being able to describe their feelings by 12 years. Children need to feel that they are valued by their friends and family. Self-concept means our knowledge of who we are. This sense of self forms a basis for an effective concept of self to develop during adolescence (see the section on Self-concept on page 278 for further details).

Over to you

Try the 'I am' test. Ask children to describe who they are; 6-year-olds will probably just say their name and where they live. They may be able to tell you other factual things like who their brothers and sisters are. Eight- or 9-year-olds may be able to tell you about things they are good at or things they like – they can explain who they are in more depth. By 12, children may say things like 'I'm quite good at sport, but not as good as Nisha – she's faster than me.' By 12, children may begin to work out how they fit in with others. Try asking children of different ages and see what kind of answers you get.

Moral development

Children's beliefs about what is right and wrong are strongly influenced by the beliefs of the people that they live with and mix with. The way children talk about what is right and wrong is influenced by their level of intellectual development. The theorist Kolberg published ideas that children and adults develop six different stages of moral thinking. These stages are outlined below:

1 **Punishment and obedience.** Things are wrong if you get told off or punished for doing them. You should do what you are told because adults have more power.
2 **Individualism and fairness.** You should do things that make you feel good or that you get praised for, and avoid things that get you punished. It is important to be fair to everyone; for instance, 'If I help you, you have to help me!', 'If I get pushed in a queue, then I have the right to push other people!'. There is a simple belief that everyone should be treated in exactly the same way, for example if everyone gets the same food, this must be fair. Children at this stage will find it hard to work out that 'the same food' is not fair, because it will discriminate against some people and not others. If everyone is given meat, this will be good for some people – but not for vegetarians!
3 **Relationships.** As children grow older, relationships with others become important and children begin to think about the way they are seen by others. At this stage, children start to think about good behaviour as behaviour that pleases others. Being good is about meeting other people's expectations of you. Ideas of loyalty, trust and respect come into children's thoughts and feelings. For example, a child might think 'I can trust my friend to keep a secret because they are a "good person".'
4 **Law and order.** Adolescents and adults start to think in terms of a 'whole society'. Rules and laws are seen as important so that people can get on with each other. Being good is not only about relationships with friends and family, but also about relationships with people in general.
5 and **6 Rights and principles.** When adults reach these stages, they decide what is right or wrong in terms of values and principles. Adults at stages 5 and 6 may argue that laws need to be changed. At these levels adults take personal responsibility for working out what is right or wrong.

Adolescence (11–18 years)

The word 'adolescence' is used here to cover ages 11–18 because 18 is the age when people are first allowed to vote and take on adult responsibilities.

Physical development

Girls generally start puberty before 13, but for boys this comes between 13 and 15. Puberty is a development stage which prepares the body for sexual reproduction. It is set off by the action of hormones that control sexual development and results in the development of **secondary sexual characteristics**. Both boys and girls may experience a 'growth spurt', where they grow taller at a faster rate than before.

Girls' sexual development during puberty includes the enlargement of breasts, the development of pubic hair, increased fat layers under the skin, and the start of menstrual periods. Boys will experience the enlargement of their testes and penis, the development of pubic and facial hair, and increased muscle strength. Boys' voices also 'break' and become deeper in tone. These major changes mean that adolescents look and behave very differently from children.

Secondary sexual characteristics *Physical features developed at puberty that distinguish between the sexes but are not involved in reproduction.*

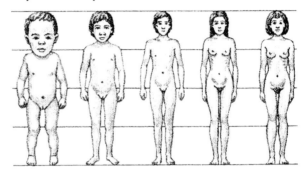

■ *Growth profiles and physical changes from infancy to adolescence*

Intellectual development

An adolescent may be able to imagine and think about things they have never seen or done. By adolescence, people can often imagine their future and how to achieve things. Children are unlikely to plan and think ahead in the same way. Piaget believed that adolescents have the ability to solve problems in an adult way. He called development after about 11 years of age the formal logical period. Although adolescents may reason in an adult way, many adolescents do not know enough to make good decisions. People continue to improve their problem-solving skills during adulthood.

Social development

Adolescents become increasingly independent of their family, and friendship groups can become more important than family for the development of social skills. This phase of development is called **secondary socialisation**.

Between 13 and 18 years of age, most adolescents will begin to explore relationships with possible sexual partners. Towards late adolescence, people will begin to think about, plan or take on job responsibilities.

The five years between 13 and 18 can involve major changes in social behaviour, as people learn to take on adult roles and adult independence. Some adolescents experience conflict with their parents during this period of change.

Over to you

There are very obvious differences in physical development. What is striking about the changes and why do you think this is?

Secondary socialisation *The values, beliefs, attitudes and behaviours that we learn during adolescence through social interaction with other adolescents.*

Emotional development

Adolescence can involve major emotional stresses as people go through rapid social and physical change. Some adolescents feel a loss of **self-esteem** as they transfer from school to work. Becoming independent from parents can involve conflict and stress. The search for love and affection from a sexual partner may not be stress-free.

Self-esteem *How well or how badly a person feels about himself or herself.*

The famous psychologist Eric Erikson (1902–94) believed that a successful adult life depended on people developing a sense of self or self-concept. During adolescence people have to work out a self-concept that will guide them through leaving home, perhaps setting up home with a sexual partner, and getting work.

Adulthood (18 onwards)

In Britain the right to vote is granted at 18 years of age, and 18 is therefore taken as the beginning of the social category of adulthood.

Physical development

Young adults are often at the peak of physical performance between 18 and 28 years of age. Most champions of highly active sport are aged between 16 and 30 years. Professional footballers and athletes usually have to retire and move into management roles during their 30s. Older adults generally tend to lose some strength and speed with age, although outside competitive sport these changes can be so gradual as to go unnoticed.

Exercise can help develop physical fitness and athletic skills. An older adult could easily achieve a personal peak of fitness at 40 or 50 years of age if they take up exercise late in life.

There are a number of age-related changes that slowly become apparent as we grow older. Many people develop a need to wear glasses to help with reading during their 40s. Some people cannot hear high-pitched sounds so well during late adulthood. Many adults show greying and thinning of hair, with hair loss being common for men.

Women are most able to conceive children in their late teens and early 20s. The risk of miscarriages and complications rises with age. Usually between 45 and 55 years of age women stop being able to have children because of the menopause. It is the time when a women's periods stop and is a normal part of growing older. However, some women may experience unpleasant symptoms such as hot sweats, depression and tiredness. One of the main problems can be loss of calcium in the bones, which means that women may be more likely to break or fracture bones. Calcium supplements are often taken. Older adults in Britain often put on weight. This middle-age spread may be caused because adults still eat the same amount of food that they did when they were younger, but they have become much less active.

The risk of disease and disability rises with age. Older adults are more likely to develop health problems than younger adults.

Intellectual development

Intellectual skills and abilities may increase during adulthood if they are exercised. Older adults may have slightly slower reaction times, but increased knowledge may compensate for this in many work situations.

Older adults may be more skilled than adolescents and young adults when it comes to making complex decisions. Some adults may develop increased wisdom as they become older.

Social development

Early adulthood is often a time when people continue to develop their network of personal friends. Most young adults establish sexual relationships and partnerships. Marriage and parenthood are important social life events that are often associated with early adulthood. The pressure to obtain paid employment and hold down a job is also a major social issue for adults. Many adults will develop skills of working alongside other people in a team in order to do their job.

Many adults experience a degree of stress in trying to cope with the demands of being a parent, a partner and a worker. Nowadays, many individuals work long hours or even take more than one job in order to achieve a high standard of living. If a person has to go to work and maintain a family home, this can create social and emotional problems. Adult life can often involve trying to balance the need to earn money with the needs of partners and other family members.

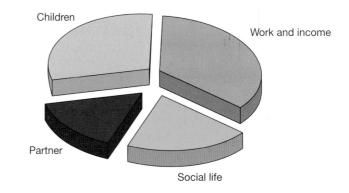

■ *Adults have to work out how to divide up their time in order to meet different needs*

Older adults may find that as well as coping with work pressures, they have to provide support for their parents and their children. Some older adults may feel that they are torn between different demands on their time. When children leave home, some pressures may be taken off parents, but some may feel that they have lost part of their social purpose when children no longer need their support.

Many people now retire from full-time paid employment in their 50s, and most people retire by their mid-60s. Retirement is seen as a positive release from pressures by some people and as an end to usefulness by others.

Emotional development

An individual's sense of self and self-esteem will continue to develop throughout adulthood. During early adulthood, many individuals may struggle to develop the confidence to share life with a partner. Some individuals may prefer to live alone or may feel that partnership relationships are too demanding. A person's previous family experience may strongly influence their expectations of a partner.

Some research suggests that adults often feel more confident and satisfied with their lives in their 30s and 40s than they did in their 20s. It may be that many young adults experience some stress in establishing a satisfying lifestyle.

One theory suggests that older adults may struggle to stay interested and involved with other people after their own family grows up. Some adults may get into 'a rut' and withdraw from active, social involvement as they get older. Successful ageing means remaining emotionally involved with other people.

Old age (65 onwards)

Most people retire by the age of 65 and the period of life after the age of 65 is generally regarded as old age. Most 65-year-olds do not see themselves as 'old', however. Some writers distinguish between the 'young-old' (65–80) and the 'old-old' (80 plus). But many 80-year-olds still claim that they are not old!

Physical changes

The period of life after 65 usually involves some reduction in the efficiency of the body:

- The heart, breathing and circulation become weaker.
- Muscles may become weaker and skin becomes less 'elastic'.
- Muscles, skin, joints and bones become less flexible, and this can mean that people become less mobile, more at risk of fractured bones and more likely to develop wrinkled skin.
- Blood capillaries in the skin are more likely to burst, meaning that bruising can happen more easily.
- Most organs in the body, such as the liver and kidneys, work less efficiently.
- Many people develop problems with arthritis.
- There may be a loss of hearing.
- The risks of impairments and disability rise with increasing age.
- Reaction times and speed of thinking slow down.

Physical health varies from person to person. Where people have poor health, their ability to remember and think things through can sometimes be affected. Life after 65 involves a general slowing down of

■ *Elderly people adjust the sorts of physical activities that they can do*

physical activity. People can still go jogging, dancing, mountain climbing, and so on, but the body becomes less flexible and less able to cope with exertion – limiting the extremes to which people can perform.

Intellectual development

Some people seem to become less able to solve problems and cope with difficult, intellectual challenges in later life. To some extent, mental abilities are influenced by physical health. The more active you are, the more alert you are.

Other people who enjoy good health, and who exercise their minds, often keep their mental abilities and continue to develop their store of knowledge. Some older people seem to increase their ability to make wise decisions. Even if thinking slows down, the opportunity to develop wisdom may increase with age.

The risk of developing dementia or Alzheimer's disease seems to increase with age; but dementia is not a part of normal ageing. There are different types of dementia, but in general dementia can cause a range of disabilities including:

■ a loss of ability to control emotion

■ difficulty in understanding other people

■ difficulties in communicating and expressing thoughts

■ loss of memory

■ difficulties in recognising people, places and things

■ problems with making sense of where they are and what is happening

■ problems with daily living activities such as getting dressed.

The reasons for dementia are not fully understood, but bad health habits like heavy drinking and smoking may increase the risk of dementia for some people. Other people may inherit a risk factor for dementia.

Social development

Older people lead varied and different lives. Many retired people have a greater opportunity for meeting and making new friends than they did while they were working. A network of family and friends can provide vital practical and emotional support. Health problems and impairments can sometimes cause social isolation.

Emotional development

People continue to develop their sense of self as life progresses. Some theorists suggest that the main challenge of old age is to keep a strong sense of self-esteem, despite the problems that can arise. Some older people may be at risk of losing their self-confidence and self-esteem because of the way others treat them. Some vulnerable elderly people suffer abuse – see page 80 in Unit 2.

The final stages of life

Physical processes

There are different theories to explain why we age and die. One theory is that the cells that make up our body have to continually renew themselves, but they can do this only a limited number of times. Eventually, body cells start to go wrong as they try to renew, and other cells die out, causing problems.

One way of understanding ageing is to look at what happens when you make photocopies. Imagine you photocopied a photograph of a face, and then photocopied your copy rather than the original page. If you keep copying your copies rather than the original, the copies will gradually fade and start to look wrong. You can copy only a limited number of times before you can no longer see the picture clearly.

Some people think that as our cells have to copy themselves, like the photocopier they can only manage the task for a limited number of times. Eventually, we lose vital parts of our pattern – and then we die.

Social issues

People think about death and dying in many different ways. Some people fear death and try not to think about it. Other people have strong religious or personal beliefs which protect them from worry. In general, older people often have less fear of dying than young adults. It may be that some older people feel ready to let go of life at a certain stage of physical decline. Some older people may prepare for their own death by thinking over their lives and the things they have achieved.

Some people who face death want to see family, friends and relatives and need social support to help them cope with dying. Other people may prefer to die alone. Each individual will have their own social and emotional needs.

Over to you

One way of trying to summarise the human story is set out below:

The genetic material in a sperm and an egg fuse together to create the genetics for a new person. This genetic plan is then influenced by the person's environment. We do not just grow physically, we also develop our social and emotional behaviour. Most people develop a sense of self – an idea about who and what they are. Our bodies are not designed to last forever, and at some age our physical abilities start to decline. The sense of self that we develop carries on until we die. Our lives influence others, and leave their mark on the history of the world. The world would not be exactly the same if you or I had never existed.

Many of the world's great religions believe that the self we have created (or soul) is 'kept on record', and that God will recreate this self in heaven or in some sort of afterlife.

Quality care depends on workers valuing and caring about other people's sense of who they are. If people do not have positive self-esteem, they may see little point living. If we have our basic needs met and a sense of self-esteem, we can go on to enjoy the whole of our lifespan.

What do you think? What would you want to add or take out from this summary of the human story?

Practice for Assessment

Carrying out this activity will provide you with underpinning evidence for P1.

You must identify the key aspects of physical, intellectual, emotional and social development that take place through the life stages.

One idea to help you to meet this outcome would be to design a board game that used the different squares on the board to identify the different life stages and to identify the key aspects of physical, intellectual, emotional and social development that occur at each life stage. You should use the theory in this section to help you to work out what titles you might choose for each square.

For merit 1

To achieve M1, your work must describe the key aspects of physical, intellectual, emotional and social development that takes place through the life stages. If you can identify the key aspects of development for the design of a board game, you could go further and go into more detail describing the issues involved in each square using short notes. Use these notes to give a short talk about the key aspects of development.

Positive and negative influences

Socialisation

Socialisation means to become social – children learn to fit in with and be part of a social group. When children grow up within a family group, they will usually learn a wide range of expectations (or norms) about how to behave. For instance, at mealtimes some families will have strict rules that everyone must sit down at the table and it is considered 'rude' if one person starts to eat before the others.

Other families may not even have set mealtimes – people may just prepare food for themselves when they feel like it. In the evenings, some families might sit round the television as a social group, while other families might all sit in different rooms doing different activities. Some families are very concerned that people take their outdoor shoes off before coming into the house, and others have no rules about shoes.

> **Socialisation** *Learning the values and normal behaviour of a group; learning to become part of a group or culture.*

 Over to you

Are, or were, any of the following expectations important in your family?

- *To say 'thank you' or 'thank you for having me' to the head of a household you visited?*
- *To give thanks in prayer before a meal?*
- *To eat hot food with your fingers?*
- *To go to bed at a fixed time – unless there is a special event or festival?*
- *Never to interrupt when an older member of the family is speaking?*
- *That children have set tasks to help adults with the housework?*
- *That male members of the household are responsible for decorating and repairing the house?*
- *That female members of the household are responsible for the washing and ironing?*

Families and similar social groups develop attitudes about what is 'normal' or right to do. Sociologists call these beliefs 'norms'. Each family will have 'norms' that cover how people should behave.

During childhood, children learn ideas about what is right or wrong. They learn the customs of their culture and family, they learn to play gender and adult roles, and they learn what is expected of them and what they should expect from others. Socialisation teaches children ways of thinking, and these ways of thinking may stay with a person for life.

Primary socialisation

Not everything that a child learns during first (or primary) socialisation within the family group is learned by copying adults. Children also spend time watching television, listening to radio and playing computer games. Children will be influenced by the things they see and hear through the media as well as their experiences within the home.

Over to you

Look at the picture of a breakfast scene below. Think carefully – how many influences on the children can you spot?

■ *Breakfast time in a family home*

Did you notice the media influence in this home? The radio sends messages about love and relationships in the songs that are playing. The television sends messages about news and opinions. The newspaper invites the reader to share its views on current events. Even the cereal packet has an advert encouraging the family to adopt a lifestyle!

Did you notice the gender roles in this home? Who is preparing the children's breakfast, and who is being waited on? What differences are there in the way the two children are playing; what toys have they chosen?

Note the ethnicity of the family. How far might social norms be the same or different for other ethnic groups?

Thinking about this scene, what do you think the children might be learning? Will the daughter tend to copy the mother's behaviour as she grows up – will she see her role as 'looking after people'? Will the son copy the father's role and expect to be waited on at mealtimes?

Socio-economic factors

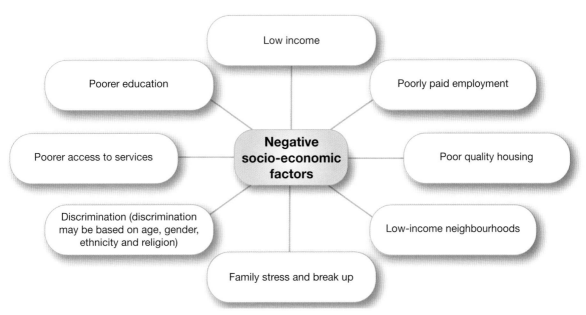

■ *Some socio-economic factors that have a negative influence on development*

Income and expenditure

Income is the money that a person gets each week to live on. Income mainly comes from:

- wages that a person is paid for working

- profits from a business if a person is self-employed

- benefits that are paid by the government to help people

- money from invested wealth such as interest on bank accounts

- money from selling property that a person owns.

In the UK, roughly one person in six lives on less than 60 per cent of an average person's income. This level of income is called a low income. People who have to live on a low income may not have enough money to cover the expenditure or cost of an average lifestyle. People on a low income may have enough money for food, for some clothing and for heating, but low income means that there is little money for interesting purchases and exciting lifestyles. People who depend on benefits have limited life choices. Fashionable clothes, modern cars, the latest electronic equipment, and so on, may not be choices that people on low incomes can afford. This may result in low self-esteem and a negative self-concept.

Key groups of people who have to live on very little money include lone-parent families, people who are unemployed, elderly people, people who are sick or disabled, single earners and unskilled couples.

There is a great deal of evidence to show that people on low incomes tend to have worse health than people who are wealthy. People who live in households where no one has a job often have worse health than people who are employed. Statistics show that people who stay poor or unemployed for most of their life often have shorter lives than wealthier people.

This difference in health and length of life is probably caused by the problems that poorer people face such as poor housing, poor diet, stress from debt and crime, and negative thinking about self (see the section on Self-concept on page 278).

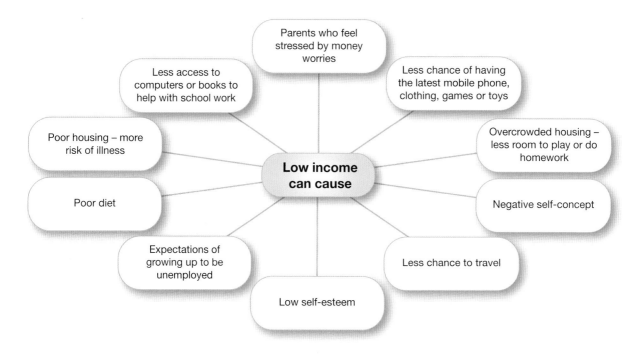

■ *Some problems a child belonging to a low-income family may face*

Environment

People with lower incomes tend to live in more densely occupied housing areas. Research shows that these areas may be more stressful to live in because of the following factors:

■ crime – including burglary and personal attacks

■ poor travel facilities

■ more chance of being woken up at night

■ noise from neighbours

■ vandalism

■ busy roads and traffic fumes creating pollution

- litter and rubbish

- graffiti.

Living in a stressful **environment** may have a negative influence on a person's self-image and self-esteem.

> **Environment** *The surroundings that a person lives in; everything around people that might influence or affect them.*

Housing

Poor housing may contribute towards a wide range of hazards to physical health and safety as well as having a negative effect on development.

Over to you

Look at the diagram below and the hazards that are listed. How do you think living in poor housing might influence a person's self-esteem?

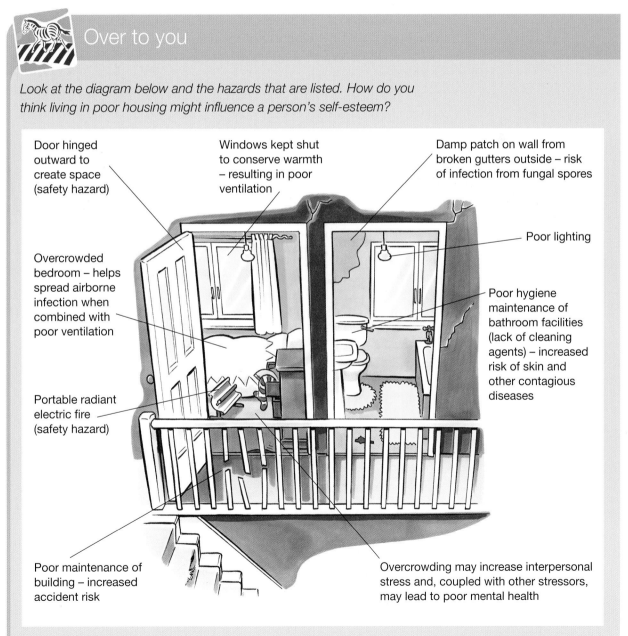

Door hinged outward to create space (safety hazard)

Windows kept shut to conserve warmth – resulting in poor ventilation

Damp patch on wall from broken gutters outside – risk of infection from fungal spores

Poor lighting

Overcrowded bedroom – helps spread airborne infection when combined with poor ventilation

Poor hygiene maintenance of bathroom facilities (lack of cleaning agents) – increased risk of skin and other contagious diseases

Portable radiant electric fire (safety hazard)

Poor maintenance of building – increased accident risk

Overcrowding may increase interpersonal stress and, coupled with other stressors, may lead to poor mental health

■ *Some hazards associated with poor housing*

Culture

> **Culture** *The beliefs, customs, values and assumptions shared within a social group. Different social groups have different cultures.*

The way we behave, the language we speak, the diet we eat, the way that we dress and our lifestyle are all part of our **culture**. Culture includes the things which make one group different and distinctive from another.

Culture gives us a set of rules or expectations which help us to understand each other, and to know how to react in certain situations. Very often we do not even know that we are working with the culture we are surrounded by; we just do 'what is normal' and fit in. Because society is made up of different sorts of people, brought up in different circumstances or places, and following different beliefs and religions, different cultures can be diverse. We tend to follow the way we were brought up, and the influences of the people around us.

Gender

It was only in 1928 that women were granted equal rights with men to vote in elections. Before that, women were considered to have a lower social status than men. Assumptions were made that women should look after children, do housework, cook and tidy and do light jobs. Men did what were considered to be the more valuable administrative, management and labouring jobs.

Great changes have come about in the nature of work and the nature of family life since 1928. Women now have equal opportunities in education and employment – the Sex Discrimination Act 1975 made it illegal to discriminate against women in education or employment. However in 2007 women's average pay was 17.2 per cent lower than men's. Women still hold fewer top jobs and seem to profit less from promotion. Women far outnumber men in jobs like nursing and primary school teaching – often these jobs are not highly paid. Men often get the more highly paid jobs, such as becoming head teachers, even within areas of work dominated by women. When it comes to domestic work, men still generally do less of the childcare, washing and cooking, although they may do more gardening and maintenance jobs.

Access to services

Low-income and unemployed people may not be able to access services as well as wealthier people. There is some evidence that in the past doctors spent more time with wealthy and well-educated people. It may be that more confident and well-educated people can influence doctors to take a greater interest in their needs. Wealthier, employed people also seem to take more notice of health education advice and have healthier lifestyles.

Wealthy people can afford private health care and health checks, so a poor or long-term unemployed person may not get their health needs met as effectively as other people.

Education

Everyone goes to school, and colleges are open to everyone. Even so, there is evidence that schools in wealthier districts achieve higher standards and sometimes offer more opportunity to their students. Some parents even move house in order to send their children to what they think is 'a good school'.

Wealthier parents often pay for their children to attend independent (private) schools, because they believe this will give their children better qualifications, skills and friends that can help with their career.

The family

The kind of family we are born into can have a great influence on our development.

A family is a social group made up of people who are 'related' to each other. Belonging to a family can have many advantages – family relationships can provide a safe, caring setting for children.

Family groups can guide and teach children, and they can provide a source of social and emotional support for adults and older family members as well as children.

Below are some positive influences that the family might provide:

- A network of people who can give emotional support and advice.
- A setting for learning social expectations (socialisation).
- A safe environment to support children.
- Financial help.
- Belonging to a family group may help people to develop positive self-esteem.
- Practical support such as babysitting or help with household repairs.
- Belonging to a family group may help people to cope with stress.
- Care for older relatives.

Families may also create stress when there are tensions between family members. (See the table on relationships on page 284 for further details of positive and negative influences.)

Real Life Care

Anil and Rick

Anil is 8 years old and was born into a family where his parents had good jobs and enough money for lots of toys, books and computers. Anil learned to play on the computer when he was only 3 years old. This has helped him to learn. Anil always has someone to talk to at home because he lives with his sister and grandparents. The family is happy and Anil can go out on his bicycle and play with friends in the local park. Anil's family are not afraid of crime in their neighbourhood. Anil is doing very well at school; he has many friends and enjoys school. Anil does not miss school very often.

Rick is 8 years old and was born into a family where both his parents had difficulty in finding work. Because Rick's parents could not get jobs, there was not much money for toys, books or computers. Rick lives in a crowded block of flats on a housing estate. Rick's mother does not let him out to play because she is afraid of the crime and drug-taking that takes place on the estate. Rick's mother has periods of depression when she does not talk to Rick. Rick is often unhappy because he has few friends and gets bored indoors. Rick often gets colds and regularly misses school.

1 How might poor housing have an influence on Rick's life? ✔

2 How are socio-economic factors working together to influence development? ✔✔

3 Looking ahead to the next section on self-concept, see if you can work out how the self-image and self-esteem of these two boys might be influenced? ✔✔✔

Think about it

List all the things you do over a week such as going to school or college, going out in the evening, and so on. How many of these things could you do without friends?

Friends

Friends are very important. Friends can help us to do practical things like housework, find a job, repair a car, and so on. Friends can also help us emotionally. They can listen to us and protect us if we feel stressed. Friends can help us sort out our worries and help us to have an interesting and enjoyable life.

Friends help us with:

- practical tasks
- emotional needs
- social life.

People without friends will probably have a harder and less enjoyable life than people with many friends.

Friends influence the things we believe and the values we hold. Early in life, our family influences us. This influence is called primary or first socialisation. Socialisation is when we learn social values. As an individual gets older, influences like school, television and friends influence our beliefs and values. This influence is called secondary socialisation. Our friends can influence the way we behave and dress. The friends we mix with during our adolescence can have a long-lasting influence on our future. If a person mixes with friends who think it is important to try hard at school, they will probably try hard too. If the person mixes with friends who take drugs, they may copy what their friends do. Some people feel under pressure to do what their friends do even if it is wrong. This is called 'peer group pressure'.

Discrimination

Discrimination is discussed fully in Unit 1 Communication and Individual Rights within the Health and Social Care Sectors, pages 23–30, and also in Unit 4 Cultural Diversity in Health and Social Care, pages 173–179.

Discrimination is a serious problem because it can:

- harm people's sense of self-esteem and value
- block people from making the most of their lives
- harm people through verbal and physical abuse
- lead to people not getting quality care and services.

The effect of socio-economic factors on development

Socio-economic factors can have a positive or negative influence on development.

Practice for Assessment

Carrying out this activity will give evidence towards P2 and D1.

This could contribute to P2.

You must identify the positive and negative influences on growth and development. Design a poster that used the information in this section to identify positive and negative influences.

For distinction 1

To achieve D1, you must explain how growth and development at each life stage can be influenced positively and negatively. If you have designed a board game to identify life stages you could try to work out how each of the issues in the table on the next page might link to each life stage in your game. You might imagine a person developing through each life stage and then explain how each of the issues listed above could work positively or negatively to affect the person's life.

Positive and negative influences of socio-economic factors

Socio-economic factors	Possible positive influence	Possible negative influence
Income and expenditure	Well-off households may be able to afford good quality housing, diet and educational opportunities.	Low-income households may experience stress and may have poorer quality housing, diet and educational opportunities.
Housing	Good housing can provide a comfortable setting to live a healthy life and study.	Poor housing can create stress and can damage physical and mental health. Overcrowded housing may make it difficult to study.
Environment	A good local environment may create a safe setting to play, explore and make friends.	Poor neighbourhoods may suffer a combination of poor housing, high rates of crime, unemployment and family disruption.
Education	Good opportunities will support the child's intellectual development and career needs.	Lack of good opportunities might mean that adults do not have the skills they need. Adults without basic skills are more likely to be unemployed.
Access to services	Well-off neighbourhoods may have good access to quality health and educational services.	Poor neighbourhoods may have less access to good quality health and education.
Family	A happy family setting may provide a wide range of support to help with physical, intellectual, social and emotional development.	Low income may create stress for families. Stress within families may affect the health and education of children.
Friends and peer pressure	Positive views may guide people to develop self-confidence and effective careers.	The beliefs of the people that a person mixes with will influence the individual. If the individual mixes with people who have negative views, they may be socialised into beliefs that could limit their opportunities.
Media and culture	We are influenced by wider social beliefs – these beliefs may lead people to develop a positive image of themselves.	People may develop negative views of themselves that may limit their opportunities because of influences in wider culture.
Gender	Some people may not experience disadvantage. Some people may not be discriminated against.	Some groups of people experience disadvantage. In the past, women did not have the same opportunities as men.
Discrimination	Some groups of people may not be subject to discrimination. Some people may be fortunate to grow up in a non-discriminatory environment.	Some groups of people such as ethnic minorities, older people and people with disabilities may experience discrimination.

Life events

Living a successful life involves coping with change. Many changes during life are predictable. We know that they will happen and sometimes we even choose to make the changes. Some examples of changes that people choose and plan for are:

- going to school or nursery for the first time
- leaving home
- marriage
- moving house
- parenthood
- changing job (employment)
- retirement
- ageing.

Some types of change can be unexpected or unpredicted. These can include:

- the birth of a new brother or sister (sibling)
- divorce
- redundancy
- **bereavement**
- serious injury
- abuse

Positive and negative effects of change

Change usually involves some level of **stress** for people. When people choose to change, for instance when they get married or start a new job, the stress may be experienced as excitement.

People may feel 'butterflies' in their stomach on their first day at work, but they may also look forward to meeting new people and learning new things. Some changes, such as the death of a friend, are experienced as being negative and these will usually cause people to feel very stressed.

Some life events change us forever. Life events that change us involve some stress. This is because change can cause:

- a sense of loss for the way things used to be
- a feeling of uncertainty about the future
- a need to spend time and/or money and/or emotional energy sorting things out
- a need to learn new things.

Stress *An in-built reaction makes us want to fight or run when we feel threatened. It is possible to be threatened but not be able to fight or run, and symptoms of stress set in when this happens.*

Some examples of predictable change

Going to school

Some people are taught at home because of travelling problems or personal needs. Most people go to school and many people will remember their first day.

Starting school can involve a sense of loss. This might be the first morning your mother and family have left you to cope with lots of other people on your own. You might cry because you miss them. You might also feel uncertain. Where are the toilets? Who should you speak to? What will happen if you do not like the food?

Starting school can also be stimulating and positive. Some children feel that it is exciting to meet new people. They might find school interesting and be proud that they are 'grown up' enough to start school activities. Starting school can be a positive experience, involving increasing independence – it all depends on how each child is helped to cope with the change.

Marriage

Many heterosexual couples live together without marrying – some go on to marry after living together for some years, but about half of all couples who live together do not marry each other.

Marriage or a civil partnership between same-sex couples involves a commitment to live with a partner permanently. It ties financial resources and the networks of family relationships together. Marriage is a big change in life, and it can involve moving house and leaving your family. This may cause a sense of loss. Many people feel some anxiety about getting married: are they marrying the right person, will they get on well together, what will living together forever be like? Learning to cope with married life takes a lot of time, money and energy. Living with a partner involves learning about his or her needs and ways. For some people, marriage is the most positive change that can happen in life. Other people regard it as involving a loss of freedom, or even as entering a relationship where one person dominates or exploits another.

Parenthood

Becoming a parent involves a major change in life. Many parents experience their relationship with their child as an intense and new emotional experience. There may be strong feelings of love and a powerful desire to protect the child. But becoming a parent also involves losses; for example, parents can lose sleep because the baby wakes them up, and they may find that they cannot go out very easily so that they lose touch with friends and social life. Parents can lose money because they have either to pay for childcare or give up full-time work to care for their child. Parents can lose career opportunities if they stay out of full-time work to bring up a family. These losses can sometimes place a relationship or marriage under stress. Sometimes a parent can even become jealous of the love and attention that a child receives from the other parent.

Becoming a parent can involve some anxiety about the new role of being a parent: 'Will the baby be healthy?', 'Is the baby safe?', 'Am I being a good parent?' New parents usually seek advice from family, friends, doctors and health visitors. Parenthood involves a lot of pressure on time, money and energy. A new infant will need nappies, clothes and toys, food, cot, high chair, car seat, and so on. An infant needs a lot of attention. Carers will need time and emotional energy to care for the child. Parents often need advice on caring skills as there is new learning involved in being a good parent and always a lot to learn about the child as a new relationship develops.

Retirement

The nature of work is changing rapidly. Many people will work as self-employed or temporary workers in the future, and retirement may become very flexible, with some people retiring early and others continuing to take on work in their late 60s and 70s. Retirement can represent a major change for people who have worked in a demanding full-time job and can have some possible negative outcomes:

- it may cause a feeling of loss of purpose

- self-concept and self-esteem will be affected without the influence of work roles

- people may lose their sense of routine

- work friends may be lost

- some people won't be prepared for the amount of leisure time they have or know what to do with it

- they may have to rely on less income.

There are many positive benefits of retirement:

- they will have more time to travel, study and take up new hobbies

- it can lead to greater freedom, and the opportunity to spend more time with family and friends

- retirement can be seen as a time of self-fulfilment, when the rewards of a lifetime's work can be harvested.

Some examples of unpredictable change

The birth of a brother or sister

Gaining a new brother or sister causes change to our relationships with parents and other family members. Children's reactions to a new member of the family can be very varied and reactions can be different depending on how old a child is and how large the family is. Very often, children have mixed emotions. Children may feel pleased that they have a new brother or sister, but they may also feel jealous that their new sibling gets attention from others.

Over to you

Ask a parent of a small child what changes have occurred since the child was born. Make a note of all the changes and put them under a PIES heading.

Positive and negative feelings associated with the birth of a sibling	
Positive	**Negative**
Feeling important because you can care for the new infant	Feeling rejected because parents spend more time with a new child
Feeling pleased because there are more people in the family	Feeling that you have been replaced and are no longer important
Feeling important because you are the older child	Feeling threatened that the younger child will compete with you for attention
Making a relationship or attachment with your new brother or sister	Feeling that your attachment to your parents is threatened

Divorce

At present, one in three marriages is likely to end in divorce. Fifty years ago many people stayed married despite being unhappy with their partners. In the past, it was often difficult to get a divorce and there were likely to be serious problems over money and finding somewhere to live following divorce, particularly for women.

Divorce is much more common nowadays, but many people who divorce go on to remarry. Each year, over a third of marriages are likely to be remarriages. Nearly a quarter of children in Britain may expect their parents to divorce before they are 16 years old.

Although many people experience divorce as a negative experience, it may often be better than living in a stressful situation. Sometimes people develop a deeper sense of self following divorce. Agencies such as Relate provide counselling services to help people to understand the emotions involved in partnerships. Counselling may help some people to decide whether it is best to divorce or not.

Bereavement

People can lose their partners at any stage of life, but as couples grow older the chances that one person will die increase. Bereavement means losing someone you loved, and it causes a major change in people's lives.

People who try to cope with a major loss often experience the following feelings:

- not being able to believe that the person is dead
- sadness and depression
- anger or guilt
- stress because they have to learn to cope with a different lifestyle.

Few people describe bereavement as a positive life event, but the final outcome need not only be sadness and grief. Over time, people can achieve a positive outlook on life again.

Life event	Emotional and care needs
Starting school/nursery	Physical needs of food, drink and activity, the need to learn about new school activities. Emotional support, involvement with other children.
Birth of a brother or sister	Learning to cope with new relationships. The need for emotional support.
Moving house	Emotional support to cope with loss of old neighbourhood, learning about new setting, physical and organisational support needed to cope with the change.
Starting employment	Learning new patterns of behaviour, making new relationships. Emotional support to cope with these changes.
Redundancy	Loss of old relationships, learning a new lifestyle, possible loss of money. The need for emotional support to cope with these changes.
Serious injury	Loss of body function, learning new ways of coping with daily living activities. Possible change of self-image, the need for emotional support.
Leaving home	Loss of old routines. Learning to live alone, learning new daily living routines.
Marriage	Loss of old lifestyle. Learning to cope with partnership and to share accommodation and finances. Learning a new relationship.
Divorce	Loss of old lifestyle, possible loss of emotional attachment, possible loss of finance and living standards. Emotional support to cope with loss.
Parenthood	Possible increase in stress – loss of sleep. Possible increase in stress on relationships with others. Emotional support to cope with change.
Retirement	As for redundancy.
Ageing	Learning to cope with reduced physical abilities. Some people may have to cope with reduced financial resources.
Bereavement	Loss of relationship. Loss of lifestyle and routines. Need for emotional support to cope with loss of relationship. Counselling may be needed.
Abuse	Risk of damage to emotional development/self-concept. Counselling and support may be needed.

Practice for Assessment

This could contribute to M2.

To achieve M2, you must explain how life events can affect the development and care needs of individuals. If you have developed a board game to identify life stages, work out where the life events described above might fit with the board game. Make notes about the way in which life events might affect a person's development and list some of the needs of people associated with the life events listed in the table above. Give a short talk based on your notes.

Self-concept

Self-esteem and self-image

Self-concept means our own knowledge of who we are. Our self-concept includes:

- **self-esteem** – how highly we value our skills and abilities
- **self-image** – how we see ourselves given the reactions of other people.

Self-concept is important for the following reasons:

- Our view of ourselves can motivate us to do things, or stop us from doing things, e.g. doing well at school or at sport.
- Our view of ourselves can create a feeling of social confidence or cause us to feel anxious with other people.
- Our view of ourselves can mean that we experience happiness or unhappiness from life experiences.
- Our view of ourselves can help us lead a successful and enjoyable life, or it can lead us into trouble and difficulties in coping with life.

If we think we are good at school or work, we will probably enjoy going to school or work. Our concept of ourselves will lead us to want to be there. If we think that we are not good at school or work, we may not want to go there. The way we think about ourselves influences what we do and how we feel.

> **Self-esteem** *How well or how badly a person feels about himself or herself.*
> **Self-image** *How a person imagines or 'images' himself or herself to be.*

■ *The way we see ourselves can influence how we choose to behave*

The beginnings of self-awareness may start when an infant can recognise their own face in a mirror. This happens somewhere about 18 months to 2 years of age, when an infant begins to demonstrate that they are separate from other people.

From this point on, children begin to form ideas about themselves. Children are very influenced by the environment and culture they grow up in; they are also influenced by the relationships they have with family and friends. As a child's ability to use language develops, this will also affect how they can talk and explain things about themselves.

People develop an increasingly detailed understanding of self as they grow older. Ways in which people may describe their self-concept are explained in the table below.

Understanding of self-concept at different life stages	
Life stage	**Self-concept**
Childhood	At first, children will only describe themselves in terms of categories such as being a boy or girl, their age and size. Later on, children will use an increasing range of categories such as hair colour, details of address, activities that they like, factual details of parents or friends.
Adolescence	Teenagers may start to explain themselves in terms of chosen beliefs, likes and dislikes, and relationships with other people.
Adulthood	Many adults may be able to explain the quality of their lives and their thoughts about themselves in greater depth and detail than when they were younger.
Old age	Some older adults may have more self-knowledge than they had when they were younger. Some older people may show wisdom in the way they talk about themselves.

 Over to you

Ask some friends or relatives about their life story. You may find that older people have more complex life stories and will talk for much longer than some younger people. This may not just be because their lives have been longer – it might also be that some older people have a more complicated self-concept.

Self-concept changes with life experience

Our knowledge of ourselves changes as we go through life. Our self-concept develops and changes because of the experiences we have. New life experiences can lead to a changed self-concept.

Influences on self-concept

Age

Because self-concept develops due to social influences, age makes a very big difference to the way children can describe themselves and the way adults think about their lives. Your self-concept will grow and change as you grow older. Some general differences in self-concept between different age groups were outlined in the table above.

Appearance

Somewhere between 10 and 12 years of age, children will start to analyse the ways in which they are like or not like others. Children start to work out how they fit in with others: do they look good or not, are they popular with others or not?

The physical shape of our body, height, weight, hair, eye and skin colour all have an influence on our self-image. Many people believe that there is an 'ideal look'. If we think we look good, then we have a positive self-image. If we think we do not look attractive, we may have a negative self-image. A negative self-image may make us feel bad or cause us to have low self-esteem.

The role of culture and the media in influencing our ideas about appearance

What we think 'looks good' depends on the culture and the beliefs of people around us. Take body shape, for example. One hundred years ago, being a bit fat was considered attractive in European culture. A woman who was very thin was seen as poor and unhealthy; a fat man was

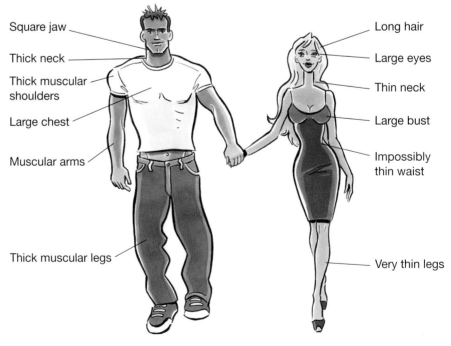

Square jaw
Thick neck
Thick muscular shoulders
Large chest
Muscular arms
Thick muscular legs

Long hair
Large eyes
Thin neck
Large bust
Impossibly thin waist
Very thin legs

■ *Ideal body shapes in the past*

considered to be someone who was successful. This began to change in the 1950s and 1960s when looking young and thin became the goal to aim for. By the 1980s, the 'Barbie doll look' became a model for some people. Very few people ever looked like Barbie, but many people came to judge themselves as attractive or unattractive in relation to these shapes.

Nowadays, television, films and magazines tend to show fitness as beautiful. Both men and women should have some muscle but little fat. People are likely to judge their attractiveness in relation to the images they see in magazines and television.

The way you look may show that you are a member of a particular kind of group. Your hairstyle, dress and behaviour can give other people ideas about your gender, age group, wealth, lifestyle, beliefs and culture.

Clothes, hairstyle, make-up and body shape are seen differently by different people. No one looks attractive to everyone. The important issue is to have a positive self-image. It can be easy to develop a negative self-image if you do not understand the way in which culture influences other people's opinions of your appearance.

? Think about it

What is the ideal body shape for a man or woman? Why is this the ideal shape? Where did these ideas come from? How many people do you see who fit this ideal? Is there a problem with having an 'ideal' shape?'

■ *No one has the same views about our appearance*

A poor self-image may cause a person to lack confidence or feel depressed about their relationships with other people.

Gender

Children seem to be able to classify themselves in terms of gender very early in life – they know whether they are a boy or a girl. Along with ethnicity (race) and age group, gender is a major social influence which affects how we understand ourselves. There are different social expectations of men and women. Men are expected to dress, think and behave differently from women. Men are expected to have different interests and habits from women.

Sociologists see being a man or a woman as like having a role in a play. People have gender roles or acts that they have to perform across life. Fifty years ago, gender roles or acts were rigidly different for men and women in Britain.

Some key differences in gender role in the 1950s	
Men	**Women**
Expected to work full time	Expected to support husband in work by undertaking household duties, washing, cleaning, cooking
Expected to provide money to pay for housing and family	Expected to care for children and older relatives as necessary
Expected to organise household and do household repairs	Expected to look after and clean home. Might do part-time or light work to improve household income if no childcare work needed
Expected to be able to fight for country if necessary	Might take on men's work if country went to war and there were not enough men to work in factories, etc.

The nature of society has changed dramatically over the last 50 years and gender roles have also changed. Both young men and women now expect to go to work and most people do not expect to fight in wars.

Some gender role differences still exist in society. Jobs which involve working with young children or cleaning are still mainly done by women. Jobs which involve engineering, building or vehicle repair are still mainly done by men.

When it comes to self-concept, women are likely to think differently from men. Career success, work and making money are standards which more men may judge themselves against than women. More women than men may see a successful life in terms of good relationships. The gender roles of 50 years ago still influence how people think of themselves today.

Look at the talking point in the margin. In a household with an adult male and female couple, how do you think the tasks below should be shared?

- Shopping
- Ironing clothes
- Making household repairs
- Painting and decorating the house
- Washing clothes
- Cooking
- Cleaning rooms

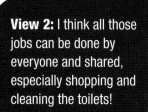

Talking point

View 1: I think that there are jobs that men can do and jobs for women. Hard jobs like plumbing and painting and decorating are for men. Women are better at shopping and cleaning.

View 2: I think all those jobs can be done by everyone and shared, especially shopping and cleaning the toilets!

- Cleaning bathrooms and toilets
- Earning money to pay bills.

Do you still see some types of activity as a male or female role?

Culture and socialisation

Different people have different customs and ways of thinking. The family and the local area or community where you grew up may have different beliefs and expectations from many other families and areas. People have different customs and ways of thinking, including the following:

- Different beliefs about food, e.g. Muslim and Jewish people do not eat pork, most Hindus do not eat beef and Buddhists are vegetarian.

- Different beliefs about education, e.g. some neighbourhoods and families think educational achievement is very important, others do not.

- Different beliefs about behaviour, e.g. some families emphasise the importance of keeping appointments, never being late and being organised for work.

- Different beliefs about marriage and gender roles, e.g. different religions and communities have different beliefs about sex and marriage.

People develop diverse beliefs, values, habits and assumptions because of the social experiences they have during their life. We classify this range of influences as cultural influences. Our culture can influence how we understand ourselves, because different cultures create different ideas about what is normal or right to do.

What you think of as being important or right or wrong will be greatly influenced by the norms of people around you. What you eat, how much you care about education, your attitude to drugs and sex will be influenced by your culture. Culture will also influence how you think about and judge yourself. Your self-esteem will be influenced by cultural beliefs about what is right and wrong.

Media

Media means things like newspapers, radio, television, DVDs, music and Internet sites. Families often influence the media that children experience, but, as children grow older, they start to choose media that interests them. We get many ideas about our culture from the media that we choose to watch, read or listen to.

Income

Being in a low- or high-income family may influence the media and cultural beliefs that we grow up with. Self-concept may be influenced by the opportunities associated with our family's income.

Relationships with family and friends

In some ways, we are all 'other people'. Our idea of self develops because of the way other people talk and act with us. Self-concept is very strongly influenced by the quality of the emotional relationships we make with others. Throughout life, relationships can strongly affect how successful and happy we are. Our self-esteem is likely to be strongly influenced by our relationships with others.

A newborn baby starting out in the world would hope to enjoy most of the positive things listed in the table below.

The effects of personal relationships at different stages of a person's life	
Good relationships	**Poor relationships**
Infancy Secure attachment between the infant and parents A rich learning environment A safe loving environment that meets the child's emotional needs	**Infancy** A failure to make a secure emotional attachment Neglect or rejection of the child
Childhood A secure home Membership of a family Socialisation into a culture Friendships with others at school A feeling of being confident and liked by other people A feeling of self-esteem because the child is good at things	**Childhood** A stressful home Angry, depressed or inconsistent parents Poor socialisation Limited friendships Feeling rejected or not liked by others Lack of confidence and self-esteem
Adolescence Independence but still with the support of the family A network of friends – sense of belonging within a group A culture shared by friends	**Adolescence** Conflict and fighting with parents and family Few friends – feelings of depression and rejection Poor self-esteem
Adulthood A network of friends and family to help and support A secure, loving, sexual relationship Good relationships with work colleagues A feeling of being secure, confident and safe with other people	**Adulthood** Feelings of isolation and loneliness Lack of support A lack of attachment to partners No social protection from stress Low self-esteem
Old age A network of family, friends and partner to provide emotional support A sense of purpose involving other people	**Old age** Few friends, no social support, isolation No social protection from stress Potential low self-esteem

Abuse

The word 'abuse' covers a wide range of behaviour. Abuse can be criminal acts of violence or acts of neglect. Children can be subjected to abuse within their family or through bullying at school. Vulnerable adults, such as people with a learning difficulty or older people, may be subjected to abuse by family members or by care workers.

Forms of abuse

- **Physical abuse** – hitting, pushing, pulling, restraining or causing pain or distress by physical actions.

- **Sexual abuse** – sexually exploiting or humiliating others.

- **Emotional abuse** – bullying, blaming, threatening and damaging others' feelings of self-worth and self-esteem (sometimes called psychological abuse).

- **Financial abuse** – taking others' property or money, theft and exploitation of others' resources.

- **Neglect** – not giving food or physical care, not giving attention.

The effects of abuse

Abuse will result in harm to an individual. In the short term, abuse might result in fear and anger or perhaps withdrawal and depression. Medium- and long-term abuse is likely to harm a person's self-image and self-esteem. In the long-term, some forms of abuse may result in self-destructive behaviour or in mental ill-health. The effects of abuse will vary from person to person, but some general medium- and long-term effects are shown in the diagram below.

Key point

The Mental Capacity Act 2005 makes it illegal to ill treat or neglect a person who is vulnerable because of limited ability to make decisions.

A loss of self-esteem

Self-destructiveness and self-harming

A lack of social confidence

Increased dependency

Abuse can cause

Copying the abusive behaviour

Mental ill-health

A negative self-concept

Attention seeking

Withdrawal from people

■ *Effects of abuse*

Education

A person's idea of who they are is strongly influenced by their experience at school. Later experiences at college or university can also confirm or change what we think about ourselves.

Education influences us because we mix with other people and may compare ourselves with them. The tasks we have to do affect our beliefs about what we are good or bad at and we may learn theories and ideas which help us to understand our lives.

Emotional health and well-being

Emotional health and well-being may depend on a clear sense of who we are and a feeling that we are special and valued. Poor physical health or mental health problems will affect a person's self-concept.

Environment

Self-concept is influenced by our environment, which can mean all the influences on us that come from other people and society, e.g. our relationships with others, culture, education, gender roles, the media. Our environment also means where we live – we may have a better self-concept if we live in a supportive neighbourhood. The housing we live in may make us feel safe, or it may make us feel stressed.

 Real Life Care

Mrs Newcome's life story

Mrs Newcome was born in 1928, married in 1950 and gave birth to a son in 1951.

'Isn't it strange, sometimes I can remember my early childhood better than I can remember things from only 10 years ago. I can still remember the smell of my mother's skin when I was little; I used to cuddle up to my mother and I felt absolutely safe – everything was perfect. Naturally, I remember my father, but it's as if he wasn't in the house very much. My father was very strict – my sister and I were not allowed to speak at the table and we were only allowed into the living room to listen to the wireless if we were quiet.

School was hard – some of the teachers used to hit you with a ruler if you weren't paying attention or didn't do your work. I had some very good friends at school – other girls that I got on with, and we used to do lots of things together. Sometimes I think about how happy I was with my family and friends. We used to go to dance clubs and that's where I met my husband. I was

in great demand! I suppose I was very attractive in those days. I left school at 15 and worked as a telephone operator because people said I was very good at speaking on the phone.

When I got married I gave up work and became a housewife. In those days we didn't think it was right for married women with children to work, but I suppose we lived in a different culture – it's all changed now.'

Mrs Newcome has described part of her early life. She would say that she had a positive self-image and a high level of self-esteem.

1 How might gender roles have influenced Mrs Newcome's development of self-concept?

2 How could a positive interpretation of appearance have contributed to the development of self-concept?

3 Try to work out what some of the reasons for a positive self-concept might be.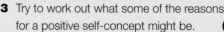

Summary of factors that influence self-concept	
Factor	**Influence**
Age	The way a person can describe who they are is influenced by learning and life experience and therefore by age.
Appearance	The way other people respond to a person may influence the self-image that they have and the way they value their self.
Gender	Fundamental issues such as gender and ethnicity will be major factors in the way a person forms a self-image.
Culture	People form an image of themselves based on ideas available in their culture.
Relationships	Self-image and self-esteem are strongly affected by the quality of relationships we have with others.
Abuse	Abuse may harm a person's view of themselves and result in low self-esteem.
Family	The quality of family relationships may have a major impact on a person's self-image and self-esteem.
Socialisation	The assumptions that people make about themselves are often based on childhood experiences associated with socialisation.
Income	Growing up in a low-income household may influence a person's way of thinking about themselves.
Media	People may compare themselves with the images of other people portrayed in the media.
Education	Educational achievement may influence a person's self-esteem.
Emotional health and well-being	A clear sense of 'who you are' and an ability to value yourself may be necessary for emotional health and well-being. Poor emotional health may cause problems with self-concept.
Environment	The neighbourhood and environment that we live in may have a major influence on our assumptions about self.

It is possible to think of the influences listed in the table working together like the circles in the diagram which follows.

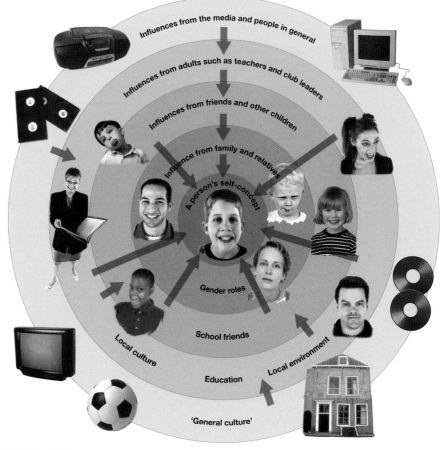

■ *Circles of influence*

Practice for Assessment

Carrying out this activity could contribute to evidence for P3.

You must identify factors that influence the individual's self-concept. One idea to help you achieve this outcome might be to design a poster diagram based on the information above.

To achieve M3, you must describe how five different factors can influence the development of the individual's self-concept. One idea to help achieve this might be to take a life story and choose five of the factors listed above in order to work out how these factors may have influenced the self-concept of the person.

Care needs

If a person is to develop as a confident individual, then they will need to develop a self-image – a clear concept of self. They will also need to 'believe in' and value themselves; in other words, they will need a sense of self-esteem. Care workers may be involved in providing a specific service to do with a care plan, but there are a range of approaches that are always needed in order to support self-concept and self-esteem needs of service users. These approaches are described in the table below:

Care needs that influence self-concept	
Approach	**Effect on self-concept**
Recognition of diversity	Each person is special and unique. Each person should be treated as an individual. Care workers need to value diverse ethnic, religious and social groups. If diversity is not valued, this may threaten a service user's self-esteem.
Active support	Service users will need active physical and emotional support. It will be important that care workers know a little about a service user's life and beliefs. Care workers will need to use active listening skills in order to provide emotional support. Emotional support might help some service users to develop their self-concept.
Promotion of independence	The development of independence during childhood and adolescence helps to support self-image and self-esteem. Older service users may need support in order to stay independent. Independence may be necessary for self-esteem.
Promotion of choice	Choices help to create a person's self-image. It may be difficult to develop or keep a working self-concept if a person does not have the opportunity to make choices.
Respect and dignity	A sense of self-esteem will depend on receiving respect and maintaining dignity during interaction with other people. Without respect and dignity, service users may develop a low sense of self-esteem.
Protection	Service users will need to feel safe. Care workers will try to create a setting that will protect the physical and emotional safety of service users. If service users feel threatened, then this may undermine self-image and self-esteem.

Real Life Care

Meeting service users' needs

Zehra is 3 years old and is looked after by a registered childminder. Zehra's physical needs for warmth and safety and food are all met, but the childminder also takes time to play with Zehra and to make sure that Zehra feels safe and happy. The social and emotional experiences that Zehra has at 3 years of age will provide a foundation for the later development of self-image and self-esteem.

Joel is a young adult with a learning difficulty. He has his own room in a hostel. Care workers undertake life-map work with Joel so that they can be effective at creating choice and promoting his independence. Life-map work involves gradually helping Joel to produce drawings that he can use to explain his views about life, including his dreams, hopes and fears. Because care workers have fully supported Joel's independence and choice and because they have shown him respect, as well as providing him with a safe place to live, Joel has developed a positive self-image and a positive level of self-esteem.

Anita is an elderly adult who now lives in a care home because she can no longer organise daily living activities

of washing, dressing and preparing food for herself. Care workers provide a safe, clean living environment that meets Anita's physical needs. Care workers also provide reminiscence discussions where service users are invited to share their memories of the past. Because Anita enjoys talking with others and because she can clearly remember her past, these discussions help Anita to keep the positive self-image that she had before she needed to come into care. Because people listen to Anita's stories and because they are interested, Anita is able to maintain positive self-esteem.

1 Identify what care needs Zehra might have apart from the need for protection. ✔

2 Identify Joel's care needs and how care workers are supporting his development of self-esteem. ✔✔

3 Identify the skills care workers are using in order to help Anita to maintain a high level of self-esteem. ✔✔✔

Assessment and care packages

Under the National Health Service and Community Care Act 1990, service users are entitled to have their needs assessed. Needs are assessed by social workers and other professional staff who assess what services an individual should have purchased for them.

> **Care plan** *A written document that outlines how the needs of an individual are to be met.*

Assessment results in a **care plan** to buy in certain services. National minimum standards require that service users' needs are assessed and a care plan is produced before people receive a service. All service users should have a care plan; for example, Standard 3 in the National Minimum Standards for Care Homes for Older People requires that a 'needs assessment' is carried out if people come into care without going through the 'care planning system'.

National Minimum Standards require that people have an individual plan for their care, which may be drawn up by providers of care. This individual plan will be based on an assessment of an individual's needs and may help staff to assess the effectiveness of care. Standard 7 (Care

Homes for Older People) states that homes must provide: 'A service user plan of care generated from a comprehensive assessment [which] is drawn up with each service user and provides the basis for the care to be delivered.' So service user needs are documented and this results in a written service user plan which explains many of the most important needs which care aims to provide for.

Many people have complex needs that result in a need for **multidisciplinary care**. For example, an older person in the community might be unable to do housework or their own shopping, might need medical attention for a leg ulcer and might also have social needs because they are lonely. This person might receive occupational therapy to help with daily living activities, home care to assist with shopping, nursing care to assist with dressing the ulcer and voluntary support to provide conversation to meet social needs.

> **Multidisciplinary care**
> *Care provided by a range of different agencies and professional carers. Examples are social work, social care, nursing, psychiatry, occupational therapy, speech therapy, medicine.*

Care needs at different life stages

Infancy

Physical and intellectual needs
Newly born babies are completely dependent on parents or carers to keep them safe, fed, washed and warm. Infants also depend on parents and carers to provide contact and stimulation in order to encourage intellectual development. Intellectual stimulation will lay the foundation for the development of a child's self-image.

Social and emotional needs
Infants need to make safe and stable relationships with carers during the first year of life. This process is called bonding – making a loving attachment. It is possible that a failure to bond or make a secure attachment in infancy might result in difficulties with relationships in later life. Having a loving relationship with a parent or carer in infancy may be essential in order to enable the development of self-esteem.

Childhood

Physical and intellectual needs
As children grow, they learn an ever-increasing range of skills like running, climbing, skipping, riding a bicycle and reading. As they gain new skills, children enjoy doing things for themselves and becoming more independent. Children will need practical opportunities to learn and develop. A child's self-image will begin to develop from interactions with other people during this stage.

Social and emotional needs
Children are still dependent on adult carers to provide a stable, loving home for them and although children will explore and experiment, carers often need to guide and supervise what they do. Adult carers will need to provide for children's physical needs and create a physically and emotionally safe environment for them.

During primary socialisation, children should feel they belong to a family or group, and they will have a need to feel loved and included in that group. The development of self-esteem will be influenced by relationships during this stage.

Adolescence

Physical and intellectual needs

Young people develop an increasing level of skill and understanding as they grow towards adulthood. Care needs will include good educational opportunities to develop practical and intellectual skills.

Social and emotional needs

The need to belong to a family or care group may still be important; adolescents will be increasingly concerned to fit in with groups of their own age. Adolescents often copy each other's style of clothing and appearance. Adolescents will be able to make independent choices about physical needs and choose their own friendship groups and lifestyle. Both self-image and self-esteem are strongly influenced by social and learning experiences at this stage.

Adults

Physical and intellectual needs

Many adults receive practical help and assistance because they cannot live completely independent lives. Adults with learning difficulties may continue to need support in order to make appropriate decisions. Adults with physical disabilities may need a range of physical and practical care, such as assisting with mobility, cooking and dressing.

Social and emotional needs

Service users will also need to feel safe, included and respected. The quality of an adult person's self-image and self-esteem will be influenced by the way other people treat them.

Older adults

Physical and intellectual needs

Many older service users need support with physical care such as getting dressed and bathing.

Social and emotional needs

Older adult service users may be at risk of not being treated with dignity and respect. Some older adults may have particular needs for supportive communication and relationships. A person's self-image and self-esteem will be influenced by the quality of the care that they receive.

Key point

The Mental Capacity Act 2005 provides new guidance and a new advocacy service to help vulnerable adults who have difficulty making choices and decisions.

The final stages of life

Physical needs

When people are dying, they will often have complex physical needs for comfort, for example pain relief, keeping the mouth moist, and so on.

Social and emotional needs

People in the final stages of life may be anxious, and will be in need of emotional support. They will often want to see friends and relatives – the need to belong is important. People sometimes need to make sense of their lives and may benefit from counselling to enable them to cope. The need to feel that life has had a value may represent a self-esteem need for many individuals.

Care needs and life stages – an overview			
Life stage	**Physical and intellectual needs**	**Social and emotional needs**	**The value of meeting needs for self-concept**
Infancy	Safety, food, warmth, physical comfort, intellectual stimulation	A first loving relationship – bonding	Good physical health and a loving relationship provide a foundation for a positive self-concept.
Childhood	A safe base from which to explore; good educational opportunities	Socialisation into the norms and beliefs of the child's culture	Childhood experiences and socialisation influence the development of self-esteem.
Adolescence	Independent self-care; educational opportunities	Secondary socialisation with friendship groups; the development of a self-concept	Interaction with other people will influence self-concept.
Adulthood	Support to lead an independent life	Social interaction – the need to 'belong' with other people and be valued by them	The need to maintain a positive self-image and positive self-esteem.
Later life	Support to maintain independence	Social interaction – as above	The need to maintain self-image and self-esteem.

Practice for Assessment

Carrying out this activity could contribute to the evidence for P4.

You must explain potential differences in the care needs of individuals at different life stages. One idea that might help with this task would be to visit different care settings and to ask about the care needs of service users. You might be able to use this section and any notes you make on your visits in order to compare and contrast differences in care needs.

To achieve a D2, you must explain how meeting individual care needs can improve the individual's self-concept. One idea to help achieve this outcome might be to use some outline details of a person in a care setting and work out how respect, choice, independence and emotional support may help to improve the person's self-esteem and self-image. You should also identify any specific care needs that the individual might be likely to have and explain how self-esteem or self-image might be improved by meeting these specific needs.

Check your understanding

1. What is a chromosome?

2. How might an average five-year-old's intellectual or thinking ability be different from that of an adult's?

3. What is meant by the term 'bonding' when talking about infants?

4. Young children often think in terms of fairness – if someone has pushed you then you have the right to push someone else – because it's fair. Adults do not usually think like this. How can you explain the difference between young children and adults?

5. List five physical changes to health that a person might expect to experience after the age of 65.

6. What is meant by socialisation?

7. List five disadvantages associated with living on a low income.

8. List three predictable life events and three life events that are likely to be unexpected.

9. List five influences on self-concept.

10. Why is it important that care workers should promote choice and independence with respect to the maintenance or development of a service user's self-concept?

7 Creative and Therapeutic Activities in Health and Social Care

Introduction

There is a wide range of creative and therapeutic activities that care settings can use to benefit service users' health and well-being. This unit looks at the different types of care settings, the different types of creative and therapeutic activities that settings use and the benefits of these activities to the health and well-being of the service user. The unit also explores suitable activities for particular client groups and will enable you to plan an activity for a group of service users. The different laws and legislation that the government has put into place to protect service providers and service users from harm or injury when taking part in these activities are explained.

How you will be assessed

This is an internally assessed unit.

In this unit you will learn about:

- creative and therapeutic activities
- the benefits of creative and therapeutic activities
- health and safety legislation, regulations and codes of practice.

Creative and therapeutic activities

In health and social care, it is important to understand the different types of care settings. Each setting will use various activities to accommodate the different needs and abilities of its service users. This section looks at the different types of care that are available and the types of creative and therapeutic activities used by settings in order to benefit the varying needs of service users for their health and well-being.

Activities

Key point

Creative means conveying a message and having the power to bring something into being.

Therapeutic means the treatment of disease or other disorder – something that may benefit health.

Different settings in health and care use a variety of activities to help people maintain and improve their health. It is important to use different activities rather than the same ones as people can often get bored with one activity. There are many activities that can assist health, such as physical activities like sport or going on a day trip with friends. This unit focuses on the creative and therapeutic activities that settings can run to meet the needs of different client groups.

Creative and therapeutic activities can help people express themselves in a variety of ways. Creative activities make good use of the techniques the different activities offer, but care settings do not use creative activities to help service users develop their skills to create a masterpiece, rather to allow service users to learn to channel their feelings, thoughts and attitudes. Therapeutic activities enable service users to relax while being able to keep a healthy mind and body. Obviously, some activities are going to be better for some groups of people than others.

Over to you

Do you enjoy any creative activities? Make a list of all the different creative and therapeutic activities that you can think of. Why do people enjoy these activities?

Drama and role play

Drama and role play are very similar activities and are often confused. Drama can be seen as an active approach that can sometimes help the service user to tell their story in order to solve a problem, understand the meaning of images and to strengthen and build relationships, and enhance communication skills. It does not necessarily mean acting out a role; it could be you expressing yourself through different roles and showing your interpretation of objects, situations, and so on. Role play, on the other hand, is more to do with taking the role of someone else and making it realistic through your adaptation and understanding of the circumstances.

Drama and role play can be used in several different ways:

- to remind people how to play
- to practise language skills
- to rehearse for real-life situations.

They can help to provide a safe and accepting environment in which clients may gain the confidence to experiment and explore areas that they may otherwise have avoided.

Drama and role play can be inexpensive activities, as it costs nothing to act out a story or scene without props and costumes. If costumes, scenery and lighting, etc. are to be used, drama is a great activity to do as a group because it involves not just the actors, but other roles that do not require being on stage, such as costume and set design and directing.

Art and craft

Art and craft activities involve painting, charcoal drawings, collage, pottery and making items such as cards and calendars. To run these creative activities you would need lots of materials. In addition, when people are painting or drawing, they often need a 'subject' (something to focus on) and so care settings may sometimes have to provide a bowl of fruit, for example, or a model will come and sit to be drawn. At other times, a group could be taken to a particular setting for the day.

Normally, art and craft activities are solo attempts, as individuals like to sketch their own drawings or make their own trinket boxes. Even though they are mainly individual activities, many people like to work with others around them. This is so that they can chat to them while they are working, perhaps showing each other their work and gaining ideas, or just for company. Once a piece has been completed, individuals sometimes like to 'show their work off' to others as this can give them a sense of achievement.

Music

We all respond to music, and music can provide a sense of release or therapy for a particular individual. Listening to music can be an individual activity or a group activity. It could benefit a group of people to sing and listen to songs together as this helps people to feel united; songs can teach children things like different colours, the alphabet, counting, and so on.

Creating music can be fun for groups to take part in, particularly if home-made instruments, which could be made first, such as shakers, drums, tambourines, musical bottles, etc. are used. Individuals could

 Over to you

Identify the types of client group that you would use drama and role play with? Who do you think would benefit the most? Why?

Which client groups would be least likely to enjoy drama or role play?

 Key point

It is very frustrating if you are trying to organise and start an activity when you do not have all the resources!

 Over to you

Think of your own experiences at school. Which art and craft activities did you enjoy doing? Why? What did you use for materials and subjects?

 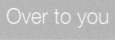 Over to you

You have been asked to lay out a table with lots of different materials for arts and crafts. What materials would you put out on the table?

Would you put out the same materials for one care setting (see the health and social care settings below for an idea of these) as you would another? Identify and describe what materials you would use for different care settings and explain why.

 Over to you

Would you use the same music for different client groups? Identify which music you would use for different groups and settings.

sing while others play the instruments, and different music can be made allowing the service users to express their feelings through loud and soft, fast and slow music.

Cooking

This is a great activity to do with service users, either as a solo or a group activity. In all settings, carers may have to supervise the cooking and use of appliances. Different items can be cooked or baked. As with art and craft activities, making sure you have the right ingredients is essential, so it is a good idea to choose the item to make in advance in order to get the ingredients required. Cooking is a good way to allow service users to enjoy their creation and achieve a sense of satisfaction when they eat their end-product. You could choose to start with something simple such as cakes or biscuits, or some groups could even cook a meal.

Over to you

Plan an activity where some service users cook the food and others make the decorations and music.

Over to you

What types of food would you let different client groups cook and prepare? How much supervision would each client group need?

Is it possible to carry out cooking activities in all care settings? Why?

■ *Cooking allows service users to enjoy their creations*

Writing

This is an activity that is mainly done individually, although when their writing is finished, some service users may like others to read their work. It gives service users the chance to express themselves and their feelings about anything on paper. This could be in the form of a piece of poetry or a story, for example. Individuals could be given a subject to write about or left to write about anything that they feel particularly strongly or are worried about.

This is a versatile activity, as it can be done in a group environment with people working on their own and then sharing their thoughts, or service users can write in the privacy of their home away from others. Groups

Over to you

Think of different topics that service users could write about. Would you use these topics for all client groups?

Are writing activities beneficial to all client groups and all settings?

could also be taken on day trips to various places for inspiration. It is also a very cheap activity, as all that is really needed is a piece of paper and a pen.

Games and quizzes

These include board games, television game shows, bingo, card games, and so on. Games could be played individually, like memory games such as pairs, or as group games such as bingo. There are a variety of game shows and quizzes on television and watching these can stimulate the mind and intellectual development. Games and quizzes can be cheap to run if they are homemade, and a variety of games can be played with a pack of playing cards, for example. Games and quizzes are suitable for all ages and abilities, but different levels of games should be played to suit the needs of the players.

Over to you

Make a game or quiz for a particular client group in a health and social care setting. Make sure you do not make it too easy or hard for the client group you are aiming it at and that everyone in the setting is able to take part if they wish.

■ *Bingo helps the memory and improves reactions*

Use of computers

Computers stimulate the mind and can be a good source of information (the Internet). They can assist in creating things and could be used for writing activities (see above). Games can be played on the computer and can help children to develop different skills. However, the use of computers can be a very individual activity, and it can be expensive to purchase a computer and any additional equipment and software.

Talking point

View 1: Computers should only be used with young people. Old people do not know how to use them.

View 2: Learning to use a computer can be therapeutic as it helps to make the mind work.

Yoga and massage

Massage and yoga aim to give inner peace and calm. Yoga aims to unite the whole body and is a system of exercises and meditation, which helps a person to become balanced in body and mind. Yoga also improves breathing and is believed to cleanse the body of toxins, improve muscle tone, reduce stress, and lower blood pressure. It can be useful for conditions such as anxiety, arthritis, headache, migraine, multiple sclerosis, osteoporosis, pregnancy, rheumatoid arthritis and more.

Key point

Massage is the rubbing and kneading of parts of the body to stimulate the circulation of the blood to reduce pain or stiffness. People with injuries or aches and pains have massages as it can relax the body and mind.

Yoga and massage can be done as a group activity, but also on an individual basis. For example, a group of friends all go for a massage, but lie on individual beds and have an individual masseuse. You can hire a yoga instructor or masseuse to visit care settings, or you can go to classes for yoga or beauty salons for massages.

Key point

Yoga comes from the Indian word for 'union'.

Over to you

In a small group, discuss which client groups you would be more inclined to do yoga and massage with. Explain why you would choose this client group over others.

The yoga instructor makes it look easy

■ *The instructor makes it look easy!*

Activities such as those mentioned above do not necessarily have to be done as a craft activity or a music activity. Activities can be combined together in order to create a fun day, a fete, charity fundraiser, play, and so on. The creative and therapeutic activities can also be linked with other activities to assist in developing health and well-being.

Health and social care settings

There are many different types of care settings for a variety of age groups, mental disabilities, physical disabilities, and so on. The way these are run and the activities they offer are all suited to the particular group and these may differ depending on where you live. As you read through the settings described below, having already explored the range of possible activities, start to think about which kinds of activity offer the most benefits in each setting as well as being the most appropriate.

Pre-school care

This is for children aged 5 years and under who are not old enough to go to school. They are sometimes held in community halls or other accessible venues. Many are attached to primary schools and provide a link for children to progress onto primary school. The sessions are normally held as separate morning and afternoon sessions, which are about 3 hours in length. The sessions show the value of play as they can provide children with the opportunity to learn basic skills such as spelling their name, counting to ten, and learning colours. The staff plan a varied curriculum of activities to help and encourage the children to learn. As children are very keen to express themselves, explore and experiment with new objects and items, pre-school is a good place to develop these interests. Studies have shown that children who go to pre-school achieve better results in later education.

Day care for children

Day care describes care for two different sets of people – children and the elderly. Day care for children involves the care of a child by a person other than their parents/guardians. This is mainly because the parents are at work. There are some varieties of day care such as crèches, or nurseries, which look after children under 5 (similar to pre-school care, although day care is not just run in morning or afternoon sessions). Places at the crèche are booked by the parents for the times they need and the crèche carries out duties such as feeding the children and, if the children are very young, then cots or beds are available for the children to go to sleep in. Children in these care environments will also learn basic skills such as spelling their name, but they mostly take part in physical activities, creative and imaginative play and indoor or outdoor play.

Childminder

A childminder is a day carer who looks after children in their home. They turn their homes into a place where the children can spend the day. Most childminders take children who are 5 years and under and, like crèches, provide food, drink and a cot should the child need it. Some childminders also look after children older than 5, so these children will be at school for the majority of the day. However, the childminder will collect the child from school. Sometimes, they also walk the child to school in the morning.

Over to you

How many different types of care settings can you think of? List as many as you can. Compare your answers with the rest of your group. Did they have some that you did not think of?

Key point

Pre-school care is sometimes called play school or playgroup.

Childminders are regularly inspected by Ofsted, the inspectorate for children and learners in England, to check that they are running everything correctly and that they are following the correct procedures.

After-school club

Similar to a childminder, an after-school club provides care for those children whose parents are still at work when they have finished school for the day. Some after-school clubs collect the children from school and provide a hot meal for them as well. These clubs are less structured than a school as they are for both older and younger children. The clubs normally provide pens and paper for the children to complete their homework or to draw, or there may be board games and televisions/DVDs.

Nanny

Another type of day care is provided by a nanny. Nannies are available not just when the parents are at work, but when they are at home as well. They provide relief for the parents/guardians and can assist with the household chores, but mainly provide welfare for the children such as making them food and providing them with entertainment and activities. Nannies are quite expensive to hire and sometimes live in with the family, so it is important that a family finds a nanny that they can get along with.

■ The nanny – one type of day care for children

Elderly day care

The second type of day care is aimed at older people or people with disabilities who live in their own homes but need additional support. Service users may attend the hospital day care centre based on their medical disabilities, as they may be recovering from an accident or an illness. They often get the chance to chat to other service users, have a meal provided and see the doctor or nurse.

A social day care centre is for the use of people who live in their own homes but may be socially isolated. They will normally attend for the whole day and are provided with a hot meal, and perhaps play some games like bingo, dominos or cards. It also enables service users to talk to others and gives them an excuse to go out. Occasionally, the centre will organise group outings or activities. Generally, it is the elderly who will use this facility.

Community group

Community groups comprise different groups and clubs that cater for various ages, genders, disabilities and interests. A social day centre, as described above, can be classed as a community group – it is a collective group of people joining together each week to share interests. Examples of other community groups include Brownies or Cubs for children, Gingerbread for lone parents, support groups for people with addictions, sporting clubs, social clubs, groups to help people get over bereavements, illnesses, etc.

Over to you

Community groups are sometimes advertised in your local paper. Have a look and see what groups are available in your area.

Residential home

Residential homes often mean clients living in a care home with other people. A residential home is simply a house with services and housemates. The accommodation typically consists of a private or shared bedroom with a private or shared bathroom and access to common rooms. Homes offer services to residents, which can include daily meals, medication management, personal care assistance and activities.

Residents can often choose whether they want a private room or a shared room and can take their own furniture and possessions (within reason) with them to make them feel comfortable and at home. Carer(s) will also live with the residents in the home. In some homes, carers work in shifts with other carers, so that the service users are never left uncared for; in other homes, staff work during the day and are on call at night if a resident activates an alarm.

Residential care is typically used and associated with older people. However, it is important to realise that residential care is also for other groups of people. Below are some examples of people that use residential care:

- Older people who cannot look after themselves.

- People with physical and mental disabilities who need practical help with dressing, mobility, eating and drinking, and personal hygiene, or people with learning disabilities who need support.

- Children with no carers, for example a child whose parents may have died or who cannot care for them.

Not all the residents are permanent. Some service users are only in a residential home for a short period of time because they have just come out of hospital and cannot do things for themselves, such as cook food, and so they stay in the home until they are well enough to take care of themselves.

In elderly residential homes, residents come and go as they please to comply with the care value base, but sometimes the home will put in place some organisation of bath nights and visiting times as a guide. Residential homes for young children or adults with mental disabilities do not allow residents to go out on their own as they may be unsafe.

Some residential homes are visited by mobile libraries and may have monthly or more regular visits from the chiropodist, doctor and physiotherapist if residents require. They may also employ a part-time activities organiser who arranges painting, quizzes and community activities.

Real Life Care

Highlands residential home

Ruby is a care assistant in Highlands residential home for elderly people. She has worked there for a number of years and knows the residents very well.

Ruby has noticed that some residents seem more forgetful and others more angry and rude with her (and other staff) when she speaks to them than they were when they first moved into the home. When Ruby talks to some of the residents, she finds out about their life and their interests before they came to the home. Most were active and enjoyed meeting friends, going on trips and doing activities at home that kept them busy. However, the home only has one television in a big room and a few books, which no one seems to read, and never organises any trips anywhere. The residents seem to keep themselves to themselves.

Ruby thinks that the residents need something to do other than the television and books. Ruby, however, doesn't know what activities would best suit the home as residents have poor circulation, arthritis and have suffered strokes.

1 Why do you think some residents are more forgetful, angry and rude with staff than they were when they first moved in? ✓

2 What advice would you give Ruby? ✓✓

3 Make a list of the activities you would suggest for the residents. Explain why you chose these activities, showing the advantages and disadvantages of each activity. ✓✓✓

Domiciliary care

This is care provided in the comfort of the client's own home. For example, it could involve a supervised living arrangement in a home environment for adults who struggle to look after themselves. The carer could help with personal hygiene (keeping clean, going to the toilet, etc.), dressing, cleaning the home, cooking meals, shopping, and transport.

Independent living

This is also known as sheltered accommodation and enables service users to maintain their independence by having their own flat or bungalow, but they also have the support of a warden who either lives on the site or can be called by using an emergency alarm. The accommodation is specially adapted to suit the residents (normally people over the age of

50 or people with disabilities) with low baths and pull cords that reach the floor, so if they fall and injure themselves, they can pull a cord, which sets off the emergency alarm.

Some independent living provides common rooms where residents can meet each other and occasionally a fete or a party will be held – it is then up to individual residents if they go or not. Other services are also available at an extra charge to the service user such as a cleaner or perhaps home meals delivery.

The service users are responsible for themselves and they are expected to do their own cooking, cleaning, shopping and washing, but they have the security of knowing that the support is there if they require it. The warden will regularly visit each flat and bungalow (perhaps once a day) to check that the residents are feeling well and to see if they have any problems. The residents can also call the **warden** if they have a problem.

> **Warden** *An official person in charge of a home or buildings who makes sure everything is maintained and that the residents are well and happy.*

Hospitals

Hospitals provide many different sorts of care to all types of service users no matter what their age, gender, ethnicity, etc. Some hospitals have more facilities and treatments than others, and patients may have to go to different hospitals for specialist treatments or even accident and emergency. Larger hospitals are able to have more departments such as physiotherapy or orthopaedics.

Hospitals are open 24 hours a day to provide care for their patients and only look after people who are ill. They provide them with food, and entertainment is limited to radios and, in some hospitals, televisions. Guests are welcome, but there are visiting hours that they may have to comply with. If service users are in hospital for long periods of time, other activities may be organised.

 Over to you

Draw up a table listing all the care settings mentioned above. For each care setting, identify all the creative and therapeutic activities that you think suit this care setting. Remember to think about the different service users and their needs in each care setting!

Are there any other creative and therapeutic activities you can think of that are not mentioned above? Which care setting would they suit?

Practice for Assessment

Carrying out this activity will give you evidence for P1, P2, P4 and M2.

You are applying for a job at your local council for the management and development of creative and therapeutic activities in health and social care settings across your town.

To show your understanding of the job, you have been asked to produce initial drafts and final plans for two creative or therapeutic activities for different clients in a health and social care setting. (P1)

Your plan must include the following information:

■ The patient/service user groups. (P1)

■ Why you chose these particular patients/service users. (P1)

■ The care setting or settings. (P1)

■ Your choice of activities or settings. (P1)

■ Reasons for your choices. (P1)

■ Identify the materials you need. (P1)

■ Select dates when the activities would take place. (P1)

■ Identify the relevant legislation, regulations and codes of practice linked to health and safety for each activity (see the section on health and safety legislation, regulations and codes of practice below and Unit 2 Individual Needs with the Health and Social Care Sectors). (P4)

■ Consider the safety of the patients/service users and others whilst carrying out the activities. (P4)

Once you have completed the draft plans, the council has asked you to produce final plans and then carry out the activities. (P1)

In your final plan, you will need to:

■ include a step-by-step guide to the activities (P1)

■ describe how health and safety issues were addressed for each activity. (M2)

Carry out your activities and get witness statements as evidence to show the council that you have completed the task. Write a report reviewing what you did in the activities and whether you think they went well or not, giving reasons in your answer and examples. (P2)

Benefits of creative and therapeutic activities

In the past, if you had any free time to be used for recreation, then you were considered not to be doing enough work! However, it has now been shown that this time can help us to learn new skills, keep our stress levels low, recover from tiredness and socialise with others. Therefore, it is important that when working in a care setting, service users (and carers) take part in some creative and therapeutic activities.

However, it is important when deciding what activity to do that you consider your environment, surroundings and the type of clients and staff that you will be working with. You must make sure that you are aware of the different needs that each service user has and how it will benefit them. There is no point in doing an activity with a group that is not capable of doing the activity or will not get any enjoyment from it.

Needs of patients/service users

The first thing to consider when running an activity in health and social care is the needs of those whom you will be doing the activity with. It is hard to list needs for everybody in society as we all have different and individual needs. However, when you relate needs to service users, you can be more specific.

Physical needs

These are the needs that we have to keep our body working. In a health and care setting, you will encounter people who have had an accident, an illness or perhaps they were born with a disability that affects their physical health. Also, as children develop and individuals get older, they develop physical needs.

Over to you

Look at the activities and client groups discussed earlier in the unit. Which activities would you use with which client groups?

Real Life Care

Colin and Stephanie

Colin and Stephanie are both physically disabled and live in domiciliary care.

Colin is 57 and had a stroke a couple of years ago, which left the left side of his body very weak. He finds it extremely hard to move his left arm and left leg and takes a long time to move around.

Stephanie is 19 and was in a motoring accident three months ago – her leg had to be amputated. She is currently using crutches and a wheelchair to help her mobility while she adapts to her disability.

1 Identify the physical needs that Colin and Stephanie each have. ✓

2 Plan an activity that you would do with Colin and an activity that you would do with Stephanie. You need to include the materials that you will require. ✓✓

3 Are they the same activities? Would the activities you chose for Colin and Stephanie suit other client groups? Explain why. ✓✓✓

Intellectual needs

These are the needs that we have to keep our brain working properly. As people get older, many suffer from memory loss. This could be short term (forgetting everyday things, for example going shopping and forgetting to buy a particular item like milk) or long term (forgetting where you live). Therefore, an intellectual need would be to stop or help a service user from suffering from memory loss.

Sometimes memory loss can occur because of boredom. If an individual is bored intellectually and they are not stimulating their mind, then they are likely to lose their memory as they are not exercising it. The mind is rather like a muscle: when you are exercising and keeping fit, your muscles feel nice and toned; however, if you stop exercising for long periods of time, your muscles go loose and relaxed. In the same way, the mind has to be regularly used to work effectively. Sometimes when service users go into care environments, they do not exercise their minds as effectively as they should and get bored.

Real Life Care

Tendai

Tendai is a student and has been on work placement in different care settings for different client groups. Tendai has noticed that some service users have nothing to do in their care environments and are bored, but the staff are unaware of this. Tendai wants to help the service users in the placements where she has visited but does not know what activities to suggest.

1 Choose a care setting and a client group and identify what creative and therapeutic activities Tendai could suggest for the service users to do to meet their intellectual needs. ✓

2 Analyse the benefits of these activities on the service users. ✓✓

3 Evaluate whether you could use these activities on other client groups. ✓✓✓

Language needs

This is the need that we have to communicate with others. We all want to be able to communicate with one another. If we did not communicate with each other, than no one would know what anyone else is doing and we would all feel very isolated and lonely.

Think about it

Could you imagine if we had no way of communicating with one another? How would we ever get things done?

Over to you

List all the different ways that we communicate with each other. Now, working with a partner, try to communicate a message without using the methods that you identified. How hard is it? Did your partner manage to understand your message?

However, just because somebody cannot speak the same language as you, it does not mean that you cannot communicate with them. How many different ways of communicating did you think of in the activity above? How many were non-verbal ways of communicating?

Over to you

Identify creative and therapeutic activities you could do to communicate with service users who do not speak the same language as the carer or other service users.

Are these activities the same for all client groups or are some more relevant to particular client groups than others?

Emotional needs

Emotional needs that are met make us feel relaxed and happy. For many individuals, being separated from loved ones can be very depressing. Someone who needs to have an operation or treatment may have to stay in hospital over a period of time. This can be upsetting for the service user (and their family) as they will miss their family and friends and be placed in an unfamiliar environment. For small children, this can be very confusing and distressing as their parents may not be able to remain with them at the hospital all the time, and so it is essential that these needs can be met with creative and therapeutic activities.

Real Life Care

Colin and Stephanie's emotional needs

Re-read the Real Life Care of Colin and Stephanie above.

1 Identify the emotional needs that they both have.

2 Describe what activities you could do with Colin and Stephanie to meet these needs.

3 Evaluate the effectiveness of these activities. Are there any other activities that might be better?

Social needs

Social needs are those that help us to make friends and build relationships with people. When people move into care environments such as residential homes, independent living or hospitals, it can be very upsetting as they are moving to new surroundings where the individual does not know anybody. They could be leaving the home that they have lived in for a long time and also moving away from their friends, not knowing who anyone is or where anyone is. It can be very lonely for the service users and they will need plenty of activities to welcome them into their new home and environment.

Real Life Care

Colin and Stephanie's social needs

Re-read the Real Life Care of Colin and Stephanie above.

1 List the different social needs for Stephanie and Colin.

2 Consider some activities that would meet their needs.

3 Compare these activities with other activities. What benefits do they provide Stephanie and Colin with?

Real Life Care

Read about Dan, and then answer the questions below.

Dan is an elderly man whose wife died six months ago. He recently moved from his home into an independent living, ground-floor flat after he had a fall and found that he could no longer manage the stairs. Dan had lots of friends where he used to live, but now he rarely sees them as his flat is 20 miles away and he does not drive. Dan has two children but they both live long distances away and do not visit Dan very often. Dan misses his family and friends and is very lonely.

Dan has seen some other residents around but is too scared to talk to them. The warden is concerned about Dan and has noticed that he is not interacting much with the other residents. The warden is thinking of having a fun day but does not know what to do or how to organise it. Can you help?

1 In groups, identify what Dan's physical, emotional and social needs are.

2 Decide which two different creative and therapeutic activities would help Dan to meet his needs.

3 Give detailed reasons for your choice and identify the materials you would need.

Benefits

Carers in health and social care settings like to choose activities that they know their clients will enjoy doing, because if an individual does not like a particular activity, then they will not carry out the activity properly. Therefore, it is important to make sure that the service user is going to enjoy the activity that has been set up for them. However, service providers do not just do creative and therapeutic activities because their patients enjoy them! They can actually be beneficial.

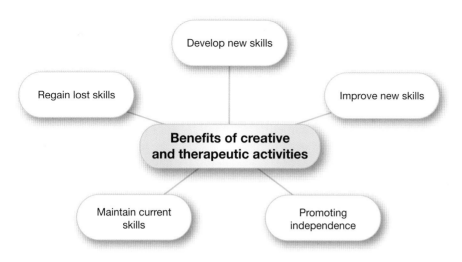

■ *Benefits of creative and therapeutic activities for service users*

Develop and improve new skills

Service users can benefit from creative and therapeutic activities as these can help them to develop new skills such as learning how to cook. This could be beneficial to clients with mental disabilities as being able to cook is an important life skill.

Children can develop lots of new skills as they are constantly learning and developing physically, intellectually, emotionally and socially, whereas adults and elderly service users find it harder to learn and develop because they are used to their own ways of doing things. However, by finding the right activity to suit their needs, such as watercolour painting, older people can develop new skills.

Real Life Care

The hospital play worker

Trish works as a hospital play worker and regularly visits children on the wards. She spends all week planning different activities such as role playing doctors and nurses with the children by getting them to act as the doctor and explaining to them the different conditions and illnesses, which helps them to understand why they are in hospital. This can help the children develop new skills and improve the skills they have already learnt by interacting and communicating with other children and adults, learning about their illnesses and emotionally coping with their poor health.

The children enjoy Trish's activities which stop them from being bored and take their minds off their illness.

1 Identify the skills that the children are learning and developing from Trish.

2 Suggest other activities Trish could do with the children to help them in the hospital. ✓✓

3 Could these activities be carried out on other client groups to help them develop skills? Give reasons to support your answer. ✓✓✓

By carrying out these or similar activities, service users can improve their newly found skills. This, in turn, leads to improved confidence and self-esteem and can promote the independence of the client to try new things and to carry on the activities on their own in private if they wish.

Maintain current skills and regain lost skills

By doing creative and therapeutic activities, service users are enabled to maintain the skills they already have. For example, Jerome is an adult who attends pilates and yoga every week. He is very flexible and can touch his toes easily. However, Jerome broke his leg and was not able to attend his classes for six months. When Jerome was fully recovered, he returned to his classes but discovered that he could not touch his toes anymore. It took him a further two months before he could touch his toes again.

Physical skills

The physical benefits of creative and therapeutic activities are that by doing exercise, such as yoga or walking, service users can keep supple and fit. Such activities help to develop new physical skills, strengthen muscles and improve mobility.

Many play and care settings for children encourage creative play as it offers so many benefits. It helps children to develop their fine motor skills, for example using their hands to hold paintbrushes, pencils or other tools. Other coordination skills can be learnt during physical activities and can help children to sleep better at night after they have burnt off energy by playing and concentrating on particular activities.

People with physical and mental disabilities will use therapeutic activities in the same manner as children, as these can assist in their recovery or coping with everyday life. For service users with physical disabilities, such activities can assist in regaining the movement that they possibly once had. For example, someone who has lost the use of their arm may use massage to stimulate and strengthen the muscles again. They then may use a creative activity to help stimulate their fine motor skills. Likewise, for a service user with mental disabilities, therapeutic activities can help to develop coordination and skills that are essential for life.

Physical exercise for adults and elderly people helps to keep the joints moving and yoga would maintain and increase suppleness, which is the flexibility of joints. This, in turn, would help to prevent broken bones and dislocation of joints.

Intellectual and language skills

Creative and therapeutic activities can help develop a child intellectually by helping them to learn about different colours, learn about different shapes, how to use tools such as paintbrushes, scissors and glue, help concentration and learn about different textures and materials.

The activities can help to stimulate the brain by providing opportunities to think, problem solve and reason. Activities such as quizzes, board games and reading are excellent for intellectual development as they

Over to you

Which activities would you suggest for a child to develop their fine motor skills? What equipment would you need?

Would you carry out the same activities for other client groups who were developing their fine motor skills?

enable the brain to think, remember and find solutions and tactics for particular games. Studies have found that elderly individuals who stay intellectually active by doing relevant activities are less likely to suffer from diseases and illnesses such as dementia and Alzheimer's than those who do not regularly stimulate their brain.

Some creative and therapeutic activities can develop the imagination. Role play is excellent for the imagination as it allows the individual to express their feelings and to show their perception of the role.

Imaginative activities such as drama and role play can also help to develop communication skills and improve speech, as individuals take on the roles of characters and move, talk and communicate in the personality of those they are pretending to be.

Emotional skills

Creative and therapeutic activities allow people to express their feelings. Letting a child play during these activities can enable them to express themselves in different ways, for example they could pound the play dough in an aggressive manner or mould it in a gentle way. This also allows them to gain confidence and self-esteem if they are pleased with their end-product, are praised and rewarded for their efforts and have a feeling of satisfaction and achievement afterwards.

From an emotional perspective, taking part in creative and therapeutic activities can assist individuals who are distraught, upset, grieving, and so on to be able to cope with the pain they are feeling. It can also relieve stress and tension as service users develop coping strategies by using particular activities as a way to escape reality, take their mind off their problems and express themselves without the judgment of others.

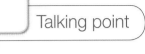
Talking point

View 1: Imaginative activities are for young children when they are playing mums and dads. They don't provide any benefits for older children or adults.

View 2: Imaginative activities can vary from play writing to acting and can provide intellectual stimulation, emotional and social benefits for all client groups.

■ *Children express themselves through activities*

Social needs

Children are likely to make friends while taking part in creative and therapeutic activities and will learn to help each other when their peers are unable to create something in a particular way. They learn to be independent and are able to work on their own but are still able to have fun and enjoy themselves with others.

Other client groups use these activities to form and develop friendships. By taking part in an activity, it enables people to work together in a team environment and allows people to interact with one another. It helps individuals who find it hard to talk to others as it gives them a common theme and interest.

Real Life Care

Adrian and his children

Adrian is a lone parent who has been divorced for approximately six years. His two children, Stuart (8 years) and Charmaine (6 years), live with him. Adrian finds it hard to go out and meet people because he cannot afford childcare.

Adrian is very lonely and finds that he misses adult company. His children have also told him that they wish they went out more and could play with other children their own age.

When a colleague at work told Adrian about a community group for lone parents, Adrian thought it sounded perfect. Adrian goes twice a week and he can take his children with him. They organise trips to go

bowling and have discos, as well as other activities. Adrian is pleased as it allows him to speak to other parents and adults in the same situation as him, and his children can play with the other children there.

1 Identify Adrian's needs before he joined the community group. ✓

2 Compare Adrian's needs with his children's. Are they the same or different? ✓✓

3 Explain how Adrian's and his children's needs have been met. Include examples in your answer. ✓✓✓

Practice for Assessment

Carrying out this activity will gve you evidence for P3 and M1.

Using your plans for two creative activities that you produced as evidence for P1, P2, P4 and M2:

- identify the potential benefits of each activity for the service user(s) (P3)
- explain how each creative/therapeutic activity could benefit the service user(s). (M1)

Choice of activity

The choice of activity that you make is very important and depends on several factors. Therefore, you need to understand what activities benefit client groups in different ways and which activity you would choose based on the needs and abilities of the client groups.

Potential benefits and therapeutic value of activities

Many settings use activities to help and assist their clients and service users to learn and develop skills that will improve their health and well-being. The table below contains a summary of some activities mentioned in this unit and their potential benefits and therapeutic value.

The potential benefits and therapeutic value of a range of activities	
Drama and role play	Provides intellectual and language benefits – develops communication skills, imagination and improves speech. Can also provide social benefits, as it can enable friendships to be formed through interaction with other service users.
Art and craft	Provides emotional benefits – allows service users to express themselves freely. A sense of satisfaction and achievement can be felt from good work, leading to gaining confidence and self-esteem.
Photography	Provides emotional benefits allowing the world to be shown through the eyes of the service user. A sense of satisfaction and achievement can be felt from good work leading to increased confidence and self-esteem.
Music	Making music can develop and improve social skills – working with others to make music. Emotional benefits include freedom of expression in the making of music and release of tension and stress. It can provide intellectual benefits as concentration is placed on timing of notes.
Cooking	An individual or a team effort. In a team environment, it can enhance communication and language. A great sense of achievement is felt when done successfully. Can lead to increased independence and confidence.
Movement and exercise	Social benefits – can lead to friendships being formed. Physical benefits – can improve mobility, muscle strength, tone and body fitness. Can be relaxing.
Writing	A way to help refine motor skills in holding a pen, but mostly assists the emotional release of thoughts and mind, which provides intellectual stimulation by concentrating and thinking about the content of the writing.
Games and quizzes	A good way of stimulating the brain by concentrating and thinking of strategies and answers. Can also add to developing social skills by strengthening friendships in the games and lead to satisfaction and achievement if successful.
Use of computers	Intellectual development requiring concentration – stimulates the brain to work. Leads to the discovery of new information. Also, promotes physical development in the form of fine motor skills when typing.
Yoga	Mainly physical development, as it increases suppleness and flexibility, but social friendships can be formed in group activities. Can also provide emotional and intellectual benefits due to relaxation techniques allowing body and mind to become free from thought.
Massage	Mainly physical development and can increase blood circulation and muscle tension. Can also provide emotional benefits due to relaxation techniques. Social skills may also be enhanced and communication and language improved through conversations with masseuse.

Practice for Assessment

Carrying out this activity will provide evidence for P3 and M1.

The local council liked your draft plans of the activities for service users that you prepared earlier in the unit. They have narrowed down the choice of applicants to two people, including you.

To help the council to decide whom they should employ, they have asked that you identify the potential benefits of your activities to the service users that you have chosen. (P3)

Explain these benefits in more detail with examples. (M1)

Age

When you go to the local park, you will often see children running around and playing. They have lots of energy and enjoy using this liveliness rather than sitting still and reading a book for a long period of time. Therefore, when choosing an activity for a child based on their age, a more physical activity would be appropriate, but this could incorporate intellectual ideas.

■ *Children love to use their energy*

Older teenagers and young adults are conscious of their image and want to look cool in front of their friends. Therefore, if you choose to do an activity that they perceive as uncool, such as yoga or playing bingo, they may not want to take part as they feel that they would look silly. A good mix between physical and intellectual activities will help them to learn and develop new skills, while improving the skills they already have.

Some elderly people will be limited to what their body will let them take part in due to physical disabilities, and so playing games such as musical chairs may not be appropriate. Elderly people will prefer to do activities that involve less physical movement than the kind of activities that children will be doing.

Gender

In the past, it was thought that men should do rough physical activities, such as rugby and football, while women should choose less physical activities based inside the home. This may have been due to the time that each gender had to spare, as we have discovered in Unit 4 that women on average tend to do more housework than men. However, as times are changing, women are starting to do more physical activities alongside men, and it is impossible to say that an activity should just be for men or just for women.

Over to you

In class, discuss which creative and therapeutic activities would suit the different age groups.

In groups, choose an age group and plan an activity which meets the service users' needs.

■ *Women take part in physical activities*

Talking point

View 1: I think that activities should be based on the gender of the service user. It is silly to think that a man is going to want to take part in a yoga class.

View 2: You should give both men and women the opportunity to say whether they want to join in with an activity or not, as we are all equal.

Over to you

For each of the following activities, note down the gender and age of the people most often associated with it: squash; badminton; cards; yoga; cooking; photography; painting; disco dancing; rugby; reading; chess; computers; board games; football.

How would you react if you were asked to be involved in an activity that was considered 'inappropriate' for your gender? How would other people react to you? How do you think a teenager would react to being asked to play chess, or a woman asked to play football?

Culture

When planning activities you will also need to consider all aspects of a person's culture such as their beliefs, religion, way of life, and so on. For example, if a person is a strict vegetarian, it is unprofessional to ask them to join in a cooking activity where they will be cooking meat.

An activity which one person may enjoy doing or is their family tradition may not be the case for others. It is very unlikely that people will start to join in new activities that are completely different to ones that their family and friends participate in, so it is important to run activities that will not make people feel excluded from the culture that they know.

Real Life Care

Sunita's religion

Sunita is a Muslim who enjoys regular visits to the day care centre. Every month the day care centre runs a special activity for service users to take part in. Sunita is upset as this month the activity is swimming, which she will not be able to take part in as it is a mixed gender activity – Sunita's religious beliefs do not allow her to swim in a pool at the same time as members of the opposite sex.

1 What would you suggest the day care centre do to take account of Sunita's religion and culture? ✓

2 Explain which activities would be more suitable for Sunita. ✓✓

3 Suggest ways in which the day care centre could avoid excluding people from activities in the future. ✓✓✓

Talking point

View 1: Service users with mental disabilities are dangerous and should not be allowed to do any creative activities because they cannot be watched all the time.

View 2: Service users with mental disabilities have creative needs just like everybody else.

Social background

The social background of the individual should be taken into account when planning suitable creative and therapeutic activities as this could affect the activities you run. For example, if you are working with a client who has a history of self-harm, then you should probably avoid activities that involve the use of scissors or other tools that they could hurt themselves with; alternatively, you could make sure that a member of staff stays with the client while they are carrying out the activity.

Patients'/service users' preferences

Of course, the ultimate factor that you must consider when planning an activity is whether it is something that the patients and service users would want to do. One way would be to ask the patients and service users who the activity is intended for whether they would like to do it. It would be a waste of your time if you were to plan an activity and organise the equipment, transport, venue, and so on, only to find out that the service users did not want to do the activity!

Over to you

For each of the activities below, write down the type of person or client group and which care setting you think it is most suited to. Give reasons for your choice.

Drawing; painting; fishing; gardening; dancing; swimming; cooking; card games; flower arranging; watching television; massage; yoga; drama; music; writing.

Practice for Assessment

This could contribute to P2, D1, and D2.

The council has decided from your reports throughout this unit that you are the best candidate for the job. They are very impressed with your activity plans for your chosen service users and have decided that you should carry out your plan.

Carry out your activities in your work placement or another suitable environment. You will need to get an appropriate member of staff to complete a witness statement for you. (P2)

Once you have completed your activity the council would like a detailed evaluation on how it went.

You will need to write a report which covers the following points:

- What did you think went well?

- What went badly?

- Were the activities suitable for the service users?

- Was the setting right?

- Were the equipment and materials used appropriate for the service users?

- Did the service users enjoy the activities?

- Did the activities meet the needs of the clients? (P2).

You will also need to include a section on each of the following:

- What benefits did the service users gain from the activities?

- If you were to do the activities again, what changes would you make? What would you do differently?

- Taking into account the individual needs of the service users, describe how you could improve your activities. (D1)

- Explain why you think it was necessary to implement specific health and safety measures, linking these measures to the legislative requirements, regulations and codes of practice. (D2)

Health and safety legislation, regulations and codes of practice

It is important when carrying out any activity in care settings that you comply with the current health and safety legislation in order to protect the service provider from causing harm to anyone and also to protect the service user from injury or harm.

For information on the Management of Health and Safety at Work Regulations 1999, see Unit 5 Anatomy and Physiology for Health and Social Care, page 231; food safety legislation is discussed in Unit 9 The Impact of Diet on Health, page 400; other relevant legislation is covered in Unit 2 Individual Needs within the Health and Social Care Sectors, pages 90–98.

Check your understanding

1. Explain what is meant by the term 'creative activity'.
2. Explain what is meant by the term 'therapeutic activity'.
3. Name three health and safety laws or regulations that are important when carrying out creative and therapeutic activities.
4. Name a symbol you should look for when buying toys.
5. Suggest the physical, intellectual, language, social, and emotional benefits of an arts and crafts activity for small children.
6. Give examples of activities that you could carry out in a residential home.
7. Describe the needs of physically disabled adults.
8. Explain what activity you could carry out with adults with physical disabilities to meet these needs.
9. What does COSHH stand for?
10. Explain what activities you would carry out in the following settings and whether you would use them in other settings: pre-school care, day care, residential homes, domiciliary care, community groups, independent living, hospitals.

8 Working in the Health and Social Care Sectors

Introduction

This unit explores how health and social care provision is organised in the UK. It looks closely at two examples of working in partnership, investigating the benefits of a team approach to health care provision. You will also have the opportunity to read about the many job roles available in the health and social care sector, and then be able to examine the care skills required by all health care providers.

How you will be assessed

This is an internally assessed unit.

In this unit you will learn about:

- health and social care provision
- working in partnership
- working in the health and social care sectors.

Health and social care provision

This section looks in more detail at the health and social care provision that is available in the four countries that make up the UK – England, Wales, Scotland and Northern Ireland.

Key elements of health and social care provision

The health and social care sector in the UK is divided into the following care providers:

- **Statutory health care.** Health care that must be provided by law to all members of the population, e.g. maternity facilities, general practitioners (GPs), ambulance service.

- **Private health care.** Health care that is paid for by the service user not through government funds, e.g. some dental services, some fertility treatments, paying for BUPA health care carer.

- **Voluntary health care.** Health care provided by charities and voluntary organisations, e.g. home meal deliveries, Macmillan nurses.

- **Informal health care.** Health care provided by the service user's family, friends or neighbours.

More detailed descriptions of these care providers can be found in Unit 3 Vocational Experience in a Health or Social Care Setting.

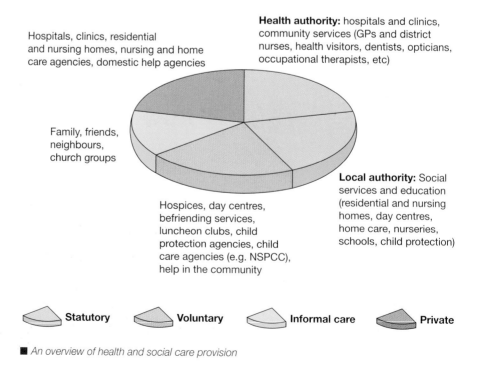

Hospitals, clinics, residential and nursing homes, nursing and home care agencies, domestic help agencies

Health authority: hospitals and clinics, community services (GPs and district nurses, health visitors, dentists, opticians, occupational therapists, etc)

Family, friends, neighbours, church groups

Local authority: Social services and education (residential and nursing homes, day centres, home care, nurseries, schools, child protection)

Hospices, day centres, befriending services, luncheon clubs, child protection agencies, child care agencies (e.g. NSPCC), help in the community

Statutory Voluntary Informal care Private

- *An overview of health and social care provision*

Social services

Social care services look after the health and welfare of the population. We are all likely to become clients of social services at one time or another. Some of the main client groups that may require social services include children or families under stress, people with disabilities, people with financial or housing problems and older people who need help with their daily living activities.

Social care services are usually run by local authorities, sometimes working in partnership with local National Health Service (NHS) providers. Many local authorities often work together to run social care services. Not all of them have the money to run every type of service necessary, so they may join with another local authority to share the responsibility. The services available from social services include:

- adoption and fostering
- Blue Badge parking scheme
- carers
- child protection
- day care facilities
- family support
- home helps
- nursing homes
- occupational therapy
- personal care at home.

The role of social services has changed over the years. Many social service departments have limited resources available, so they tend to assess the needs of individuals and buy in resources when necessary.

Over to you

Think of all the reasons for and against social services paying for private organisations to care for the elderly.

Real Life Care

The dilemma

Mrs Able's health is beginning to fail and she will soon need to go and live in a residential care home. She has no family to support her. Before she retired, she had worked as a school dinner lady for very many years, and she is unable to afford a private residential care home. The social service department pays for and runs one home in her area, but it is full – there is a waiting list that she could be placed on. Mrs Able's social worker has found her a small room in a privately run residential home instead, but it is in an area unfamiliar to her. The room in the private home will cost social services more than their own home would.

1 Will Mrs Able receive the same care wherever she lives? ✓

2 Should Mrs Able be able to choose where she lives? ✓✓

3 If you were the social worker, where would you place Mrs Able? ✓✓✓

Social workers are employed by social services to assess the needs of people requiring help from social services, for example children, people with physical or learning disabilities, people with mental health problems and the elderly. Once a social worker has assessed a need for a service, funds should be allocated and the service provided. Due to high demand and limited funds not all services can be paid for by social services; it is in these circumstances that voluntary organisations and charities can offer help and support.

The NHS

The birth of the NHS

In the early nineteenth century, health care was the responsibility of the family not the government. People had to look after their own health and that of the older members of their family. Those who had no family support were looked after in workhouses, which were run like prisons and their inmates seen as a burden on the state. The governments of the time did not understand the need for public health programmes, consequently people died from diseases such as cholera and smallpox. Women received no maternity care, so many babies and women died in childbirth.

■ *A workhouse in the nineteenth century*

During the nineteenth century, Britain developed as an important industrial power, with more and more people going to work in factories and industries throughout the country. Unfortunately, at the beginning of the twentieth century, there was still a very high infant death rate and people were dying in large numbers due to poor sanitation, poor housing and inadequate health care. The government was slow to act. It was not until after the First World War that the government realised the importance of health care to ensure the population was fit enough to work and when necessary to fight.

In 1942, the Beveridge Report set out to tackle five aspects of health: want, disease, ignorance, squalor and idleness. Beveridge wanted a health service that was free for everyone from 'cradle to grave'. The scheme would be paid for by a compulsory taxation system – taking money from workers' wages. This would pay for areas such as medical care, unemployment benefit, orphans, the elderly and maternity services. Beveridge's scheme was designed to share wealth more evenly through the whole population. Finally, six years later in 1948, the National Health Service (NHS) was set up based on Beveridge's ideas.

Development of the NHS

The NHS developed rapidly and became a model of health care provision throughout the world. People could now receive 'free health care' wherever they needed it most. For more information on the development of the NHS, see Unit 3 Vocational Experience in a Health or Social Care Setting, pages 121 and 127.

Over the last 60 years the NHS has changed in many ways. The most recent change is set out in the NHS Plan published in 2000. The Department of Health introduced the plan to radically change the NHS over the next ten years. The NHS Plan includes:

Over to you

Ask a grandparent or elderly relative what changes they have noticed to the NHS in their lifetime. Do they remember the start of the NHS?

- giving more power and information to patients

- more hospitals and beds

- more nurses and doctors

- shorter waiting lists

- cleaner wards

- better food

- improved care for the elderly

- tougher standards for NHS organisations and better rewards for the best.

To achieve the plan, hospitals are now judged on a set of performance targets and given a star rating to show users how good their local facilities are. The star system is designed to encourage poor scoring services to improve and high scoring hospitals to maintain their excellent facilities. Three stars means that the hospital does very well against targets and is run well; two stars means the hospital is performing well overall but its performance is inconsistent; one star shows some areas for concern. A hospital with no stars is one that either fails against government targets or is not run very well. A low star rating does not mean that a hospital is unsafe or that it does not contain some very good clinical services.

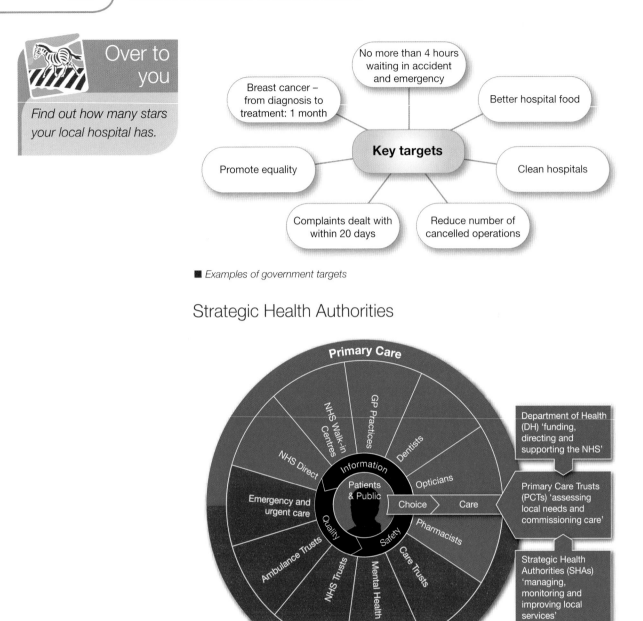

■ Examples of government targets

Strategic Health Authorities

■ The structure of the National Health Service in England

Source: *About the NHS, www.nhs.uk*

There are 28 Strategic Health Authorities (SHAs) in England which are responsible for managing the NHS in your local area and are closely linked to the Department of Health. SHAs are responsible for:

■ developing plans to improve health services in their local area

■ making sure local health services are of a high quality

■ providing more local health services

- making sure that national priorities, e.g. diagnosing and treating breast cancer quickly, are also implemented in local health services.

The structure of the NHS in Wales, Scotland and Northern Ireland is looked at later in this unit.

Real Life Care

Lynda

Lynda is 40 years old. Recently, she noticed a small lump in her right breast. When visiting a friend in her local hospital, she spotted a mobile Well-Woman Clinic parked in the car park which was open for women to drop in and ask questions. After talking to a sympathetic nurse, Lynda agreed to have a mammogram (x-ray) of her breast lump, the results of which indicated that she needed a sample of the lump to be taken (a biopsy) for testing. The biopsy showed that Lynda did not have breast cancer, but that the lump was only a harmless cyst.

1 What might have happened to Lynda if she had not gone into the Well-Woman Clinic? ✓

2 Describe some of the reasons why Lynda may have found it hard to go for screening. ✓✓

3 A Well-Woman Clinic may screen hundreds of women who do not have cancer. Screening costs a lot of money. Do you think that preventative screening is cost-effective? ✓✓✓

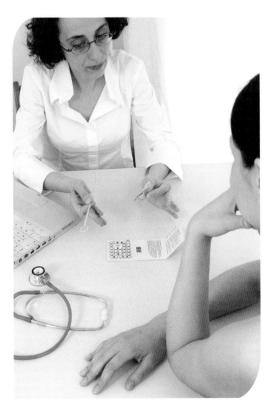

■ A Well-Woman Clinic

Primary Care Trusts

Primary Care Trusts (PCTs) are local health organisations responsible for managing health services in your area. They are large organisations that usually serve 100,000–300,000 people. They work with local authorities to provide health and social care services to make sure the community's needs are met. PCTs now receive 75 per cent of the NHS budget. As they are local, they are in the best position to understand the needs of their community. PCTs are responsible for:

Over to you

Try to find the address of your local Primary Care Trust – the NHS website will help you. To access this website, go to www. heinemann.co.uk/hotlinks and enter the express code 3322P.

- providing and managing services such as hospitals, doctors, dentists and mental health services
- getting health and social care systems working together to benefit service users
- developing new services in their local area
- providing the public with information about services in their area
- registering and dealing with complaints about service providers
- buying and selling land and buildings to raise funds.

Primary health care

Primary health care is provided by the people you normally see when you first have a health problem. It may be your GP or dentist, an optician or your local pharmacist. NHS Walk-in Centres and the phone line NHS Direct are also part of primary health care. Their aim is to prevent illness from getting any worse, and to refer service users to secondary health care when necessary.

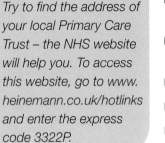

Real Life Care

Hayley

One Sunday morning, 4-year-old Hayley complains to her mother, Karen, that she has a sore throat. Karen notices that Hayley also has a swollen, spotty tongue. She phones NHS Direct to ask if she should wait until her GP's surgery opens in the morning or whether she needs to see a doctor sooner. The nurse at NHS Direct asks Karen several detailed questions, and suggests that she takes Hayley to see an emergency doctor today. The emergency doctor diagnoses scarlet fever and prescribes antibiotics. Hayley makes a good recovery.

1 List some of the positive and negative aspects of the NHS Direct service. ✓

2 Before NHS Direct, what would have been Karen's options for finding a diagnosis for Hayley? ✓✓

3 Discuss the difference between a discussion with a nurse at NHS Direct and a face-to-face consultation with a doctor. ✓✓✓

Secondary health care

If a problem cannot be sorted out through primary care, or if there is an emergency, the next stop will be a hospital. Secondary care is about the care given in hospitals, day care surgeries and outpatient clinics.

Integrated care

Integrated care involves primary and secondary health care working together to plan and provide services in partnership, not as two different organisations. By working together, they should be able to improve the delivery of care to people depending on their needs. This approach is called 'Whole Systems Working' and takes place when:

- services are organised together
- all service providers recognise that their actions have an impact elsewhere
- users experience services that are seamless and the boundaries between providers are not noticeable.

Mental Health Trusts

Mental health services are provided through primary health care providers such as GPs and secondary health care providers in the form of specialist units. This could include counselling, psychiatric therapies, community and family support. For example, someone suffering from bereavement, depression, stress or anxiety can get help through primary care services. If they need further support, they may be referred for specialist care. This specialist care is provided by Mental Health Trusts whose services range from psychological therapy to very specialist medical services for people with severe anxiety problems.

Talking point

View 1: Integrated care ensures that someone receives all the care they need, despite the cost to the NHS and social services.

View 2: Integrated care is expensive and it involves too many care providers for just one person.

Real Life Care

June

June is 86 years old and is visiting her GP for a routine check-up. While in the surgery, she stumbles and falls. The surgery's nurse is able to offer her first aid and pain relief while they wait for the ambulance to arrive. June is treated in hospital for four weeks with a fractured neck of the femur. When she is well enough to go home, she will be cared for by her district nurse and GP as well as an occupational therapist, who will assess her home circumstances, and a physiotherapist, who will help her become fully mobile again.

1 Identify the primary and secondary care June has received. ✔

2 If her condition worsens, which other health care professionals could be involved in her treatment? ✔✔

3 Would social services get involved in June's care? If so, why? ✔✔✔

Real Life Care

Zac

Zac is 12 years old and very overweight for his age. His mother has taken Zac to the GP as he is constantly thirsty and always tired. The doctor suspects Zac may have diabetes and does some blood tests. When the results come back, they show that Zac could be developing diabetes, so the doctor refers Zac to the hospital paediatric department for further tests.

1 Identify the primary and secondary care Zac has received. ✓

2 If Zac develops diabetes, he will need health care throughout his life. What other types of health care provision might he need as he grows up? ✓✓

3 How can the Primary Care Trust ensure Zac receives integrated care? ✓✓✓

Over to you

Research the case of Victoria Climbie to highlight poor communication by health care providers.

Children's Trusts

Children's Trusts bring together all services for children and young people in an area. They were developed to ensure that providers of children's services work and communicate together. Following cases of children dying as a result of health care providers not communicating with each other, Children's Trusts aim to listen to children and focus on improving child health care provisions. Examples of good child health care provision are Sure Start, the Children's Fund and Connexions. By 2008, every area should have a Children's Trust.

Real Life Care

Sasha

Sasha is 15 years old. She lives with her mother and two younger brothers. Sasha often gets very aggressive and has been in trouble with the police on many occasions – she now has an anti-social behavioural order (ASBO). This means that she must stay at home in the evenings and is not allowed to hang around her local shopping arcade as she used to do. As part of her ASBO, she has been allocated a Connexions worker. The Connexions worker is working with Sasha to help her find ways of coping with her anger and to talk about the problems she experiences at home. Sasha now joins in many activities arranged by the Connexions team and has been on several organised trips to help her work with other people. Her Connexions worker has helped Sasha apply for a course in animal management at her local college – this will be the first time in two years that Sasha has been in education.

1 Find out about your nearest Connexions. What facilities does it offer? ✓

2 What factors may be contributing to Sasha's behaviour? ✓✓

3 How will Connexions help Sasha in the future? ✓✓✓

Health and social care settings

Day nurseries and play schools

Day nurseries and play schools are designed to meet the needs of children before they are old enough to go to school. They offer facilities for children to play and learn in a safe, supervised manner. (For more information on these settings, see Unit 7 Creative and Therapeutic Activities in Health and Social Care, page 301.)

Schools

In the UK, by law, all children must be educated from 5 to 16 years old. In this time they will be taught to read and write and to use numbers correctly as well as many other important skills. Most parents choose to send their children to a school for their education, where they will learn how to communicate with other children and adults as well as receiving the education prescribed by the government. Some parents choose not to send their children to school, but to educate them themselves at home.

Schools are provided for by the government, which ensures that every child has access to education. Besides state-run schools there are also schools that ask the parents to pay for the child's education. Fee-paying or independent schools are usually able to offer a wider choice of subjects with fewer students in each class than state-run schools. However a child is educated, their schooling will remain important for the rest of their lives.

Special schools

Special schools offer facilities to children with different needs. Some special schools are adapted to allow easier access and offer specialised teaching for students with learning difficulties and physical disabilities.

Hospitals

The NHS and the private health care sector both provide hospitals. They offer a wide range of services that are designed to meet the health needs of its surrounding population.

Residential homes

Residential homes provide accommodation, care and support for the elderly. They do not look after people who require nursing care, but house people who can no longer cope at home.

Day centres

Day centres offer the elderly somewhere to go during the day. By attending a day centre, an elderly person will have the opportunity to meet with other people as well as take part in a wide range of organised activities such as flower arranging, writing classes and computer courses.

■ *Day centres offer a range of activities*

Domiciliary care

Domiciliary care is offered in the service user's home. It can be anything from gardening and housework to helping with personal hygiene and dressing.

Access to health and social care settings

Over to you

Can you think of a time when you or a family member have experienced being referred to another health care service?

Whenever you use a health care service, such as visiting your GP, pharmacist or dentist, you are accessing that service. Health care services are usually accessed by a process known as a referral. There are three different types of referral:

- **Self-referral.** A person chooses to ask for help or to go to a service provider such as their GP or dentist.

- **Professional referral.** A care practitioner puts a client in contact with another service provider who offers specialist care, e.g. a GP may refer a client to a physiotherapist to improve their mobility.

- **Third-party referral.** A person is put in contact with a service by a friend, neighbour or relative or a non-care practitioner, e.g. a manager at work may suggest an employee visit the works counsellor for an appointment.

Over to you

If you had woken this morning with a bad earache and felt you needed to see your GP, what factors might prevent you from seeing the doctor for an appointment immediately?

Barriers to access

Sometimes people are unable to access the health facilities that they need. This could be due to a variety of reasons known as barriers to access.

Since the NHS offers free care to all, it can seem hard to believe that not everyone in the UK has the same access to the same services. However, for many reasons some people find it difficult to access services – these reasons are known as barriers to referral.

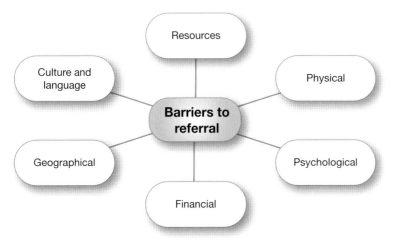

■ *Barriers to referral*

Geographical barriers

Geographical barriers for some service users may include:

■ lack of local health facilities, e.g. service user living in rural location, too many people using a service

■ lack of transport to health facilities.

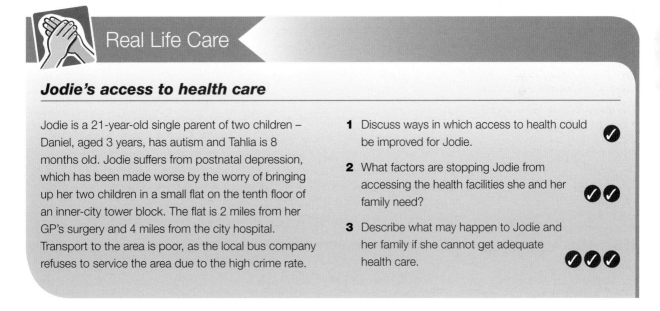

Real Life Care

Jodie's access to health care

Jodie is a 21-year-old single parent of two children – Daniel, aged 3 years, has autism and Tahlia is 8 months old. Jodie suffers from postnatal depression, which has been made worse by the worry of bringing up her two children in a small flat on the tenth floor of an inner-city tower block. The flat is 2 miles from her GP's surgery and 4 miles from the city hospital. Transport to the area is poor, as the local bus company refuses to service the area due to the high crime rate.

1 Discuss ways in which access to health could be improved for Jodie. ✓

2 What factors are stopping Jodie from accessing the health facilities she and her family need? ✓✓

3 Describe what may happen to Jodie and her family if she cannot get adequate health care. ✓✓✓

By looking carefully at the Real Life Care above, you may be able to identify some geographical barriers that might prevent Jodie from receiving the care she and her family need. Jodie lives in a high-rise block, so she may have problems with lifts not working – this could result in her having to carry the children up and down the stairs. As there is no transport close to her housing estate, she will find it difficult to visit her GP or the hospital to receive help and support for her depression and Daniel's autism.

Physical barriers

Physical barriers may include:

- inadequate access to buildings for service users with poor mobility or wheelchair users
- service users too weak as a result of illness to attend a health facility
- service users too young to access services without help.

Many people who require services have mobility difficulties. They may be elderly or wheelchair users and consequently find it hard to get to services. Service settings must be designed to give adequate access to wheelchair users. Jodie will need to use a pushchair to transport Tahlia, so it would be very difficult for her if the hospital did not allow pushchairs inside or only had push-open doors. It would be awkward for her to carry Tahlia to appointments.

Psychological barriers

Psychological barriers may include:

- fear, e.g. the service user is too scared to leave home
- anxiety
- depression
- the service user's own belief that they cannot be helped
- the service user failing to recognise their need for help, perhaps even ignoring the problem
- a lack of understanding about how health facilities can be used.

Psychological barriers occur when service users are too scared and worried to use the services they need. Jodie has postnatal depression. She might feel unable to talk to her GP or health visitor as she may think that they will consider her an incompetent parent who is unable to care for her children. Fear and anxiety about health are common in all of us. Have you ever been worried about visiting the dentist or telling your problems to your GP? If a person suspects that they have a serious problem, they might even decide to ignore it, hoping it will go away, or pretend it does not exist. Some people are too proud to use a service, for example older men often have difficulty talking to young female nurses about their personal problems.

Financial barriers

Financial barriers may include a service user's inability to pay for:

- transport to health facilities
- prescriptions
- disability aids
- health care not provided free by the NHS.

Even though the NHS is 'free', lack of money may still be a barrier to receiving appropriate service facilities. Jodie may be on income support and unable to afford to travel to a hospital or her GP. Not all services are available in all areas, for example she may need to take Daniel to a specialist pre-school that teaches children with autism, but the nearest school may be many miles away.

In recent years, it has become difficult to receive dental treatment on the NHS due to the lack of NHS dentists. Therefore to receive treatment, people may have to pay. Charges and fees make some services only accessible to people with enough money to pay for them.

Cultural barriers

Cultural barriers may include:

- no staff from the service user's culture

- language barriers

- the service user not being permitted to wear the traditional clothing of their culture

- the service user not being allowed to worship as necessary

- care only being available from members of the opposite sex, which might cause offence to some service users.

The UK is a culturally diverse country and is home to people from a wide range of ethnic and religious backgrounds. Therefore, it is very important that service facilities are accessible to everyone including those for whom English is not their first language. Cultural beliefs about who should provide care and how illness is dealt with may prevent some communities from using services. For example, Muslim women may feel humiliated and degraded if examined by a male nurse or doctor, and should be treated by female staff wherever possible. If a GP's surgery does not have both male and female doctors, then this may mean that Muslim women will not be able to access the facilities, which could result in serious health problems.

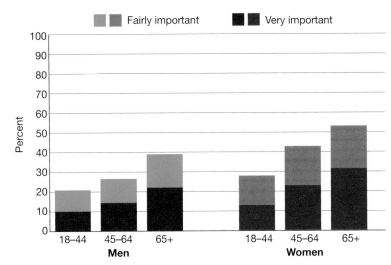

■ The importance of seeing a GP of your own ethnic group, by age and sex of respondent

Language and communication barriers

Language and communication barriers may include:

- the service user not being able to understand the care worker's language
- no translators or interpreters available to communicate between the service user and care worker
- the use of jargon
- lack of health promotion information in the appropriate language.

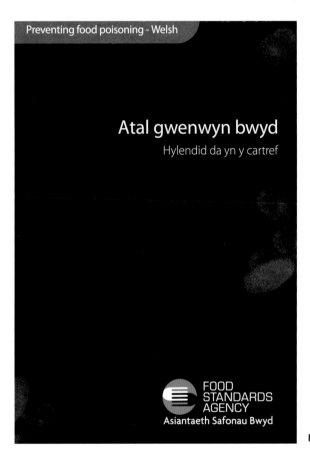

Preventing food poisoning - Welsh

Atal gwenwyn bwyd

Hylendid da yn y cartref

FOOD STANDARDS AGENCY
Asiantaeth Safonau Bwyd

Language can be a barrier to accessing health facilities. If you are unable to understand signposts, leaflets and information about health care provisions, you will be unable to access the relevant services you would need. Many service providers print leaflets and information in several languages to accommodate the needs of local communities.

People with hearing or visual impairments also need help to access the health care they need, either through the provision of information on tapes and videos or in Braille and large print format.

The use of jargon and technical language can cause barriers too. For example, an elderly gentleman who is having an operation may be sent instructions to be 'NBM'. When he arrives at the hospital, without clear 'jargon-free' information, he may not realise that this stands for nil-by-mouth and that he should not eat before his operation.

■ *A health information leaflet about food poisoning printed in Welsh*

Over to you

Imagine that you are on holiday abroad with your friend when they have a minor accident that requires hospital treatment. Neither you nor your friend speaks the local language, and you do not know how the local health system works. How could you access health facilities?

What resources could the local health services have in place to help foreign visitors understand how to access care?

Practice for Assessment

Carrying out this activity will provide underpinning knowledge for P2 and M1. Read about Simone, and then answer the questions below.

Simone is 30 years old and married with two children. She has been a wheelchair user all her life. She is able to drive a car and has recently started her own fashion business. She works very hard, often working Saturdays and late into the evenings. She lives about 6 miles from the nearest town, choosing the quiet country life over a busy city. The village where she lives has a bus service once an hour. She also has her two elderly parents living at home with her and her husband.

Draw a detailed spider diagram identifying all the possible reasons why Simone may be unable to access the health facilities she and her family need. (P2)

Using some of the barriers you identified above, explain with examples how these barriers affect Simone accessing health facilities. (M1)

Countries

England

In England, the provision of both health and social care is the responsibility of the Secretary of State. The NHS is responsible for the organisation of health care facilities, and local authorities are responsible for the organisation of social services.

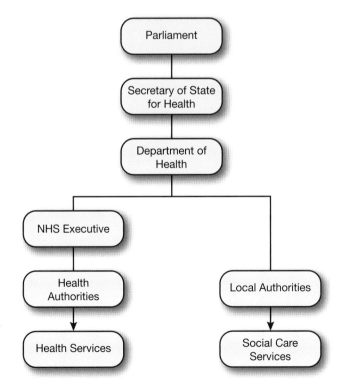

■ *The structure of health and social care in England*

Wales

Health and social care services in Wales are organised in a similar way to England. The Secretary of State for Wales is answerable to the National Assembly for Wales for health and social care provision.

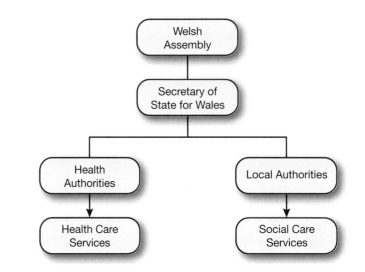

■ *The structure of health and social care in Wales*

Scotland

The Secretary of State for Scotland is responsible to the Scottish Parliament for health and social care services in Scotland. Health and social care services are run separately by local authority boards that are accountable to the Scottish Executive Health and Development Departments.

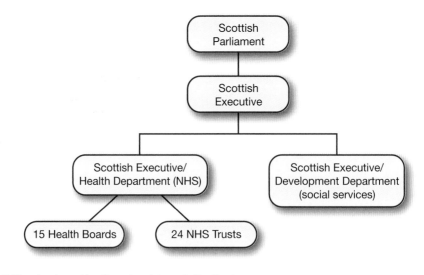

■ *The structure of health and social care in Scotland*

Northern Ireland

In Northern Ireland, health and social care services are organised together – this is a good example of integrated care. The department responsible for the provision of health and social services is the Department of Health, Social Services and Public Safety, which is part of the Northern Ireland Office.

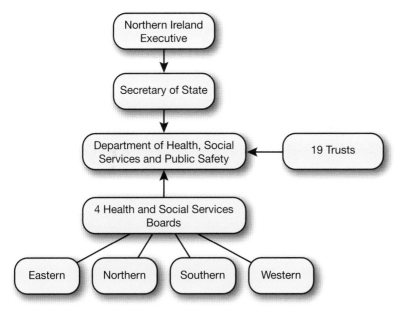

■ *The structure of health and social care in Northern Ireland*

Practice for Assessment

This could contribute to P1.

Choose one of the four countries of the UK and describe how health and social care services are provided in your chosen country. Look on the Internet to add to the information outlined above (a list of relevant websites is given on www.heinemann.co.uk/hotlinks).

Working in partnership

Health care professionals rarely work alone but more often than not as part of a team. This team consists of many different care workers with different roles working together in partnership to provide the best care for a service user. This section looks in detail at two very different examples of a working partnership, both in the community and hospital-based. It mainly considers how Primary Care Trusts liaise with other NHS trusts, how service users and carers are involved in the planning of care, and how a variety of agencies work together.

Working in partnership: example 1

■ *Health care professionals work together as a team to provide the care needed by service users*

 Real Life Care

James

James, aged 26, has learning difficulties and visual impairment as a result of being born with Down's Syndrome. He attends a day centre for five days a week. He lives in a small residential home with four other adults and a carer. The home is run by the local authority's social services department.

1 List all the care professionals and organisations that would be involved in James' care. ✔

2 Divide your list into two columns labelled NHS and Social Services. ✔✔

3 Identify who is responsible for paying for the care that you have identified. ✔✔✔

Now that James has reached adulthood, most of his care is based in the community. When he was growing up, he would have had involvement with a great variety of care providers and organisations that would try to manage his care to ensure that he developed to the best of his ability.

Social services will be responsible for James' housing needs and has consequently placed him in a residential home, where he can learn to live independently or with the minimum of support. A residential care worker will be responsible for his day-to-day living requirements, with tasks such as dressing, washing, cooking and shopping. James will be allocated a social worker who makes sure that James receives any financial entitlements as well as ensuring that he is housed in a safe and appropriate setting. He will also have a key worker. The key worker's responsibilities include:

- helping James to keep in touch with his family

- helping him order and collect his medicines

- helping James to buy new clothes

- organising and attending individual programme planning (IPP) meetings to plan things formally with James

- communicating with the rest of the team to ensure that James receives the support and care to which he is entitled.

The key worker will play an important part in James' life as they will build up a relationship with him so that they can act as an **advocate** for him, ensuring he receives all the care he needs.

James' local Primary Care Trust (PCT) will be responsible for ensuring that he has a doctor caring for his health when he is ill. The doctor will also be responsible for contacting the local PCT to provide James with the specialist care he needs. The PCT should also provide access to a dentist and optician as well as a pharmacist to dispense his prescriptions. When James is fit and well, he will not need as much care from the PCT. He may be undergoing more specialist care which will be provided by the local NHS Trust.

The NHS Trust is responsible for hospitals and the specialists that work within them. In the case of James, he may be under the care of:

- a speech therapist who will help him develop his use of language and communication skills

- an ophthalmologist who will care for his eyesight

- an occupational therapist who will be responsible for ensuring that he has all the appropriate appliances and equipment available to him to ensure that he leads as normal a life as possible. The occupational therapist may work in the community and visit James in his home to assess more accurately what he needs to help him with everyday living.

There are other agencies that may be involved in James' care. The RNIB (Royal Institute for the Blind) is a charitable organisation that helps

Advocate *A person who acts on someone else's behalf. In care work an advocate tries to understand and argue from a client's perspective.*

Key point

Local NHS Trusts may comprise several trusts such as Mental Health Trusts and Children's Trusts.

people who are blind or have visual impairments. The RNIB offers support and advice and can provide equipment that helps visually impaired people live successful lives. The Down's Syndrome Association is a charity that works with people who have Down's Syndrome and their carers. It offers support and advice and provides information about the syndrome to help increase public awareness of the condition.

Working in partnership: example 2

Usha's fertility treatment (see below) was performed in a private infertility clinic. Fertility treatment is very expensive and, consequently, can be very difficult to receive through the NHS. Private health care offers services that are often not available to NHS clients. Private treatments can be costly, but it can be argued that they offer an increase in the choices available to service users. Usha is now pregnant and expecting twins.

During her pregnancy, Usha may have needed genetic counselling, which would be provided by the NHS Trust. Genetic counselling involves looking at all the possible choices available to a couple when one of them carries genes that may affect the health of their baby. Usha carries a gene for haemophilia which may affect a male baby, resulting in a disease that will require extensive treatment throughout his life. A genetic counsellor can offer support, advice and information that will prepare Usha and her partner for the possibility that a male baby may be at risk.

Throughout her pregnancy, Usha was cared for by the PCT, which provides a doctor and midwife who managed her care together. Usha would have planned to have her babies in a hospital that had a special care baby unit, as twins often need extra support after they are born. Kishan and Mahiya

Talking point

View 1: The NHS should offer fertility treatment no matter how much it costs.

View 2: Private fertility clinics take the burden off the NHS so money can be used for other treatments.

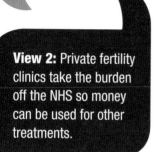

Real Life Care

Usha and her twins

Usha is 36 years old. She was unable to conceive normally and paid to have fertility treatment. She carries a genetic condition called haemophilia that could result in her babies having a blood disorder. Usha went into premature labour at 32 weeks of her pregnancy and needed to have a caesarean section. The babies – a boy called Kishan and a girl called Mahiya – were taken to the special care baby unit (SCBU) straight after their birth. They remained in SCBU for four weeks before being discharged home. At home, Usha was visited by her midwife to check her recovery after the operation. She was also seen by her

GP who prescribed painkillers. When the babies came home, Kishan required a continual oxygen supply being pumped into his lungs until he was big enough to breathe without it. The family were visited regularly by a community paediatric nurse.

1 List all the care professionals and organisations that were involved in Usha and her babies' care. ✔

2 Divide your list into three columns – PCT, NHS, Private. ✔✔

3 Identify who is responsible for paying for the care that you have identified. ✔✔✔

were born by caesarean section and nursed in a SCBU. They were cared for by midwives, neonatal nurses, nursery nurses, audiologists (test hearing), radiographers (take x-rays) and paediatricians, to name but a few. These health professions are the responsibility of the NHS Trust.

Once the babies were discharged home, they needed extra care offered within the community. This care was undertaken by a community paediatric nurse who planned and carried out their care until they were well enough to be cared for by the PCT's health visitor. Usha also received visits from a midwife and her GP to ensure that she was recovering well from her operation. Any medication required by Usha or the babies was provided for by the PCT's pharmacist.

There are several voluntary organisations that are set up to help new mothers and families with new babies and multiple births. The National Childbirth Trust (NCT) is a charity that helps pregnant women and their partners, as well as new parents, adjust to parenthood. They offer a range of services from general information about parenthood and breastfeeding advice to social support for new mothers. The Twins and Multiple Births Association (TAMBA) helps families to adjust to having more than one baby by putting them in contact with other families in the same situation. Both these organisations are run by volunteers.

Involving clients in decision making

Teams as large as those responsible for James and Usha's needs must all work together to ensure that they receive 'joined-up care', that is, care which is seamless and flows from one carer to another. The best way to do this is to write a care plan that every carer and organisation can work towards. When drawing up care plans, it is necessary to involve the client in the planning process. Care plans should:

- involve the client as much as possible, empowering them to make their own decisions
- be written down in a clear manner using terminology that is understood by all care providers
- be clear about who is going to do what
- assess the individual's needs and set realistic goals
- list the actions necessary to meet the set goals
- be reviewed and evaluated, changed and updated regularly, with the involvement of the client.

In the case of James, he may find it difficult to make his wishes understood clearly enough to be totally involved in the planning process. In cases where the service user has communication difficulties, it may be necessary to involve an advocate who can speak for them. As Kishan and Mihiya were children, their care plans would be written by the community paediatric nurse who would involve their parents in the decision-making processes.

Key point

Empowering a client or service user means allowing them to take control of their own lives, that is, giving them the power and information to make their own decisions and choices.

Purpose of working in partnership

The many different service providers working in partnership ensures that clients receive care that meets all their physical, social, emotional and spiritual needs. This holistic approach to care allows the client to feel empowered and in control of their own health needs. The Department of Health believes that working in partnership is so important that it has written a policy document entitled 'Making partnerships work for patients, carers and services users' (Department of Health, 2004). This policy outlines a framework for the Department of Health, the NHS and social care and the voluntary and community sectors to work together.

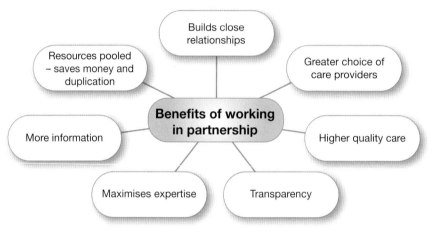

■ *The benefits of working in partnership*

Advantages for the client

When teams work together to provide care, there are many advantages for the client:

■ The client is treated as a whole person, not just a collection of illnesses or labels. For example, James had several physical needs, but his key worker would ensure that the team also considered James' social, emotional and spiritual needs as well.

■ The client feels empowered and in control of their own care provision. Even people with severe communication problems can be involved in the planning of their own care.

■ The client will have the chance to receive a wider choice of the services available.

■ There is an opportunity to build up relationships with several carers, resulting in clients feeling able to discuss their problems and fears openly.

Advantages for the care provider

Teams working together does not just bring advantages to the client; it benefits every member of the team:

- Each care provider has their own expertise, which through collaboration they can use to improve the care given.

- Several carers with different ideas could share ideas, which may result in new ideas being developed. Teams can work together to develop new and improved forms of care, thereby maximising the use of the expertise available.

- It reduces the chances of repeating care, where several carers perform similar roles. For example, in the case of Usha, the paediatric community nurse will perform some of the jobs which are usually the responsibility of the community midwife.

- Resources can be pooled, such as sharing equipment and facilities, which prevents duplication of resources.

When partnerships fail

If care providers work independently of each other, each providing the care they feel is necessary without consulting other members of the team, this may result in the client losing their independence, personal choices and control over their own care. When clients see care providers contradicting each others' advice and disregarding their wishes, the client may give up on their own care and lose their ability to choose the best options for themselves. For example, in the case of Usha, if the hospital midwife had suggested one type of pain relief, the community midwife another type and the doctor a third type, Usha may have felt frustrated that no one knew what the other person was doing. The effect of this could be that Usha lost trust in the team.

When partnerships fail, the client will receive care that is contradictory, even unnecessary, and may feel isolated and abandoned by their care team.

Practice for Assessment

Carrying out this activity will provide evidence for P3, M2 and D1.

Think carefully about service providers in your local area.

Describe two examples of several different service providers working in partnership to provide care. (P3)

Explain how the two examples of health and social care service providers working in partnership benefits service users. (M2)

Review your work on barriers to access to services. Explain how these barriers may be overcome by effective partnership working. (D1)

Working in the health and social care sectors

Working in health and social care is not just about working in a hospital or a residential home. There are many different settings that require people to do a variety of jobs and look after service users with various needs and requirements. In large care settings, such as a hospital, the different departments will link together to provide the overall care for a patient. This unit investigates working in the health and social care sectors by focusing on the different job roles that are available and the skills and requirements you would need.

Job roles

Different types of care require different types of people in a variety of jobs to deliver this care. There are two main types of care:

- **Direct care**, e.g. nurses, doctors, counsellors – people who work and provide care directly to the client.

- **Indirect care**, e.g. medical receptionists, cleaners, and porters – people who work in care settings to provide a service to support the direct carers.

The way a person behaves in their job can determine whether they deliver a good service to service users or not. You will need to understand what particular job roles entail and what skills and requirements are called for to do these roles. You should also be able to recognise the developments that are available to you in the workforce and the guidance you will receive, such as legislation and policies.

When investigating working in health and social care sectors, it is important to look at a variety of roles in the different sectors and the care skills and the requirements needed for each role. An overview of care skills and requirements needed for working in the health and social care field in general is given below together with an in-depth look at particular job roles.

Care skills

In health and social care settings, it is essential that staff in their particular areas and fields of work all have certain skills in order to make sure that they are capable of doing their job and that everyone is doing things in the same way as others in their job. This is important as everyone working in the same way with the right skills will mean that health and social care environments can all work together to improve the health and well-being of service users.

Over to you

On a sheet of paper make three columns headed Health settings, Social settings and Early years settings. Under each column, list as many different jobs as you can think of for each setting. Which setting has the most jobs?

Staff working in health and social care areas have to follow the care value base (see Unit 1 Communication and Individual Rights within the Health and Social Care Sectors, page 35). The care value base sets out the principles of good care practices such as maintaining confidentiality and treating service users with respect and dignity. It is important for all health and social care organisations to promote these values as it could make a difference to a service user.

Organisations also like their staff to have good communication and interpersonal skills and to be supportive towards one another, as working in a health and social care environment can be rewarding but there are also sad and difficult times. Staff should also be supportive, patient and understanding towards service users as they are going through times of change and can often feel lonely and unsupported.

Care settings also have policies and procedures that staff are expected to follow, as these set out the skills that a person needs to have to be able to carry out particular tasks and the manner in which they must done (see Unit 4 Cultural Diversity in Health and Social Care, page 188). For example, working in a hospital, it is essential that staff follow the correct procedure for giving somebody an injection. If staff did not follow the correct way of doing this task, for example not using a clean needle, then the patient or other patients could be cross-infected.

Real Life Care

Kim's care skills

Kim has worked for about six years as a nurse at the local hospital. Because she has been there a long time, Kim has let some of her care skills slide – she thinks to herself, 'I don't have time to wash my hands before I attend to the patients, and I don't have time to change the bed from that patient who has left to the new patient coming in. Oh well, it doesn't matter anyway.'

1 Describe what you would say to Kim if you worked with her. ✓

2 Explain what skills you think Kim needs to improve. ✓✓

3 Analyse why these skills are important. ✓✓✓

Requirements

As with all jobs, no matter what industry you are in, it is very important to make sure that you arrive on time for your work. Some jobs allow flexibility, for example you might have to be in work between 8 am and 8.30 am, or as long as you work 20 hours a week, it does not matter when you work them. However, even though you may have this flexibility, when working with other people, whether they are staff or service users, they expect you to be punctual and work to your timetable.

Many jobs, especially in health and social care settings, have uniforms that you have to wear to work. Sometimes the setting provides the uniform; at other times, you will have to buy the uniform yourself or put down a deposit for it. Other organisations and jobs have dress codes such as no jeans and trainers. Most jobs will, however, expect you to dress appropriately. For example, a counsellor working with children would not be expected to wear a very smart suit as this might make the children feel inferior or uncomfortable. On the other hand, scruffy and dirty clothes could give out the wrong message and might cause the children not to respect you. Most counsellors wear smart, casual clothes such as jeans and a shirt.

Another attribute that is often required in the workplace is a positive attitude to the job that you are doing. If you are constantly negative and downhearted towards your job, it can make others feel down, and if you are working with the general public, it might make them not want to come back.

Real Life Care

Sarah and Lisa

Sarah is a medical receptionist at the local hospital. She has worked in the job for five years but dislikes it intensely. Sarah really wants to be a nurse and is just doing this job while she finishes her training.

Lisa is an elderly lady who has recently moved to the area. She has a fear of hospitals and avoids going to the hospital if she can. However, Lisa has to attend the hospital for a blood test.

When Lisa arrives, she goes to reception to sign in. Sarah makes Lisa wait for a few minutes while she finishes a sandwich and her conversation on the phone and then when she speaks to Lisa, she is grumpy and almost rude. When Sarah is later asked about her behaviour, Sarah says she does not care, as she is not going to be doing this job for much longer anyway.

1 Describe what personal attributes and skills Sarah is lacking. ✓

2 Analyse whether you would employ her as a nurse if you had seen the way Sarah treats people as a receptionist. ✓✓

3 Evaluate how this would make Lisa feel. Explain what effect this would have on Lisa's physical, intellectual, emotional and social needs. ✓✓✓

Types of jobs

Nurse

Role
A nurse can work in a variety of care settings such as GPs' surgeries, schools, hospitals and in the armed forces. However, their main role remains the same in all settings: to care for ill or injured people and those who have a disability. They do this by providing health care and advice to the service users and their families.

■ *A nurse can work in many settings*

Generally, the role of a nurse is to observe patients and monitor their progress, support patients who are anxious about treatment and give advice to patients and their families. Some nurses can administer drugs to patients, dependent on their condition, and can give injections. They work very closely with other care professionals such as doctors to make sure that the service users are getting the right care for their condition. They might change the dressing on wounds, x-ray broken bones and administer splints.

In different settings, nurses will perform different tasks from one another. For example, in accident and emergency a nurse will assess patients as they arrive at the hospital and treat their injuries and wounds. A nurse in theatre will prepare a patient for an operation and help them to recover afterwards. A nurse in a GP's surgery will carry out an overall assessment of new patients to the practice, and they can take blood tests and give advice and prescriptions for items such as contraception.

Skills

The skills and personal qualities required to become a nurse include excellent people skills, as nurses work with the general public. It is important to be able to work as a team and understand the nurse's role alongside other health care staff but still be able to use their own **initiative** and work independently.

Nurses also need to be able to remain calm and think clearly in stressful and busy times and be mentally fit because, as well as making people better, not all patients make a full recovery.

Hospital nurses need to be adaptable and flexible as they are often expected to work shifts since hospitals are open round the clock, seven days a week. Nurses take it in turns to work nights and weekends.

Over to you

In a small group, think of the many different areas and environments that a nurse works in. Compare your answers to the rest of the class. Have you thought of some that others did not?

Initiative *Being able to carry out a task without being asked – seeing what needs to be done and getting on with it.*

Requirements

To be a nurse, you must go to university to study. There are four different areas of nursing:

- Children's nursing (paediatrics).
- Adult nursing.
- Mental health nursing.
- Learning disability nursing.

To go to university to study and train for the Diploma in Nursing, you must have five GCSEs (A–C) including English, or equivalent qualifications. A levels, or an equivalent, including a science such as Biology, are required to study for the degree.

There are other routes into nursing such as a foundation degree, which is a two-year course preparing students for health care roles, the NVQ route, and the NHS cadet schemes, which can lead to a pre-registration nursing programme.

Counsellor

Role

A counsellor is someone that you can go to when you feel you need to talk to someone about something that is worrying you. Counsellors give people the opportunity to work through their feelings and listen very carefully to what the clients are saying.

Bereavement *Suffering because of the death of a much-loved person. It can involve strong emotions of disbelief, denial, anger and guilt.*

Counsellors can specialise in different areas such as helping people to overcome addictions, helping people with **bereavement** (death of family member or a friend) or marriage guidance. They can also focus on a particular age group such as children.

Skills

To be a counsellor it is essential that you have excellent communication skills and be able to listen well. You must be able to empathise with the client but not become too attached. Counsellors also have to be very good at making people feel comfortable in this environment and be able to work with lots of different types of people.

Requirements

It is unusual for people to become counsellors in their early 20s as counselling draws on life experiences. Most people start their counselling career by working in the voluntary sector gaining experience. Most professional organisations such as colleges and universities ask that you have a Level 4 Diploma in Counselling to become a counsellor and they also like you to be registered, as this shows your professionalism and clients can make sure that you are a good counsellor. However, it is not compulsory to have any qualifications to become a counsellor.

Over to you

In a small group, try to think of as many different counselling groups as you can and the sorts of issues that people go to counsellors about.

Look in the local telephone directory and see what organisations counsellors work in. Make a list of all the different settings and industries you can find.

Medical receptionist

Role

Medical receptionists work in health environments such as GPs' practices, hospitals, dental surgeries and health centres. The duties that medical receptionists perform can vary from organisation to organisation. However, in general, they would often check-in the patients that are seeing the GP and find their medical file; make appointments for people requesting to see a nurse, or doctor; greet and direct patients and service users to the correct areas of the building; and sometimes type letters and update patient records on their database.

Skills

Medical receptionists must be well organised and efficient as they are dealing with clients' details. They must also be able to communicate effectively with different people of different ages, religions, etc. and respect the confidentiality of patients' information.

Requirements

There are no minimum qualifications that you need to become a medical receptionist. However, some settings may ask for GCSEs or equivalent qualifications. Qualifications aside, medical receptionists must like working with the general public and alongside other members of staff in a team environment.

■ *A medical receptionist's duties vary from setting to setting*

Porter

Role

Porters play a very important role in hospitals, as they move patients around the hospital, for example moving a patient from the ward to theatre for an operation. They can use wheelchairs or trolleys, or they move the patient in their bed.

Porters do not just move patients to and from different areas of the hospital; they transport the deceased to the mortuary; they could take meals to patients; bring fresh laundry to wards and remove dirty laundry to be cleaned; move furniture; deliver post; transport new supplies and dispose of waste.

Skills

A porter must be fit and have stamina, as much of the work involves walking around the workplace (which, if it is a hospital, can be very large). As they are transporting patients, delivering items and assisting staff with their needs, it is important to be able to communicate well with others and be polite and friendly. Furthermore, it is important that porters remember the value of confidentiality, as often patients will confide in them and so also will visitors who are looking for friends and family.

Requirements

Literacy *The skill of being able to read and write competently.*

To become a porter, there are no formal qualification requirements, but employers do prefer the applicant to have a good level of **literacy** because the nature of the work involves transporting individuals or items around the workplace and it is essential that they be moved to the correct place. Sometimes, candidates are required to complete a physical fitness test or a medical examination and generally have to be over the age of 18, although there is no strict age limit.

Porter jobs are very popular and it can sometimes help to have experience of the role before applying, so some candidates do voluntary work at their local hospital or health centre to give them a better understanding of the requirements, skills and role of the job.

Real Life Care

Sandy the hospital porter

Sandy is a hospital porter and has worked at the hospital for a long time. She is a much respected member of the hospital as she knows where every department is and is very helpful to staff, service users and their friends and families. Sandy enjoys her job thoroughly as it helps to keep her fit and healthy.

1 Identify and describe the main roles of Sandy's job. ✔

2 Explain the requirements of being a porter in a hospital. ✔✔

3 Analyse the skills and qualities that Sandy needs to be a good porter. ✔✔✔

Paramedic

Role

A paramedic works in the ambulance service, and paramedics are the first health care staff to the scene of an emergency call. They respond to all sorts of incidents such as road accidents or sporting accidents. They are trained to make sure the patient is stable and then get them to hospital for treatment as quickly as possible.

Skills

Paramedics need to be very calm at the incident scene as they are normally scenes of shock and panic. They need to be able to think clearly in stressful situations and to make important decisions in the heat of the moment. Additionally, paramedics have to be able to work as part of a team and require excellent communication skills in order to deal with the patients and other members of the public.

Requirements

Most paramedics become an ambulance technician first for at least a year before becoming a paramedic. To become an ambulance technician, you must normally be over 21 and have at least four GCSEs (grade A*–C). You must then do an intensive training course that lasts about 8–12 weeks to become a paramedic. Sometimes, people go to university to do a degree in paramedic science, which can then help them go straight into being a paramedic.

Cleaner

Role

Every working environment, whether in health and social care settings or in other areas, needs a cleaner. The role of a cleaner is simply to remove the dirt and grime from the place of work such as the building, rooms and facilities. They do this to provide a safe environment to work in and make it a healthy and pleasant place to be.

Cleaners in health and social care settings are particularly important as much health and social care work is based on **hygiene**. It is essential to have a clean hospital as it prevents the spreading of diseases. Likewise, in a residential home, facilities must be cleaned regularly to ensure the home is a safe place to live in and to prevent cross-infections.

A cleaner may work together with other cleaners in large organisations such as hospitals and be given particular roles to do; alternatively, they may work individually on one room or small building. Cleaners have to use specialist chemicals and equipment to be able to disinfect the building and utensils. They must make sure that they do each job properly as there could be serious health consequences to the service providers and service users if a cleaner only uses water to clean a floor, for example, instead of the correct chemicals and solution. Some cleaners work outdoors and travel to different sites, but transport is normally provided.

Key point

To be a paramedic, you have to be able to stand the sight of blood and gruesome injuries.

Over to you

Do you think that anyone could be a paramedic? Discuss what sort of person would make a good paramedic. What type of person would not be suited to being a paramedic?

Hygiene *Principles and practice of cleanliness and health.*

Cleaners may wear uniforms or overalls to protect their skin and clothing from the chemicals that they are using and use various types of cleaning equipment, from dusters to industrial cleaning hoses and machines.

Skills

A cleaner needs to be reliable and responsible as the workplace and facilities must be kept clean. They need to have good teamwork skills but be able to work independently and competently without supervision. A cleaner must be fairly fit because of the demanding physical nature of the work involved.

The work cleaners do needs to be efficiently done and to a high standard, and so they must be focused on the task in hand. Furthermore, a cleaner must be proud of their work and want to provide a good quality of service.

Due to the nature of the role, cleaning normally takes place in unsociable hours as this is the time when few or no people are around and the cleaning can be done effectively. This means that a cleaner must be flexible and able to work different times of the day such as very early mornings and late evenings.

Requirements

Most cleaners learn and train on the job, as each cleaning role is different depending on the care setting – different items have to be cleaned in various ways using a range of chemicals and solutions. Therefore, there are no formal qualifications required to become a cleaner, although literacy and **numeracy** skills are essential when reading instructions for chemicals and cleaning solutions. However, a number of qualifications, such as NVQs and apprenticeships in cleaning and support services, are available, and these can be studied while in employment as a cleaner.

Numeracy *Number skills; being able to add, substract, multiply and divide.*

Nursery nurse

Role

Nursery nurses care for children aged 8 and under. They can work in settings such as schools, nurseries and crèches, hospitals, residential or day nurseries, or even in the child's own home.

Their duties and tasks depend on the age group that they are caring for. For example, babies require a lot of physical care such as giving them baths, feeding and dressing them and changing their nappies, while older children require more play activities to develop their language skills and personal development.

Skills

Nursery nurses must have lots of patience! This is because children take longer to understand things than adults, and you may have to explain something several times to a child before they understand what you want them to do. Nursery nurses also need to be aware of the different beliefs and values of the children in their care and take this into consideration when planning activities for the children to do. It is important to be friendly and enthusiastic as this will help settle the children and form good relationships with them and their parents. Nursery nurses also need good writing skills, as they have to write about the children's development on reports to the parents and other health care professionals that they might be working alongside.

Requirements

To be able to work unsupervised with children, nursery nurses must have the Council for Awards in Children's Care and Education (CACHE) Diploma in Child Care and Education or S/NVQ in Early Years and Education Level 3.

■ *A nursery nurse*

Care Assistant

Role

Care assistants provide care to those who need help with the everyday activities in their lives. This could involve helping the service user to wash and dress or perhaps assisting them with their cleaning and laundry. The carer can also help service users with **budgeting**, paying the bills and letter writing. The type of service that a care assistant provides depends on whether the service user has any disabilities or on the environment that they live in. For example, care assistants may work in the individual's home or in residential homes or day centres. In some environments, it might be appropriate for the carer to set up activities that lots of people can do. Another important part of the job is to help service users with their emotional and social needs.

Talking point

Would-be nursery nurse: I would like to be a nursery nurse. I think it sounds like good fun.

Friend: But you don't like children!

Budgeting *Working to a budget – working out how much income a person has and how much is spent on food, bills etc.*

Real Life Care

Care assistant Chi Wai

Chi Wai is a care assistant for Kevin, an elderly man who lives on his own and has no family in the area. Chi Wai visits Kevin three days a week and does all Kevin's laundry and housework. Kevin likes it when Chi Wai comes round as he gets to talk to Chi Wai about his week.

1 Identify and describe the skills and requirements you think Chi Wai needs when he is working with Kevin. ✓

2 Explain why it is important to have these attributes. ✓✓

3 Evaluate how Kevin would feel if he did not have a care assistant. ✓✓✓

Skills

Care assistants need to have a range of skills such as being able to cook and help wash, dress and feed service users if they require it. They must remain calm and patient with the service users as they encourage them to do things for themselves and assist in their lives.

Requirements

There are no special qualifications to be a care assistant. GCSEs or an S/NVQ in Care Level 2 or BTEC First in Health and Social Care would be an asset. Other requirements would be a desire to work with people and being a good listener.

Midwife

Role

Midwives support pregnant women and their families before, during and after the birth of their babies. Their main duties and tasks are to monitor the health of the mother and inform her of the possible options of delivery. They can give advice on how to stay healthy during pregnancy, such as not smoking and drinking alcohol, and also run **antenatal** classes for pregnant women and partners so that they can explain the process of giving birth and teach parents techniques of how to give birth.

> **Antenatal** *Before birth, i.e. when a woman is pregnant.*

Skills

Midwives go out to visit patients in their own homes or the patients will come into health centres, GPs' surgeries or hospitals to see their midwife. As they are working one to one with their clients, midwives need to be reliable and dependable. Midwives also need to be good communicators and to develop a good rapport with their service users to be able to make them feel comfortable.

Requirements

To become a midwife, you will need to have either a degree or a Level 4 Diploma in Midwifery, or become a nurse first and then take a course to become a midwife, although many Universities have stopped doing this.

To be accepted onto the degree and diploma courses, you must be over 17 years of age and have at least 5 GCSEs (grade A*–C) and at least two A Levels in relevant subjects or alternative qualifications such as the BTEC National Diploma Health and Social Care.

When midwives have qualified, they must register with the Nursing and Midwifery Council as this then proves that they have qualified in the approved way and so employers can check their suitability.

■ *What did you do today?*

Occupational therapist

Role
Occupational therapists help patients who have disabilities to develop and improve their skills, recover from the disability or to maintain the skills they already have. They help people to perform the everyday activities that we take for granted such as being able to walk or getting dressed, showing a client how to use crutches or how to put socks on when they cannot reach their toes because their leg is in plaster. They often treat elderly patients who may have suffered from a stroke and have mobility problems, or they can assist service users who have had accidents such as two broken legs. Occupational therapists work one to one with the service user either in their own home or at the health centre, day centre, hospital or GP's surgery.

Skills
Occupational therapists' work requires them to deal with many different people from a variety of backgrounds and so they need to be able to relate and communicate with service users effectively. They should also

be good motivators and have an encouraging personality as it can be depressing and demoralising for service users who have a disability to have to use special equipment to perform a task that everyone else can do without thinking about it.

Requirements

To become an occupational therapist, you need a degree in this area. To join the degree course, you must have five GCSEs (grade A*–C) and two A Levels of which at least one must be science-based, or equivalent qualifications, such as BTEC National Health and Social Care.

Dietician

Role

Dieticians are experts in the nutritional value of food and drink. They advise people on the best diet to follow to maintain good health. Dieticians help people to understand the effects of food and drink on their health and well-being.

A dietician may work in various settings with different individuals. They may work in hospitals, working out new diet plans for individuals who have particular illnesses or disabilities and need to eat certain foods. Dieticians may also work with sports people to ensure that they are eating and drinking the correct food to give them the energy they need for their particular sport.

They may also work with the media to promote awareness of food and health issues (the television programme 'You are What You Eat' is a good example of this) and work with food companies and supermarkets giving nutritional advice on products.

Skills

It is important for a dietician to have a non-judgemental and friendly approach, as for some individuals food can be a very stressful topic. Dieticians spend most of their time with their clients and so they need good communication skills and an ability to translate the nutritional information into a language that their service users understand. Dieticians also require good team skills, as they will be working with others to meet the needs of the service users, and also have a good scientific knowledge of food and drink products and their contents.

Requirements

Dieticians must have a degree or postgraduate Diploma in Nutrition and Dietetics. To study for these qualifications at university, applicants must have at least two A Levels in Chemistry and another science, or equivalent qualifications such as BTEC National Diploma Health and Social Care, as well as three GCSEs (grade A*–C), including English and Maths. Adults entering a degree course can be accepted by taking an access course.

Manager of a residential home

Role

A manager of a residential home is the person in charge of its day-to-day running. They have to manage and monitor budgets, help people in their everyday activities such as eating and drinking, enable the home to interact with the local community, manage other staff and ensure that all staff are properly trained and following all the rules set out in the codes of practice and policies.

This is a very responsible role as every person in the home, whether staff or residents, is under the manager's overall care. It is the manager's responsibility to make sure that everyone is happy and that their well-being is maintained.

Managers are also responsible for the administrative aspects of the job, such as paying the staff and bills, and ensuring the maintenance of the building and updating parts of it when needed.

Skills

A manager of a residential home must be organised and keep up to date with paperwork and the latest laws and policies. They must be a good leader as they are in charge of staff, and therefore they also require teamwork skills and an ability to communicate effectively with both staff and service users.

Managers need to be creative and use their initiative to think of new activities to keep service users interested and active. Good literacy and numeracy skills would be an advantage together with a desire to run a care environment efficiently, while always promoting good practice, independence and a warm, friendly environment.

Requirements

If they are looking for a job as a new manager of a home, most candidates will be required to have experience of managerial roles and also experience in the care sector. They may be required to have S/NVQs in Care or other appropriate qualifications, such as the registered managers award.

Hospital play worker

Role

When children are in hospital as patients, they can get very bored as there are not a lot of things for them to do. Therefore, some hospitals employ play workers or play specialists to entertain children and to help them to understand and deal with the things that are happening to them.

The play worker will use different activities such as creative, therapeutic or physical activities to help the children to settle into the hospital and prepare them for treatment such as injections or operations. They also provide support for the families as they can tell them how to play with the child when they leave hospital.

Skills

Play specialists work as part of a team with other direct care providers such as physiotherapists, nurses, occupational therapists, doctors and so on. Therefore, it is essential that they are able work in a team and to communicate effectively with the children, staff and families of the service users.

If you want to become a play worker, you will need to enjoy working with children! A good sense of humour and fun is essential for play workers as they sometimes need to take the child's mind off the treatment they are having. They need to be imaginative, as they plan their own activities, and to be well organised, but it is up to them to arrange how equipment should be used. On the negative side, play workers need to be able to cope emotionally with the sad times that can occur in hospitals.

Requirements

To become a qualified play worker, you will need a qualification in child care, nursing, teaching, occupational therapy or art, drama or music therapy. You have to be over 20 years old and have worked for at least three years with children. In addition, you will be expected to work towards the Professional Diploma in Specialised Play for Sick Children and Young People and then register as a play worker so that future employers can check you are properly qualified.

 Over to you

Look back over the list of jobs that you made for each setting. Pick one or two from your list and research the job roles, care skills and requirements that you need to be able to do each job.

Alternatively, pick a job from the list below to research:

Mental health nurse; health visitor; nursing assistant; doctor; dentist; optician; physiotherapist; medical laboratory technician; social worker; community workers; mobile meals staff; care arranger; family support; assistant youth worker; childminder; nanny; foster parent.

Present your findings to the rest of the class. Perhaps you could make an information sheet or poster to show the rest of the class.

 Over to you

Look in newspapers, magazines, the Internet and other sources to find jobs that you would like to do in the health and social care sector. What skills and attributes do you need to do these jobs? Do you think that you have the skills to be able to do them? What roles in health and social care do you think you are not suitable for?

Practice for Assessment

Carrying out this activity will give you evidence for P4, P5 and M3.

You have been asked to make a brochure advertising the world of health and social care for teenagers making their career choices.

You need to research two different job roles in health and social care and write a description of them including the requirements of the jobs. (P4)

Explain these requirements in detail for each of the job roles. Include requirements such as appearance, attitude, confidence, punctuality, ability to work alone or in a team, qualifications, and empathy with others. (M3)

Add a section about the skills needed for each job role. (P5)

Workforce development

In the health and social care sector, new technology and methods of practice are constantly being updated and improved. A long time ago, doctors used leeches to suck the poison out of the patient's body. Could you imagine if we did that today! Therefore, it is important that the people caring for us stay up to date with their knowledge and care for us in the way that we would expect to be cared for.

Requirements and regulations of Sector Skills Councils

In the UK, Sector Skills Councils (SSCs) are independent organisations in many different sectors. They tackle the skills and productivity needs of their sector, and have four key goals:

- To reduce skills gaps and shortages.
- To improve productivity, business and public service performance.
- To increase opportunities to boost the skills and productivity of everyone in the sector's workforce, including action on equal opportunities.
- To improve learning supply, including apprenticeships, higher education and national occupational standards.

Skills for Health is the SSC for the health sector. It works with employers and other organisations to ensure that those working in the sector have the right skills to support the development and delivery of health care services. They do this by running training programmes to help people work as a team and make sure the job roles cover all the tasks that need to be done. If there are too many tasks for each job role to cover, then new jobs are created to ease the workload and make a framework (structure) that people can work to.

National occupational standards

One of the main functions of Skills for Health is to develop national occupational standards (NOS). These define what good practice is in the way people work, and helps bring together the skills, knowledge and values needed based on the requirements of the job. The standards can be used by individuals to help them develop their skills, by people who offer education and training, and by employers and agencies to improve the overall quality of their services.

■ The areas that the national occupational standards cover

NOS are the foundation on which NVQs and SVQs are developed and provide the legal requirements for all health and social care staff to ensure they are fully trained and qualified to the appropriate level and relate directly to the job that the person is training for.

Agenda for Change and NHS Knowledge and Skills Framework

Agenda for Change outlines the new pay, terms and conditions for the NHS and is the biggest overhaul of NHS pay, terms and conditions in over 50 years.

The new pay system will ensure that all staff are paid fairly and that career progression is easier for people to achieve. Agenda for Change ensures that staff will be paid for the jobs they are doing and the skills and knowledge they apply to these jobs, because some members of staff work harder than others for the same pay.

Some of the benefits of Agenda for Change may include:

■ a system that is fair

■ recognition and reward for the skills and competencies staff acquire throughout their career

■ a system that should improve recruitment to health and social care settings.

To assist with personal development and career progression, the NHS Knowledge and Skills Framework (NHS KSF) was created as part of Agenda for Change. It was designed to form the basis of a review of how well an individual is developing in their job. It looks at how individuals are applying their knowledge and skills to meet the demands of the post, and gives them a 'Personal Development Plan' suggesting the learning and development that needs to take place by the next review. It is a good way of monitoring an individual's and a department's performance.

Induction and transition

When you start a new job, you do not just turn up on the first day and get on straightaway with the everyday tasks. You will need to learn how to do them all first! Even if you are doing a similar job to one you did before in another department, everyone has their own way of doing things and you have to learn how to do them according to their policies and procedures.

To help you settle into your new role, you will be inducted into the new methods and tasks that you will be doing in your job. You will be shown how to maintain safety at work, that you understand the organisation and what your duties will be.

People are also inducted into their roles at work during times of transition. For example, a care assistant needs to be inducted with new procedures for washing clients in the bath that have recently been introduced.

Continuing professional development and competence

Some organisations require that staff stay up to date with new procedures and methods. This is particularly important when teaching students. For example, teachers, nurses or doctors who are training students to become workers in health and social care settings must be fully aware of all the latest techniques and equipment in order to be able to educate the learners effectively. Therefore, staff are encouraged to go on training programmes and continue their professional development by learning new methods or reminding them of particular techniques.

Ways of monitoring performance

We have already mentioned above that the NHS KSF is a good way of monitoring performance of individuals, staff, departments and organisations. However, another way of monitoring an employee's performance is to carry out an **appraisal**. In health and social care settings, this might involve observing the employee carrying out their day-to-day duties in the workplace followed by a discussion about their role and performance. Targets might be set for the employee to meet before the next appraisal, which could be in six months or, in other organisations, a year or longer.

The main purpose of an appraisal is to discuss the employee's strengths and weaknesses, what their needs are, including any training required, and sometimes to decide whether the employee should be given a pay rise.

Key point

Induction means showing someone a new way of doing something, and teaching them the correct methods of carrying out a task.

Appraisal *A workplace appraisal involves a meeting and discussion between employer and employee about their worth and performance.*

The appraisal is conducted on a one-to-one basis with the employee having a chance to speak to their supervisor or manager about their job role in an honest manner. It is also a chance for the supervisor to tell the employee how well they have been performing.

Guidance

To help you to perform in your chosen profession as efficiently and effectively as possible, different rules and procedures exist for you to follow. These may be different depending on the environment and sector that you work in. However, you will need to be aware of the types of rules and regulations that there are. They include the following:

- **Legislation** – laws made by Parliament that apply to everybody in the UK.

- **National minimum standards** – the Care Standards Act 2000 sets out different standards for different organisations such as care homes for older people, children's homes and boarding schools. These standards form the basis for judgements as to whether a health and social care organisation is working properly.

- **Codes of practices** – these are lists of rules that tell care workers what to do in their profession. They are made by the regulatory body for the particular care setting, and so all residential homes, for example, will follow the same code of practice.

- **Charters** – a charter informs service users of what to expect from the service that they are using. It also tells them how to access this service and what to do if it does not meet their expectations.

- **Organisational policies and procedures, terms and conditions** – the organisations and companies that employ you make these. They may have particular policies and procedures for certain activities and tasks as well as terms and conditions, which can vary from individual to individual.

For a more detailed look at these rules and regulations, see Unit 4 Cultural Diversity in Health and Social Care, page 183.

Practice for Assessment

This could contribute to P6, M4 and D2.

You have been asked to write a report describing the relevant guidance and potential workforce development activities for the two job roles in your brochure. (P6)

Include examples to explain the importance of relevant guidance and potential workforce development activities for health and social care workers. (M4)

Explain how workforce development and guidance help to maintain a competent health and social care workforce. (D2)

Check your understanding

1. Identify three different jobs for each of the following sectors: health care, social care and early years.

2. Choose one of the jobs that you identified above for each sector and describe the job role including the care skills that are needed in the role.

3. What does secondary care mean?

4. Give one example of guidance that you have to follow whilst in the workplace, and explain why this is important.

5. Describe what an induction is, and why they are carried out.

6. Give one example of how to continue professional development or competence. Explain why this is an important part of working in health and social care sectors.

7. Describe the difference between a code of practice and a charter.

8. Why might someone from an ethnic minority have difficulty accessing care?

9. Explain the difference between an employee and an employer.

10. Suggest ways of monitoring an employee's performance in the workplace.

9 The Impact of Diet on Health

Introduction

It is important for workers in health and social care to understand the principles of nutrition, not only to help maintain the nutritional status of the people they care for but also to maintain good nutritional status themselves. The aim of the unit is to help you to develop your knowledge and understanding of nutrition.

How you will be assessed

This is an internally assessed unit.
In this unit you will learn about:

- the dietary needs of individuals at different life stages
- the effects of unbalanced diets on the health of individuals
- specific dietary needs of patients/service users
- food safety and hygiene.

Dietary needs of individuals at different life stages

It is important to recognise that people's dietary needs change during their lifespan. A suitable balanced diet for a small child will not be suitable for an adult or older person, so needs must be taken into account when caring for different individuals.

Life stages

Infancy (0–3 years)

At birth, babies rely only on milk to meet their nutritional requirements. Breast milk is the ideal food for newborns because it contains nutrients for all the baby's needs in the right amounts. Although it is low in iron and copper, the baby has enough of these stored until it starts eating solid foods. In addition, breast milk provides immunity and is clean, readily available and does not have to be prepared. Some mothers are either unable or choose not to breastfeed and use formula milk, which is modified cow's milk. This must be made up to the right concentration to prevent damage to the immature kidneys. The equipment used must be sterilised to prevent infection.

Weaning should not be done before about 6 months of age as doing it early may cause later obesity or allergies. Different foods can be introduced gradually such as cereals, then fruit and vegetables and egg yolk and finely minced meat. By about 12–18 months, the toddler should be eating the same food as the rest of the family, with no extra salt or sugar added. It is usually advised that up until the age of 2 years, children should be given whole milk, but after this they can be given semi-skimmed milk. Skimmed milk should not be given until the age of 5. The amount of milk drunk will decrease as the child eats more and more solid food.

Childhood (4–10 years)

Children between 4 and 10 years of age tend to be very active and are growing fast. Although their energy requirements are not as high as adults', they need almost the same amount of some vitamins and minerals. Some children seem to have big appetites – this is not due to greed but to the fact that they have high nutritional needs. During childhood, children should be encouraged to eat healthy meals consisting of meat, fish or eggs and potatoes, pasta or rice, with plenty of vegetables and fruit. They should not eat too many sweets, crisps, biscuits and fizzy drinks, as these can lead to obesity and tooth decay.

Adolescence (11–18 years)

The nutritional needs of adolescents are greater than for any other age group. This is because they have large appetites and are still growing. It is important that people in this age group are encouraged to eat sensibly at regular intervals and not to go through phases of overeating or starving themselves in order to lose weight. In addition to encouraging healthy eating, they should be advised to maintain a regular amount of physical activity. Again they should not eat too many sweets, crisps, biscuits and fizzy drinks.

Over to you

Make a list of your favourite foods and drinks. Compare your list with a partner. Do you both enjoy the same kinds of foods? Are there any foods that one of you likes and the other really dislikes? Why do you think this is?

Why is it important to enjoy your food?

Adulthood (19–65 years)

During adulthood nutritional needs reduce with age. In general, adults need to eat a healthy diet consisting of complex carbohydrates such as bread, potatoes, rice or pasta, protein such as meat, eggs, cheese or fish, and fruit and vegetables. Fatty and sugary foods should be kept to a minimum and adults should be advised to take physical activity on a regular basis. Alcohol intake should be limited as it contributes extra kilocalories to the diet.

Pregnancy and breastfeeding

During pregnancy and breastfeeding a woman's nutritional needs are increased to provide nutrition for the growing baby and for making breast milk after the baby is born. Although there is a belief that being pregnant means that a woman can 'eat for two', only about an extra 200 kilocalories are required in the last three months of the pregnancy, and about 450–570 kilocalories during breastfeeding. This is to give the mother the energy she needs to carry the extra weight of the baby and to make breast milk. Women planning to become pregnant should be advised to eat a diet rich in folic acid to prevent damage to the foetus, particularly spina bifida.

Old age (65 years +)

Although, in general, there is not much difference in the energy needs of adults and older adults, as we age we become less mobile and our energy requirements decrease. Appetite also decreases, so it is important that older adults have a diet that provides concentrated sources of protein, vitamins and minerals. Gentle exercise should also be encouraged. Elderly people who live alone often cannot be bothered to cook a hot meal for one person, so they should be encouraged to eat foods that do not require much preparation but are high in nutrients. Taste buds become less efficient in older people so they may require extra flavouring in their food. However, adding salt can raise blood pressure, so herbs and spices can be used.

Recommended daily amounts of megajoules/kilocalories in males and females				
Age range	**Males**		**Females**	
	Megajoules	**Kilocalories**	**Megajoules**	**Kilocalories**
0–3 months (formula fed)	2.28	545	2.16	515
4–6 months	2.89	690	2.69	645
7–9 months	3.44	825	3.20	765
10–12 months	3.85	920	3.61	865
1–3 years	5.15	1230	4.86	1165
4–6 years	7.16	1715	6.46	1545
7–10 years	8.24	1970	7.28	1740
11–14 years	9.27	2220	7.92	1845
15–18 years	11.51	2755	8.83	2110
19–59 years	10.60	2550	8.10	1940
60–64 years	9.93	2380	8.00	1900
65–74 years	9.71	2330	7.99	1900
75+ years	8.77	2100	7.96	1810
Pregnant			+0.80*	+200*
Lactating:				
1 month			+1.90	+450
2 months			+2.20	+530
3 months			+2.40	+570
4 – 6 months			+2.00	+480
6+ months			+1.00	+240

* = last trimester (three months) only

1 megajoule = 1000 kilojoules; 1 kilojoule = 4.18 kilocalories

Source: DEFRA (1995) *Manual of Nutrition*, 10th edition.

Concept of balanced diet

Intake and needs

There is not one single food or type of food that provides all the nutrients that the human body needs to function efficiently. A balanced diet will depend on the types of food eaten over a period of time and the nutritional needs of the particular individual. The wider the variety of foods eaten, the more nutrients will be provided by them. It is now known that some health problems are caused by dietary intake, such as too much fat causing heart disease and too much salt contributing to strokes.

Dietary needs will vary for each individual. As you have seen from the information above, dietary needs will differ according to age, but other factors will come into play. Such factors include:

■ the level of exercise taken

■ the type of job a person does

■ religious or cultural decisions

■ likes and dislikes

■ a person's health

■ availability of food.

These will be discussed further later in the unit.

Dietary Reference Values

In 1991, the Committee on Medical Aspects of Food Policy (COMA) published Dietary Reference Values (DRVs), which were designed to provide guidelines by which doctors and nutritionists would be able to assess the adequacy of the diets of different groups of people. From this, three different values were set for most nutrients, as shown in the table below.

Dietary Reference Values	
DRV	**Definition**
Estimated Average Requirement (EAR)	An estimate of the average need for food energy or a nutrient. Most people will need more than this average and many will need less.
Reference Nutrient Intake (RNI)	The amount of a nutrient that is enough for almost every individual, even those with high needs. The RNI is generally much higher than most people need. The RNI supplies enough of a nutrient for at least 97.5% of the population.
Lower Reference Nutrient Intake (LRNI)	The amount of a nutrient considered to be sufficient only for the small number of individuals with low nutrient needs (only about 2.5% of the population).

Over to you

Dietary Reference Values for vitamin C (mg per day)			
Age	**LRNI**	**EAR**	**RNI**
0–12 months	6	15	25
1–10 years	8	20	39
11–14 years	9	22	35
15+ years	10	25	40
Pregnant women	20	35	50
Breastfeeding women	40	55	70

Source: Adapted from *Dietary Reference Values – A Guide* (1991), HMSO

1 What is the average requirement for vitamin C for people aged 11–14?

2 A pregnant mother asks you how much vitamin C she should consume daily. What would you advise her?

3 You are planning a school lunch. How much vitamin C should you include to make sure that most people's needs are met?

4 A survey shows that a group of 12-year-olds has an average intake of 16 mg of vitamin C a day. Do you think they need to increase the amount of vitamin C in their diet?

Energy balance

It is important that there is energy balance in the diet. The diet should contain a variety of foods so that energy comes from different sources. As you will see later in the unit, different food groups provide different amounts of energy per gram of the food, and balancing these will help to provide an overall healthy diet.

Nutrient deficiencies and malnutrition

Maintaining good health depends on the consumption of sufficient amounts of nutrients and energy. Malnutrition can describe undernutrition or overnutrition. Undernutrition is the result of not taking in enough energy or nutrients and if this continues over a length of time, starvation and other deficiency disorders will occur. Most particularly, children who suffer from undernutrition can suffer from physical stunting or mental retardation. Overnutrition results from an excessive intake of energy of one or more nutrients and can result in medical problems such as obesity, heart disease or diabetes. Further information on these and other nutrition disorders will be covered in more detail later in the unit.

The Balance of Good Health

The Balance of Good Health is based on the government's Eight Guidelines for a healthy diet. It forms the basis of the Food Standards Agency nutrition strategy. The guidelines are shown below:

1. Base your meals on starchy foods

2. Eat lots of fruit and veg

3. Eat more fish

4. Cut down on saturated fat and sugar

5. Try to eat less salt – no more than 6g a day

6. Get active and try to be a healthy weight

7. Drink plenty of water

8. Don't skip breakfast

■ *Eight Guidelines for a Healthy Diet (Source: Food Standards Agency)*

The balance of good health is set out in pictorial form to show the recommended balance of foods in the diet. If people follow the recommended amounts as shown on the plate and make sure that they choose different foods, they should ensure that they have a balanced diet.

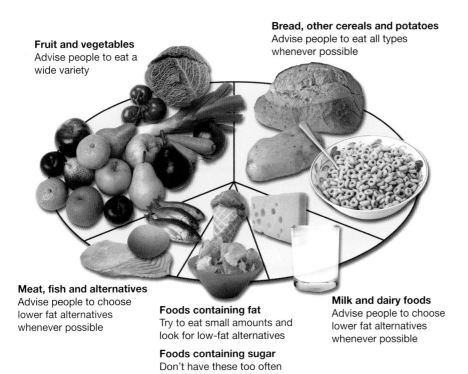

Fruit and vegetables
Advise people to eat a
wide variety

Bread, other cereals and potatoes
Advise people to eat all types
whenever possible

Meat, fish and alternatives
Advise people to choose
lower fat alternatives
whenever possible

Foods containing fat
Try to eat small amounts and
look for low-fat alternatives

Foods containing sugar
Don't have these too often

Milk and dairy foods
Advise people to choose
lower fat alternatives
whenever possible

■ *The Balance of Good Health*

Nutritional value of the main food groups		
Food	**What's included**	**Main nutrients**
Bread, other cereals and potatoes	Other cereals means foods such as breakfast cereals, pasta, rice, oats, noodles, maize, millet and cornmeal. This group also includes yams and plantains. Beans and pulses can be eaten as part of this group.	Carbohydrate (starch), fibre, some calcium and iron, B vitamins
Fruit and vegetables	Fresh, frozen and canned fruit and vegetables and dried fruit. A glass of fruit juice also counts. Beans and pulses can be eaten as part of this group.	Vitamin C, carotenes, folates, fibre and some carbohydrate
Milk and dairy foods	Milk, cheese, yoghurt and fromage frais. This group does not include butter, eggs and cream.	Calcium, protein, vitamins A, B12 and D
Meat, fish and alternatives	Meat, poultry, fish, eggs, nuts, beans and pulses. Meat includes bacon and salami and meat products such as sausages, beefburgers and pâté. These are all relatively high-fat choices. Beans, such as canned baked beans and pulses are in this group and they are a good source of protein for vegetarians. Fish includes frozen and canned fish such as sardines and tuna, fishfingers and fishcakes. Aim to eat at least one portion of oily fish such as sardines and salmon each week.	Iron, protein, B vitamins, especially B12, zinc, magnesium
Foods containing fat	Food containing fat: margarine, butter, other spreading fats and low-fat spreads, cooking oils, oil-based salad dressings, mayonnaise, cream, chocolate, crisps, biscuits, pastries, cakes, puddings, ice cream, rich sauces and gravies	Fat, including some essential fatty acids, but also some vitamins. Some products also contain salt or sugar.
Foods and drinks containing sugar	Foods and drinks containing sugar: soft drinks, sweets, jam and sugar, as well as foods such as cakes, puddings, biscuits, pastries and ice cream	Sugar, with minerals in some products and fat in others.

Source: Food Standards Agency (2001) *The Balance of Good Health*

Message	Recommendations

Eat lots	Try to eat wholemeal, wholegrain, brown or high fibre versions where possible. Try to avoid:
	■ having them fried too often
	■ adding too much fat
	  (e.g. thickly spread butter, margarine or low-fat spread on bread)
	■ adding rich sauces and dressings
	  (e.g. cream or cheese sauce on pasta)

Eat lots – at least 5 portions a day. Fruit juice counts as only one portion however much you drink in a day. Beans and pulses count as only one portion however much you eat in a day.	Eat a wide variety of fruit and vegetables. Try to avoid:
	■ adding fat or rich sauces to vegetables
	  (e.g. carrots glazed with butter or parsnips roasted in a lot of fat)
	■ adding sugar or syrupy dressings to fruit
	  (e.g. stewed apple with sugar or chocolate sauce on banana)

Eat or drink moderate amounts and choose lower fat versions whenever you can.	Lower fat versions means semi-skimmed or skimmed milk, low-fat (0.1% fat) yoghurts or fromage frais, and lower fat cheeses (e.g. Edam, half-fat cheese and Camembert). Check the amount of fat by looking at the nutrient information on the labels. Compare similar products and choose the lowest, e.g. 8% fromage frais may be labelled 'low fat', but it is not actually the lowest available.
Eat moderate amounts and choose lower fat versions whenever you can.	Lower fat versions means things like meat with the fat cut off, poultry without the skin and fish without batter. Cook these foods without added fat. Beans and pulses are good alternatives to meat as they are naturally very low in fat.
Eat foods containing fat sparingly and look out for the low-fat alternatives.	Some foods containing fat will be eaten every day, but should be kept to small amounts, e.g. margarine and butter, other spreading fats (including low-fat spreads), cooking oils, oil-based salad dressings and mayonnaise.
Foods and drinks containing sugar should not be eaten too often as they can contribute to tooth decay.	Foods containing fat such as cakes, biscuits, pastries and ice cream should be limited and low-fat alternatives chosen where available. All foods and drinks containing sugar should be eaten mainly at mealtimes to reduce the risk of tooth decay.

Although the main components of the diet should be healthy, people can still eat less healthy foods, but in smaller quantities. This is sometimes known as the 80/20 rule – 80% of the time people should eat healthily and they can then eat less healthily 20% of the time. It does not necessarily mean that people have to vary their diet daily – as long as they can achieve a good balance over a week or two-week period. Another pictorial representation is sometimes shown as a pyramid.

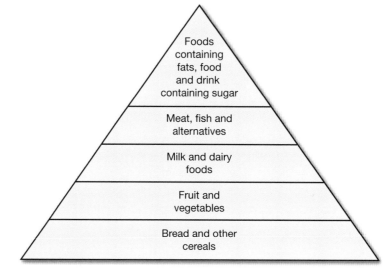

■ *The food pyramid*

Components of a healthy diet

Nutrients

A balanced diet is made up of proteins, carbohydrates, fats, vitamins, minerals, fibre and water. Carbohydrates, proteins and fats are known as **macro**nutrients because they are required in the body in large amounts. Vitamins and minerals are known as **micro**nutrients because they are needed in relatively small amounts.

Carbohydrates

Carbohydrates (CHOs) are made up of carbon, hydrogen and oxygen. There are three main groups of carbohydrates in foods. These are sugars, starches and cellulose and related products (fibre). They provide the main source of energy in the diet. Foods high in carbohydrates include grains, pulses, fruit and vegetables, and should make up about 55 per cent of the diet.

Sugars are referred to as simple carbohydrates. There are many different types of sugars. Glucose is found naturally in fruit and plants and in the blood. As carbohydrates in food are broken down, the final result is glucose, the molecules of which are small enough to pass from the blood into the cells to provide energy. Glucose syrups are used in the manufacture of cakes, sweets and jams. Fructose is found in some fruit and vegetables and honey. It is the sweetest sugar known. Glucose and fructose are known as **mono**saccharides or simple sugars.

Sucrose is commonly known as table sugar. It occurs naturally in sugar cane and sugar beet and in some fruits and root vegetables such as carrots. Lactose occurs in milk and is less sweet than glucose or sucrose. Sucrose and lactose linked together both consist of two single sugar units (monosaccharides) to form a **di**saccharide.

Starches are known as **poly**saccharides, which means that they are made up of many monosaccharide sugars linked together. Most common forms of starch are cereals such as oats, wheat, barley, rye and rice and potatoes. Pasta and bread are made mainly of wheat. One gram of starch provides approximately four kilocalories of energy.

Non-starch polysaccharides are also known as cellulose or fibre. This is found in the fibrous structure of plant material such as cereals, fruit and vegetables. It is classed as a carbohydrate, but it cannot be digested and absorbed by humans. It is a very important part of the diet as it has a role in the maintenance of good health. It has the following functions:

■ It encourages chewing.

■ It adds bulk to the diet and helps with digestion.

■ It helps to prevent constipation.

■ It helps to prevent bowel disorders.

Proteins

Proteins are made up of carbon, hydrogen, nitrogen and oxygen. Most also contain sulphur and some contain phosphorus. Proteins are essential components of all cells and they have two main functions – to regulate body processes or to provide structure in the body. They also help to make antibodies and enzymes. Protein is needed in the body for growth and repair, but any excess taken in will be used to provide energy. Proteins are made up of chains of amino acids. About 20 amino acids are needed in the body and of these, eight are said to be essential. This does not mean that they are more necessary than the others, but that they cannot be made in the body so have to be obtained from the food eaten. Protein should make up about 15 per cent of the diet.

Proteins can be divided into animal and vegetable. Animal proteins are called high biological value proteins because they contain all eight essential amino acids. These include meat, fish, cheese and eggs. Plant proteins are called low biological value proteins because they are usually deficient in one or more of the essential amino acids. When these foods are mixed in the same meal, they will complement each other and become a complete protein. An example of this is baked beans on toast. Bread is deficient in one essential amino acid and beans are deficient in another, so by eating them together you can have a complete protein meal. Low biological value foods include pulses such as beans and peas and soya or tofu. Tofu is the most complete vegetable protein. Food combining is a way that vegetarians and vegans can obtain complete proteins in food. The following diagram shows how this can be done:

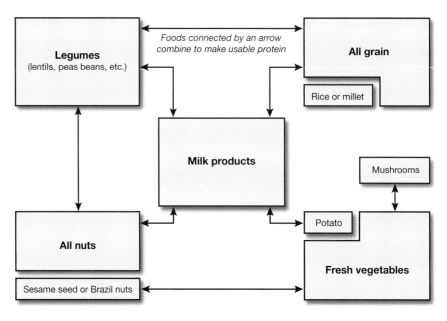

■ *Combining foods for more complete protein*
Source: Patrick Holford (1997) The Optimum Nutrition Bible, Piatkus

In addition to proteins found naturally in animal or plant food, there are alternatives to meat that have been developed by the food industry:

■ Texturised vegetable proteins have been developed from plant proteins and are considered suitable for use by vegetarians. These are made from soya beans and are produced as soya mince or chunks. They are fortified with vitamins and minerals.

■ Mycoprotein is another acceptable alternative to meat. It is produced from a fungus and one well-known product is Quorn. The fungal microorganism is grown, harvested and processed, and is produced as slices, chunks, mince, sausages and burgers.

Fats

Fats are compounds of carbon, hydrogen and oxygen. Some of the fats consumed by humans are visible, that is, they can be easily seen, such as the fat on meat. Others are invisible and these are generally a component of a food such as milk and nuts. Fats have several important functions in the body:

■ Fats provide a concentrated source of energy in the diet.

■ They also help to provide insulation against the cold by preventing heat loss.

■ They protect body organs such as the kidneys.

■ They help to transport and store Vitamins A, D, E and K.

■ They provide taste to food and make it easier to eat.

Over to you

Try to identify some other sources of visible and invisible fat in foods.

The main sources of fat in the western diet come from animal and dairy products. These are called saturated fats and are solid at room temperature. Examples of these are butter and margarine as well as suet and the fat on meat. They are less healthy than vegetable fats because they contain cholesterol, which contributes to heart disease. Fats should make up 30 per cent of the diet, but no more than 10 per cent should be saturated fats.

Plant fats are usually liquid at room temperature and examples of these are oils such as olive and sunflower. They are known as unsaturated fats. They are less likely to contribute to heart disease because they do not have the same effect of blocking the blood vessels as animal fats have. Olive oil is particularly identified as an oil that helps to prevent against heart disease.

Essential fatty acids are now known to be very important in the prevention of heart disease. They are the Omega 3 and Omega 6 fatty acids, but those in seeds such as pumpkin seeds, linseed and oily fish such as mackerel, sardines, tuna and salmon are known to be particularly beneficial. Omega 6 fatty acids are found in cereals, eggs, poultry and in evening primrose and borage oils.

Hydrogenation

'Hydrogenation is one of the processes that can be used to turn liquid oil into solid fat. The final product of this process is called hydrogenated vegetable oil, or sometimes hydrogenated fat. It's used in some biscuits, cakes, pastry, margarine and other processed foods.'

During the process of hydrogenation, trans fats may be formed. This means that foods that contain hydrogenated vegetable oil (always declared in the ingredients list) may also contain trans fats.

The trans fats found in food containing hydrogenated vegetable oil are harmful and have no known nutritional benefits. They raise the type of cholesterol in the blood that increases the risk of coronary heart disease. Some evidence suggests that the effects of these trans fats may be worse than saturated fats.

So, as part of a healthy diet we should try to reduce the amount of foods we eat that contain hydrogenated or saturated fats and replace them with unsaturated fats. And it's also important to reduce the total amount of fat we eat.

Biscuits, cakes, pastries, meat pies, sausages, hard cheese, butter and foods containing coconut or palm oil all tend to be high in saturated fats, so try not to eat too much of these.

Foods that are rich in unsaturated fats include oily fish, avocados, nuts and sunflower, rapeseed and olive oils.

Trans fats are also naturally found at very low levels in foods such as dairy products, beef and lamb.

Source: www.eatwell.gov.uk

Key point

'Interestingly, nutritionists are now finding that Omega-6s and Omega-3s will only maintain their status as "good" fats when you get relatively balanced amounts of both. Unfortunately, most western diets today are heavy on Omega-6s, often at the expense of Omega-3s. This means that, except as an adjunct to certain health conditions, Omega-6 supplements are probably not necessary.'

Source: wholehealthmd.com

Vitamins

Until the beginning of the twentieth century, it was believed that the only necessary components of the diet were proteins, carbohydrates and fats. However at this time, it was established that there were other elements that were also essential. Vitamins are very important in the body because they help enzymes to work properly. Vitamins cannot be made by the body and they are essential to life. There are two types of vitamins: water soluble and fat soluble. The water soluble vitamins are the B vitamins and Vitamin C. The fat soluble Vitamins are A, D, E and K. The table below shows the sources and functions of the vitamins in the diet.

Sources and functions of vitamins

Vitamin	Chemistry	Principal sources in diet	Function	Effect of shortage	Practical notes
A – Retinol	Organic compound, soluble in fat and oil	Fish oil, liver, butter, cheese, eggs, milk, fruit and veg	Night vision, keeps skin and epithelial linings healthy	Night blindness, itching, thickening of horny layer, dry skin	Stored in liver, excess can be harmful
B_1 – Thiamin	Organic compound, soluble in water	Bread, nuts, cereals, flour, meat, eggs, potatoes, poultry, milk	Release of energy from carbohydrates (CHO), digestion, correct functioning of nerves, building of blood, growth	Beri beri, apathy, poor appetite, pins and needles in legs, depression	Some may be lost in cooking, cannot be stored
B_2 – Riboflavin	Organic compound, soluble in water	Milk, liver, kidney, cereal, yeast, meat extracts, eggs, cheese	Release of energy from CHO	Cracking at corner of mouth, soreness of tongue, light sensitivity	Susceptibility to sunlight – bottles of milk on doorstep
B_3 – Niacin	Organic compound, soluble in water	Meat extract, yeast extract, wholemeal bread, eggs, liver, cereals	Release of energy from CHO, healthy skin and nervous system, cell metabolism	Pellagra, redness of skin, exfoliation of hands and face, diarrhoea, memory loss, irritability, insomnia	Depleted by physical and mental stress

▶ Continued from previous page

Vitamin	Chemistry	Principal sources in diet	Function	Effect of shortage	Practical notes
B_5 – Pantothenic acid	Organic compound, soluble in water	Animal products, cereals, legumes	Releases energy from fat and CHO, healthy immune system	Weakness, depression, resistance to infection	Microorganisms in small intestine can make this
B_6 – Pyridoxine	Organic compound, soluble in water	Meat, green veg, bran, wholemeal flour, eggs, bananas	Protein metabolism, converts tryptophan to niacin, formation of haemoglobin	Fatigue, nerve dysfunction	
B_{12} – Cyanocobalamin	Organic compound, soluble in water	Widely distributed in animal foods	Involved in manufacture of red blood cells in bone marrow, healthy nervous system	Pernicious anaemia, red sore tongues, degeneration of nerve cells	
C – Ascorbic acid	Organic compound, soluble in water	Blackcurrants, citrus fruits, green veg, peppers, tomatoes	Formation of bones and teeth, essential in blood, wound healing, immune system, skin and gums	Scurvy, incomplete cell repair, bruise easily, physical and mental stress	Not stored in body, lost in cooking, possibly carcinogenic in large doses
D	Organic compound, soluble in fat and oil	Fish liver, oily fish, eggs, milk, margarine, sunlight	Absorption of calcium in intestine, regulates calcium and magnesium in bone tissue	Rickets, osteomalacia, spontaneous fractures	Produced in skin by sun, stored in liver, excess can be harmful, good for nails
E	Organic compound, soluble in fat and oil	Eggs, cereal oils, veg oils, nuts, seeds	Maintains healthy muscular system, anti-oxidant, protects cell membranes	Poor muscle, circulatory and nerve performance	Babies fed low E content formula can have low stores, some people cannot absorb or utilise
K	Organic compound, soluble in fat and oil	Green veg, fish liver oils, alfalfa tablets, molasses, yoghurt	Blood clotting	Rare – babies may need supplement at birth, diarrhoea	Can be made by intestinal bacteria
Folic acid		Yeast, leafy green veg, meat, avocado, bananas	Produce red blood cells and tissue cells, normal growth, healthy gastrointestinal tract	Megaloblastic anaemia, neural tube defects	Can result from poor diet, decreased absorption in gastrointestinal disease

Minerals

Minerals are elements that are found in the earth and the sea. About 15 of them are essential to normal health and some are needed in quite large quantities while others are trace minerals and are only needed in very small quantities. The tables below show the sources and functions of both.

Sources and functions of minerals

Mineral	Function	Food sources	Deficiency symptoms	Notes
Calcium	Builds strong bones and hard teeth. Essential for blood clotting. Helps muscles and nerves to work. Activates certain enzymes	Milk, cheese, bread, flour and green vegetables. For some the bones in canned fish are important	Rickets, osteomalacia, muscle cramps	Blood level controlled by parathyroid glands. Requires vitamin D for absorption
Iron	Needed by all cells. Needed to form haemoglobin in red blood cells. Needed to form myoglobin in muscles	Meat (offal), bread, flour, cereal products, potatoes and vegetables	Anaemia, fatigue, brittle fingernails	Absorbed by body relative to need. Vitamin C increases absorption of iron
Phosphorus	Helps build bone and teeth. Needed by nerve fibres. All cells need it. Concerned in release of energy from food	Present in nearly all foods		
Magnesium	Essential constituent of all cells. Needed for enzymes involved in energy utilisation, healthy heart arteries, protein production and nerve function	Wholegrains, seafood, green vegetables	Growth failure, leg cramps, nervousness, confusion, anger easily	Deficiency likely from diarrhoea. Extra needed during lactation
Sodium chloride	Maintains balance of body fluid (sodium works with potassium). Maintains blood pressure, aids muscle contraction and nerve transmission	Naturally in eggs, meat, vegetables, milk. Added to many processed foods	Muscle cramps	Salt lost by body in diarrhoea. Control regulated by adrenal gland. Salt lost in sweat. Restriction needed in renal disease
Potassium	Balance of fluids in body (with sodium). Needed for muscle and nerve function. Controls pH of blood	Potatoes, fruit (especially bananas), vegetables and juices	Irregular heart beat, muscle weakness	Most is absorbed. Excess is excreted by kidneys. Excess can cause heart failure

Sources and functions of trace minerals

Mineral	Chief functions in body	Significant sources	Deficiency symptoms	Toxicity symptoms
Cobalt	Part of vitamin B_{12}, nerve cell function, blood formation	Vitamin B_{12} containing foods – meat, milk and milk products	Only as Vitamin B_{12} deficiency in humans	Unknown nutritionally, occasional exposure damages skin and red blood cells
Copper	Necessary for absorption and use of iron in forming haemoglobin. Part of several enzymes. Helps to form protective covering of nerves	Meat, drinking water	Anaemia, bone changes (rare in humans)	Vomiting, diarrhoea
Chromium	Associated with insulin and required for release of energy from glucose	Meat, unrefined foods, fats, veg oils	Diabetes-like condition – inability to use glucose normally. Associated with coronary artery disease	Unknown as nutritional disorder. Occupational exposure damages skin and kidneys
Fluorine	Involved in formation of teeth and bones. Helps make teeth resistant to decay	Drinking water, tea, seafood	Tooth decay	Discoloration of teeth, nausea, diarrhoea. itching, chest pain, vomiting
Iodine	Component of thyroxine which helps to regulate growth, development and metabolic rate	Iodised salt, seafood, plants grown in most parts of the country and animals who eat the plants	Enlargement of thyroid gland (goitre), weight gain, mental and physical retardation of infants	Enlargement of thyroid gland, depressed thyroid activity
Manganese	Facilitator with enzymes of many cell processes	Widely distributed in foods	(in animals) poor growth, nervous system disorders, reproductive abnormalities	Nervous system disorders
Selenium	Part of an enzyme that works with vitamin E to protect body compounds from oxidation	Seafood, meat, grains	Anaemia (rare), heart disease	Digestive system disorders. Loss of hair and nails, skin lesions, nervous system disorders; tooth damage
Zinc	Part of many enzymes. Associated with insulin. Involved in making genetic materials and proteins, immune reactions. Transport of vitamin A. Taste perception, wound healing. Making sperm, normal development of foetus	Protein containing foods – meats, fish, poultry grains, vegetables	Tendency to atherosclerosis, raised ammonia levels, reduced insulin concentration. Growth retardation, abnormal collagen synthesis, decreased DNA synthesis. Impaired cell division and protein synthesis. Diarrhoea, vomiting. Reduced copper absorption, night blindness. Delayed onset of puberty, small gonads in males. Reduced synthesis and release of testosterone, abnormal glucose tolerance, reduced synthesis of adrenocortical hormones. Altered thyroid function	

Water

Although people can live for many days without food, they cannot live for more than a few days without water. Water makes up about 55–60 per cent of the body's weight and is an essential part of all body cells, also helping in many chemical reactions in the body. It helps to carry nutrients to the cells and waste away from them. It helps to regulate body temperature, digest food and lubricate joints. Excess water leaves the body via urine, faeces, sweat and breathing. The kidneys regulate water levels in the body and hormones control the amount of water excreted by monitoring the concentration of the blood.

Nearly all foods contain water, particularly apples, pears, melons, cucumbers, cabbage and tomatoes. Water is also present in cottage cheese, white fish and boiled rice.

People who live in temperate climates such as Britain should have at least eight glasses of water a day. If they eat good quantities of foods that are high in water content, they can easily do this. People who live in hot climates or who take a lot of exercise must make sure that they drink more than this.

Diet variation during life stage development

Babies

Breast and bottle feeding have already been mentioned earlier in the unit, but at about six months, babies start to need more nutrients than can be supplied by milk alone. Weaning is the term used to describe the introduction of solid food to babies. It should not be started before the end of the first six months of age because the baby's kidneys are not mature enough to cope with solid food before this. Early weaning is also thought to contribute to obesity in later life.

The process of weaning	
Stage	**Weaning process**
Stage 1 6-8 months	Approximately 500-600 mils breast or formula milk a day. Start with spoonfuls of baby rice, mashed potato or puréed vegetables such as carrot, peas or parsnips. It may take some time for babies to get used to the spoon.
Stage 2 8-10 months	Minimum of 500-600 ml breast or formula food a day. Gradually increase the amount of food given according to the baby's appetite and increase the number of times solid food is given up to three feeds a day. Introduce food with soft lumps. Do not give nuts as infants may choke or be allergic.
Stage 3 10-12 months	Minimum of 500-600 ml breast or formula milk per day. Minced or finely chopped food should be given to introduce different textures. Two to three servings a day of starchy foods and fruit and vegetables at at least two meals are recommended. Finger foods such as toast, strips of pitta bread, carrots and apple can be introduced, as well as one serving of a protein group food per day such as soft meat, fish or well cooked eggs. Avoid sweet foods and adding sugar and salt to food.
Stage 4 12 months and over	Continue to give about 500-600 ml of breast or formula milk a day. A good mixed diet of chopped and minced food should be given by this stage, including 3 meals and 2-3 healthy snacks in between each day.

Babies should be encouraged to start drinking from a cup at about 6 months of age and, ideally, should not be given bottles after the age of 12 months. Prepared baby foods are available in shops or they can be home made. It is important not to add salt to homemade food and it is also advisable not to add sugar, unless there is a need for it in small amounts in puréed fruit, which may be sharp for babies.

Children and adolescents

Schoolchildren grow very fast and are very active. This results in them having large appetites. Children should be encouraged to eat meals that are not too heavy but have concentrated sources of vitamins and minerals and protein to help with growth and development. Obesity can be a problem in children that will remain a problem in adulthood. Some studies in the USA seem to point to the fact that 80 per cent of obese children become obese adults. On this basis, children should be encouraged to eat plenty of fruit and vegetables along with protein and carbohydrate, and discouraged from eating too much fatty and sweet foods. Sugar only provides calories and has no nutritional benefit. Training young palates to enjoy healthy foods is more likely to encourage healthy eating for life. Publicity about the food provided in schools and the television series 'Jamie's School Dinners', resulted in changes being announced in September 2005 by the Secretary of State for Education about what food should be provided in school canteens and what should be banned.

 Over to you

The School Meals Review Panel is an expert advisory group on school meal standards. It first met in May 2005. It was set up by the government in response to a campaign by TV chef Jamie Oliver to improve the quality of school meals. It has announced detailed nutritional standards for school meals.

Carry out some research to find out what the nutritional standards are. Do you think that such standards will work? If so, why? If not, why not?

Adolescents probably have the highest needs of any other group of people. They generally have big appetites and should be advised to eat as healthily as possible. There is perhaps less parental influence over what adolescents eat, and this can lead to snacking on high fat and sugar food and drinks. When adolescent obesity occurs it is often as a result of a poor diet and lack of exercise. It is important to encourage regular healthy eating rather than periods of dieting which can be dangerous and lead to nutritional deficiency.

Adults

In developed countries, adults are more likely to suffer from overnutrition than undernutrition. Food is plentiful and readily available and there is a lot of hidden sugar and salt in ready-made meals. Heart disease is the commonest cause of death in Britain and one of the causes of this is eating food high in saturated fat. A high salt intake contributes to strokes and adults should be advised not to cook with salt and not to add salt at the table.

A healthy well-balanced diet for adults is one that is high in complex carbohydrates such as bread, potatoes, pasta and rice, moderate amounts of meat or alternatives (oily fish about three times a week will help to prevent heart disease) and plenty of fruit and vegetables. Alcohol should be limited to 3–4 units per day for men and 2–3 units per day for women. Alcohol provides 7 calories per gram, 3 calories per gram more than proteins and carbohydrates and only 2 calories per gram less than fats.

During pregnancy and breastfeeding, a woman's diet should contain sufficient energy, protein, iron, calcium, folate and vitamins C and D. This is to ensure the normal growth and development of the foetus. Insufficient intake will mean that the foetus will use the mother's stores and she may become undernourished. Pregnant women should be advised to avoid certain foods and alcohol. Birth defects can occur from eating foods high in vitamin A and so liver should be avoided. Soft cheeses and pâtés should also be avoided because of the risk of them being contaminated with listeria, a bacterium that can be harmful.

There is some debate over whether women should drink any alcohol during pregnancy. However, in March 2008 the government recommended that pregnant women should avoid alcohol, even though there is no firm evidence that drinking small amounts of alcohol is harmful. Alcohol consumption during pregnancy can result in Foetal Alcohol Syndrome (FAS).

Key point

Children with FAS may have the following characteristics or exhibit the following behaviours:

- small for gestational age or small in stature in relation to peers
- facial abnormalities such as small eye openings
- poor coordination
- hyperactive behaviour
- learning disabilities
- developmental disabilities (e.g. speech and language delays)
- mental retardation or low IQ
- problems with daily living
- poor reasoning and judgement skills
- sleep and sucking disturbances in infancy.

As people age, their nutritional needs decline. This is because body weight decreases as does energy expenditure. People tend to eat less and so they may become deficient in certain vitamins or minerals. Older people should be encouraged to eat little and often and to make sure that the food they choose contains concentrated amounts of the necessary nutrients. As with any age group, older people should be advised not to eat too many foods that contain saturated fat, to help prevent heart disease. Gentle exercise should also be encouraged.

People who are very active at work or take a lot of exercise will have higher needs than those who do not exercise much and have sedentary jobs. They are more likely to burn off any excess energy that they take in and their blood pressure is likely to be lower than those who do not take exercise. Keeping weight within normal limits by eating a well-balanced diet will help to prevent nutrition-related conditions.

Practice for Assessment

Carrying out this activity will provide evidence for P1, M1 and D1.

What are the differences between the components of a balanced diet for people in different age groups? (P1)

How do these components contribute to people's health at different life stages? (M1)

Why do the components of a healthy diet vary according to a person's life stage? (D1)

You should cover the following life stages in your work: infancy, childhood, adolescence, adulthood (including pregnancy and breastfeeding), and old age.

Factors influencing the diet of individuals

Religion/culture

Religion and culture will play a large part in the food that people eat. Various foods are forbidden in certain religions. In general, Jews and Muslims do not eat pork, Hindus do not eat beef and Buddhists are vegetarian. (See the table on page 398 which shows the general food rules for six different religions.)

Asian groups, particularly teenage girls, may be deficient in Vitamin D, which is known as the sunshine vitamin. Because their religion requires them to cover most of their body, they do not get the opportunity to expose their skin to the sunlight. This can result in conditions known as rickets and osteomalacia. The most common sign of this is bowed legs. They should ensure that they eat a diet that is high in Vitamin D. They may also be more at risk of becoming anaemic as a traditional Asian diet may not provide enough iron.

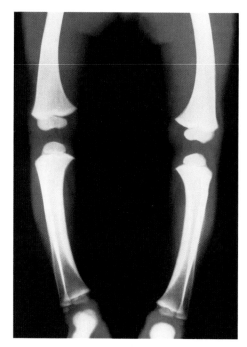

■ *Rickets can result from a lack of vitamin D in the diet*

Social class

There is some evidence to suggest that differences in social class will play a part in influencing dietary choices. In general, people from Social Classes I and II tend to eat more healthy food, and poorer people eat fewer fruit and vegetables and more high-fat, high-sugar foods (Scottish Health Survey – Eating Habits, 1998). Women (not men) in the lower social classes are more likely to be obese than women in the upper social classes. (For more information on social classes, see page 151.)

People in lower social classes generally earn less money than those in the higher social classes and because of this are more likely to substitute cheap, processed food for fresh food.

Personal preference

Personal preference plays a part in the choices an individual makes about food. This may not just be linked to likes and dislikes but other factors, for example people who choose not to eat meat because of the implications of killing animals for food. Personal preference is also influenced by taste, texture, cultural and social habits.

Peer pressure

Peer pressure can have an effect on the food choices that are made, especially by children and teenagers. Many young people develop a stereotyped view of people who eat healthy and unhealthy food and may choose less healthy options such as fast food to fit in with what their friends eat because they do not want to seem different.

Over to you

In a small group, discuss how important peer pressure is in your choice of food.

Do you eat what your friends tend to eat, or do you eat what you like and want to eat?

The media

Information publicised in the media can be another factor that influences food choice. Food scares can often be caused by reporting of facts in the press and in news bulletins. Two examples of this were the egg scare in 1988 and 'mad cow disease' in 1995. In 1988, a junior health minister, Edwina Curry, said that the majority of eggs in the UK were contaminated with salmonella. This had a huge impact on the sale of eggs – 400 million eggs and 4 million chickens were destroyed. In 1996, beef exports to Europe were banned when a link between eating beef and a brain disease, Creutzfeld Jacob Disease, was established. Again, this had a huge impact on beef sales and consumption of beef, and beef was banned from school menus.

Position in family

There is little evidence available to suggest that there is a difference in food choice depending on the position you hold in the family, but it is known that mothers will often give more protein or fruit and vegetables or larger quantities to their husband/partner or children. They will then fill up on lower quality food and their nutritional status may suffer as a result. Choice may also be related to who in the family does the shopping and cooking. If you do most of the family shopping and do not like a particular food, even if others in the family do like it you are less likely to buy it.

Geographic location

Where you live will have an effect on the diet you have. Although there is enough food in the world, it is not evenly distributed. More wealthy countries can afford to buy food and so have a greater variety than countries that are poor. Food that is grown in poor soil will contain fewer minerals and so the quality of the diet will be poorer.

Availability of food

Many developing countries suffer from poor soil conditions, flooding and drought, which result in repeated years of lost harvests. People have access to restricted diets that are high in carbohydrates and not so rich in protein and fats. This can lead to undernutrition.

In developed countries, people have access to a good variety of food. Much of it is home grown and the increase in air travel means that most foods are available all year round. As a result, the population of developed countries is more likely to suffer from overnutrition.

Other factors influenced by geographical location will be where people live and how easily they can get food. Greater variety is available in large supermarkets generally situated on the outskirts of large towns. Small corner shops in rural areas tend to have less variety and less fresh fruit and vegetables.

Over to you

Below is a list of fruit and vegetables which grow in the UK. See if you can find out which month each is 'in season':

Parsnips   *Apples*
Spinach   *Carrots*
Strawberries   *Brussels sprouts*
Rhubarb   *Pears*

Financial resources

The ability to afford food is linked to social class (see above). People who are in the higher social classes have more money to spend on food and tend to buy better quality food and eat out more. People who have low incomes are more likely to buy food that is high in salt, fat and sugar and provide concentrated sources of energy.

Practice for Assessment

Carrying out this activity will give you evidence for P2. Read about Sarah and Benita and then answer the questions below.

Sarah is 84 years old and lives in a small rural village with only one shop. Her family all live more than three hours away and she does not see them very often. She has good neighbours, but most of them work full time and the village is very quiet on weekdays. She no longer drives and the local bus service only comes through the village every two hours. The bus journey to the nearest town with a large supermarket takes one-and-a-half hours. Sarah has arthritis and a heart condition and cannot carry heavy things. She is on a very low income as she only has her state pension to live on. She spends a lot of her time watching daytime television.

Benita is 75 years old and lives in a luxury flat in a town centre. She was widowed seven years ago. Her husband was the managing director of a large company. As well as her state pension, she also receives a substantial pension from her husband's firm. Benita is very active and still drives her car. Most of her family live within 30 minutes' drive of her home. Her town has very good services and there are three large supermarkets within 15 minutes' drive of her flat. There is also a farmers' market in the town centre every Tuesday. Benita has a lively social life and is often out and about meeting friends and family.

Identify five socio-economic influences from the two case studies above. What influence could they have on Sarah's and Benita's diets?

Effects of unbalanced diets on the health of individuals

Medical conditions related to unbalanced diets

Malnutrition

A balanced diet is based on the consumption of appropriate amounts of nutrients and energy. Malnutrition can result from people eating too much or too little of some nutrients over a period of time. Insufficient intake can result in undernutrition or starvation and excessive intake can result in overnutrition and obesity.

Overnutrition

There are some conditions that are related to eating too much of a certain nutrient. Coronary heart disease occurs as a result of eating too many foods such as animal proteins that are high in saturated fats. Fatty deposits build up in the coronary arteries in the heart and this can lead to the formation of a clot that will stop the supply of blood to part of the heart muscle which then dies. This is known as a heart attack. Symptoms of a heart attack can include shortness of breath and pain in the chest, jaw and left arm.

Obesity results from eating too much food. Any food that is eaten in excess will ultimately be converted to fat and stored in the body, which leads to overweight and obesity.

Type 2 diabetes, also known as late or adult onset diabetes, is today seen in children as young as 9 years old. It is caused by eating too much fat and sugar in the diet. The pancreas is either unable to produce enough insulin to allow the cells to absorb glucose from the blood or the body becomes resistant to the insulin that is produced. Symptoms of Type 2 diabetes include thirst, excessive urination and extreme tiredness.

Undernutrition

Undernutrition can result from a general lack of nutrients, particularly protein and energy, or from a lack of a particular nutrient. Two conditions that are seen in underdeveloped countries and that particularly affect children are kwashiorkor and marasmus. The differences between them can be seen in the table below.

Differences between marasmus and kwashiorkor

Birth and breastfeeding

Nutritional marasmus	Kwashiorkor
Starts as early as 5 months	Starts at about 12 months
Early abrupt weaning onto formula or breast milk subsititute	Late gradual weaning and stopping breastfeeding
Dirty dilute formula	Starchy family diet with insufficient protein
Repeated infections especially of the digestive tract	Acute infections
Starvation therapy	
Signs and symptoms: Commonest severe form of protein energy malnutrition Diet very low in protein and calories often due to early weaning Usually occurs at less than one year Growth very retarded and weight very low Muscles and fat wasted giving an 'old man look' Vitamin deficiency Dehydration	*Signs and symptoms:* Protein energy malnutrition. Occurs between ages 1 and 3 years in children from poor rural areas displaced from the breast by the next child and given a low-protein porridge diet (cassava and plantain) Growth failure, low weight, oedema (swelling) of feet, legs, face and hands Wasted muscles but still have fat Misery and apathy Hair turns orangeish, straightens and pulls out easily Skin becomes lighter on the face Stools are loose Anaemia Flaky skin on legs and buttocks, pain and ulcers, may lead to gangrene Liver large and fatty Deficient in vitamins A and B, zinc, potassium and magnesium

■ *A child suffering from nutritional marasmus*

■ *Children suffering from kwashiorkor*

Specific nutrient deficiencies

Anaemia

Anaemia is caused by iron deficiency. Iron is used for making red blood cells and in the body's use of oxygen. Symptoms include:

■ fatigue/lack of energy

■ weakness

■ brittle fingernails.

Tooth decay

Tooth decay or dental caries cannot be strictly be described as undernutrition, as it is caused by an excess of sugar in the diet. Sticky deposits called plaque are deposited on the teeth. Plaque is acid and over time it will dissolve the enamel on teeth, causing cavities. If the cavities remain untreated, they can kill the tooth's nerve and blood supply and eventually the whole tooth will die. It is important that sugary foods and drinks are kept to a minimum and good dental hygiene is observed.

Rickets

Rickets is caused by Vitamin D deficiency, which controls calcium metabolism. The elderly, adolescents and women who have repeated pregnancies may suffer from osteomalacia (the adult form of rickets) because they absorb too little calcium from a low calcium diet. There is also some ethnic evidence of a difference in Vitamin D metabolism.

In children, long bones are not calcified enough and their legs bend, and they tend to have very tiny chests. The four main plates of the skull are not ossified – this is known as the hot-cross bun sign in newborn babies.

Night blindness

Night blindness is caused by a lack of Vitamin A. It is also known as xeropthalmia or dry eye. In its early stages, it can be cured by providing sufferers with Vitamin A supplements such as palm oil or other foods high in Vitamin A. However, in its later stages it is incurable and leads to complete blindness and in some cases death.

Beri beri

Beri beri is Vitamin B_1 or thiamin deficiency – this vitamin is needed to metabolise carbohydrates. Symptoms of beri beri include some or all of the following:

- neuritis
- headache
- fatigue
- poor memory
- diarrhoea
- anxiety
- insomnia
- depression
- irritability
- eczema
- dermatitis
- acne
- enlarged heart muscle weakness
- wrist and ankle drop – no strength to keep them up
- tenderness in calf muscle.

Scurvy

Scurvy is known as Vitamin C deficiency and only occurs when fresh food, especially citrus fruits, are not available. Symptoms include swelling of gums and teeth falling out, bleeding and slow wound healing.

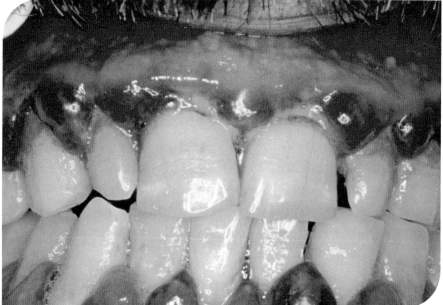

■ *Scurvy*

Real Life Care

Dan is 16 and has been having trouble with his teeth. He is a bit embarrassed because, when he cleans them, his gums bleed. He thinks that might mean bad breath, but he does not know who to ask. He is also annoyed that he has had a cold for about a month which will not go away. His nose is red and runny all the time.

He lives with his parents, but he hardly ever eats at home. He is always out and only seems to grab a can of cola and some chocolate when he is hungry.

Sometimes he has a bit of fish or a burger from the burger van in the town square when he can be bothered. His skin is a bit spotty, too. In fact, he has decided he looks a bit grey – he will have to do something about his appearance because he wants to ask Jodie out this weekend.

1 Why do you think that Dan is having the kind of health problems that he describes?

2 What would you suggest he does?

3 What might be the long-term effects on his health if he does not follow your advice?

Practice for Assessment

This activity will provide evidence for P3 and M2.

Choose two medical conditions related to unbalanced diets to research in detail. Find out the signs and symptoms of the two conditions and state how they are related to unbalanced diets. (P3)

Once you have completed your research, explain how unbalanced diets could have resulted in the two conditions that you have identified. (M2)

Specific dietary needs of patients/service users

Conditions with specific dietary requirements

Coronary heart disease

People who suffer from coronary heart disease should modify their diet in order to prevent further damage to the heart. Sufferers should be advised to make the following changes to their diet:

- Eat at least five portions of fruit and vegetables a day.
- Reduce the total amount of fat in the diet and substitute saturated fats for poly- and mono-unsaturated fats such as vegetable and olive oils.
- Eat oily fish such as mackerel, sardines, herring, tuna, salmon two to three times a week.
- Introduce nuts and seeds into the diet.
- Maintain a healthy weight.
- Reduce the amount of salt in the diet to a maximum of 6 grams per day.
- Drink alcohol in moderation – 1–2 units per day.
- Take exercise – a minimum of 30 minutes three times a week.

Obesity

The best way to combat obesity is to maintain a diet low in fat and sugar and high in complex carbohydrates and fruit and vegetables. Regular exercise will also help to burn up any excess energy intake.

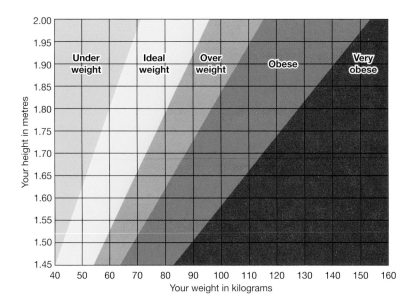

■ *A height and weight chart*

Over to you

Jodie is 16 years old and always worried about her weight, because that is all her friends seem to talk about. She is 160 centimetres tall and weighs 55 kilograms. Her friend Natasha is taller than her. She is 170 centimetres tall and weighs about the same. They both do lots of sport; in fact, they are training for the school's athletics championship at the moment.

In pairs, look at the height/weight chart, and see if you think either girl is overweight or underweight. Would you advise them to diet?

Type 2 diabetes

People who suffer from Type 2 diabetes can do a lot to help the levels of blood glucose by maintaining a diet low in fat and sugar. Complex carbohydrates should form a part of the diet, as low carbohydrate diets can be high in fat. There is a relatively high incidence of coronary heart disease in diabetic sufferers in the UK.

Lactose intolerance

Lactose intolerance is an inability to digest lactose, the sugar found in milk and milk products. It is particularly common in people of African and Asian origin and can lead to digestive disturbance such as cramps, diarrhoea and wind. Milk should be avoided in the diet, but often sufferers can tolerate yoghurt and cheese because the lactose is converted to lactic acid during manufacture.

Food allergies

Allergic reactions to food vary in intensity, and similar symptoms and illnesses can be triggered by different allergens as well as the same allergens causing very different reactions in different people. Symptoms can include eczema, asthma, urticaria (hives) and other health problems. Anaphylaxis is an extreme reaction which must be treated by adrenaline injections. Failure to treat this promptly can result in death. Avoidance of food that causes allergies is the only way to prevent the onset of symptoms.

Genetic disorders

Certain genetic disorders can cause problems that can be relieved by diet. Cystic fibrosis is a disorder that causes thick, sticky mucous to coat the pancreatic duct. Pancreatic enzymes needed to digest food cannot pass into the small intestine and sufferers are given these enzymes in powdered form sprinkled onto their food.

Phenylketonuria is a rare inherited condition in which there is a build up of phenylalanine in the body. Phenylalanine is an amino acid – a building block of protein. A low-protein diet is essential for sufferers and has to be supplemented with artificial protein that does not contain phenylalanine. If this diet is not followed, learning difficulties can result.

Religion/culture

The table below shows the main dietary rules for some world religions.

Dietary rules for six religions						
Foods	**Roman Catholic**	**Jewish**	**Sikh**	**Muslim**	**Hindu**	**Buddhist**
Eggs	✓	No blood spots	Some	✓	Some	✓
Milk/yoghurt	✓	Not with meat	✓	Not with rennet	Not with rennet	✓
Cheese	✓	Not with meat	Some	Some	Some	✗
Chicken	Some people do not eat meat during Lent	Kosher	Some	Halal	Some	✗
Lamb		Kosher	✓	Halal	Some	✗
Beef		Kosher	✗	Halal	✗	✗
Pork		✗	Rarely	✗	Rarely	Some
Fish	✓	Must have scales and fins	Some	Halal	Must have scales and fins	✗
Shellfish	✓	✗	Some	Halal	Some	✗
Animal fats	✓	Kosher	Some	Some halal	Some	✗
Alcohol	✓	✓	✓	✗	✗	✗
Cocoa/tea/coffee	✓	✓	✓	✓	✓	✓ No milk
Nuts	✓	✓	✓	✓	✓	✓
Pulses	✓	✓	✓	✓	✓	✓
Fruit	✓	✓	✓	✓	✓	✓
Vegetables	✓	✓	✓	✓	✓	✓
Fasting		Yom Kippur		Ramadan		

Some people choose not to eat meat and become vegetarian or vegan. Vegetarians do not usually eat meat, poultry, game or fish. However, most will eat eggs and dairy products. Vegetarians will be healthy as long as they eat a varied diet and combine plant proteins, as shown in the diagram on page 378.

Vegans eat no animal foods at all and have to be careful about the plant proteins they eat to ensure that they have a balanced diet. There is a possibility that they may suffer from vitamin B_{12} deficiency as this is mainly found in animal products, although yeast extract is a good source.

Two-day plan

Sometimes it is necessary for people who have been newly diagnosed with a nutrition-related disorder to be given advice about how they should change their diet to suit their needs. Creating a two-day plan that will give them ideas about the foods they should be eating with suggestions for possible suitable alternatives will help them to adjust to a new way of eating.

Over to you

This will help you to prepare for P4 of your assessment opportunity.

Keep a food diary for two days of all the food and drink that you have consumed, making sure that you do not cheat! Swap your diary with a partner and make a table of all the foods consumed according to the five food-group headings. Analyse what has been eaten and drunk over the 48-hour period.

Make recommendations to your partner about what changes they could make to their diet. Do they eat five portions of fruit and vegetables a day? Do they eat a lot of high-fat/sugar/salt snacks? Do they drink eight glasses of water a day?

Devise a two-day healthy eating plan for your partner to follow. After the two days, find out the following information:

- *How easy was it to follow the plan?*
- *What did they enjoy?*
- *What did they not enjoy?*
- *Could you make any changes to the plan to include any of your partner's preferences?*

Practice for Assessment

Carrying out this activity will provide evidence for P4, M3 and D2.

Now that you have practised analysing your two-day plan on each other, you can practise further by devising a two-day plan for two different service users who have specific dietary needs. You can make up a small case study for each of the service users, or you can ask two people you know who suffer from the conditions to keep a two-day food diary for you that you can use to devise the two-day plan.

Devise a two-day food plan for two different service users suffering from two different dietary conditions. (P4)

Describe why the identified specific dietary needs require dietary adjustment for the two service users. (M3)

Explain how the two-day diet plan meets the dietary needs of the service users. (D2)

Food safety and hygiene

Safe practices

Hygiene control

Control of hygiene when working with food is essential. This is because food must be kept safe. This is done by:

- protecting food from contamination by harmful bacteria
- preventing bacteria from multiplying to dangerous levels
- destroying harmful bacteria in or on food by thorough cooking
- disposing of harmful food safely.

The basic rules of food hygiene are outlined below:

- Always wash your hands before touching food, particularly after visiting the toilet, after touching animals, your own skin and hair, and after touching raw food.
- Always cover any break in the skin of your hands, or sores or spots, with a waterproof adhesive dressing (preferably a highly coloured one so you notice it if it comes off).
- No smoking during the preparation of food.
- Avoid preparing food if you have any illness (particularly skin, nose or throat infections and sickness and diarrhoea).
- Do not allow animals into the food preparation area.
- Cover food to protect it from flies and other insects.
- Wrap all food waste and dispose of it in a covered waste bin.
- Clean as you go. Wash surfaces with hot water and detergent.
- Wipe spills up immediately with kitchen tissue and place this in a covered bin.
- Serve food as soon as possible after preparing it.
- Never allow raw food to come in contact with cooked food; common ways in which cooked food is contaminated from raw food are through the hands, knives and working surfaces.
- Wear clean clothing and be clean yourself.
- Do not cough or sneeze over food.

■ The basic rules of food hygiene

Temperature control

Control of temperature is very important in the cooking and storage of food. The Food Safety (Temperature Control) Regulations 1995 sets out the safe temperatures for the storage, heating and chilling of food, as shown in the table below.

Temperatures for safe storage, heating and chilling of food	
Method	**Temperature**
Freezer	−18°C to −22°C
Refrigerator	Legal requirement 8°C; good practice 5–6°C
Hot holding food	Hot food must be maintained at a temperature of 63°C
Reheating commercially manufactured food that has been cooked once during manufacture	Temperature of reheated food must reach a minimum of 82°C

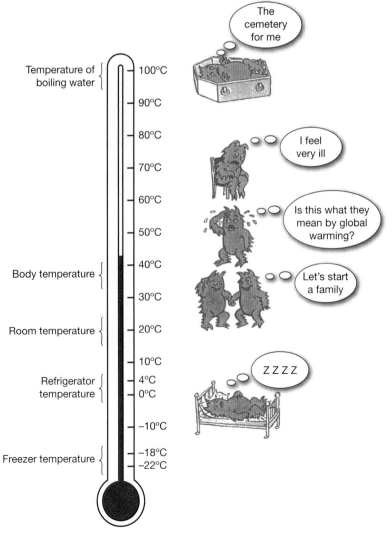

■ *Bacteria and temperature*

Pest control

A food pest is any animal that can live on or in food, causing damage or contamination. The main types of pests are:

- insects such as flies, cockroaches and weevils
- birds
- rodents such as rats and mice.

Flies land on food and carry bacteria on their bodies. In addition, they defecate on food and regurgitate half-digested food from a previous meal onto the food. They can also lay eggs and their dead bodies can be found in food.

Cockroaches can deposit faeces on food and spread bacteria, and small insects such as weevils live in stored foods and food products such as flour and cereals.

Rodents such as mice and rats carry bacteria and pass these on by either walking on the food or on work surfaces. Mice particularly have a tendency to urinate on food.

Some birds can also carry bacteria. Food can be contaminated by droppings and feathers and by insects that they carry on their bodies. Some birds will contaminate milk by pecking through the foil tops of bottles left on the doorstep.

Protecting premises where food is stored or manufactured is the most important way of preventing possible infection of or damage to food. The owner of the premises must ensure that the building is kept in good repair with no obvious points of entry for pests. Food pests tend to like warm, dark, damp undisturbed places, so it is important for food storage and preparation areas to be cool, clean and dry.

Effects of unsafe practices

Food can be contaminated in a variety of ways – both physical and chemical. Physical contaminants include bones, shells or pips and stalks from food, food packaging, nuts or bolts from equipment, jewellery, hair, fingernails, plasters, dust and dirt, and insects and their droppings and eggs.

Chemical contamination can be caused by cleaning chemicals, if they are not kept separate from food and food preparation areas, and agricultural chemicals, for example on fruit and vegetables if they have been sprayed. They must be cleaned thoroughly or peeled before eating.

Leftover food or drink from metal containers should always be transferred to a non-metallic container and stored covered in a refrigerator. Acidic and salty food can attack the metal once a can is opened, which then affects the food.

Biological contamination is contamination by bacteria or viruses where they multiply on the food to dangerous levels, or by moulds which cause

toxins on food. When they are eaten, they cause illness. Some of the
more common types are set out in the table below.

Food poisoning			
Microorganism	**Source**	**Symptoms**	**Incubation period**
Salmonella	Raw poultry, eggs, raw meat, milk, animals, insects and sewage	Abdominal pain, vomiting, diarrhoea, fever	12–36 hours
Staphylococcus aureus	Unpasteurised milk, people	Abdominal pain or cramp, vomiting, low temperature	1–6 hours
Clostridium perfringens	Raw meat, animal and human waste, soil, dust, insects	Abdominal pain, diarrhoea	12–18 hours
Clostridium botulinum	Raw fish and meat, vegetables, smoked fish, canned fish and corned beef	Difficulties in breathing and swallowing, paralysis	12–36 hours
Bacillus cereus	Cereals, soil and dust	Abdominal pain, diarrhoea and vomiting	1–5 hours or 8–16 hours depending on the form of the food poisoning

Source: Chartered Institute of Environmental Health

Food-borne diseases (illness spread by food or water)			
Microorganism	**Source**	**Symptoms**	**Incubation period**
Campylobacter	Raw poultry, raw meat, milk, animals (including pets)	Diarrhoea, often bloody, abdominal pain, nausea, fever	48–60 hours
E. coli	Human and animal gut, sewage, water and raw meat	Abdominal pain, fever, diarrhoea, vomiting, kidney damage or failure	12–24 hours or longer

Source: Chartered Institute of Environmental Health

Legislation, regulations and codes of practice

Food safety legislation requires that establishments preparing and
serving food ensure that food is safe to eat. Three of the main laws and
regulations are:

- the Food Safety Act 1990
- the Food Safety (General Food Hygiene) Regulations 1995
- the Food Safety (Temperature Control) Regulations 1995.

Food Safety Act 1990

The Food Safety Act is the main piece of legislation that governs the safety of food. The Act says that it is illegal to sell or keep for sale food that is unfit for people to eat or causes food to be dangerous to health, or is not of acceptable content or quality, or is labelled or advertised in any way that misleads the consumer. If prosecuted, people who work with food must show that they have taken all reasonable steps to avoid causing any of the above.

Food Safety (General Food Hygiene) Regulations 1995

These regulations cover the basic hygiene principles that businesses must follow and relate to staff, premises and food handling. They affect anyone who owns manages or works in a food business, whether it is a caravan in a lay-by selling tea, coffee and snacks, or a five-star hotel. The regulations cover the following:

- The supply and selling of food in a hygienic way.
- Identification of possible food hazards.
- Control of identified hazards to prevent harm to customers.
- The establishment of effective control and monitoring procedures to ensure that harm does not come to customers.

Food Safety (Temperature Control) Regulations 1995

These regulations cover the following aspects of food hygiene:

- The stages of the food chain that are subject to temperature controls.
- The temperatures at which certain foods must be kept.
- Which foods are exempt from specific temperature controls.
- When the temperature controls allow flexibility.

The safe temperatures are set out in the table above (page 35).

Hazard Analysis Critical Control Point (HACCP)

HACCP is a universal food safety system. It aims to protect food from contamination by:

- identifying critical points in the food handling process that might cause contamination
- putting controls in place to prevent microbiological, chemical and physical contamination of food
- monitoring the critical points to ensure that contamination does not occur.

This means that all potential hazards at each stage of food handling, from delivery of raw products to the serving of fully prepared food, must be identified. The whole process is designed to ensure that any problems can be dealt with before they cause any problems or illness.

The hazard control chart for pre-cooked meat is shown below.

Stage	Hazards What can go wrong?	Controls How can I prevent it going wrong?	Monitoring How can I check my control?	Corrective action What do I do if things are not right?
Hazard Flow Chart for				
Delivery				
Storage				
Preparation				
Cooking				
Serving				

■ *Hazard flow chart for pre-cooked meat*

Practice for Assessment

Carrying out this activity will contribute to P5 and M4.

Identify what safe practices should be followed when preparing, cooking and serving food. (P5)

What might be the results of following unsafe practices when preparing, serving and cooking food? (M4)

Check your understanding

1. What does 'weaning' mean and approximately when should it be started? Why is it important not to start weaning to early?

2. What factors will influence the dietary needs of individuals?

3. What are the government's Eight Guidelines for a healthy diet?

4. What are macronutrients and micronutrients and why are these terms used?

5. What are the functions of fibre in the diet?

6. Why are vegetable proteins called 'low biological value proteins'?

7. Essential fatty acids are considered to be important in the diet. Give examples of which foods contain them.

8. Explain the differences in the food choices of Jews, Muslims and Hindus.

9. Name two conditions that occur through overnutrition. Why do they occur?

10. Explain what rickets is.

11. What aspects of food hygiene do the Food Safety (General Food Hygiene) Regulations 1995 cover.

12. What is HACCP and what are its aims?

Glossary

Abuse A term which covers a wide range of negative and damaging behaviour, including hitting, humiliation, exploiting, stealing from or neglecting others.

Active listening Active listening involves being interested, hearing, remembering and checking what you have understood with another person.

Advocate An advocates argues a case for another person. In law an advocate argues a legal case for a client. In care work an advocate tries to understand and argue from a client's perspective.

Antenatal The period of time before birth. Some health centres and community groups provide antenatal classes to assist the families with what to expect when having the baby. It can teach the mother techniques such as breathing to assist them when they are in labour.

Appraisal This is to estimate how valuable something is. So in terms of having an appraisal in the workplace, it is a discussion with staff to find out how they are coping in the workplace and what problems they are having, and to work out how valuable their work is to the setting.

Attachment The close relationship that a baby has with his or her carers.

Bereavement The feelings experienced on the death of a person you loved and coming to terms with the loss. It often involves strong emotions of disbelief, denial, anger, guilt and resisting change.

Body language The language of non-verbal communication; the messages we send with our body.

Body movements The speed and type of people's movements sends messages to others. Movements of the hands, eyes, head and body may communicate emotions such as anger and happiness.

Bonding Forming an emotional attachment to a person. Infants usually form an attachment to carers during the first year of life.

Budgeting This involves taking into account all the money you have over a period of time, such as a month; it includes all your incomings (money coming in) and your outgoings (money spent on bills, food, etc). Budgeting means setting a limit of how much to spend on each thing based on how much money you have, and sticking to it.

Care plan A written document that outlines how the needs of an individual are to be met.

Care planning A process of working out how a person's needs can be met, which involves service users and carers.

Carer Anyone who provides care for another person or people.

Charters Documents that set up or explain the rights that people may expect from a service.

Chromosome This is the genetic material that directs human development. Human cells have 23 pairs of chromosomes.

Class A social grouping whose members share economic, social and cultural characteristics.

Codes of practice A set of principles which can be used to guide and measure the quality of care practice.

Coherent Logical and consistent.

Communication barriers Blocks or barriers which prevent communication. Examples might include blocks which prevent people from receiving a message, or making sense of a message or understanding a message.

Communication cycle The process involved in building an understanding of what another person is communicating.

Conduction The transmission of heat or electricity directly through a substance.

Confidence An individual's confidence in his or her ability to achieve something or cope with a situation. It may be influenced by self-esteem.

Confidentiality To keep secure and private information about service users. This is an important care value.

Contraception Ways of preventing pregnancy.

Convection Transference of mass or heat within a fluid caused by the tendency of warmer and less dense material to rise.

Creative This means conveying a message and having the power to bring something into being.

Culture The customs, beliefs and ways of thinking that people learn as they grow up. These customs identify people as belonging to a group. Different social groups have different cultures.

D

Dementia This covers a range of illnesses involving the degeneration (wasting) of the brain. Dementia is not part of normal ageing; most very old people show no signs of the illness.

Demography The study of population and the way it increases and decreases over time. This is carried by looking at the different factors that could affect this, such as the fact that we all live much longer now than we used to 100 years ago.

Di This means two, as in the case of a disaccharide.

Direct care This is care that is given on a face-to-face basis.

Disability The consequences of an impairment or other individual difference in a given social setting.

Disability Discrimination Act 1995 An Act of Parliament that created rights for people with disability.

Disability Rights Commission An organisation which aims to protect the rights of disabled people

Discrimination This is treating a person less favourably than others because of assumptions about the group that they belong to.

Diversity The way in which people are different from one another. Key differences include gender, age, ethnicity, class, religion and sexuality.

E

Embryo The developing baby during the first eight weeks of life in the womb.

Employee A person who is hired by another person (employer) to do a job and get paid for carrying out the job.

Employer A person who hires people (employees) to do a job for them. They pay the employees for carrying out and completing the job.

Emulsify To disperse the particles of one liquid evenly in another.

Environment The surroundings that a person lives in; everything   around people that might influence or affect them.

Ethnic group People of the same race or nationality who share a distinctive culture.

Ethnicity The social and cultural categories which people use to explain what race they are.

Extended family A family that consists of parents, their children and other relatives such as grandparents and uncles and aunts.

Eye contact Eye contact is an important source of non-verbal communication.

F

Facial expression The face is an important source of non-verbal communication.

Family A social group made up of people who are related to each other.

Foetus The developing baby within the womb from eight weeks to birth.

G

Gender The social role associated with being male of female.

General Social Care Council (GSCC) An organisation responsible for the codes of practice and the registration of social care workers.

Genes The biological set of instructions which influence the development of people. Genes interact with the environment to create individual people. Differences in people are always due to this interaction of genes and environment.

Gestures The sending of non-verbal messages using the arms, hands and fingers.

GSCC Code of Practice A list of statements that describe the standards of practice required of social care workers.

H

Holistic Treating the whole person and looking at all aspects of their health: physical, intellectual, social and emotional.

Hygiene This is the principles and practice of cleanliness and health. It can involve following different procedures and codes of practice to meet the different levels of hygiene expected in different settings such as schools and hospitals.

I

Indirect care Services provided to support direct care, e.g. the ambulance service.

Initiative This means being able to carry out a task or activity without being asked to do it or being constantly reminded how to do it. It involves seeing what needs to be done and doing it without being asked; it also involves having the ability to think of new ideas and methods.

Interpersonal interaction This includes every type of communication between people.

Interpreters Interpreters communicate meaning from one language to another.

L

Labelling Using a word or a simple description in making assumptions about a person.

Legislation This is the laws that the government makes. There are many laws that cover different areas, such as disability, race, human rights, and so on.

Life events Common events that happen to people within a society. Examples include going to school, starting work, retirement and bereavement.

Life stages Socially defined periods which are used to identify developmental stages such as infancy, childhood, adolescence and adulthood.

Listening The ability to build an understanding of another person's views. Listening involves more than just hearing the sound of another person's voice.

Literacy The skill of being able to read and write competently.

Lone-parent families A family consisting of one parent and children.

Low income Having to live on less than 60% of the average person's income.

M

Macro This means large or large scale, as in the case of macronutrients.

Menopause The end of menstruation in women – usually some time between the ages of 45 and 55.

Micro This means very small, as in the case of micronutrients.

Monitoring Checking how something is working, such as a policy, an activity, or a member of staff.

Mono This means one, as in the case of monosaccharides (simple sugars).

Multicultural 'Multi' means many and 'culture' refers to the features that make groups different from each other. Therefore, multicultural means many different cultures and groups in one area.

Multidisciplinary care Care provided by a range of different agencies and professional carers. 'Multi' means 'many' and 'disciplinary' refers to different professional disciplines – for example: social work, social care, nursing, psychiatry, occupational therapy, speech therapy, medicine.

Muscle tension Tension within the muscles of the face, neck, or arms may send messages about our emotional state.

N

National Health Service (NHS) The government-run service which provides doctors (GPs), hospitals and community health services.

National Minimum Standards of Care A series of regulations for different care services that define expected standards.

NHS Plan A plan to 'modernise' and improve the National Health Service.

Non-invasive Not involving the introduction of instruments or other objects into the body.

Non-verbal communication Our eyes, faces and bodies send messages to others. Our tone of voice also sends messages which are distinct from the verbal content of a conversation.

Nuclear family A family consisting of parents and their children who share a residence and cooperate economically and socially.

Numeracy This refers to the ability to use numbers for carrying out calculations such as adding, subtracting, multiplication and division.

P

Patient's Charter A document that sets out the rights and standards people can expect from the NHS.

Peripheral On the outer limits.

Permeable Allowing something to pass through, such as gas and liquids.

Personal space The space between people when they communicate.

Piaget Jean Piaget (1896–1980) was famous for his early research on child development. He believed children's intellectual development could be described in four stages.

Poly This means many or much, as in the case of polysaccharides.

Postnatal The period after the birth of a baby.

Posture The way a person positions his or her body. Posture is part of an individual's non-verbal communication.

Prejudice This is to pre-judge other people or groups, based on fixed negative views about them.

Procedure A set way for carrying out a task. Procedures are often set up to protect clients' rights and safety.

Psychologist A person who studies human behaviour.

R

Race Relations Act 1976 (amended 2000) An Act of Parliament which makes discrimination on the basis of race illegal.

Reconstituted families A family that is made up of children from previous family groups. The couple are not the parents of each child in the family.

Reincarnation Some religions believe that when you die, your soul leaves your body and incarnates (enters) another body.

Religion This is a belief in a god or gods, or other supreme beings. It involves having faith and expressing that faith in various ways, such as praying and celebrating festivals. People grow up with different religious traditions.

Rights Certain rights exist under laws or international conventions. Other rights exist by virtue of the values that guide care practice or society.

S

Secondary sexual characteristics Physical features developed at puberty that distinguish between the sexes but are not involved in reproduction.

Secondary socialisation The values, beliefs, attitudes and behaviours that we learn during adolescence through social interaction with other adolescents. This socialisation comes after the first socialisation that involves learning beliefs, attitudes and behaviours within a family environment.

Secular This refers to something that has no connection with religion or church. A secular belief, for example, is something that people believe in but is not religious.

Self-concept An understanding of who we are. It may be difficult to cope with life as an adult if you do not have an understanding of this.

Self-esteem How much a person values him or herself and his or her life. High self-esteem may help a person to feel happy and confident. Low self-esteem may lead to depression and unhappiness.

Self-fulfilling prophecy This describes the process of labelling, which involves ascribing a name to someone. When you are labelled the label itself becomes embedded so that you end up becoming what the label suggests.

Self-image How a person imagines, or 'images', himself or herself to be.

Service user plan of care The individual plan of care which may be drawn up with a service user within a care setting.

Sex Discrimination Act 1975 (amended 1986) An Act of Parliament designed to prevent discrimination on the basis of gender.

Sexuality This refers to a person's sexual orientation – whether they are heterosexual, bisexual or homosexual. It can also mean what sex we are – whether we are a male or a female.

Signers People who communicate spoken language into sign language and sign language into spoken communication.

Social class A group of people who share a common position in society. Class membership is linked with occupation, income, wealth, beliefs and lifestyle.

Socialisation Learning the values and normal behaviour of a social group or culture in becoming part of it.

Socio-economic Socio-economic factors are those that affect how we live and work. Factors include poverty, employment, class and housing.

Stereotyping Making assumptions about people using a fixed set of ideas.

Stimulate This means to awaken or to rouse, encourage, work up or urge particular things. When people talk about stimulating the mind, this means keeping the mind active and making it work hard.

Stress An in-built reaction makes us want to fight or run when we feel threatened. It is possible to be threatened but not be able to fight or run, and symptoms of stress set in when this happens.

Susceptibility The ability to be influenced by something.

T

Therapeutic This is the treatment of disease or other disorder, something that may benefit health.

Translation This involves changing recorded material from one language to another.

Turn taking Learning to take turns within group discussion so the group members do not all speak at once.

V

Value base A system of values which should guide a care worker's behaviour.

Values Beliefs about what is valuable or to be valued when working with others.

Vegan People who do not eat or use animal products in any way.

Vegetarian People who do not eat killed meat or fish but will eat milk, eggs and dairy produce.

Verbal communication Spoken communication using words.

Victimised A person who stands up for their rights and is mistreated because of this. An example could be a woman being paid less than a man even though they both started the job on the same day with exactly the same qualifications and experience. The woman complains and this results in her being dismissed from the job.

Voice tone The way a person's voice sounds, such as 'soft' or 'harsh'.

Warden This is an official person in charge and looks after something, such as a building or homes. They will make sure that everything is maintained and that the people living there are all happy and well.

Index

PATIENT INFORMATION

Patient Name: **G. P. Name:**

Date of Birth:

Contact in Emergency		Allergies	Admission Date and Time	
Admitting Nurse/Key Worker	**Primary Nurse**	**Physio (Date Referred)**	**O.T. (Date Referred)**	**Care Manager (Date Referred)**

THIS PERSON PREFERS TO BE CALLED

.... Home Telephone Number ....

is [   ] years old   and is Married/Widowed/Divorced/Separated/Single/Other

He/She lives   Alone [   ] With

> **Name:**
>
> **Relationship:**

Language spoken .... Religion ....

Admitted from: Home/Part III/Nursing Home/Warden Controlled/Hospital

Important telephone numbers:

Name/Relationship	Number

What health event has brought this person into hospital?

NAME .... **COMMUNITY HOSPITAL** ....

EVALUATION

Date	No		Signature

Let the web do the work!

Why not visit our website and see what it can do for you?

Free online support materials

You can download free support materials for many of our IT products. We even offer a special e-alert service to notify you when new content is posted.

Lists of useful weblinks

Our site includes lists of other websites, which can save you hours of research time.

Online ordering – 24 hours a day

It's quick and simple to order your resources online, and you can do it anytime – day or night!

Find your consultant

The website helps you find your nearest Heinemann consultant, who will be able to discuss your needs and help you find the most cost-effective way to buy.

It's time to save time – visit our website now!

www.heinemann.co.uk/vocational

And what's more, you can register now to receive our FREE information-packed eNewsletter. Register today at www.heinemann.co.uk/vocnews.

(t) 0845 630 44 44   (f) 0845 630 77 77   (e) myorders@pearson.com   (w) www.heinemann.co.uk

Heinemann